Children's Literature

Edinburgh Critical Guides to Literature
Series Editors: Martin Halliwell, University of Leicester and
Andy Mousley, De Montfort University

Published Titles:
Gothic Literature, Andrew Smith
Canadian Literature, Faye Hammill
Women's Poetry, Jo Gill
Contemporary American Drama, Annette J. Saddik
Shakespeare, Gabriel Egan
Asian American Literature, Bella Adams
Children's Literature, M. O. Grenby

Forthcoming Titles in the Series:
Eighteenth-Century Literature, Hamish Mathison
Contemporary British Fiction, Nick Bentley
Contemporary American Fiction, David Brauner
Victorian Literature, David Amigoni
Crime Fiction, Stacy Gillis
Renaissance Literature, Siobhan Keenan
Modern American Literature, Catherine Morley
Scottish Literature, Gerard Carruthers
Romantic Literature, Richard Marggraf Turley
Modernist Literature, Rachel Potter
Medieval Literature, Pamela King
Women's Fiction, Sarah Sceats
African American Literature, Jennifer Terry

Children's Literature

M. O. Grenby

Edinburgh University Press

Edinburgh University Press Ltd
22 George Square, Edinburgh

Typeset in Ehrhardt
by Servis Filmsetting Ltd, Manchester, and
printed and bound in Great Britain by
Antony Rowe Ltd, Chippenham, Wilts

A CIP record for this book is available from the British Library

ISBN 978 0 7486 2273 3 (hardback)
ISBN 978 0 7486 2274 0 (paperback)

Contents

Series Preface

The study of English literature in the early twenty-first century is host to an exhilarating range of critical approaches, theories and historical perspectives. 'English' ranges from traditional modes of study such as Shakespeare and Romanticism to popular interest in national and area literatures such as the United States, Ireland and the Caribbean. The subject also spans a diverse array of genres from tragedy to cyberpunk, incorporates such hybrid fields of study as Asian American literature, Black British literature, creative writing and literary adaptations, and remains eclectic in its methodology.

Such diversity is cause for both celebration and consternation. English is varied enough to promise enrichment and enjoyment for all kinds of readers and to challenge preconceptions about what the study of literature might involve. But how are readers to navigate their way through such literary and cultural diversity? And how are students to make sense of the various literary categories and periodisations, such as modernism and the Renaissance, or the proliferating theories of literature, from feminism and Marxism to queer theory and eco-criticism? The Edinburgh Critical Guides to Literature series reflects the challenges and pluralities of English today, but at the same time it offers readers clear and accessible routes through the texts, contexts, genres, historical periods and debates within the subject.

Martin Halliwell and Andy Mousley

Acknowledgements

An introduction to children's literature might be written in many different ways. The particular approach I have adopted here derives from my experiences teaching in the School of English at Newcastle University. I am very grateful therefore to all the students who have taken my 'Beyond Wonderland' undergraduate module since it first began. Their responses to the course, and their comments about how difficult it can be for those new to the subject to find their bearings, have shaped my thinking about what a new introduction might try to do. But I am equally grateful to the community of postgraduate students in the Children's Literature Unit at Newcastle. Their suggestions and criticisms, given as a group and individually, in person and by correspondence, have helped this book very much, and I have greatly enjoyed the challenge of responding to their forthright assessments. More than this, their own master's and doctoral projects have prompted me to think in different ways about children's literature. Above all, the enthusiasm and commitment of all the students in the Children's Literature Unit has been an inspiration.

My colleague Professor Kim Reynolds has read some sections of this book and, as ever, her advice has been constructive, astute and erudite. Dr Jenny Litster has taken the time to talk with me about my plans, and has generously shared her bright ideas and detailed knowledge. The anonymous reviewers of the proposal made many useful comments. All of the errors that remain are entirely my own.

I must also thank Dr Andy Mousley for suggesting that I should write this book, and, with Dr Martin Halliwell, for commissioning me to do so. Jackie Jones and James Dale, at Edinburgh University Press, have been sympathetic editors. I am very grateful for the patience and forbearance of them all.

Finally, and above all, thank-you to Mary.

Chronology

The timeline lists only those children's books mentioned in this *Edinburgh Critical Guide*. The chapters in which the texts are discussed are given in brackets. Where the year of first publication is uncertain, an approximate date has been given.

1617   Evaldus Gallus, *Pueriles Confabulatiunculae: or Children's Dialogues* (School)

1672   James Janeway, *A Token for Children* (Introduction; Moral Tales; Family)

1673   Benjamin Keach, *War with the Devil* (Introduction)

1686   John Bunyan, *Divine Emblems*, also known as *A Book for Boys and Girls* or *Country Rhimes for Children* (Introduction; Poetry)

1692   Roger L'Estrange, *Fables of Æsop* (Fables)

1693   Cotton Mather, *The Wonders of the Invisible World* (Fantasy)

1700   Anon., *The Friar and the Boy*, a new version (Poetry)

1708   Joseph Jackson, *A New Translation of Æsop's Fables* (Fables)

1712	Thomas Gills, *Useful and Delightful Instructions* (Poetry)
1715	Isaac Watts, *Divine Songs Attempted in Easy Language for the Use of Children* (Poetry)
1719	Daniel Defoe, *Robinson Crusoe* (Adventure)
1722	James Greenwood, *The Virgin Muse* (Poetry); Samuel Croxall, *Fables of Aesop and Others* (Fables)
1726	Jonathan Swift, *Gulliver's Travels* (Adventure)
1727	John Wright, *Spiritual Songs for Children* (Poetry)
1734	Mary Barber, *Poems on Several Occasions* (Poetry)
1740–50	Jane Johnson, home-made verses and stories (Poetry)
1743	John Vowler, 'The Young Student's Scheme' (Poetry)
1744	Mary Cooper, *Tommy Thumb's Pretty Song Book* (Poetry)
1749	Sarah Fielding, *The Governess; or, Little Female Academy* (School)
1751	John Marchant, *Puerilia: Amusements for the Young* (Fables; Poetry)
1758–63	Christopher Smart, *Jubilate Agno* (Poetry)
1760	Anon., *The Top Book of All, for Little Masters and Misses* (Poetry)
1765	Anon., *The History of Goody Two-Shoes* (School; Adventure); Anon., *Mother Goose's Melody, or Sonnets from the Cradle* (Poetry)
1770	Anon., *The Prettiest Book for Children* (Fantasy); Christopher smart, *Hymns for the Amusement of Children* (poetry)
1774	Anon., *The Lilliputian Magazine; or, Children's Repository* (Moral Tales)

1780   Anon., *Virtue and Vice: or, the History of Charles Careful, and Harry Heedless* (Moral Tales)

1781   Dorothy Kilner, *The Holyday Present* (Family)

1782   Ellinor Fenn, *School Occurrences* (School)

1783   Mary Ann Kilner, *Jemima Placid* (Moral Tales)

1784   Dorothy Kilner, *The Life and Perambulations of a Mouse* (Fantasy); Joseph Ritson, *Gammer Gurton's Garland, or, the Nursery Parnassus* (Poetry)

1786   Arnaud Berquin, *The Children's Friend* (Moral Tales; Family); Sarah Trimmer, *Fabulous Histories* (Fables; Family; Fantasy)

1788   Mary Wollstonecraft, *Original Stories from Real Life* (Moral Tales)

1789–94   William Blake, *Songs of Innocence and Experience* (Poetry)

1790   Christian Gotthilf Salzmann, trans. Mary Wollstonecraft, *Elements of Morality* (Moral Tales)

1792–96   John Aikin and Anna Laetitia Barbauld, *Evenings at Home* (Moral Tales; Family)

1796   Maria Edgeworth, *The Parent's Assistant; or, Stories for Children*, including 'The Purple Jar' (Moral Tales) and 'The Barring Out' (School)

1804–05   Ann and Jane Taylor (and others), *Original Poems for Infant Minds* (Poetry)

1805   Sarah Catherine Martin, *The Comic Adventures of Old Mother Hubbard and her Dog* (Poetry); William Godwin, *Fables Ancient and Modern* (Fables)

1806   William Roscoe, *The Butterfly's Ball and the Grasshopper's Feast* (Poetry)

1810   Ann and Jane Taylor, *Signor Topsy-Turvey's Wonderful Magic Lantern* (Poetry)

1847   Frederick Marryat, *Children of the New Forest*
        (Family; Adventure)

1848   Cecil Frances Alexander, *Hymns for Little Children*
        (Poetry); Heinrich Hoffmann, *Shock-Headed Peter*
        (Introduction; Poetry)

1850   Elizabeth Wetherell, *The Wide, Wide World*
        (Family)

1853   Lewis Carroll, 'Solitude' (Poetry)

1854   Henry Wadsworth Longfellow, *The Song of
        Hiawatha* (Poetry); Louisa Charlesworth, *Ministering
        Angels* (Moral Tales); W. M. Thackeray, *The Rose
        and the Ring* (Fantasy)

1856   Charlotte Yonge, *The Daisy Chain* (Moral Tales;
        Family)

1857   Thomas Hughes, *Tom Brown's Schooldays* (School)

1858   F. W. Farrar, *Eric, or Little by Little, a Tale of Roslyn
        School* (School); R. M. Ballantyne, *The Coral Island*
        (Adventure)

1861   R. M. Ballantyne, *The Gorilla Hunters* (Adventure)

1862   Coventry Patmore, *The Children's Garland* (Poetry)

1863   Charles Kingsley, *The Water-Babies* (Fantasy);
        Henry Wadsworth Longfellow, 'Paul Revere's Ride'
        (Poetry)

1864   Jules Verne, *Journey to the Centre of the Earth*
        (Fantasy; Adventure)

1865   Lewis Carroll, *Alice's Adventures in Wonderland*
        (Introduction; Poetry; Fantasy)

1867   Hesba Stretton, *Jessica's First Prayer* (Moral Tales);
        Horatio Alger, *Ragged Dick; or, Street Life in New
        York* (Moral Tales)

1868   Louisa May Alcott, *Little Women* (Family)

1869   Louisa May Alcott, *Little Women Part Two*, known as *Good Wives* in the UK (Family)

1870   Edward Lear, *Nonsense Songs, Stories, Botany, and Alphabets* (Poetry; Fantasy)

1871   George MacDonald, *At the Back of the North Wind* (Fantasy); Lewis Carroll, *Through the Looking Glass* (Fantasy; Poetry); Louisa May Alcott, *Little Men* (School)

1872   Christina Rossetti, *Sing-Song: A Nursery Rhyme Book* (Poetry); Susan Coolidge, *What Katy Did* (Family)

1873   Charlotte Yonge, *The Pillars of the House* (Family); Jules Verne, *From Earth to the Moon Direct* (Fantasy); Jules Verne, *Twenty Thousand Leagues Under the Sea* (Fantasy; Adventure); Susan Coolidge, *What Katy Did At School* (School)

1875   O. F. Walton, *Christie's Old Organ, or Home Sweet Home* (Moral Tales)

1876   Edward Lear, *Laughable Lyrics* (Poetry); Lewis Carroll, 'The Hunting of the Snark' (Poetry); Mrs Molesworth, *Carrots: Just a Little Boy* (Moral Tales; Family)

1877   Anna Sewell, *Black Beauty* (Fables)

1879   Frances Hodgson Burnett, *Haworth's* (Moral Tales)

1880   Joel Harris Chandler, *Uncle Remus: His Songs and His Sayings* (Fables); G. A. Henty, *The Young Buglers: a Tale of the Peninsular War* (Adventure)

1881–82   Talbot Baines Reed, *The Fifth Form at St. Dominic's* (School)

1882   F. Anstey, *Vice Versa; or, A Lesson to Fathers* (Fantasy); Mark Twain, *The Prince and the Pauper* (Adventure)

1882–83   Elizabeth Whittaker, 'Robina Crusoe, and her Lonely Island Home', in *The Girl's Own Paper* (Adventure)

1883	Robert Louis Stevenson, *Treasure Island* (Adventure)
1884	G.A. Henty, *By Sheer Pluck* (Adventure); Mark Twain, *The Adventures of Huckleberry Finn* (Adventure)
1885	Henry Rider Haggard, *King Solomon's Mines* (Adventure); Robert Louis Stevenson, *A Child's Garden of Verses* (Poetry); Robert Louis Stevenson, *Kidnapped* (Adventure)
1886	Frances Hodgson Burnett, *Little Lord Fauntleroy* (Moral Tales); L. T. Meade, *A World of Girls* (School)
1887	Walter Crane, *The Baby's Own Aesop* (Fables)
1892	G. A. Henty, *Those Other Animals* (Fables); L. T. Meade, *Four on an Island* (Adventure)
1893	G. A. Henty, *Beric the Briton: a Story of the Roman Invasion* (Adventure)
1895	Kenneth Grahame, *The Golden Age* (Family); Mrs Molesworth, *Sheila's Mystery* (Family)
1896	Eugene Field, *Love Songs of Childhood* (Poetry)
1898	Mrs. George Corbett, *Little Miss Robinson Crusoe* (Adventure)
1899	E. Nesbit, *The Treasure Seekers* (Family); Rudyard Kipling, *Stalky & Co.* (School)
1900	L. Frank Baum, *The Wonderful Wizard of Oz* (Fantasy)
1901	Bessie Marchant, *Three Girls on a Ranch: A Tale of New Mexico* (Adventure); E. Nesbit, *The Wouldbegoods* (Moral Tales; Family; Adventure); Rudyard Kipling, *Kim* (Adventure)
1902	John Masefield, 'Sea Fever' (Poetry); Rudyard Kipling, *Just So Stories* (Fables); Walter De la Mare, *Songs of Childhood* (Poetry)

1903   G. A. Henty, *With Kitchener in the Soudan* (Adventure); Kate Douglas Wiggin, *Rebecca of Sunnybrook Farm* (Family)

1904   First performance of J. M. Barrie, *Peter Pan, or The Boy Who Wouldn't Grow Up* (Family)

1905   Frances Hodgson Burnett, *A Little Princess*, originally published as *Sara Crewe* in 1887 (Moral Tales; School)

1906   Angela Brazil, *The Fortunes of Philippa* (School); E. Nesbit, *The Railway Children* (Family)

1907   Hilaire Belloc, *Cautionary Tales for Children* (Introduction; Poetry)

1908   First of Frank Richards, *Greyfriars* stories in *The Magnet* (School); Kenneth Grahame, *The Wind in the Willows* (Fables; Fantasy); L. M. Montgomery, *Anne of Green Gables* (Family); L. T. Meade, *The School Favourite* (School)

1909   L. M. Montgomery, *Anne of Avonlea* (School)

1911   J. M. Barrie, *Peter and Wendy* (School; Family; Fantasy)

1913   Alfred Noyes, 'The Highwayman' (Poetry); Eleanor Hodgman Porter, *Pollyanna* (Family); Walter De la Mare, *Peacock Pie* (Poetry)

1915   'Charlie Chaplin's Schooldays' in *Boy's Realm* magazine (School); Bessie Marchant, *Molly Angel's Adventures* (Adventure)

1916   Alec Waugh, *The Loom of Youth* (School)

1916–17   Eleanor Farjeon, *Nursery Rhymes of London Town* (Poetry)

1918   Angela Brazil, *For the School Colours* (School)

1920   Dorita Fairlie Bruce, *Dimsie Goes to School* (School)

1924	A. A. Milne, *When We Were Very Young* (Poetry)
1927	A. A. Milne, *Now We Are Six* (Poetry)
1929	Erich Kästner, *Emil and the Detectives* (Adventure)
1930	Arthur Ransome, *Swallows and Amazons* (Adventure); Hergé, *Tintin au pays des Soviets* (Adventure)
1931	J. B. Morton, 'Now We Are Sick' (Poetry)
1932	Laura Ingalls Wilder, *Little House in the Big Woods* (Family)
1933	Elinor Brent-Dyer, *Exploits of the Chalet Girls* (School)
1934	Elinor Brent-Dyer, *The Chalet School and the Lintons* (School); Geoffrey Trease, *Bows Against the Barons* (Adventure); P. L. Travers, *Mary Poppins* (Fantasy)
1935	John Masefield, *The Box of Delights* (Fantasy); Laura Ingalls Wilder, *The Little House on the Prairie* (Family; Adventure)
1937	Eve Garnett, *The Family From One-End Street* (Family); J. R. R. Tolkien, *The Hobbit* (Fantasy; Adventure); Release of Walt Disney's first animated feature film, *Snow White and the Seven Dwarfs* (Fantasy)
1939	DuBose Hayward, *The Country Bunny and the Little Gold Shoes* (Fables)
1940	James Thurber, *Fables for Our Time* (Fables)
1941	Enid Blyton, *The Twins at St. Clare's* (School); W. E. Johns, *Worrals of the W.A.A.F.* (Adventure)
1942	Enid Blyton, *Five on a Treasure Island* (Adventure); Laura Ingalls Wilder, *The Long Winter* (Family)
1945	E. B. White, *Stuart Little* (Fantasy); George Orwell, *Animal Farm* (Fables)

1946	Enid Blyton, *First Term at Malory Towers* (School)
1947	Laurence Maynell, *The Old Gang* (School)
1949	C. Day Lewis, *The Otterbury Incident* (Adventure); Geoffrey Trease, *No Boats on Bannermere* (School)
1950	Anne Barrett, *Caterpillar Hall* (Fantasy); Anthony Buckeridge, *Jennings Goes to School* (School); C. S. Lewis, *The Lion, the Witch and the Wardrobe* (Family; Fantasy; Adventure)
1951	J. D. Salinger, *The Catcher in the Rye* (Moral Tales)
1952	Mabel Esther Allan, *The School on Cloud-Ridge* (School); E. B. White, *Charlotte's Web* (Fables)
1954	Lucy Boston, *The Children of Green Knowe* (Fantasy)
1954–55	J. R. R. Tolkien, *The Lord of the Rings* (Fantasy)
1955	C. S. Lewis, *The Magician's Nephew* (Fantasy); Rosemary Sutcliff, *Outcast* (Adventure); William Mayne, *A Swarm in May* (School)
1956	Ian Serraillier, *The Silver Sword* (Adventure)
1957	Eleanor Farjeon, *The Children's Bells* (Poetry)
1958	Catherine Storr, *Marianne Dreams* (Fantasy); E. W. Hildick, *Jim Starling* (School); Philippa Pearce, *Tom's Midnight Garden* (Fantasy)
1959	Cynthia Harnett, *The Load of Unicorn* (Adventure)
1960	John Knowles, *A Separate Peace* (School)
1961	John Rowe Townsend, *Gumble's Yard* (Family)
1963	Ann Holm, *I Am David* (Adventure); Maurice Sendak, *Where the Wild Things Are* (Fantasy); Ted Hughes, *How the Whale Became* (Fables)
1964	Leon Garfield, *Jack Holborn* (Adventure); Louise Fitzhugh, *Harriet the Spy* (School); Nina Bawden,

On the Run (Adventure); Roald Dahl, *Charlie and the Chocolate Factory* (Poetry)

1965   Alan Garner, *Elidor* (Fantasy); Susan Cooper, *Over Sea, Under Stone* (Adventure)

1966   William Mayne, *Earthfasts* (Fantasy)

1967   Henry Treece, *The Dream-Time* (Adventure); Ursula Le Guin, *The Wizard of Earthsea* (Fantasy)

1969   Penelope Farmer, *Charlotte Sometimes* (Fantasy); Russell Hoban, *The Mouse and His Child* (Fantasy)

1970   Betsy Byars, *The Summer of the Swans* (Moral Tales); Charles Causley, *Figgie Hobbin* (Poetry); E. B. White, *The Trumpet of the Swan* (Fantasy); Judy Blume, *Are You There God? It's Me, Margaret* (Moral Tales); Roald Dahl, *Fantastic Mr Fox* (Fables)

1971   Robert O'Brien, *Mrs Frisby and the Rats of* NIMH (Fables)

1972   Helen Cresswell, *Lizzie Dripping* (Fantasy); Mary Rogers, *Freaky Friday* (Fantasy); Richard Adams, *Watership Down* (Fantasy); Richard Peck, *Don't Look and It Won't Hurt* (Moral Tales)

1973   Penelope Lively, *The Ghost of Thomas Kempe* (Fantasy); Susan Cooper, *The Dark is Rising* (Adventure)

1974   Bernard Ashley, *The Trouble with Donovan Croft* (Moral Tales); Jill Murphy, *The Worst Witch* (Fantasy); Louise Fitzhugh, *Nobody's Family is Going to Change* (Family); Michael Rosen, *Mind Your Own Business* (Poetry); Robert Cormier, *The Chocolate War* (School)

1975   Judy Bloom, *Forever* (Moral Tales); Roald Dahl, *Danny the Champion of the World* (School); Robert O'Brien, *Z for Zachariah* (Fantasy)

1976   Richard Peck, *Are You in the House Alone?* (Moral
        Tales); Roger McGough, 'First Day at School'
        (Poetry)

1976–78 Alan Garner, *The Stone Book Quartet* (Family)

1977   Betsy Byars, *The Pinballs* (Family); Gene Kemp,
        Cricklepit Combined School (School); Gene Kemp,
        The Turbulent Term of Tyke Tiler (School)

1978   Aidan Chambers, *Breaktime* (School); Anne
        Digby, *First Term at Trebizon* (School); First episode
        of Phil Redmond's television series, *Grange Hill*
        (School); Jan Needle, *My Mate Shofiq* (Moral tales);
        Louis Sachar, *Sideways Stories from Wayside School*
        (School)

1979   Deborah Hautzig, *Hey, Dollface* (School); Katherine
        Paterson, *The Great Gilly Hopkins* (Moral Tales;
        Family); Ogden Nash, *Custard and Company*
        (Introduction); Robert Cormier, *After the First Death*
        (Adventure)

1980   Anne Digby, *Boy Trouble at Trebizon* (School);
        Arnold Lebel, *Fables* (Fables); Gene Kemp, *Dog
        Days and Cat Naps* (School); Robert Leeson, *Grange
        Hill Rules OK?* (School)

1981   Cynthia Voigt, *Homecoming* (Family); Peter
        Dickinson, *The Seventh Raven* (Adventure); Shel
        Silverstein, *A Light in the Attic* (Poetry)

1982   Gillian Cross, *The Demon Headmaster* (School);
        Roald Dahl, *Revolting Rhymes* (Introduction; Poetry)

1983   Aidan Chambers, *The Present Takers* (School);
        Susanne Bösche, *Jenny lives with Eric and Martin*
        (Family)

1984   Francine Pascal, *Sweet Valley High* (School); Ted
        Hughes, *What is the Truth? A Farmyard Fable for the
        Young* (Fables; Poetry)

1985   Beverley Naidoo, *Journey to Jo'burg* (Adventure); David Macaulay, *Baaa* (Fables)

1986   Diana Wynne Jones, *Howl's Moving Castle* (Fantasy); Jack Prelutsky, *The New Kid on the Block* (Poetry)

1987   Anne Fine, *Madame Doubtfire*, known as *Alias Madame Doubtfire* in the USA (Family); Jenny Pausacker, *What Are Ya?* (School); John Mole, *Boo to a Goose* (Poetry); Louis Sachar, *There's a Boy in the Girls' Bathroom* (School)

1988   Janet and Allan Ahlberg, *Starting School* (School)

1989   Allan Ahlberg and Fritz Wegner, *Heard it in the Playground* (Poetry); Anne Fine, *Goggle-Eyes* (Family); Bruce Coville, *My Teacher is an Alien* (School); Jean Ure, *Plague 99* (Fantasy); Leslea Newman, *Heather Has Two Mommies* (Family); Morris Gleitzman, *Two Weeks With the Queen* (Family)

1990   Jamie Rix, *Grizzly Tales: Cautionary Tales for Lovers of Squeam!* (Introduction); Ursula Le Guin, *Tehanu* (Fantasy)

1990–92   Adèle Geras, *Egerton Hall Trilogy* (School)

1991   Berlie Doherty, *Dear Nobody* (Moral tales); Jacqueline Wilson, *The Story of Tracy Beaker* (Family)

1992   Jackie Kay, *Two's Company* (Poetry); Mick Gowar, 'Rat Trap' (Poetry)

1993   Robert Westall, *Falling into Glory* (School); Alida E. Young, *Losing David* (Introduction)

1994   Benjamin Zephaniah, 'According to My Mood' (Poetry)

1995   Gary Kilworth, *The Brontë Girls* (Family); William Mayne, *Cradlefasts* (Fantasy)

1995–2000   Philip Pullman, *His Dark Materials* (Introduction; Family; Fantasy; Adventure)

1995–2003   Garth Nix, *Old Kingdom* series (Fantasy)

1997   Vivian French and Korky Paul, *Aesop's Funky Fables* (Fables)

1997–2007   J. K. Rowling, *Harry Potter* series (School; Fantasy)

1998   Morris Gleitzman, *Bumface* (Family)

2000   Anthony Horowitz, *Stormbreaker* (Adventure); Beverley Naidoo, *The Other Side of Truth* (Adventure)

2001   Terry Pratchett, *The Amazing Maurice and His Educated Rodents* (Fantasy)

2003   Melvyn Burgess, *Doing It* (School)

2004   Michael Morpurgo, *The Orchard Book of Aesop's Fables* (Fables)

2005   Charlie Higson, *Silverfin* (Adventure); Joshua Mowill, *Operation Red Jericho* (Adventure)

2006   Geraldine McCaughrean, *Peter Pan in Scarlet* (School); Susan Cooper, *Victory* (Adventure)

2007   David Gilman, *Danger Zone: The Devil's Breath* (Adventure)

Introduction

The aim of this *Critical Guide* is to deepen understanding of individual children's books, and of children's literature as a whole, by examining the history of the form and, especially, the generic traditions that have emerged over the course of the last three hundred years. The idea is not that a great deal of detailed information about particular books or authors will be found here. Specific texts will certainly be discussed, often in some depth. But this short survey is primarily intended as an introduction to the subject, providing a sound foundation for further study. This is a book that explores how particular texts and authors fit into the wider pattern.

Each of the main chapters examines one of the major genres of children's literature. These genres have existed since children's literature was first established as a separate part of print culture in the seventeenth and eighteenth centuries, and sometimes even before that. What a short study like this cannot do is to provide a complete account of children's literature. After all, it is a vast subject: texts have been read by children from the very earliest periods of recorded history to today, across all continents and there are important genres besides those covered here. To attempt to consider all this would be preposterous – as preposterous as trying to cover all of 'adult literature' in a few dozen pages. Some limits, then, have been necessary. First, in general it is only the children's books of Britain and North America that will be considered here. Occasionally, some authors from outside these geographical limits have been discussed – Jules

Verne from France and Erich Kästner from Germany, and Beverley Naidoo from South Africa, not to mention Aesop – but these are usually authors who have become implanted in the Anglo-American tradition. Comparing Anglo-American texts with work from the wider world – from European or Asian literature, from colonial and post-colonial traditions – is fascinating, and criticism is beginning to explore these connections, but it would not have been possible in such a short book as this.

The second limit is generic. Children have consumed, and still consume, a huge variety of material – from fiction to textbooks, from Shakespeare to the scriptures, from verse to adverts, from picturebooks to computer games. Taken in its widest sense, the term 'children's literature' covers all these forms, and many others. Some are so expansive, and have generated so much critical discussion, that they demand a whole book to themselves – fairy stories and folk tales, for example – and so they do not feature here. Others are only partially represented by this book's seven chapters: for instance war stories and historical novels are subsumed into the chapter on adventure stories. Still others do not feature at all: comics, plays and films for example. Important as the range of material is, and absorbing as it may be to trace the adaptation of texts from one medium to another, this study will concentrate only on those texts which appear in book form, those which have been intended primarily for children, those which have been intended to entertain children at least as much as to instruct them, and those which have a high textual, as opposed to graphic, content. Thus comics, films and games are excluded under the first clause; some adults books which have been widely read by children are excluded under the second; school-books and ABCs are omitted under the third; and picturebooks and pop-up books are left out under the fourth. There are a few exceptions to these general rules. Some picturebooks and television programmes are discussed, but only when they fall squarely within one of the main genres under discussion, and have made an important contribution to their development.

The third limit is chronological. Texts have been produced for children since Roman times, and very probably before. Children in medieval and Renaissance Britain were certainly provided with a wide range of reading material, books produced primarily for older readers that they were permitted or encouraged to read, as well as texts designed especially for them.[1] But should we consider this children's literature? The critic Peter Hunt certainly thought not, arguing vociferously that children's literature is properly comprised only of texts that were 'written expressly for children who are recognizably children, with a childhood recognizable today'. Books of 'no interest to the *current* librarian or child', he insisted, even if they were actually written for children once, are not rightly part of our subject, and ought to be the preserve of historians and bibliographers.[2] There is an undeniable logic to this argument, although a number of critics responded to Hunt with indignation and incredulity.[3]

More questionable is Hunt's attack on what he thinks an erroneous assumption, that there is a 'flow, a stream of history, that connects all books written for children, and that we in the present can learn from the past about books for children'.[4] Hunt may well have been correct that because notions of childhood have altered over time, so the purposes and practice of children's literature will have changed, meaning that children's books do not now do the same things that they once did and that we should not, therefore, try to place them in a continuum. But generic continuities certainly do exist in the minds of authors and illustrators, and publishers anxious to contract only books that will sell. A school story published today will be written for a wholly different kind of child than a school story written in the sixteenth century, but the producers of the twenty-first century text will nevertheless be inheriting traditions, expectations and perhaps limits from a long succession of previous practitioners. J. K. Rowling's *Harry Potter* novels, for example, are evidently part of the long history of evolution of the school story, with literary genes having been passed on by, amongst many other ancestors, the television programme *Grange Hill*, the school stories of Enid Blyton, Frank Richards, Angela Brazil, L. T. Meade, Thomas Hughes, Maria Edgeworth and Sarah Fielding, whose *The Governess* (1749) is often cited as the first school story. But even Fielding did not magic her formula out of nothing, for she too drew on a tradition of children's books set in schools that dated back to the Renaissance or even before. What is true of school stories is true of the other genres in this book too, although sometimes in less obvious ways. The continuities between Judy Blume writing in

America in the 1970s, and Maria Edgeworth, say, writing in Britain almost two centuries before, may not be immediately apparent, but both were writing moral tales of a sort, and the generic continuities outweigh the differences of style and subject. In each intervening generation the formula has been modified in many new ways, so much so that today's children might find little to interest them in the moral tales or school stories of the eighteenth, or even the nineteenth, century. But this does not undermine the unavoidable importance of past children's books in the formation of today's children's literature, nor, therefore, the relevance of tracing these generic genetics.

There is still, though, a need to delimit the chronological range of children's literature, and the survey offered in this book begins only in the late seventeenth century. The decision for this starting point is not based on any claim about relevance to today's children, but on the notion that children's literature began to be presented and recognised as a distinct part of print culture in Britain and America only in the decade or so on either side of 1700. This is not to say that texts written earlier were not enjoyed by children, nor that there are not clear stylistic and thematic links between what classical, medieval and Renaissance children were reading and what would follow. But it is to say that children's literature began to be widely understood as a separate product only in the half-century or so following 1660, when Puritan authors realised how effective it could be in furthering their campaign to reform the personal piety of all individuals, adults and children alike.

James Janeway's *A Token for Children* (1672) is perhaps the classic example of a Puritan children's book. His morbid, not to say traumatic, account of the 'Joyful Deaths of Several Young Children' (as part of the full title puts it) is, in terms of tone and subject, very far from today's children's literature (although a 1990s series taking a similar subject, *Sweet Goodbyes*, can seem eerily equivalent).[5] But his insistence that a work of imaginative literature can be as important to a child's future as any exclusively didactic or devotional text was an important foundation for modern children's literature. After all, the same principle could very easily be applied to secular concerns. That children's literature developed when, where and how it did was due not so much to the daring of pioneering publishers or the genius of avant-garde authors but to the emergence of a new market: affluent parents who were willing to invest in their children. Above all, eighteenth-century children's books, however pious and conservative they also were, were fundamentally designed to enlist fiction and verse to expedite the secular, socio-economic advancement of their readers.

Puritan writers like Janeway were also modern in their conviction that their writing would be most effective if children enjoyed reading it. We might like to think that children would not have taken pleasure from rigid piety and accounts of childhood deaths, but the evidence we have suggests otherwise. Autobiographies can speak of 'delight in reading, especially of Mr. Janeway's *Token for Children*', and when one young reader, as late as 1821, described *A Token for Children* as 'the most entertaining book that can be', it was surely not (or not only) because he had enjoyed reading about pious prigs expiring in agonies.[6] Indeed, if we can get past the religiosity, it is not so difficult to see why some Puritan texts would have been attractive to child readers. John Bunyan's *A Book for Boys and Girls* (also called *Country Rimes for Children* or *Divine Emblems*, 1686) contained poems which, though remorselessly devout, were light in tone and cleverly constructed to draw in the reader. 'The Boy and Watch-Maker' tells of a golden watch given to a boy by his father, but which does not work. It is an alluring subject, and frustratingly familiar. Only the third stanza, the 'Comparison', explains the poem's meaning: the boy is a Christian soul and the watch is divine grace within his heart. The watch does not tell the time because it has not been well-cared for. The analogy is spelled out in language that is kindly and approachable (and, incidentally, reminds the modern reader of Philip Pullman's *His Dark Materials*, 1995–2000, with its golden compass rather than watch):

> Do not lay ope' thy heart to Worldly Dust,
> Nor let they Graces over grow with Rust.
> Be oft renew'd in th' Spirit of thy mind,
> Or else uncertain thou thy Watch wilt find.[7]

The verses function as a sort of riddle, evidently designed to entertain as well as reform. The same might even be said of Benjamin

Keach's *War With the Devil* (1673), a dialogue in verse between a 'Youth' and his 'Conscience'. The text is as undeviating as any hell-fire sermon, but it still contains almost comic elements as the two characters berate one another. Youth treats Conscience as if he was an annoying, old-fashioned friend: 'I'd have you know,' says Youth, 'that I | A Person am of some Authority; | Are you so saucy as to curb and chide | Such a brave Spark, who can't your Ways abide?'[8] Even *A Token for Children* has its attractions. The language could be powerful and moving, Janeway being surprisingly tender with his death-scenes. The child-centric nature of these texts was deliberately designed to be attractive to children too. Each narrative revolves around a single child, the adults playing only minor roles. In this sense, Janeway's characters were not so different from Lewis Carroll's Alice or Pullman's Lyra. Janeway's children are wiser and nobler than any adult, and frequently admonish them. This appealed, no doubt, to children's fantasies of empowerment. They were heroic too, battling valiantly against sin in a way neatly demonstrated by an illustration to Keach's *War With the Devil* in which the 'youth in his converted state' single-handedly stands up to the armed assault of a band of sinners and the Devil himself. One might even speculate that the protagonists' deaths in Janeway dramatised another common children's fantasy: the desire to be lost from parents so that the adults realise how much they miss their children when they are gone.

In numerous ways, then, the origins of modern children's literature can be seen in the books produced by the Puritans for children, however unpalatable we might think them today. Any attempt to trace continuities in children's literature, though, is open to criticism. It might seem too teleological, as if all the literature of the past is to be understood and appraised only as it has contributed to form the literature of the present. And it might seem to be canon-building. This would be particularly regrettable since children's literature (largely because its study began in earnest only at a time when canons were becoming unfashionable) has remained comparatively free of the sort of 'Great Tradition', or division into 'important' and 'marginal' books, that has afflicted adult literature. The best antidote to teleology is the appreciation of all texts on their own merits, and in their own contexts, without defining them in terms of their difference from, let alone inferiority to, what was to come. This is the approach taken in this book. If Maria Edgeworth can be understood as the ancestor of Judy Blume, this is not to say that any relative value is embedded in the comparison, nor that the connections between them should be read in only one direction. Reading Edgeworth in the light of Blume can be just as enlightening as reading Blume in the light of Edgeworth. This explains why some of the chapters in this study take a broadly chronological approach while others dart backwards and forwards through the history of a genre.

Similarly, a strong preventative against the stealthy material-isation of a children's literature canon is the inclusion of an extensive array of material from the most neglected corners of the field. While it is true that by looking at fiction and poetry, rather than work appearing in more undervalued and ephemeral media (comics, or textbooks), this book concentrates mostly on the sort of texts that are likely to feature on university children's literature courses, it is also a survey that features a great many non-canonical works. Alongside the sorts of authors who feature in most histories of children's books other much less well-known works are discussed, from early eighteenth-century collections of children's verse to largely forgotten 'problem novels' published in 1970s America, and from Victorian monthly magazines stories to picture-books from the Harlem Renaissance. The inclusion of such a wide range of texts has not been prompted by any particular ideological agenda or canonic iconoclasm. Rather it reflects a conviction that the history of children's literature is by no means described only by those books that are still well-known today. As with literature for adults, the history of children's literature is littered with books, and whole sub-genres, that were once hugely popular but are now neither read nor widely known. Yet in many cases, these obscure works were extremely important in constructing generic traditions that shape children's books today. A good example are the caution-ary tales popular in the eighteenth and early nineteenth centuries: long-forgotten stories and poems warning about the horrible fates befalling naughty children. These texts were no longer in fashion even when they were parodied by Heinrich Hoffmann's *Shock-Headed Peter* (1848), Lewis Carroll's *Alice's Adventures in Wonderland* (1865) and Hilaire Belloc's *Cautionary Tales for*

Children (1907). But somehow they have remained ingrained in the fabric of children's culture. Authors like Ogden Nash, Roald Dahl and Jamie Rix were still riffing on them at the end of the twentieth century (*Custard and Company*, 1979; *Revolting Rhymes*, 1982; *Grizzly Tales: Cautionary Tales for Lovers of Squeam!*, 1990).

One further dilemma that must confront anyone now attempting to write a concise account of children's literature is how best to do justice to the increasing amount, and sophistication, of the scholarship devoted to it. Much innovative and searching criticism of children's literature has now accumulated. It has been possible to mention only a small fraction of it in the footnotes and the Guide to Further Reading. Some of the best criticism presents careful new readings of particular texts. Some concentrates on authors, or publishers, or readers. Some is concerned more with how children's books can be positioned in larger contexts: social or political history say, or discourses of gender, race or child development. Some critics have taken a more abstract approach, seeking to pose, or solve, theoretical problems about the very nature of children's literature. How, for instance, is childhood to be defined, and how has this changed over time? Is there such a thing as children's literature in any case? Might it be more accurate to speak of a boys' literature and a girls' literature? Can children's literature exist for an audience that ranges from infants to pre-teens to young adults and beyond? And is it perhaps really produced for the adults who commission, write and buy it, rather than any actual children?

The current status of children's literature studies, and some possible future directions, are briefly considered in the conclusion to this book, but by and large, this study is not designed to provide a survey of current methodologies, nor is it overly concerned with problematising the concept of children's literature. No one particular kind of analysis is favoured, but rather different critical approaches are taken when they seem to offer important insight into how each major genre has developed. The fundamental argument presented here is simply that a book written for children should be treated no differently than a book for adults. Both can make equally serious artistic statements. Both have a place in particular literary traditions. And both may be analysed without theorising about how the intended audience, rather than the text itself, determines meaning. The challenges of children's literature are many, and they are complex and fascinating. But the greatest challenge, which all of the best children's literature criticism meets, is to give children's books the kind of careful, nuanced and disinterested critical attention that for many years was reserved only for books written for adults.

NOTES

1. See Gillian Adams, 'Medieval Children's Literature: Its Possibility and Actuality', *Children's Literature*, 26 (1998), 1–24.
2. Peter Hunt, *Criticism, Theory and Children's Literature* (Oxford: Blackwell, 1991), pp. 67 and 61. Emphasis added.
3. For instance, Perry Nodelman, 'The Second Kind of Criticism', *Children's Literature Association Quarterly*, 17 (1992), 37–9; Richard Flynn, 'The Intersection of Children's Literature and Childhood Studies', *Children's Literature Association Quarterly*, 22 (1997), 143–5; Susan R. Gannon, 'Report from Limbo: Reading Historical Children's Literature Today', *Signal. Approaches to Children's Books*, 85 (1998), 63–72.
4. Peter Hunt, 'Passing on the Past: The Problem of Books That Are for Children and That Were for Children', *Children's Literature in Education*, 21 (1996–97), 200–2 (p. 200).
5. For instance Alida E. Young, *Losing David* (London: Lions, 1993), about an HIV-positive girl and a boy with leukaemia.
6. *An Account of the Life of the Late Reverend Mr David Brainerd* (Edinburgh: William Gray, 1765), p. 3: Brainerd was born in Connecticut in 1718; *The Sunday Scholars' Magazine*, quoted in Gillian Avery, 'The Puritans and Their Heirs' in *Children and Their Books: A Celebration of the Work of Iona and Peter Opie*, ed. Gillian Avery and Julia Briggs (Oxford: Oxford University Press, 1989), pp. 95–118 (p. 113).
7. John Bunyan, *A Book for Boys and Girls* (London: printed for N.P., 1686), pp. 54–5.
8. Benjamin Keach, *War With the Devil, or, The Young Man's Conflict with the Powers of Darkness in a Dialogue* (London: Benjamin Harris, [1673] 1676), p. 15.

CHAPTER I

Fables

The classic fable is a short, fictional tale which has a specific moral or behavioural lesson to teach. This lesson is often explained at the end of the tale in an epigram or 'moral'. Some are about humans: 'The Boy Who Cried Wolf' for instance. But most feature animals as their main characters, representing human beings, or perhaps particular types of people or kinds of behaviour. In these 'beast fables' the animals are generally fairly lifelike – except that they can often talk – and they do not usually encounter humans. This distinguishes them from animals in fairy tales, often enchanted in one way or another, who interact with humans and live what are essentially human lives. Like fairy tales, fables probably had their origins in an oral folk tale tradition and were not originally intended only for children. Also like fairy tales, fables subsequently came to be associated primarily with the young. Fables are still being written, mainly for children, but sometimes with the hope of appealing to a mixed-age audience. These modern fables can be much grander affairs that the short, allegorical animal stories that first defined the genre. They are often novel-length, with many characters and intricate plots, like Robert O'Brien's *Mrs Frisby and the Rats of* NIMH (1971). They can have complicated themes and enigmatic meanings, like E. B. White's *Charlotte's Web* (1952). Sometimes they seek to give much more scientifically accurate representations of animal life, as in Richard Adams' *Watership Down* (1972). They have sometimes taken their lessons from a much wider range of animals than generally feature in Aesop, as in *Those Other Animals* (1892) by G. A. Henty, who preferred to draw lessons from animals 'whose good points have been hitherto ignored' – like the bacillus – and 'to take down others from the pedestal upon which they have been placed'.[1] And often they are very political, as with George Orwell's *Animal Farm* (1945). But what is more remarkable than the developments within the fable tradition are the continuities. However sophisticated the fable has become it remains fundamentally a didactic form, designed to draw in its readers through a compelling story and appealing, even cute, characters, and to teach important lessons through allegory. It is this consistency, within a general pattern of evolution, that this chapter will trace.

There are good reasons for regarding fables as the first children's literature. They were written down as early as two thousand years BCE on the cuneiform tablets used by the Sumerians in what is now Iraq and Iran. According to Gillian Adams, the fact that fables were written on unbaked clay tablets in relatively unformed writing demonstrates that they were used by children in school lessons.[2] Fables were used for education from a very early period in India too. A collection called the *Panchatantra* had been composed at least as early as the sixth century BCE, and certain fables were later extracted into a separate collection for use by children, usually known as the *Fables of Bidpai* (or *Pilpay*). Bidpai is a learned Brahmin who tries to overcome the stupidity of three princes by encasing their lessons in short narratives. They were widely translated – into Arabic, then Greek (which was the version which circulated widely in medieval Europe), and, by the eighteenth century, English. Most famous in the West are the fables associated with the name Aesop. Aesop was probably a real historical figure, a slave living somewhere in Asia Minor in the sixth century BCE who may later have moved to Greece. He is mentioned by Plato, Plutarch, Herodotus and other Greek writers, and there is a record of a collection of his tales, by Demetrius of Phalerus, now destroyed, being in the Great Library of Alexandria in the fourth century BCE. But the first collection of fables attributed to Aesop that still exists dates only from the Roman period, a collection assembled by the poet Phaedrus in the first century CE. Fables were apparently central to the education of Roman children. As well as Phaedrus' collection of Aesop (called the *Romulus*), they might have read another by Babrius (also first century CE, written in Greek verse) or by Avianus (compiled in around CE 400). All these continued to be read by children throughout medieval Europe.

The relationship between all the different fable traditions is incestuous, with versions of the same narratives, characters and morals cropping up in Indian, Greek, Roman and other later collections, such as the French 'Reynard the Fox' series (c.1175–1250). However, by the later medieval period in Britain, almost all fables were being marketed as having come from Aesop. Sir Roger L'Estrange nicely summed up the situation in his important edition of 1692:

> the Story is come down to us so Dark and Doubtful, that it is Impossible to Distinguish the *Original* from the *Copy:* And to say, which of the Fables are *Aesops*, and which *not;* which are *Genuine*, and which *Spurious*.[3]

From the fifteenth century many different collections were published under Aesop's name, mostly, apparently, for a sophisticated, adult audience. William Caxton's 1484 translation (one of the first books printed in Britain) was in large format and expensive; Robert Henryson's *The Morall Fabillis of Esope in Scottis Meter* (1570) was addressed to 'worthie folk' and 'lordis of prudence'; and John Ogilby's *The Fables of Aesop* (1651) and Jean de La Fontaine's French *Fables Choisies* (1668–93) were written in stylish and sophisticated verse. But throughout the Renaissance period in Britain, Aesop's *Fables* was also the text most commonly used in schools to teach elementary English.[4] Indeed, Sir Roger L'Estrange admitted that he had started to amass his late seventeenth-century collection by pilfering 'the Common *School-Book*'.

More importantly, L'Estrange redesigned the fable to suit children's abilities and needs, as he saw them. He complained that fables had previously been,

> Taught in All our Schools; but almost at such a rate as we Teach *Pyes* [magpies] and *Parrots*, that Pronounce the Words without so much as Guessing at the Meaning of them: Or to take it Another way, the Boys Break their Teeth upon the

Shells, without ever coming near the Kernel. They Learn the *Fables* by *Lessons*, and the Moral is the least part of our Care in a Childs Institution.

For L'Estrange, the potency of the fable lay in the way instruction could be combined with the pleasure of a short narrative: 'it is beyond All Dispute,' he wrote, 'that the Delight and Genius of Children, lies much toward the Hearing, Learning, and Telling of Little Stories'. The writer for children should therefore always be 'Indulging and Cultivating of This *Disposition*, or *Inclination*, on the *One* hand, and the Applying of a Profitable *Moral* to the *Figure*, or the *Fable*, on the *Other*'. By these means, 'These very Lessons Themselves may be Gilt and Sweeten'd, as we Order Pills and Potions; so as to take off the Disgust of the Remedy.'[5] This provides another reason for believing that fables should be regarded as the earliest form of modern children's literature, for L'Estrange's theory of the fable foreshadows the 'instruction and delight' strategy proudly employed fifty years later by John Newbery, so often regarded as the first publisher to offer children entertainment intertwined with education.

Perhaps equally beholden to L'Estrange and the fable tradition was the educational theory so influentially advocated by John Locke in his *Some Thoughts Concerning Education* of 1693, only a year after the publication of L'Estrange's Aesop. Locke practically paraphrased L'Estrange's ideas. He famously likened the child to a *tabula rasa* (blank tablet or slate), but this was merely a restatement of L'Estrange's view that '*Children* are but *Blank Paper*, ready Indifferently for any Impression'. And Locke's lament at the lack of safe and useful reading matter for children, although there was so much 'perfectly useless trumpery', recalls L'Estrange's even more contemptuous assertion that his fables replaced nothing better than 'Insipid *Twittle-Twattles*, Frothy *Jests*, and Jingling *Witticisms*'. Even more strikingly, Locke maintained that there were only two books available that were suitable for the education of children: *Raynard the Fox* and *Aesop's Fables*.[6] Although some were to complain that because fables were 'a palpable Falsehood, and a mere Fiction', they accustomed children to deceit (which, *ipso facto*, was a bad thing, but also 'abates much of the Pleasure of reading the

Story')[7], Locke's endorsement ensured that the fable flourished throughout the eighteenth century and beyond. Reworked collections appeared every few years.[8]

Increasingly, these new collections were designed solely for children. Joseph Jackson justified his own 1708 venture into print by claiming that L'Estrange's collection 'seems rather designed for part of the furniture of a statesman's closet, than the satchel of a school-boy' so that the fables have 'not so fully attained the chief aim of their publication viz. the Instruction of Youth.' His, by contrast, would be concise, direct and well-illustrated so as to enable 'an easier reception into the understanding, or at least root it deeper in the memory of every juvenile reader'.[9] A century later, in his *Fables Ancient and Modern* (1805), William Godwin repeated the Lockean position, that 'fables were the happiest vehicle which could be devised for the instruction of children in the first period of their education', but argued that, if they were to be appealing and effective, revisions were necessary. He developed the characters of the animal protagonists and introduced humans to interact with them. Attempting 'to make almost all my narratives end in a happy and forgiving tone', he replaced the customary abrupt manner and pithy morals with a more discursive style and protracted lessons. 'The Ass in the Lion's Skin' exhibits his method very well. Godwin's fable is around five times as long as the traditional version, with a beginning, middle and end to the narrative, and it is buttressed by geographical notes ('All this happened in a country where lions lived; I suppose in Africa'). Moreover, whereas in the standard version, an ass dons a lion's pelt to scare his master and other animals, Godwin's ass uses the pelt to punish boys who have been tormenting him. The moral comes some way before the fable's end and is also made more relevant to children: 'Cheats are always found out.' The narrative closes not with the ass being beaten, but with a much more tender rapprochement with the children, bordering on sentimentality: 'now, instead of running away the moment they came in sight, he would trot to meet them, would rub his head against them to tell them how much he loved them, and would eat the thistles and the oats out of their hand: was not that pretty?'[10]

Many later writers sought to make their fables more directly appealing to children by abridgement not extension. Walter Crane's

Baby's Own Aesop (1887) distilled them into limericks, and the morals into snappy maxims, and relied heavily on his beautiful full-page illustrations to fascinate the reader. Here is 'The Crow and the Pitcher' for example:

> How the cunning old Crow got his drink
> When 'twas low in the pitcher, just think!
> Don't say that he spilled it!
> With pebbles he filled it,
> 'Till the water rose up to the brink!

Crane's moral is 'Use your wits'.[11] Each generation makes its own refinements. The attempt to contemporise fables is evident for example even in the (rather clunky) title of *Aesop's Funky Fables* (1997). Its publishers trusted jointly to Korky Paul's 'wild and inventive illustrations' and Vivian French's 'catchy rap-rhythms and witty retelling' to 'make these the funkiest fables around!' Here is the start of 'The Lion and the Mouse':

> Squeak squeak
> Nibble nibble
>   Rummage rummage
>   Pitter patter
>   Pitter patter
>   Pitter –
> EEEEEEEEEEEEEEEEEEEEEEEEEEEEK!
> Oh no no no no no no no!
> Oh my pitter patter heart oh my whiskers
> That are trembling!
> Mr Lion
> Please don't eat me!
> Let me go!

Aesop's Funky Fables are much less didactic than most previous versions too. Indeed the morals are entirely omitted.[12]

Comparing L'Estrange to Godwin to Crane to *Aesop's Funky Fables* reveals some fairly obvious changes in style, format, language and tone. What are often even more revealing about society's changing attitudes to childhood and children's literature are slight variations in the content of the fables and the sometimes subtle shifts of emphases in the morals. The well-known 'The Boy Who Cried Wolf' is an interesting example. In Michael Morpurgo's 2004 version the lesson is that 'No one believes a liar even when he is telling the truth.'[13] But three hundred years earlier, for L'Estrange, the moral had been 'He must be a very Wise Man that knows the True Bounds, and Measures of Foolling [*sic*]'. His further 'Reflexion' explains that the boy's error was not in joking about the danger of wolves, but in taking the joke too far. Despite its hazards, L'Estrange insists that raillery remains 'the very Sawce of Civil Entertainment': an important part of how society functions smoothly and how the individual relates to the community.[14] By 2004 (and well before, in fact) the fable's moral had become much more straightforward and more literal: more 'childish' one might say. According to the critic David Whitley this is because in the mid-eighteenth century authors influenced by Locke began to see that fables were the perfect medium for encouraging children to work out the lessons for themselves, decoding the allegory or the illustrations to discover simple lessons. Fables were regarded as 'a testing ground for ideas about what children needed from a story and the most appropriate ways for this to reach them', Whitley concludes.[15] Yet if the morals have been simplified since the eighteenth century, we cannot say for certain that the fables themselves have become more 'childish'. It is now a standard part of 'The Boy Who Cried Wolf' that the boy ends up being eaten along with his sheep, and this is what happens in Morpurgo's apparently very traditional 2004 retelling. We might be tempted to regard the bland conclusion of the version in *Aesop's Funky Fables* – with the boy climbing a tree to escape the wolf but being forced to spend the rest of his days feeding the chickens and chopping wood so that he 'never had time to play' – as a modern palliation of Aesop's savagery, perhaps in deference to parental anxieties about violence in books for the young.[16] In fact, though, the boy is not eaten in most seventeenth- and eighteenth-century versions, and it is likely that the wolf's consumption of the boy is actually a contamination from fairy tales such as 'Little Red Riding Hood'. Aesop's fables have evolved in fascinating, but not predictable, ways.

By the end of the nineteenth century new, post-Aesopic collections of fables were appearing. Probably the most successful are Joel Chandler Harris's *Uncle Remus* stories (from 1879) and the *Just So Stories* (1902) and *The Jungle Books* (1894–95) by Rudyard Kipling. These are not so obviously didactic as the Aesopian fables, and they are bound together into much more sophisticated framing narratives, but they retain the same basic format: short narratives about individual animals representing a particular type of person or behaviour. An alternative tradition was the novel-length animal story designed to illustrate more substantial lessons through more sustained narratives. Early examples include Dorothy Kilner's *The Life and Perambulations of a Mouse* (1783) and Edward Kendall's *Keeper's Travels in Search of his Master* (1798), but the form came of age in the late Victorian and Edwardian periods with books like Anna Sewell's *Black Beauty* (1877), Richard Jeffries' *Wood Magic* (1881) and Jack London's *The Call of the Wild* (1903). For the critic John Goldthwaite what these books represent is 'the beast fable suddenly shedding its ancient moralizing intent and taking on the affective weight of modern prose fantasy.'[17]

But in fact there had always been a substantial crossover between the fable and the animal story. Sewell's intention in *Black Beauty: the Autobiography of a Horse* was to reveal the mistreatment that horses receive from humans. But even if it was not designed exclusively for children, it retains many of the characteristics of the fable. Much of the text concentrates on the best methods to train and manage a horse, but the same lessons are allegorically applicable to humans. The advice given to Black Beauty by his mother, the reason why he lives a more or less contented life that ends happily, is decipherable in the same way as Aesop's warning not to cry wolf: 'do your work with a good will, lift your feet up well when you trot, and never bite or kick even in play.'[18] Likewise, the abuse Sewell chiefly complains of is the 'bearing rein', and although this was genuinely a nineteenth-century practice designed to enhance horses' appearance but causing them discomfort and shortening their lives, it also functions as part of the fable. Black Beauty and his fellow horses rebel against it, causing damage and preventing their mistress from getting to the Duchess' garden party. Sewell did not append a moral, but it is evident nonetheless: brutally to impose restrictions, especially if just for the sake of appearances, will always be resented and counterproductive (or, more Aesopically: 'So violent Threat and Rigour often fail, | Where milder courses oftentimes prevail').[19] Sewell means the lesson to be applied to children as well as to horses, and even perhaps to wives, for it is Lady W—— who favours the bearing rein, and Black Beauty's groom complains bitterly that it is the job of her husband to prevent her cruelty: 'if a woman's husband can't rule her . . . I wash my hands of it.'[20]

In fact, a century before *Black Beauty*, Sarah Trimmer had already happily planted fable elements into a sustained animal story in *Fabulous Histories* (1786). It tells the parallel stories of a family of birds and another of humans: hence its alternative title, *The History of the Robins*, under which it remained in print until well into the twentieth century. Trimmer was adamant that her novel should be considered not 'as containing the real conversations of birds (for that it is impossible we should ever understand), but as a series of FABLES, intended to convey moral instruction'. The two human children, Harriet and Frederick, and the four nestlings, Robin, Dicky, Flapsy and Pecksy, learn roughly the same general lessons: that 'In a family every individual ought to consult the welfare of the whole, instead of his own private satisfaction' and that God has created the world so that all animals are interdependent and that to hurt or kill other creatures without reason is to transgress against the '*divine principle* of UNIVERSAL BENEVOLENCE'. There were more specific lessons too, often taught through inset fable-like vignettes. The robins meet many other birds, learning from their various failings how one ought to behave. The magpies talk all at once so no-one can understand what they say; the chaffinch is condemned for telling tales; the cuckoo denounced for stealing other birds' nests. In another Aesopian episode, the young robins learn that appearances can be deceptive when they find that a man spreading seeds on the ground for them is no philanthropist, but a bird-catcher. Meanwhile Harriet and Frederick learn from other humans: Mrs Addis, who dotes on her pets to the neglect of her own children, and Edward Jenkins who tortures animals, eventually being killed by his own horse. But as in the conventional fable, nature has much to teach humans too. A visit to a beehive leads his mother to ask whether Frederick would fight as well for his monarch as the bees do for their Queen?[21]

The cosmological role of animals, and the relationship between animals and humans, naturally became a frequent subject for these expanded fables. Trimmer's Christianity dictated that mankind had dominion over animals, but although no animal rights campaigner or vegetarian, she insisted that God was in all animals and that they should be treated kindly ('I often regret that so many lives should be sacrificed to preserve ours,' says the children's mother, 'but we must eat animals, or they would at length eat us').[22] Two centuries later, the same pantheistic theme was taken up by Ted Hughes in his *What is the Truth? A Farmyard Fable for the Young* (1984), though with the environmentalist implications brought much further to the fore. The book is composed of the animal poems that an assortment of humans recite to God and his Son when they visit Earth one night. Each is beautiful and moving in its way. But, God insists, they miss the Truth, which is that 'I was those Worms . . . I was that Fox. Just as I was that Foal. . . . I am each of these things. The Rat. The Fly. And each of these things is Me. It is. It is. That is the Truth.'[23]

If Trimmer and Hughes emphasised the interconnectedness of human and animal life, many modern fabulists have preferred to show animals and humans at war. The fundamental lesson of these fables has been that humans are beasts, both in the sense that we are part of the natural world too and should seek to preserve it, and that humans can be as cruel and uncaring as any animal. Roald Dahl's extended fable, *Fantastic Mr Fox* (1970), is typical in its representation of the way in which 'civilisation' has alienated humans from their natural state, a happier and (ironically) more humanitarian way of life that Dahl's animals still inhabit. Boggis, Bunce and Bean are three repulsive farmers who decide to kill a fox who has been poaching their poultry. With their guns and their mechanical diggers they drive him and his family underground, laying waste to the landscape and forcing all the local animals to the brink of starvation. Mr Fox saves the animals' lives by tunnelling to Boggis's chicken shed, Bunce's storeroom and Bean's cider cellar, and the animals live happily in a new underground utopia while the farmers camp in vain at the foxhole ('And so far as I know, they are still waiting.'). What has happened, the reader realises, is that the humans have become rude, nasty and unpleasant, as only Dahl could make them, and as savage as any wild beast, while the animals have become civilised. Mr Fox is convivial, inviting all the animals to his feast. He is chivalric, treating his wife courteously (if somewhat patronisingly). And he is moderate, taking only what he needs from the unlimited stores he has obtained. While the farmers and their employees are outside in the rain ('armed with sticks and guns and hatchets and pistols and all sorts of other horrible weapons') Mr Fox's tunnels have led him physically and symbolically closer to human habitation, until he ends up in the basement of Bean's own house. Morally he is far more civilised too. When a badger questions him about his theft of the farmers' food Mr Fox replies 'My dear old furry frump . . . do you know anyone in the *whole world* who wouldn't swipe a few chickens if his children were starving to death?' By the end of the book, Mr Fox even talks of his poaching as 'shopping'. Besides, the farmers are trying to *kill* the animals, he points out, 'But *we're* not going to stoop to *their* level.' *Fantastic Mr Fox* marries the characters and satire of Aesop with Dahl's uniquely grotesque misanthropy to produce a playful fable about a kind of 'progress' that has brought little but greed, vindictiveness and natural devastation.[24]

John Goldthwaite attributes the rise of the animal story in the late nineteenth century to the advent of 'empire, electricity, and later the automobile, and, perhaps most importantly, of urbanization'.[25] These developments severed people's links with nature but simultaneously encouraged a nostalgic Arcadianism that created the demand for books like Beatrix Potter's *The Tale of Peter Rabbit* (1901) or Kenneth Grahame's *The Wind in the Willows* (1908). Critics have seen the latter in particular as depicting nature threatened equally by technology (Toad's motor car) and the lower classes (the stoats and the weasels who invade Toad Hall), but offering a consoling fantasy in which the 'good' animals (Badger, Rat, Mole) finally rally round to save 'Toad from his extravagances, and the aristocracy from the masses' and 'the English countryside from the forces of industrialisation and exploitation.'[26] But if nostalgia for the rural was often an essentially conservative impulse, by the 1960s the desire 'to get ourselves | Back to the garden', as Joni Mitchell put it in her 1969 song 'Woodstock', had become more politically radical. This new Arcadiaism was still derived from anxiety about the ills of modern, urban, consumerist society, but its fables attack rather than defend existing power structures. Increasingly inflected with environmentalist concerns, they are often more dystopian than consoling. A fine example is David Macaulay's picturebook *Baaa* (1985) in which sheep move into the city after the last humans have somehow disappeared. When over-population results in shortages, their leaders can only pacify the flock by feeding them a product called 'Baaa'. We gradually discover that this must be made of sheep. The population necessarily declines until only two are left: 'one day they met for lunch', the book chillingly concludes.[27] *Baaa* is a satire on the logic of the consumer society and, more generally, is designed to demonstrate how quickly civilisation can alienate creatures – ovine and human – from their true nature.

This is also the basic theme of one of the most complex and successful modern children's fables, Robert O'Brien's *Mrs Frisby and the Rats of* NIMH (1971). It tells of a colony of rats captured for research in a scientific institution ('NIMH': probably based on the American N.I.H. – National Institutes of Health). The injections they are given render them super-intelligent and long-lived, and they escape. Once free, they build for themselves a new society, reading human books, harvesting a share of the crops of the farmer Mr Fitzgibbon, and even harnessing his electricity supply. They help Mrs Frisby, a mouse, by moving her home out of the way of Farmer Fitzgibbon's plough. Like Trimmer long before him, O'Brien was happy to draw attention to the fable-like nature of his novel. Chapter three, 'The Crow and the Cat', recalls Aesop's 'The Mouse and the Lion', with Mrs Frisby saving Jeremy the crow from Dragon the cat by gnawing through the string in which Jeremy is tangled. It is a synecdoche of the whole novel, for eventually Mrs Frisby is integral to the survival of the rats too, warning them of the arrival of the pest exterminators.

This description might make *Mrs Frisby and the Rats of* NIMH sound twee, but the book is actually exceptionally intelligent and surprisingly powerful. Despite their abilities, the rats are rather pitiful creatures, unsure of who they are. By the experiment they 'were set apart from even our own kind', recalls Nicodemus, their leader. Should they 'go back to living in a sewer-pipe . . . eating other people's garbage' just because 'that's what rats do', he asks?

'Where does a group of civilized rats fit in?' Their answer is extraordinary, taking the novel much further beyond its satire on animal experimentation. Their plan, inspired by reading about the rise and fall of the ancient Egyptians, Greeks and Romans, is to establish a new civilisation, but unlike all previous rat societies, it will not be based on stealing food, but on their own farming of the land in an area remote from human habitation. This utopianism emphasises how the novel as a whole functions as a much larger fable than anything in Aesop. There is perhaps the implication that all human societies are based on theft too, but above all, it is the foolish vanity of human civilisation that is emphasised. It is sign-posted by the farmer's name: 'Fitz', from the French 'fils', meaning son (usually associated with illegitimate descent), and 'gibbon', pointing to mankind's simian ancestry. An equivocal attitude to progress permeates the whole novel, from the arrogance of the NIMH scientists (whose treatment of animals would have been roundly condemned by Trimmer or Sewell) to the attitude of Jenner's break-away group of rats who want to live like humans, stealing whatever is necessary from them and threatening to 'find out where they keep the dynamite and use it on them.' It is best summed up in a short, inset fable that Nicodemus tells. Mrs Jones keeps her house clean with a broom and mop until she buys a vacuum cleaner which does the job quicker. Soon all the neighbouring houses have vacuum cleaners and a factory opens up. Its pollution makes the houses dirtier than they were before, so that Mrs Jones has to work twice as long to keep her house *almost* as clean as it had been before she had bought the vacuum cleaner.[28] In its way, *Mrs Frisby and the Rats of* NIMH is as political a fable as George Orwell's *Animal Farm*.

Such a strong political slant in a fable was nothing new. Seventeenth- and eighteenth-century collections of Aesop had been very specific in their satire, offering commentaries on recent political events and controversies. One of Aesop's fables tells how the pigeons were so harassed by a kite that they asked a hawk to be their protector, only to find that the hawk 'makes more Havock . . . in Two Days, than the *Kite* could have done in Twice as many months.' The Tory L'Estrange easily converted this into a attack on the 'Glorious Revolution' of 1688–89 when the English had invited

William III to take the throne from James II.[29] Samuel Croxall managed to use the same fable to argue a contrary political point of view in 1722. James Thurber's *Fables for Our Time* from 1940 are the direct descendants of these, combining historical specificity with a general moral application. Here is 'The Rabbits Who Caused All the Trouble':

> Within the memory of the youngest child there was a family of rabbits who lived near a pack of wolves. The wolves announced that they did not like the way the rabbits were living. . . . One night several wolves were killed in an earthquake and this was blamed on the rabbits, for it is well known that rabbits pound on the ground with their hind legs and cause earthquakes. On another night one of the wolves was killed by a bolt of lightning and this was also blamed on the rabbits, for it is well known that lettuce-eaters cause lightning. The wolves threatened to civilize the rabbits if they didn't behave, and the rabbits decided to run away to a desert island. But the other animals, who lived at a great distance, shamed them, saying, 'You must stay where you are and be brave. This is no world for escapists. If the wolves attack you, we will come to your aid, in all probability.' So the rabbits continued to live near the wolves and one day there was a terrific flood which drowned a great many wolves. This was blamed on the rabbits, for it is well known that carrot-nibblers with long ears cause floods. The wolves descended on the rabbits, for their own good, and imprisoned them in a dark cave, for their own protection.
>
> When nothing was heard about the rabbits for some weeks, the other animals decided to know what had happened to them. The wolves replied that the rabbits had been eaten and since they had been eaten the affair was an internal matter. But the other animals warned that they might possibly unite against the wolves unless some reason was given for the destruction of the rabbits. So the wolves gave them one. 'They were trying to escape,' said the wolves, 'and, as you know, this is no world for escapists.'
> *Moral: Run, don't walk, to the nearest desert island.*[30]

In America in 1940 this might have been read as an anti-appeasement fable designed to bring the USA into the Second World War by allegorising the Nazi conquest of Austria, Czechoslovakia and Poland. From our perspective it is difficult not to read it as a veiled representation of the persecution of Jews in Nazi Germany. One critic has (anachronistically) suggested that the subject is the Soviet takeover of Hungary in 1956.[31] The multiplicity of possible meanings is a symptom of the fable's universality. Certainly it works as a general statement about the ease with which minorities can be blamed for disasters. The very slightly feasible allegation that the rabbits caused the earthquake quickly descends into the absurd contention 'that carrot-nibblers with long ears cause floods'. The mordant humour (the 'internal matter' – a play on the rabbit's edibility) adds to the effect. At their best, then, irrespective of the links with their original context, Thurber's fables are as generally relevant as Aesop's. He did not originally write his fables for the young, but as the distance from the specific events and attitudes that they satirise has increased, so too has their suitability for children.

It might be argued that Thurber, Orwell, O'Brien, Dahl and most other modern authors were, with their fables of toleration, cooperation and conservation, maintaining what was basically a progressive, liberal tradition dating back to Aesop. Aesop's world had been one of competition and predation, but the small or slow often triumphed over the big or fast ('The Hare and the Tortoise'), animals thrived by mutual aid ('The Lion and the Mouse') and selfishness was roundly condemned ('The Dog in the Manger'). Tolerance of difference has also been a traditional concern of fables. Sewell's *Black Beauty* has been read as an attack on slavery as much as cruelty to animals.[32] More obviously engaged with the politics of race are Harris' 185 *Uncle Remus* stories (from 1879), although they are not now much read, at least in the original versions, because of their white author's ventriloquism of what he affected to think were the speech patterns of black slaves. This can certainly be regarded as extremely patronising and insulting, yet when we consider that Harris was writing about an astute black narrator who tells his own stories to the son of his white owners, and thereby is perhaps able to influence the future of the plantation, the picture becomes more complicated. In any case, the stories themselves, mostly recounting the victories of the trickster Brer Rabbit over his more powerful enemies, seem to offer a coded account of resistance to authority. As Harris put it in his introduction to *Songs and Sayings* (1881), the fables he collected were 'thoroughly characteristic of the Negro',

> and it needs no scientific investigation to show why he selects as his hero the weakest and most harmless of all animals, and brings him out victorious in contests with the bear, the wolf, and the fox. It is not virtue that triumphs, but helplessness; it is not malice, but mischievousness.[33]

Likewise, the language used by Rudyard Kipling in his account of why the 'Ethiopian' – 'really a negro, and so his name was Sambo' – is black is unpalatable now, but can be read as an attempt to explain and play down – or perhaps celebrate – racial difference. Just as the leopard with whom he shares this *Just So Story* chooses his own spots, so the 'Ethiopian' devises for himself his 'nice working blackish-brownish colour, with a little purple in it, and touches of slaty-blue' so that he too may hunt more effectively.[34]

One of the moral lessons that fables have traditionally been intended to teach is about the difference between surface and substance, appearance and reality, and this may help to explain why race – frequently represented in terms of skin colour – has always been a subject for them. Samuel Croxall's 'The Blackamoor', for instance, included in his 1722 collection, tells of a foolish man's wish to wash his black slave white. The attempt attracts derision, and the valuable 'Æthiopian' is killed in the process.[35] One of Ted Hughes' fables, 'How the Polar Bear Became' (1963), written in the manner of Kipling's *Just So Stories* and in some ways a corrective to 'How the Leopard Got His Spots', offers a more complex investigation of the politics of appearance. The Polar Bear routinely wins the animals' beauty contest on account of her beautiful white fur. This makes her increasingly vain and she longs to get away from the other animals who dirty her coat. The Peregrine Falcon, who usually comes second in the contests, devises a plot to remove his rival. He tells her of a country that is 'so clean it is even whiter than you are' and he shows her the way.

She lives at the North Pole still, with the company of only her sycophantic admirers, the seals. In some ways, this is a piece of whimsy, gently teasing Darwinism, and lacking a clear moral. It might be read as a satire on vanity. But because of the Polar Bear's whiteness there is a political dimension too. The other animals did not win the contest because they were 'all the wrong colour . . . black, or brown, or yellow, or ginger, or fawn, or speckled'. But when the Polar Bear's pride in her whiteness and her purity leads her to exile herself to the barren icecap, it is all the other animals who inherit the fruitful world. Racial arrogance is sterile, isolating and self-destructive.[36]

If Hughes, Kipling and Croxall tackled issues of race indirectly, other fabulists aimed to make their fables more overtly about racial politics. One of the best examples is *The Country Bunny and the Little Gold Shoes* (1939), a picturebook written by DuBose Heyward (a white author best known for his depictions of black culture in the American South of the 1920s) with illustrations by Marjorie Flack. It tells of the five rabbits who deliver all the Easter eggs. When one of them grows old, the Grandfather Bunny chooses a replacement, always wise, and kind, and swift. It is the dream of the book's heroine, 'a little country girl bunny with brown skin and a little cotton-ball of a tail', to become one of them, but 'all of the big white bunnies who lived in fine houses, and the Jack Rabbits with long legs who can run so fast' laughed at her chances. Their scorn is only deepened when she gives birth to twenty-one babies and has to spend all of her time rearing them. But then when a replacement Easter Bunny is needed, it is she who impresses the Grandfather with her wise, efficient and kind household management. She becomes the Easter Bunny and is even given the hardest job of all, to deliver an egg to a boy who has been ill for a year but never complained, and who lives beyond rivers and hills at the top of the tallest mountain. Her perseverance in this almost impossible task wins her the magic golden shoes, which allow her to complete the delivery, and she returns home to her happy family. *The Country Bunny* celebrates the triumph of poverty over affluence, the country over the town, the female over the male, and the small over the big. Above all, it is a fable about race, telling of the eventual victory of the 'country girl bunny with a brown skin' over the 'big white bunnies'. The only element that jars with this ideological positioning is the affluence, whiteness and maleness of the Grandfather Rabbit and of the uncomplaining child (at least in the illustrations), especially since they seem to represent God and Christ respectively.[37]

It is possible, then, to argue that the fable is an inherently liberal or even radical genre. But there is a strong streak of conservatism too. Many of Aesop's fables seem designed to teach readers to be happy with what they have. In Michael Morpurgo's twenty-first century version, for instance, the moral of 'The Town Mouse and the Country Mouse' is 'Better to be happy with what you need than risk everything for more.'[38] In earlier periods, especially times of social upheaval, this kind of warning against ambition was often more explicitly political. The Reverend H. G. Keene's *Persian Fables, for Young and Old* (1833), published by the evangelical Society for Promoting Christian Knowledge in the year after the Great Reform Act, openly advocated resignation, humility and contentment with one's lot. 'The Ambitious Crane', wrote Keene, teaches that 'The wisest thing we can do, is to follow the pursuits that belong to our station', while the moral of 'The Greedy Cat' was 'Poverty may have its hardships; but wealth and greatness have their troubles and alarms.'[39] Today, this advocacy of passive contentment remains in place, but it is often presented, much less politically, as self-actualisation: be happy with who you are, rather than be content with your rank in life. Morpurgo's moral for 'The Wolf and the Donkey', for instance, is 'Stick to what you know and be true to yourself.'[40] Indeed, a number of recent fabulists have moved away from traditional moral and social didacticism, preferring fables that read like Zen parables and that advocate personal awareness and fulfillment. The closing tale in Arnold Lobel's Caldecott-winning *Fables* (1980), 'The Mouse at the Seashore', is a good example. It tells of a young mouse's determination to see the sea despite his parents' warnings of the danger. On his journey, he is duly attacked by cats, dogs and birds, but finally arrives:

> The moon and the stars began to appear over the ocean. The Mouse sat silently on the top of the hill. He was overwhelmed by a feeling of deep peace and contentment.

Lobel's moral is 'All the miles of a hard road are worth a moment of happiness.'[41] More mystical than moral or practical, this represents another stage in the evolution of the fable. Yet the basic form of the fable has remained the same: the anthropomorphism, the economy of expression, the single precept, the small story teaching a wider truth. What is striking about the fable is both how little the form has changed over the many centuries of its existence, but how easily it has been adapted to suit the attitudes, anxieties and priorities of different periods.

SUMMARY OF KEY POINTS

- Fables can be regarded as the earliest form of modern children's literature, used by children in ancient Sumer, India, Greece and Rome, and throughout medieval Europe.
- Fables can take many forms, and vary widely in length and sophistication, but they have consistently been used to teach important lessons using an engaging, allegorical story with appealing characters.
- Familiar fables have been constantly reworked and re-presented to suit changing cultural and political values, and changing ideas about the nature of childhood and children's literature. New fables have also been devised to express new anxieties.
- Fables have often been used to teach both specific and generalised political lessons.
- Perhaps because of their traditional use of animal characters, fables have frequently addressed environmental concerns.
- Perhaps because they have traditionally taken the difference between surface and substance as a theme, fables have often investigated questions of racial and ethnic difference.

NOTES

1. G. A. Henty, 'To the Reader', *Those Other Animals* (London: Henry and Co. [1892]), p. v.

2. Gillian Adams, 'Ancient and medieval children's texts', in *International Companion Encylopedia of Children's Literature*, ed. Peter Hunt, 2nd edn, 2 vols (London: Routledge, 2004), vol.1, pp. 225–38 (p. 226).

3. Sir Roger L'Estrange, *Fables of Æsop and Other Eminent Mythologists with Morals and Reflexions* (London: R. Sare *et al.*, 1692), p. i.

4. See Adams, 'Ancient and medieval children's texts', pp. 233–4 and 'Medieval children's literature: its possibility and actuality', *Children's Literature*, 26 (1998), 1–24. See also Nicholas Orme, *English Schools in the Middle Ages* (London: Methuen, 1973), Edward Wheatley, *Mastering Aesop: Medieval Education, Chaucer and his Followers* (Gainesville, FL: University Press of Florida, 2000), and *The Norton Anthology of Children's Literature*, ed. Jack Zipes *et al.* (New York: W. W. Norton, 2005), pp. 387–8.

5. L'Estrange, *Fables of Æsop*, pp. 7 and 2–3.

6. John Locke, *Some Thoughts Concerning Education* (London: A. and J. Churchill, 1693), section 148, pp. 183–4; L'Estrange, *Fables of Æsop*, p. 3.

7. John Marchant, *Puerilia: Amusements for the Young* (London: P. Stevens, 1751), p. iv. Jean-Jacques Rousseau made the same point later in *Julie; ou, La Nouvelle Héloïse* (1761): *Eloisa: or, a Series of Original Letters*, 4 vols (London: R. Griffiths, T. Becket and P. A. De Hondt, 1761), vol. 3, p. 288.

8. For more details see Jayne Elizabeth Lewis, *The English Fable: Aesop and Literary Culture, 1651–1740* (Cambridge: Cambridge University Press, 1996), and Anja Müller, 'Picturing Æsops: re-visions of Æsop's Fables from L'Estrange to Richardson', *1650–1850*, 10 (2004), 33–62.

9. Joseph Jackson, *A New Translation of Æsop's Fables, Adorn'd with Cutts; Suited to the Fables* (London: Thomas Tebb, 1708), pp. vii–viii.

10. William Godwin (writing as 'Edward Baldwin'), *Fables Ancient and Modern. Adapted for the Use of Children* (London: Thomas Hodgkins, 1805), pp. iii–iv.

11. Walter Crane, *The Baby's Own Aesop* (1887), rpt in *Norton Anthology of Children's Literature*, p. 401.

12. Vivian French and Korky Paul, *Aesop's Funky Fables* (London: Puffin, [1997] 1999), back cover and pp. 24–5.

13. 'The Wolf and the Shepherd's Son', Michael Morpurgo, *The Orchard Book of Aesop's Fables*, illustrated by Emma Chichester Clark (London: Orchard Books, 2004), p. 96.

14. 'The Boy and false Alarms', L'Estrange, *Fables of Æsop*, pp. 73–4.

15. David Whitley, 'Samuel Richardson's *Aesop*', *Opening the Nursery Door: Reading, Writing and Childhood 1600–1900* (London: Routledge, 1997), pp. 65–79 (pp. 75 and 79).

16. French and Paul, *Aesop's Funky Fables*, p. 23.

17. John Goldthwaite, *The Natural History of Make-Believe: A Guide to the Principal Works of Britain, Europe and America* (New York: Oxford University Press, 1996), p. 253.

18. Anna Sewell, *Black Beauty, his Grooms and Companions; the Autobiography of a Horse. Translated from the Original Equine* (London: Puffin, [1877] 1994), p. 4.

19. 'Of the Sun and the North-Wind', Anon. *Æsop's Fables, With Their Morals: in Prose and Verse* (London: J. Hodges, 1741), p. 132.

20. Sewell, *Black Beauty*, p. 113.

21. Sarah Trimmer, *Fabulous Histories. Designed for the Instruction of Children, Respecting Their Treatment of Animals* (London: T. Longman *et al.*, [1786] 1798), pp. vii–viii, 69, 172, 110–12, 144, 119–20.

22. Trimmer, *Fabulous Histories*, p. 115.

23. Ted Hughes, *What is the Truth? A Farmyard Fable for the Young*, with drawings by R. J. Lloyd (London: Faber & Faber, 1984), p. 121.

24. Roald Dahl, illustrated by Quentin Blake, *Fantastic Mr Fox* (London: Puffin, [1970] 1996), pp. 80, 58–9 and 79.

25. Goldthwaite, *Natural History of Make-Believe*, p. 251.

26. Tess Cosslett, *Talking Animals in British Children's Fiction, 1786–1914* (Aldershot: Ashgate, 2006), p. 180.

27. David Macaulay, *Baaa* (1985), rpt in *Norton Anthology of Children's Literature*, pp. 1068–96, pp. 1095–6.

28. Robert C. O'Brien, *Mrs Frisby and the Rats of* NIMH (London: Puffin, [1971] 1975), pp. 124, 118–19, 137, 151 and 146.

29. L'Estrange, *Fables of Æsop*, p. 21.

30. James Thurber, *Fables for Our Time and Famous Poems Illustrated* (London: Hamish Hamilton, 1940), p. 69.

31. Marie Fernandes, *The Animal Fable in Modern Literature* (New Delhi: B. R. Publishing Corporation, 1996), p. 137.

32. Moira Ferguson, 'Breaking in Englishness: *Black Beauty* and the politics of gender, race and class', *Women: A Cultural Review*, 15 (1994), 34–52.

33. Joel Chandler Harris, *The Complete Tales of Uncle Remus*, ed. Richard Chase (New York: Houghton Mifflin, [1955] 2002), p. xxv. See Goldthwaite, *Natural History of Make-Believe*, pp. 251–86, for a long and enthusiastic discussion of the Uncle Remus stories.

34. 'How the Leopard Got His Spots', Rudyard Kipling, *Just So Stories* (London: Puffin, [1902] 2004), pp. 45–6.

35. Samuel Croxall, *Fables of Aesop and Others Newly Done into English* (London: Thomas Astley, [1722] 1728), pp. 315–16.

36. Ted Hughes, *How the Whale Became and Other Stories* (London: Puffin, [1963] 1982), pp. 40–6.

37. DuBose Heyward, with pictures by Marjorie Flack, *The Country Bunny and the Little Gold Shoes. As told to Jenifer* (London: Collins, 1956), pp. 2–4.

38. Morpurgo, *Orchard Book of Aesop's Fables*, p. 89.

39. Rev. H. G. Keene, *Persian Fables, for Young and Old* (London: John W. Parker, 1833), pp. 68 and 87.

40. Morpurgo, *Orchard Book of Aesop's Fables*, p. 75.

41. Arnold Lobel, *Fables* (New York: HarperCollins, 1980), p. 40.

CHAPTER 2

Poetry

This chapter is intended as a concise overview of the development of verse for children since the late seventeenth century. The first problem to confront is the difficulty of determining what children's poetry actually is. It is a problem that has defeated many poets and critics.[1] Is it a question of subject matter? Or language, tone, form or style? Or is it a question of the audience that the poet intended to reach? If so, what about those poems that were written for adults, but have since become 'anchored to the children's verse tradition by a kind of gravitational pull' as one recent anthologist puts it?[2] Certainly, anthologies of children's verse have always been full of poems that were originally intended for adults, like James Greenwood's compilation *The Virgin Muse* (1722), designed for 'young gentlemen and ladies' but providing them with the work of Milton and Dryden. Indeed, some anthologies, like Coventry Patmore's *The Children's Garland* (1862), have made a boast of excluding any poem first written for children. And many children have enjoyed 'adult verse'. Anne of Green Gables, for instance, particularly loved 'poetry that gives you a crinkly feeling up and down your back' by eighteenth-century poets now read by few adults let alone children.[3] Then of course gender, class, location and age will have played a part in determining what constitutes children's poetry, and its definition will have changed over time. Probably the majority of the verse that was once thought perfectly suited to the needs or wants of children would now be neither enjoyed by them nor prescribed for them by adults.

This is certainly the case with almost all the verse written for children before the Victorian period. Modern anthologies sometimes include a smattering of eighteenth-century and Romantic-era poems, but they generally get into their stride only with Robert Browning ('The Pied Piper of Hamelin', 1842) and Edward Lear (*A Book of Nonsense*, 1846), or in America, Henry Wadsworth Longfellow (*The Song of Hiawatha*, 1854). Earlier children's poetry is generally now characterised as 'concerned with religious and moral education', with the corollary 'that actual childhood is being completely bypassed'.[4] Even Morag Styles, whose history of children's poetry champions several early texts, takes this line. She contends that until Robert Louis Stevenson's *A Child's Garden of Verses* (1885), 'Children's verse was still weighed down by adults' determination to instill a code of good manners, conventional behaviour and religious observance in the young.'[5] Pre-nineteenth-century children's poems, as the introduction to *The Oxford Book of Children's Verse in America* puts it, 'appear to twentieth-century eyes wholly impossible for children.'[6]

The earliest verse written solely for children was undeniably extremely devout. John Bunyan's *Country Rhimes for Children* (1686), more often known as *Divine Emblems* or *A Book for Boys and Girls*, and Isaac Watts' *Divine Songs Attempted in Easy Language for the Use of Children* (1715) are the best-known examples. Both writers were concerned primarily with children's inherently sinful nature and used their poetry to remind readers about the imminence of death. They were determined to discipline and educate the reader, using poetry as the vehicle. But if Bunyan and Watts emphatically do not participate in our modern concept of childhood, they do share many of our poetic values. Styles, for instance, commends Bunyan's 'lyrical use of language', and Patricia Demers speaks highly of Watts' 'graceful prosody and sweetness of tone' and 'inimitable gentleness'. Their conscious fashioning of their verse to suit children's tastes and abilities has also been admired. Heather Glen is impressed by Bunyan's efforts to see the world as a child might see it; Styles congratulates Bunyan on understanding 'children's need for play'. Demers argues that 'only a poet of great compassion and delicacy' – like Watts – 'would have attempted to relate the major events of Christian salvation in the form of a lullaby', as he does in 'A Cradle Hymn':

> Hush, my dear, lie still and slumber!
> Holy angels guard thy bed!
> Heavenly blessings without number
> Gently falling on thy head.
>
> . . .
>
> 'Twas to save thee, child, from dying,
> Save my dear from burning flame,
> Bitter groans, and endless crying,
> That thy blest Redeemer came.[7]

Both texts, but most obviously Bunyan's, derive from the tradition of the emblem book in which the verse 'epigram' was supposed to explicate an accompanying picture. Although emblems were widely used during the Catholic Counter-Reformation to elucidate the bible and theology, in the Protestant tradition it was important that the pictures should be taken from the natural world and from ordinary life. This helps to explain the friendly and familiar tone of Bunyan's and Watts' verse.[8] The direct engagement with the child reader links Bunyan and Watts with the work of many of today's children's poets who are also usually anxious to speak of real life to real people, and who often use verse and illustration in conjunction, much like the emblem books. Indeed, Bunyan's and Watts' poetry lasted much longer than the strict Puritan religiosity from which it had arisen. After a steady start, Watts' verse sold well even into the nineteenth century, inspiring William Blake's *Songs of Innocence and Experience* (1789 and 1794) and remaining well enough known in the 1860s for it to be parodied in Lewis Carroll's *Alice* books. Imitations proliferated during the eighteenth century, authors generally offering their work as an addition to Watts' verses not as a replacement. Perhaps the best was Christopher Smart's final work, written from prison, *Hymns for the Amusement of Children* (1770), a collection of emblems chiefly remarkable, critics have suggested, for a syntactical difficulty that forces the reader actively to engage with the text.[9] Smart's *Jubilate Agno* ('Rejoice in the Lamb', composed

1758–63), written from the madhouse, is probably his best known piece, and some see it as an important harbinger of the 'golden age' ushered in by *Alice's Adventures in Wonderland* a century later in 1865. Amongst other strange verse it contained Smart's poem in praise of his cat, Jeoffry, still sometimes anthologised despite its very eccentric religious fervour: 'For he is of the tribe of Tiger. . . . For he is a mixture of gravity and waggery . . . . For the divine spirit comes about his body to sustain it in complete cat. . . . For by stroking of him I have found out electricity'.[10]

By and large, though, this kind of devotional verse has been marginalised from the standard histories of children's books because of its ardent and, to some, oppressive piety. But there is certainly a case for saying that early collections of poetry for children, such as John Marchant's two-hundred page *Puerilia: or, Amusements for the Young* (1751), ought to be considered as just as important in the history of children's literature as the much more celebrated mid-eighteenth-century innovations in prose produced by John Newbery. One definition of children's literature might be that it concerns itself with children's lives and views the world from their point of view. Marchant said he would do just that, providing verse for children that is 'adapted to their own Way of thinking, and to the Occurrences that happen within their own little Sphere of Action', as well as being composed 'in as pleasant and humorous a Stile' as he could manage. Hence his poems are about dolls and cricket, ice-skating and new dresses, though they remain devout.[11] John Wright's even earlier *Spiritual Songs for Children* (1727) is also interesting. One poem, 'A Poetical Exercise on the Author's Journey into Middlesex, and to the famous City of London', is a scathing attack on the impiety of metropolitan life, but also offers a description of the city that must have been intriguing to many children:

> *London*! What's *London*? Tis a World of Pride,
> Frizels and Furbelows on ev'ry Side;
> Patches like Moles, and powder'd Wiggs like Snow,
> Ladies like Peacocks with their Gallants go.[12]

With its talk of the 'Beasts and Birds, Fishes and Serpents keen' that can be seen in the natural history collections at Gresham

College, the armour at the Tower of London, the 'Mad, Distracted, and . . . Lunatick' at Bedlam, and the '*Jews* and *Gentiles*' who 'worship their own Way, | Some chant with Organs, and with Whirlgigs pray', the poem is a sort of a travelogue in the tradition of Thomas Boreman's slightly later *Gigantick Histories* books about the 'Curiosities of London' (1740–43) or even modern picture-books like Richard Scarry's, or the *Curious George* series (1941–66) by H. A. and Margret Rey.

However, it is a mistake to imagine that early modern children's encounters with verse were limited to the religious and moral poetry designed especially for them. In fact, verse was everywhere in seventeenth- and eighteenth-century Britain and America, and it would have permeated children's lives in a way that, perhaps, poetry has not done since. It is surely not an overstatement to say that most children led a much richer poetic life in the seventeenth and eighteenth centuries than they do today. The availability of secular and irreligious verse to children is hinted at in Watts' preface to *Divine Songs*. 'Verse was at first design'd for the service of God,' he argued, but 'it hath been wretchedly abused since.'[13] Likewise, Marchant's preface gives an insight into what verse was available to children and how they may have used it: 'no sooner can they read,' he wrote, 'but they are furnished with the most filthy Ribaldry, which they are instructed to con and get by Heart, and when they can sing it to some ordinary Tune, they are made to thrill it with their little Voices in every Company where they are intro-duced'.[14] As for Bunyan, he ashamedly admitted that his boyhood reading had included many ballads.[15] We can only understand the devotional and moral children's poetry that Bunyan, Watts, Marchant and others produced if we recognise it as a reaction to children's immersion in much more profane verse.

Ballads were part of oral culture, but by the sixteenth and seven-teenth centuries in England a great many were in print, either in small anthologies ('garlands'), singly in short pamphlets, or on single large sheets of paper illustrated with simple woodcuts ('broadsides'). Although some were religious, others contained accounts of legendary figures (like Robin Hood), commemorated topical events (such as murders or political scandals), or offered short verse narratives. Some were perfectly designed to appeal to children. For example, *The Friar and the Boy*, in print since the six-teenth century, tells of a mistreated boy's sudden empowerment when he acquires a magical charm that makes people break wind uncontrollably. He uses it without compunction to gain vengeance against his cruel stepmother:

> And then a cracker she let fly,
> That almost shook the ground.
> She blush'd as they made merry sport,
> The little boy reply'd,
> My mother has a good report
> You hear at her backside,
> Sure had there been a cannon-ball,
> With such a force it flew,
> It would have beaten down the wall,
> Perhaps the chimney too.[16]

The Friar and the Boy is characteristic of many ballads in its coarse-ness, as well as its longevity. But it is also typical for its clear narra-tive and its use (in most eighteenth-century versions) of the simple but compelling 'ballad metre': organised in quatrains, rhyming a-b-a-b, and with four accented syllables in the first and third lines, and three in the third and fourth.

Besides their encounters with ballads many early modern chil-dren would have come across a great deal of poetry in their educa-tion. John Locke, in *Some Thoughts Concerning Education* (1693), had recommended *Aesop's Fables* and *Reynard the Fox* as the books most likely to draw children into learning and both these, by the eighteenth century, were generally published in verse. The educa-tional programme set out half a century later by John Vowler in 'The Young Student's Scheme' (1743) was much more demanding, but retained a place for poetry and was itself set out in verse form. 'I'll tell you, Sir, how I design | My Point in Learning to attain', the poem begins, before listing the details of the self-imposed curricu-lum: scripture, history, geography, astronomy and, on '*Thursdays* I'll Poetry rehearse, | Those Songs and Hymns I've learnt in Verse.'[17] If from the social elite, it is likely that this conscientious student's Thursday lesson would have included mostly Greek and

Latin poetry, although by the middle of the eighteenth century many educationalists were insisting that 'boys should begin with the *English* poetry' (usually the work of Edmund Spenser and John Milton, James Thomson and Alexander Pope).[18] Vowler wrote in verse, he said, because it 'was easier learnt and longer retain'd by Children than Prose'.[19] In accordance with this widely-held view, it is quite likely that pupils would have found some of their textbooks for geography, history and many other subjects (not to mention religion) also set out in verse. By the early nineteenth century, children's books were teaching almost every subject through poetry. Charlotte Finch's *The Gamut and Time-Table in Verse*, for instance, sets out to explain the theory of music through cheerful lines like these: 'Then of Demisemiquavers, thirty-two in a line, | With the Ten and six semiquavers make even time.'[20] It was not only children from affluent backgrounds who were receiving an education through poetry. Thomas Gills's *Useful and Delightful Instructions by Way of Dialogue Between the Master and his Scholar . . . Composed in Verse* (1712) was 'recommended to the Use of Children of both Sexes, train'd up in the Charity-Schools'.

Besides its use in school, there is evidence that mothers were using poetry in the more informal education of their children at home. The classic example is Jane Johnson, the wife of a Buckinghamshire clergyman, who, in the 1740s, produced a collection of home-made cards and books to help teach her children to read. On one card, for instance, Johnson meticulously drew two women and one man in very elegant dress, placing above them these verses, presumably her own invention, designed to amuse and instruct (in national prejudices, if nothing else):

> Such short Gowns as these, are much used in France,
> And the Men and the Women cut capers and dance.
> The Ladys they Paint, and their backsides they show.
> The Men hop and skip, and each one is a Beau
> Would you see men like monkeys, to France you must go.[21]

It is not unlikely that many other elite and middle-class mothers (and fathers) also wrote verse for their own children. Certainly, many eighteenth-century women writers included poetry directed at their children in their published collections. Part of her 1734 *Poems on Several Occasions*, for instance, was Mary Barber's 'Written for My Son, and Spoken by Him at His First Putting on Breeches' (boys wore petticoats, like their sisters, until they were 'breeched' at around five or six years old).

Even children unlucky enough to lack poetic parents would still have encountered verse at home through, if nothing else, what we now call nursery rhymes. Their history is extremely obscure, largely because they originally circulated in oral form, but what is known has been very clearly set out by Iona and Peter Opie. As they explain, the earliest published references to such still familiar verses as 'Boys and Girls Come Out to Play' and 'The Lion and the Unicorn' are often in eighteenth-century mock-serious discussions of their supposed political or philosophical meanings. Only towards the end of the century were they being collected by scholars genuinely interested in this poetry as folklore. Seventy-nine nursery rhymes were collected into *Gammer Gurton's Garland, or, the Nursery Parnassus* in 1784 by the antiquarian Joseph Ritson. Nursery rhymes had been published especially for children well before this though. Mary Cooper's *Tommy Thumb's Pretty Song Book* (c.1744) had contained 'Bah, Bah, a black sheep', 'Who did kill Cock Robin' and many other nursery classics. *Mother Goose's Melody, or Sonnets from the Cradle*, probably first published in the mid-1760s, by John Newbery or his nephew, was advertised as containing 'the most celebrated songs and lullabies of the old British nurses; calculated to amuse children, and to excite them to sleep.'[22] Other similar collections rapidly followed, becoming popular in both Britain and America. Some verses that were apparently original, written especially for these volumes but very much in the style of the traditional nursery rhymes, were also included. In *The Top Book of All, for Little Masters and Misses* (c.1760), for instance, this satire on boastfulness appeared, under the title 'Telling *Tommy Thumb* a Story':

> Little, pretty, Jacky Nory,
> Telling Tommy Thumb a Story,
> How he's gotten into Breeches,
> And his Pockets full of Riches,

> And how he shall on Cock-horse ride,
> With Sword and Gun girt by his Side,
> And that he will with his great Gun,
> Kill all the French when they do run,
> And with his Sword he will them cut,
> As small as Herbs for Porridge Pot;
> Nay more he vows, and which is worse,
> He'll cut them smaller than a Horse,
> And with one Blow cut off a Head,
> And send the Backside for to beg.
> But pray, says Tom, first kill that Mouse,
> That eats my Cakes, and stinks the House.
> Not I, says Jack, Lud, how it frights,
> Let's run away before it bites.[23]

Jacky Nory's insistence that he has 'gotten into Breeches' would have spoken specifically to a boy's pride at going through that rite of passage. Moreover, even though some slight moral warning against vanity does remain, it was clearly designed primarily to amuse. Evidently by the 1760s and '70s, the market could accommodate poetry that was both especially for children and more or less exclusively entertaining.

By the end of the eighteenth century then, child readers had an enormous range of verse available to them, some of it written especially for them, some of it 'inherited' from adults; some of it derived from folk traditions, much of it newly-minted; some designed to instruct, some to entertain. Access to these different kinds of verse would have been dependent on age, affluence, gender, religion, education, literacy and location. The number of volumes of children's poetry began to increase in the early nineteenth century. New varieties developed too: amongst others, nonsense verse, narrative poems and sentimental verse. Fundamentally, though, the children's poetry of the nineteenth and twentieth centuries, even these ostensibly new kinds of verse, may be regarded as continuations of traditions that had emerged in the eighteenth century. Religious verse certainly survived. Not only were Bunyan and Watts still read, but much more of a similar style was produced. Most of it is now forgotten, save only, perhaps, those poems that lived on as hymns:

Cecil Frances Alexander's 'All Things Bright and Beautiful' and 'Once in Royal David's City', for example, first published in 1848 in her *Hymns for Little Children* (likewise Christina Rossetti's 'In the Bleak Midwinter', 1872, and Eleanor Farjeon's 'Morning Has Broken', 1931). The sort of simple rhymes that featured in *Tommy Thumb's Pretty Song Book* and *Gammer Gurton's Garland* provide another example of a verse tradition that has survived from the early modern period (or before) into the present. They have continued to evolve, through what Iona Opie calls 'the process of fission and fusion . . . the alteration of words and phrases through misunderstanding, failure of memory, or deliberate innovation', so that children still recite versions, or at least modern counterparts, as playground rhymes.[24] The cadences, colloquiality and jumbled (and often subversive) values of this kind of children's popular or 'street' poetry have also been self-consciously taken up by a variety of modern poets. Eleanor Farjeon sought to replicate the feel of nursery rhymes in much of her early twentieth-century children's poetry (*Nursery Rhymes of London Town*, 1916–17), and a good proportion of A.A. Milne's verse is in the same tradition: 'I think I am a Muffin Man. I haven't got a bell, | I haven't got the muffin things that muffin people sell'.[25] More recently, authors of so-called 'urchin verse', popular, especially in Britain, since the 1970s, have set out to reproduce the voices, subjects and general spirit of playground rhymes. This is from Allan Ahlberg's *Heard it in the Playground* (1989):

> We seen 'em in the cloakroom, Miss –
> Ann Cram and Alan Owen
> Tryin' to have the longest kiss –
> They had the stopwatch goin'![26]

This kind of poem, written by an adult in imitation of children's own 'street' verse, deliberately carnivalesque but still just noticeably infused with an adult's sensibility, is a direct descendent of the account of 'Jacky Nory, | Telling Tommy Thumb a Story' published over two centuries earlier.

Another verse tradition that began early but continues still is the cautionary tale. Many were included in the most successful collection of the early nineteenth century, *Original Poems for Infant Minds* (1804–5), written largely by the sisters Ann and Jane Taylor. Here boys who play truant from school end up being torn apart on mill-wheels, and girls who raise false alarms are burned in raging fires. The aim is instructive of course, but the lack of proportion between the calamitous punishment and the minor crime is ludicrous today and may well have been laughable to many readers even when these verses were first published. The neatness of the verse that contains these moral fables only emphasises their absurdity. It is no surprise, then, that parodies were produced, most famously Heinrich Hoffmann's *Struwwelpeter*, translated from the German as *Shock-Headed Peter* in 1848. What is more curious is that others – Hilaire Belloc (*Cautionary Tales for Children*, 1907) and Roald Dahl (*Revolting Rhymes*, 1982), for example – were eager to write similar parodies long after the original moral verses had become extinct. They were, it seems, expecting that many of their readers were still being berated in verse. Moreover, however tongue-in-cheek their poetry was, it was not wholly lacking a didactic dimension. Hoffmann admitted that he wrote such poems as 'The Dreadful Story of Harriet and the Matches' to impress the reader 'more than hundreds of general warnings', as well as to amuse.[27] Similarly, the Oompa-Loompas' songs, gloating over the fate of each sinning child in Dahl's *Charlie and the Chocolate Factory* (1964), are very droll but also expressive of the author's genuine disdain for over-indulged children: 'Augustus Gloop! Augustus Gloop! | The great big greedy nincompoop!', sing the Oompa-Loompas as he is apparently drowned in a lake of molten chocolate. They explain:

> How long could we allow this beast
> To gorge and guzzle, feed and feast
> On everything he wanted to?
> Great Scott! It simply wouldn't do![28]

With its vestigial didactic impulse, and its celebration of salutary violence, Dahl's poetry is not so very different from original cautionary verse of the early nineteenth century, which itself owed much to Puritan warnings of the wages of sin: 'There is a dreadful

Hell, | And everlasting Pains, | There Sinners must with Devils dwell | In Darkness, Fire, and Chains.'[29]

The history of nonsense verse reveals another pattern of gradual evolution rather than sudden innovation by iconoclastic geniuses.[30] Edward Lear and Lewis Carroll were undeniably brilliant, but there were many antecedents. Whimsical anthropomorphic poems like William Roscoe's *The Butterfly's Ball and the Grasshopper's Feast* (1806), or verses based on folk characters, such as Sarah Catherine Martin's *The Comic Adventures of Old Mother Hubbard and her Dog* (1805), are two possible sources. And, as Styles notes, even in the eighteenth century, nonsense 'was already a thriving form in chap-book culture'.[31] One such chapbook was *The World Turned Upside Down*, in which verses and images depicted such inversions as fish turned anglers and stags turned huntsmen. The verse could be comic. In an early nineteenth-century version, a man attempting to eat himself remarks 'If I once get my legs in | As far as my knees, | The rest will slip down | With a great deal of ease'.[32] It was also somewhat subversive, proffering that fantasy that the disempowered might one day become dominant. Being largely subordinate themselves, children may well have enjoyed *The World Turned Upside Down* long before a version was published especially for them in 1810. This was *Signor Topsy-Turvey's Wonderful Magic Lantern* by Ann and Jane Taylor. Although the subversion was constrained – the power inversions being presented as slides projected by a comical travelling showman – a rebellious element did remain. The hare in 'The Cook Cooked', enraged by the idea that '*hares* should be nutrition', 'brew'd sedition' and fomented a conspiracy of all the other animals in the larder. Other episodes were more in the tradition of moral literature. 'Children at War, and Cats and Dogs at Peace' attempted to shame children into good behaviour by demonstrating that their petulance was just as ludicrous as a fish wanting to live out of water, say.[33] Although both the subversion and the morality are lacking from Lear's verse, the foundations of the nonsense, especially in his early work, remain largely the same: the distortion, exaggeration or inversion of reality. His Jumblies (*Nonsense Songs, Stories, Botany, and Alphabets*, 1870), for instance, go to sea in that least watertight of objects, a sieve, while the Owl and the Pussycat – an unusual ménage in itself – buy, for a shilling, the metal loop put through a pig's nose for their wedding ring, though which one of them wears it, and how, is not made clear. What Lear added to the formula, and Carroll developed further, were more and madder logic reversals, the inclusion of ludicrously irrelevant characters and objects, many neologisms and bad puns, and much linguistic experimentation. The technique was to reach its zenith in the two Alice books (1865 and 1871) with poems like 'The Lobster Quadrille' and 'Jabberwocky'.

Curiously, in the 1870s, both Lear and Carroll seem to have retreated from their earlier playfully experimental verse, preferring to encase their nonsense within longer narratives. Lear's 'The Dong with the Luminous Nose' (from *Laughable Lyrics*, 1876) is a self-pitying account of a heartbroken creature who fashions for himself a nose like a lamp so that he may search for his lost Jumbly Girl. The nonsense of Carroll's *The Hunting of the Snark* (1876) is more like the world of Samuel Beckett's *Waiting for Godot* (1952) than *Through the Looking-Glass*. Carroll called it 'An Agony in Eight Fits', and he sends his miscellaneous characters on a grim, apparently dangerous and largely unexplained quest to find a Snark. The poem's final statement (the single line that came suddenly to Carroll, inspiring him to write the poem), 'For the Snark *was* a Boojum, you see', somehow conveys both their fear and frustration at the futility of the voyage.[34] Whether light or dark in tone, it was Carroll's and Lear's technical ability to write really compelling verse that allowed such flights of nonsense. The rhythm, rhyme and pace of the poetry carries the reader on even when the words themselves make no sense. This is the paradox at the heart of good nonsense poetry: that the apparent freedom, and even randomness, have to be carefully restrained and regulated within firm verse structures if they are not to disorientate the reader. Only the best nonsense verse written since – by A. A. Milne, Mervyn Peake and Spike Milligan in Britain, say, or Ogden Nash and Shel Silverstein in America – can match these two halves of Carroll's and Lear's achievement: the poetic proficiency, and the linguistic inventiveness and inversion of the normal.

With roots in the early modern period, but its most celebrated and enduring examples materialising in the mid-nineteenth century, the history of the children's narrative poem parallels the history of nonsense verse. Longfellow's *The Song of Hiawatha* (1855) or 'Paul Revere's Ride' (1863) are classic examples, and their strong narratives and driving rhythms clearly show their antecedents in the ballad tradition. The former derived its complicated metre from ancient, orally transmitted Finnish verse-narratives. The latter plainly signalled its author's aspiration to the ballad tradition with its first stanza:

> Listen, my children, and you shall hear
> Of the midnight ride of Paul Revere,
> On the eighteenth of April, in Seventy-five;
> Hardly a man is now alive
> Who remembers that famous day and year.[35]

As in the early modern period, many of the nineteenth- and twentieth-century ballads best loved by children were not necessarily originally written for them. Somehow, at least as far as anthologists of children's poetry have been concerned, they have crossed an invisible divide and become part of children's literature. Thus, not only are poems such as Robert Browning's 'How They Brought the Good News from Ghent to Aix' (1845) and John Masefield's 'Sea Fever' (1902) now more likely to be found in collections of children's than adult verse, but, apparently purely because of their strong narrative, melodramatic tone, and driving rhythm, children's anthologies feature more recondite and even disturbing material such as Samuel Taylor Coleridge's 'Rime of the Ancient Mariner' (1798) or Alfred Noyes's intense account of a woman tied up, sexually assaulted and killing herself, 'The Highwayman' (1913). Other poets have deliberately set out to capture the spirit of early modern popular literature. For example, some of the poetry of Charles Causley, celebrated as 'probably the greatest exponent of the modern ballad', is very much in the tradition of texts like *The Friar and the Boy*, both in its playfulness and delight in bodily function:

> King Foo Foo sat upon his throne
> Dressed in his royal closes,
> While all around his courtiers stood
> With clothes-pegs on their noses.

> 'This action strange,' King Foo Foo said,
> 'My mind quite discomposes,
> Though vulgar curiosity
> A good king never shoses.'
>
> But to the court it was as clear
> As poetry or prose is:
> King Foo Foo had not had a bath
> Since goodness only knoses.[36]

The ballad form is extremely adaptable, and, if it is less popular than it once was, good examples were still being published even in an age when free verse and 'street poetry' celebrating the quotidian above the extraordinary, have come to dominate. Mick Gowar's 'Rat Trap' (1992), for example, is a reworking of Browning's 'The Pied Piper of Hamelin' (1842), promising to reveal what actually happened. In this version, the plague of rats is invented by the mayor to distract the townspeople from his rapacious regime. The Pied Piper – more usually employed for 'Street theatre, kid's parties' – is hired to exterminate the rats, which he does by arming all the boys with sticks and leading them in a 'Rat-killing Bash-up, and barbecue'. In part, this is conventional postmodernism, using the intertextuality for humour, voicing the reader's likely scepticism about the sort of supernatural events Browning describes, and generally trying to destabilise the authority of traditional narrative poetry. It might also be taken as a wry fable, commenting on the propensity of corrupt men to blame nature for their failings. But it is more sinister too. After the massacre of the rats, 'A taste for blood-letting started to grow', and the Piper threatens to lead the boys against the city elders: 'Let's finish the job we started today: | Cleanse Hamelin Town properly!':

> A forest of sticks was raised in salute.
> In reply, the Piper lifted his flute . . .
> 'I give in,' said the mayor. 'I'll pay you your fee.
> But first, our dear children. You must set them free
> From this terrible spell.
> Just look at them – there!

How their lips seem to snarl,
How their eyes seem to stare.'
The Piper just grinned: 'Some things can't be undone:
We've taught them the pleasure of killing for *fun*.[37]

Much may be read into the poem's description of the scapegoating of an innocent group described as vermin, and the ability of a charismatic leader to beguile a mob into mass violence and the overthrow of the legitimate, if incompetent, government. For more astute readers, the parallels with the rise of Nazism in 1930s Germany will be inescapable.

Given its worldly cynicism, it is surprising to find that Gowar's 'Rat Trap' ends like this:

> And so saying, the Devil
> > went
> > > back
> > > down
> > > > to
> > > > Hell.[38]

It might be said that the sudden introduction of the supernatural neutralises the poem's political satire. But it is the arrangement of words to resemble steps that seems most curious. Playing with layout and typography is characteristic of much modern children's poetry: Benjamin Zephaniah's 'According to My Mood' (1994), for example, mixes different fonts and upper and lower case letters, and adds punctuation marks and misspellings, to argue that 'I have *poetic* license, i WriTe thE way i waNt.'[39] But Gowar's device is rather twee and resembles nothing so much as A. A. Milne at his most saccharine – the sort of poem that was satirised with pitiless precision by J. B. Morton:

> Hush, hush, nobody cares,
> Christopher Robin
> > has
> > > fallen
> > > > downstairs.[40]

Opinion is divided on Milne's two books of poetry, *When We Were Very Young* (1924) and *Now We Are Six* (1927). Although they were and remain hugely successful, both in terms of sales and their absorption into popular culture, some critics have derided what they see as their sentimentality, whimsicality, idealisation of childhood and the cosy world they present of upper middle class British life. Others (including Milne himself) have sought to defend the poems by pointing out how easy it is to misread them. 'Vespers', for instance, depicts Christopher Robin kneeling at the end of his bed, piously praying for his mother, father and nursemaid. This might be thought a corny representation of what Humphrey Carpenter has called the 'Beautiful Child', a Victorian idealisation of a child 'distinguished . . . by an almost heavenly innocence'. But, as Carpenter goes on to say, although Christopher Robin 'occasionally repeats one of the formulas he has been taught', he is not actually praying, and is constantly being distracted by the material world around him:

> *God bless Mummy*. I know that's right.
> Wasn't it fun in the bath to-night?
> The cold's so cold, and the hot's so hot.
> Oh! *God bless Daddy* – I quite forgot.

Carpenter argues that the poem reveals Milne's hostility to formal religion, and that its ending – an emphatic '*God bless me*' – reveals the natural and ruthless egotism of children, exploding any notion of childhood innocence or holiness.[41] Certainly 'Vespers' is an extremely sensual poem, for it is always the child's delight in what he has seen, heard or touched that distracts him from his prayers.

Childhood angst is also quite often observable in Milne's poetry, lurking behind the façade of sentimentality. It is tempting to read the famous poem 'Disobedience', for example, as an expression of a boy's Oedipal anxiety. It begins by telling the reader that James James Morrison Morrison Weatherby George Dupree 'Took great | Care of his Mother, | Though he was only three.' When she disobeys his injunction not to go down to the end of the town 'if you don't go down with me', she goes missing and, despite the reward offered by King John (who somehow enters the poem from another compartment of the boy's imagination), 'She hasn't been heard of since.' The poem dramatises a boy's fear that his mother will desert him for the adult world (she wears a 'golden gown' to make her disobedient trip, both its goldenness and gowniness being more likely to appeal to men than boys). The curious final stanza, which the reader is instructed to recite 'very softly', is a funeral dirge for lost mothers (it even replaces the term itself with 'M*****'). Only with its very final word does the poem offer reassurance, especially if it is being read aloud by a child in the company of a parent, reaffirming the child's centrality with a capitalised, shouted, 'ME!'[42]

Neither the sentimentality of Milne's verse, nor its attempt to recapture what it was like to be a child, was entirely new. The poetry of Robert Louis Stevenson, whose *A Child's Garden of Verses* was published in 1885, is a clear influence, so too perhaps was the work of Christina Rossetti (*Sing-Song: A Nursery Rhyme Book*, 1872) and their American counterpart, Eugene Field (*Love Songs of Childhood*, 1896). With their direct address to the child reader, and idealisation of childhood, all were the heirs of the best eighteenth-century poets like Christopher Smart and William Blake. Neither subject matter, nor form, nor tone would rule out Smart's 'Hymn for Saturday' (1770), for example, from *A Child's Garden of Verses* or *Now We Are Six*:

> Now's the time for mirth and play,
> Saturday's an holiday;
> Praise to heaven unceasing yield,
> I've found a lark's nest in the field.[43]

What Stevenson did pioneer, and Milne developed, was the representation of the individual child's anxieties, particularly the worries of sensitive and solitary children. Many of Milne's poems deal with loneliness and isolation ('Halfway Down', 'Come Out With Me', 'Solitude'), which seems to reflect a perception on Milne's part that childhood is a state in which one is largely ignored – requiring the compensation of imaginary friends perhaps, such as Winnie-the-Pooh. An entire section of Stevenson's *A Child's Garden of Verses* (1885) is called 'The Child Alone'. They too tell of imaginary

children: not actual street-urchins, but not brought up by nurse-maids, and not the owners of extensive private grounds, and certainly not adults. It is written, by and large, in free verse, rather than in traditional metres and rhyme structures. Slang, the vernacular, and children's authentic speech-patterns have replaced more self-consciously poetic language. All this sounds radical, an impression supported by the criticism that 'urchin verse' has provoked. Commentators have worried that the price of accessibility is ephemerality and disposability, and that the squibbishness of modern children's poetry will dissuade young readers from ever graduating onto 'real', 'classic' poetry that is (they say) beautiful and multifaceted in a way that urchin verse is not.[50] The most perceptive critics have remarked that this new kind of verse is, more than anything else, a response to the way that childhood has been culturally constructed. Poetry is regarded as being 'profound and static, delicate and reflective', says Peter Hunt, while children are now generally imagined to be the opposite: 'shallow and dynamic, robust and outgoing'. It is from this disjunction that this new form of poetry has emerged, full of 'quick, flip gags that adults assume that children will like, precisely (and demeaningly) because it is junk in adult terms.'[51] For Alison Lurie too, the danger is that by providing children with 'easier' verse, modern poets may be writing to fit a false construction of modern childhood (short attention span; low-brow tastes) and that this will be self-perpetuating, making the false construction real and infantilising generations of readers.[52]

There is probably no need to worry. For one thing, the best authors of 'urchin verse' – amongst others, Gareth Owen, Allan Ahlberg, Benjamin Zephaniah and Michael Rosen (whose collection, *Mind Your Own Business*, is sometimes said to have begun the trend in 1974) – have produced poetry which is colloquial, quotidian and accessible, but which is also thought-provoking and multi-layered, sensitive and artistic. Here, for instance, is Roger McGough capturing the feelings of a child on his or her first day at school:

> A millionbillionwillion miles from home
> Waiting for the bell to go. (To go where?)
> Why are they all so big, other children?

So noisy? So much at home they
must have been born in uniform.
Lived all their lives in playgrounds.
Spent the years inventing games
that don't let me in. Games
that are rough, that swallow you up.
And the railings.
All around, the railings.
Are they to keep out wolves and monsters?
Things that carry off and eat children?
Things you don't take sweets from?
Perhaps they're to stop us getting out
Running away from the lessins. Lessin.
What does a lessin look like?
Sounds small and slimy.
They keep them in glassrooms.
Whole rooms made out of glass. Imagine.

I wish I could remember my name
Mummy said it would come in useful.
Like wellies. When there's puddles.
Yellowwellies. I wish she was here.
I think perhaps my name is sewn on somewhere
Perhaps the teacher will read it for me.
Tea'cher. The one who makes the tea.[53]

If the wordplay here is a little feeble, blatantly introduced to tickle young readers (or listeners), there is ample compensation in the careful creation of a mood of bewilderment and suppression. The uniforms, the railings, the loss of identity (except through a sewn-on label) make the school into a prison camp, but in which even fellow inmates seem agents of oppression. All readers will be able to associate with this child, stuck half-way between the cosiness of mother, home and yellow wellington boots, and the strangeness of school with its strange lexicon and new social networks. This is a poem that might defamiliarise the surroundings of those who have already become habituated to school, prompt a sense of autobiography, or even encourage empathy with those just arriving. Like many of the best of these poems, it somehow manages to be menacing and cheerful, instructive and fun.

In any case, 'urchin verse' has not dominated late twentieth- and early twenty-first century children's poetry as much as its critics contend. Other, more traditional forms have co-existed. Notable British children's poets of the same period include Ted Hughes (*What is the Truth*, 1984) and John Mole (*Boo to a Goose*, 1987). And 'urchin verse' is, in any case, largely a British development. Shel Silverstein (*A Light in the Attic*, 1981) and Jack Prelutsky (*The New Kid on the Block*, 1986), amongst a few others, have provided a sort of American equivalent, but Glenna Sloan, in her survey of American verse, has found that most American children's poetry 'stays well within its traditions'.[54] Moreover, new forms of verse have already developed out of, and away from, the kind of poetry being written by Rosen, McGough and others in the 1970s and '80s. Jackie Kay, for example, uses the colloquial language, free verse forms and everyday subjects of the 'urchin' school – probably to an even greater extent than McGough or Rosen, for she employs Scots dialect and takes racism and broken families as two of her principal themes. But the jokiness has faded, replaced by an exploration of the complications of modern life and their effects on the developing consciousness. Her verse is still wry but is no longer whimsical. Here is part of 'What Jenny Knows' from Kay's first collection, *Two's Company* (1992):

> 'I didn't come out of my mummy's tummy.
> No I didn't,' I says to my pal Jenny.
> But Jenny says, 'you must have,
> How come?' And I replies,
>
> 'I just didn't. Get it. I didn't.'
> 'Everybody does' says Jenny,
> who is fastly becoming an enemy.
> 'Rubbish,' I say. 'My mummy got me.
> She picked me. She collected me.
>
> I was in a supermarket,
> On the shelf and she took me off it.'
> 'Nonsense,' says Jenny. 'Lies.'

The speaker explains to Jenny that she is adopted:

> 'I know That!' says Jenny,
> 'But you still came out
>
> Somebody's tummy. Somebody
> had to have you. Didn't they?'
> 'Not my mummy. Not my mummy,' I says.
> 'Shut your face. Shut your face.'[55]

It is an everyday conversation between two friends in which nothing is resolved or revealed, but in which a world of conflicting emotions and loyalties are exposed. It is poetry of the street, or the playground, about real children and their real concerns, but it is not jokey or ephemeral. Like all of the best children's poetry of recent decades, it has not reacted to Victorian and Edwardian sentimentality with a too ardent commitment to earthiness and obviousness. Just as Watts or Smart could be gentle and engaging while remaining religious, or Lear and Carroll absurd while remaining decorous and controlled, so Kay and the best contemporary children's poets combine subtlety with immediacy, and realism with weightiness.

In the mid-1980s, Donald Hall wrote in his introduction to *The Oxford Book of Children's Verse in America* that 'contemporary fashions in children's verse, which favour humor and nonsense, will one day seem as quaint as pieties about dead children.'[56] The poetry of the 'urchin' school does not yet seem quaint, and much fine humorous and nonsense verse continues to be written. But the poetry of Kay, and of most of the other poets discussed in this chapter, show how inappropriate it is to organise children's verse into fashions and fads that come and go. The question of what makes good children's poetry has been much discussed and never resolved. For some the key characteristic is the immediate appeal to the senses, without the need for reflection, memory or learning.[57] For others, good children's poetry must have 'simplicity without stupidity'.[58] Some might think that the most important thing is for poems to see things from a child's point of view (even if others point out the impossibility of the endeavour). What is clear, though, is that good children's poetry has been written throughout the last three centuries, and that it is the continuities that are more striking than the changes.

SUMMARY OF KEY POINTS

- Verse was more pervasive in pre-modern culture than today and children would have encountered poetry in almost all aspects of their daily lives: at school, in their devotions, in their homes and on the streets. By the mid-eighteenth century, much of this poetry was being published especially for children and was designed to entertain them.
- Much children's poetry has been condemned as sentimental and twee, but it is sometimes more cynical and satirical about childhood than it first appears, and can explore children's (and adult's) anxieties in surprising depth.
- Poetry written recently to be more accessible and relevant to children has been condemned by some critics as unsophisticated and ephemeral, but the best of this verse is as subtle and weighty as it is punchy and immediate.
- What actually constitutes children's poetry has always been uncertain, and subject matter, original intended audience, language and genre do not offer certain guidance.
- Changing constructions of childhood have affected ideas of children's verse, but formal, tonal and stylistic continuities are often more striking than the innovations.

NOTES

1. For some thoughts on definition see John Mole, 'Questions of Poetry', *Signal*, 74 (1994), 86–92 and Glenna Sloan, 'But is it poetry?', *Children's Literature in Education*, 32 (2001), 45–56.
2. Neil Philip, 'Introduction', *The New Oxford Book of Children's Verse* (Oxford: Oxford University Press, 1996), p. xxv.
3. L. M. Montgomery, *Anne of Green Gables* (Wordsworth Classics, [1908] 1994), p. 45.

4. Peter Hunt, *Children's Literature* (Oxford: Blackwell, 2001), p. 295.
5. Morag Styles, *From the Garden to the Street. An Introduction to 300 Years of Poetry for Children* (London: Cassell, 1998), p. 1.
6. Donald Hall (ed.), *The Oxford Book of Children's Verse in America* (New York: Oxford University Press, 1985), p. xxiv.
7. Styles, *From the Garden to the Street*, p. 9; Patricia Demers, *From Instruction to Delight: An Anthology of Children's Literature to 1850*, 2nd edn (Don Mills, Ontario: Oxford University Press Canada, 2004), p. 77; Heather Glen, *Vision and Disenchantment* (Cambridge: Cambridge University Press, 1983), pp. 10–11; Isaac Watts, *Divine Songs Attempted in Easy Language, for the Use of Children* (London: Richard Ford, [1715] 1727), pp. 47–50.
8. Christopher Hill, *A Turbulent, Seditious and Factious People: John Bunyan and his Church 1628–1688* (Oxford: Clarendon Press, 1989), pp. 267–74.
9. Mark Booth, 'Syntax and Paradigm in Smart's *Hymns for the Amusement of Children*', in *Christopher Smart and the Enlightenment*, ed. Clement Hawes (New York: St. Martin's Press, 1999), pp. 67–81.
10. Smart, *Jubilate Agno* (written 1758–63, published 1939), in *From Instruction to Delight*, ed. Demers, pp. 273–4.
11. John Marchant, *Puerilia: or, Amusements for the Young* (London: P. Stevens, 1751), pp. v–vi.
12. John Wright, *Spiritual Songs for Children: or, Poems on Several Subjects and Occasions* (London: Joseph Marshall, 1727), pp. 7–11.
13. Watts, *Divine Songs*, p. [xv].
14. Marchant, *Puerilia*, p. vi.
15. John Bunyan, *A Few Sighs from Hell, or The Groans of a damned Soul* (London: Ralph Wood, 1658), pp. 156–7.
16. *The Friar and Boy . . . Part the First* (no publication details but c.1760), pp. 11–12.
17. John Vowler, *An Essay for Instructing Children on Various Useful and Uncommon Subjects* (Exeter: printed for the author, 1743), p. 38.

18. James Barclay, *A Treatise on Education* (Edinburgh: James Cochran, 1743), p. 131.
19. Vowler, *An Essay for Instructing Children*, p. viii.
20. Charlotte Finch, *The Gamut and Time-Table in Verse* (London: Dean and Munday, c.1825), p. 35.
21. Set 21, no. 9, Jane Johnson MSS., Lilly Library, Indiana University, Bloomington, Indiana, online at http://www.dlib.indiana.edu/collections/janejohnson/ [accessed 16 August 2007].
22. *The Oxford Dictionary of Nursery Rhymes*, ed. Iona and Peter Opie (Oxford: Oxford University Press, [1951] 1997), pp. 28–36.
23. *The Top Book of All, for Little Masters and Misses* (London: R. Baldwin and S. Crowder, c.1760), pp. 7–9.
24. Iona Opie, 'Playground Rhymes', *The Cambridge Guide to Children's Books in English*, ed. Victor Watson (Cambridge: Cambridge University Press, 2001), pp. 570–1.
25. Milne, 'Busy', *Now We Are Six* (London: Egmont, [1927] 1989), p. 7.
26. Allan Ahlberg, 'The Longest Kiss Contest', *Heard it in the Playground* (London: Puffin, [1989] 1991), p. 13.
27. Humphrey Carpenter and Mari Prichard, *The Oxford Companion to Children's Literature* (Oxford: Oxford University Press, 1984), p. 502.
28. Roald Dahl, *Charlie and the Chocolate Factory* (Harmondsworth: Penguin, [1964] 1975), p. 74.
29. Watts, 'Heaven and Hell', *Divine Songs*, p. 16.
30. Noel Malcolm, *The Origins of English Nonsense* (London: Harper Collins, 1997) and Kimberly Reynolds, *Radical Children's Literature: Future Visions and Aesthetic Transformations in Juvenile Fiction* (Basingstoke: Palgrave Macmillan, 2007), pp. 45–67.
31. Styles, 'Poetry', in *International Companion Encyclopedia of Children's Literature*, ed. Peter Hunt, 2nd edn, 2 vols (London: Routledge, 2004), vol. 1, pp. 396–417 (p. 405).
32. *The World Turned Upside Down* (York: J. Kendrew, c.1830).
33. Jane and Ann Taylor, *Signor Topsy-Turvy's Wonderful Magic Lantern; or, the World Turned Upside Down* (London: Tabart, 1810), pp. 8 and 40.

34. Lewis Carroll, *The Hunting of the Snark* (1876), in *Alice in Wonderland*, ed. Donald J. Gray (New York: W. W. Norton, 1992), p. 234.
35. *The New Oxford Book of Children's Verse*, p. 29.
36. Peter Hollindale and Zena Sutherland, 'Internationalism, Fantasy, and Realism', pp. 252–88 in *Children's Literature. An Illustrated History*, ed. Peter Hunt, (Oxford: Oxford University Press, 1995), p. 284. Charles Causley, *Figgie Hobbin* (Harmondsworth: Penguin, [1970] 1979), p. 43.
37. Mick Gowar, 'Rat Trap', from *Carnival for the Animals, and Other Poems* (1992), in *The New Oxford Book of Children's Verse*, p. 325.
38. Gowar, 'Rat Trap', p. 326.
39. Benjamin Zephaniah, 'According to my mood', from *Talking Turkeys* (1994), in *The New Oxford Book of Children's Verse*, p. 334.
40. J. B. Morton, 'Now We Are Sick' (1931), quoted in *The Faber Book of Parodies*, ed. Simon Brett (London: Faber & Faber, 1984), p. 258.
41. Humphrey Carpenter, *Secret Gardens: The Golden Age of Children's Literature* (London: George Allen and Unwin, 1985), pp. 107 and 196. A. A. Milne, *When We Were Very Young* (London: Egmont, [1924] 1989), pp. 99–100.
42. Milne, *When We Were Very Young*, pp. 30–3.
43. Smart, 'Hymn xxxiii: For Saturday', in *The New Oxford Book of Children's Verse*, p. 1.
44. Robert Louis Stevenson, 'The Land of Story-Books', *A Child's Garden of Verses* (London: Wordsworth, [1885] 1994), pp. 97–8.
45. Stevenson, *Child's Garden of Verses*, pp. 139–40.
46. Lewis Carroll, 'Solitude' (1853), *The Complete Works of Lewis Carroll*, ed. Alexander Woollcott (London: Nonesuch, 1939).
47. John Goldthwaite, *The Natural History of Make-Believe* (New York: Oxford University Press, 1996), p. 28.
48. Jacqueline Rose, *The Case of Peter Pan or The Impossibility of Children's Fiction* (London: Macmillan, 1984).
49. Hunt, *Children's Literature*, p. 297.
50. Summarised in Styles, *From the Garden to the Street*, pp. 262–70.

51. Peter Hunt, 'The New Oxford: "Poetry Alive"', *Children's Literature Association Quarterly* 22 (1997), 149–50 (p. 149).

52. Alison Lurie, *Boys and Girls Forever: Children's Classics from Cinderella to Harry Potter* (Harmondsworth: Penguin, 2003), p. 157.

53. Roger McGough, 'First Day at School', from *In the Glassroom* (1976), in *The New Oxford Book of Children's Verse*, ed. Philip, p. 290.

54. Glenna Sloan, 'But is it poetry?', p. 52.

55. Jackie Kay, 'What Jenny Knew', from *Two's Company* (1992), in *The New Oxford Book of Children's Verse*, p. 336.

56. Hall, *The Oxford Book of Children's Verse in America*, p. xxiv.

57. Neil Philip, 'Introduction', *The New Oxford Book of Children's Verse*, p. xxv;

58. Styles, *From the Garden to the Street*, p. 156.

CHAPTER 3

Moral and Instructive Tales

In an essay written in 1980, Nina Bawden, the author of many successful children's books including *Carrie's War* (1973) and *The Peppermint Pig* (1975), wrote a strongly worded essay attacking what have been called the 'problem novels' of the 1970s. These were books designed mainly for teenagers in which (she said) 'fashionable social problems' were 'dragged in to satisfy some educational or social theory.' She lamented that this was what 'superficial critics consider realism to be'. Since they were part of life, Bawden accepted, such subjects as poverty and divorce, learning disabilities and racism, should certainly not be ignored by children's literature. But focusing on this kind of issue did not in itself make a book good, and it ought not to be a book's only *raison d'être*. Nor should children's books 'be used as a kind of therapy'. Why should a poor child have to read of poverty? Why should anyone think that a child from a one-parent family would feel better after reading about other children from one-parent families? 'The most important realism that children need,' she insisted, 'is the realism of the emotional landscape in which the book is set'. A children's book, she concluded, 'should be judged for the pleasure it gives, for its style and its quality', not according to how well it serves 'factions and interests and ideologies'.[1]

Bawden's essay is a good place to start this chapter since it brings up the two issues of realism (the accurate depiction of everyday life) and didacticism (instruction for a specific purpose) which will link together the very various texts discussed here. This is not to say that some fairy tales or fantasies are not didactic, nor, say, that school stories or adventure tales cannot be realistic. But there is an important and distinct tradition of children's literature, visible from the seventeenth century to today, that deals with ordinary children in ordinary situations being taught to deal with ordinary problems. It is the endurance of this tradition across centuries that can make Bawden's comments seem rather curious. What was wrong with the problem novels, she was essentially arguing, was that they tried to teach specific lessons in a context that readers would recognise as their own. In other words, they attempted to fuse didacticism and realism. But authors have always sought to do just this. 150 years before Bawden's attack, Catherine Sinclair, author of what is sometimes thought of as 'the first modern children's novel', *Holiday House* (1839), had railed against moral children's books which tried to 'stuff the memory' with 'ready-made opinions', leaving no room 'for the vigour of natural feeling, the glow of natural genius, and the ardour of natural enthusiasm.'[2] Charles Lamb similarly attacked 'the cursed Barbauld crew' (by which he meant the authors of late eighteenth-century moral tales, like Anna Laetitia Barbauld) for their dreary didactic realism which had supplanted, he said, those 'wild tales which made the child a man'.[3] This desire for 'real stories' rather than real life, and for subtly imparted values rather than explicit instruction, has been a constant theme of children's literature criticism. But just as constant, and more productive, has been the steady disregard of this criticism.

A comparison of some specific realistic, didactic texts from across the last three centuries will show more clearly exactly how durable this particular form of children's literature has been. Perhaps the most archetypal of all the teenage problem novels of the 1970s is Judy Blume's *Forever* (1975). It was the most controversial, and successful, in a sequence of books which she had began with *Are You There God? It's Me, Margaret* (1970) and continued with *Then Again, Maybe I Won't* (1971), *It's Not the End of the World* (1971), *Deenie* (1973) and *Blubber* (1974). These had dealt with boyfriends and bras (eleven-year-old Margaret prays for both), menstruation and masturbation, divorce and disability, bullying (the persecution of overweight Linda in *Blubber*) and, in *Forever*, sex. Its story is simple. At a party, the narrator, a seventeen-year-old called Katherine, meets Michael, a boy of her own age. They begin a relationship, gradually becoming more and more intimate until they become fully sexually active. They promise to stay together forever. By the end of the novel, though, Katherine, and perhaps Michael, have begun relationships with other people. Even if the book is not exactly erotic, it has undoubtedly been the book's descriptions of sex which have kept it so popular with young readers, and which have drawn so much condemnation. That *Forever* was still, in the US in 2005, in the top ten of books 'challenged' as being unsuitable for children shows how controversial its subject remains.[4]

On the surface *Forever* could not be more dissimilar from what we might call the 'classic' moral tales produced in great numbers in the late eighteenth and early nineteenth century by women such as Barbauld, Maria Edgeworth and Mary Wollstonecraft. These were generally short stories, rather than full-length novels, though many of them are about the same characters and trace their growth over a number of years. They are usually told by an omniscient third-person narrator, or sometimes given as dramatic dialogues, whereas *Forever* is narrated by Katherine. Another difference is these books' intended audience. *Forever* was designed for teenagers. Barbauld and Edgeworth wrote some of their tales for children as young as two or three, though later sequels were for readers who might, anachronistically, be described as teenagers. Above all, one might think, it is the subject matter that distinguishes the eighteenth-century moral tale from the twentieth-century problem novel. Edgeworth, for example, was careful to reassure parents in the preface to a collection of stories about the ten-to-thirteen-year-old Rosamond that she had not 'attempted to give what is called a knowledge of the world, which ought not, cannot be given prematurely'.[5] This demonstrates how keen Edgeworth was to please parents and to explain to them why her books were suitable for their children. She clearly intended the tales to be read by children and adults together. By contrast, Blume deliberately wrote about subjects which parents and children seldom discussed (a point she forcibly made with the title she chose for a collection of letters readers had sent her: *Letters to Judy: What Your Kids Wish They*

Could Tell You, 1986). Yet if we turn to Wollstonecraft, the similarities with Blume are much more striking than the differences. She had wanted to include lessons about 'chastity and impurity' in one of her collections of moral tales, for, she wrote, 'impurity is now spread so far that even children are infected'. She added that she was,

> thoroughly persuaded that the most efficacious method to root out this dreadful evil . . . would be to speak to children of the organs of generation as freely as we speak of other parts of the body, and explain to them the noble use which they were designed for, and how they may be injured.

Wollstonecraft left out such material only after being convinced that her views would 'not have sufficient weight with the public to conquer long-fostered prejudices.'[6] But it is noticeable that, like Blume two hundred years later, Wollstonecraft felt that to talk openly about taboo subjects was the best way to encourage healthy development.

Edgeworth, more prim that Wollstonecraft, did not make reference to sex in her moral tales, but nor did she escape criticism. The deeply conservative Sarah Trimmer wrote in 1803 that Edgeworth's books were not sufficiently religious and added that parents sometimes have to impose good behaviour and enforce discipline rather than always letting children come to their own conclusions.[7] Again, these were the same criticisms as would be levelled at Blume's work, and it is the centrality of this idea that children should teach themselves that gives the moral tale its coherence across two centuries. The most famous of Edgeworth's moral tales is 'The Purple Jar' (1796). This short fable begins with Rosamond out shopping with her mother. Her eye is caught by a purple jar on display in the window of an apothecary's shop and she begs her mother to buy it. Her mother will purchase only one item and, because Rosamond's shoes are very worn, she steers her towards a new pair instead of the jar. Rosamond ponders her choice, but the lure of the jar proves too strong. When she returns home, she is disappointed to find that the jar itself is not purple at all, but was simply filled with an odorous purple liquid. Later, Rosamond's distress is compounded when her father withdraws his offer to take her to see a glasshouse full of exotic plants because her shoes are in such a disgraceful state. She bitterly regrets her choice. 'O mamma,' she says, 'I am sure – no not quite sure, but I hope I shall be wiser another time.'[8] Several modern critics have been appalled that, even though Rosamond's shoes hurt her feet, her mother did not intervene in her choice.[9] But the idea that children should learn their lessons on their own is every bit as central to Edgeworth's writing as it is to Blume's. Just as Rosamond's mother did not impose the lesson about value, or the importance of distinguishing between appearance and reality, so, in *Forever*, Katherine's parents trust her to find out about sex for herself (although her mother cuts out relevant articles from the paper for her and her grandmother sends her leaflets on contraception, abortion and sexually transmitted diseases). In fact the main tension of *Forever* comes from Katherine's certainty that she will always love Michael versus her parents' awareness that the relationship will falter. They are adamant that Katherine's relationship should not govern her important decisions, such as her choice of university. For the most part they allow her to work this out for herself, although on one occasion, without her knowledge, her father does autocratically arrange for Katherine to take a good job at a summer camp (where she meets her next boyfriend). Like Rosamond, Katherine eventually comes to see the wisdom of her parents' attitudes.[10] But this one instance of parental authority exposes the power relationship within the text. Despite the illusion of freedom, Blume's teenagers are in fact still subservient to their parents, just as Rosamond was to hers. What both Edgeworth and Blume actually provide is a parental fantasy in which children are allowed to learn their own lessons, but always come to the conclusions which their parents would wish.

Older and newer moral tales are also linked by their determination to appear almost hyper-realistic. Typical in its gritty and graphic subject matter, and in its attempt to heighten immediacy by carefully deploying references to such things as current television programmes, pop music hits and school text books is Richard Peck's *Are You in the House Alone?* (1976) – the book which Nina Bawden was probably attacking when she wrote against a book congratulated for 'being the first children's book with a rape in it'.

Blume's similar use of shock tactics, and teenage argot, is evident right from *Forever's* first, shocking sentence: 'Sybil Davison has a genius I.Q. and has been laid by at least six different guys.'[11] Although there is nothing like this in Edgeworth, she too strove hard for a verisimilitude which would anchor her didacticism in everyday life. *Forever* describes in detail the process of getting into university; 'The Purple Jar' gives a detailed description of the shops Rosamond visits. Both authors immerse their protagonists in material culture. In *Forever*, Blume deploys references to the purchase of new clothes, of finding bargains, of visits to cinemas and cafes, of the whole process of saving and spending money, as a way of stapling the narrative to the real world with real teenage concerns. Surprisingly, Edgeworth's tales are even more concerned with children's purchasing power. As Marilyn Butler has pointed out, 'it would usually be possible to name the exact sum in the pocket of any of Maria Edgeworth's twelve-year-olds.'[12] Edgeworth and Blume also tried as hard as they could to give realistic representations of child psychology. Edgeworth has been applauded for portraying 'the first living and breathing children in English literature since Shakespeare'.[13] She manages to give this impression by representing her characters' faults and limitations. Rosamond is solipsistic, motivated by strong but fleeting desires, and, at the end of the tale, is still appealingly unsure that she will be able to reform. Blume's Katherine is just as self-absorbed and impulsive, just as angry at her parents' refusal to see things her way, then as willing to admit that they were right.

All this ostentatious realism has several purposes. First, Edgeworth and Blume were both trying to emphasise that literature is not removed from real life and to enable the reader to see him or herself in the text. Second, they were attempting to establish a division between the young reader and adults and to give the impression that the book is somehow on the reader's side. In *Forever* this is achieved by Katherine's first-person narration, a characteristic of the majority of post-War Young Adult fiction, much of which shows the influence of J. D. Salinger's *The Catcher in the Rye* (1951). The confessional mode of these books allows readers to feel complicit in the plot and to share the narrator's resentment at adult superciliousness and interference. In a very similar way in

'The Purple Jar', the reader participates in all Rosamond's deliberations, anticipation, disappointment and regret. Indeed, when Rosamond's father refuses to let her accompany him to the glasshouse, Edgeworth does not attempt to mitigate the harshness of his edict. The sense of injustice she creates cements the bond between the reader and Rosamond. But above all, the sense of realism developed by both Edgeworth and Blume was designed to smooth the passage of the didacticism.

However, both *Forever* and Edgeworth's moral tales are more than mere vehicles for didacticism. One critic, for example, has argued that Edgeworth's tales focus on 'issues of adult authority and child empowerment', exploring 'what it's like for juveniles who seek both separation and relation' in a society in which children 'must develop their own sense of self, yet maintain the affiliative network that defines social being.'[14] Many critics have been more sceptical about Blume's place in the history of children's literature, but *Forever* is a sophisticated and satisfying text, much more than simply a 'problem novel'. It has dated quite badly, as the fact that it is now marketed as 'a teenage classic' acknowledges, but for several different reasons simultaneously. On the one hand, its attempt to capture teenage demotic language now seems rather quaint. On the other, it now seems the product of a specific historical period, after the advent of the contraceptive pill and before the onset of AIDS.

Certainly many modern readers will find it shocking that one of Katherine's friends is encouraged to go on the pill by her mother even before she has had sex: 'she said she'd feel better if she knew that I was prepared for college, in every way', recounts her rather bemused daughter.[15] Yet sex is not really the issue at the core of *Forever*. The book is principally about change and the illusion of permanence. The action of the novel takes place at the moment when Katherine is poised between one phase of life and the next, about to graduate from high school and depart for university. Many other smaller shifts make up the fabric of the book, also disturbing her previous comfortable life: her sister's arrival at puberty, the desertion of some of her friends, her grandfather's death and so on. Most obviously the disruption of the past is caused by her relationship with Michael and the commencement of her sex-life. She is desperate for the relationship always to endure, her conviction symbolised by a silver disk Michael buys her, engraved with the word 'forever' and hanging from a (heavily metaphorical) chain. The novel, then, is an account of Katherine coming to understand that however secure the past has been, she must break her self-imposed ties, freeing herself to enter a new stage of her life. Moreover, Blume suggests that what Katherine is experiencing on a personal level, society as a whole is also going through in the late 1960s and early 1970s. The permissive society's break with the past cannot be resisted, she argues. Rather, it has to be embraced, even by parents whose instinct is to protect their daughters from adult sexuality. And its consequences have to be faced, even when they are as difficult as the unwanted pregnancy of Sybil Davison, whose promiscuity Blume introduced in the novel's first sentence. *Forever* can seem morally conservative, arguing that sex should always take place within a loving environment. But it is also a novel of liberation, making the case for the acceptance of change, both personal and social.

The classic moral tales of the late eighteenth and early nineteenth centuries could also incorporate a progressive agenda within their fundamentally conservative moral universe. Almost all of them were opposed to racism and slavery, for instance, and not only because so many were written and published by religious non-conformists. Some critics have argued that moral tales often present a feminist programme. Mary Wollstonecraft's *Original Stories from Real Life* (1788), for example, can certainly be regarded as representing the sort of rational education for girls that its author would later demand in *A Vindication of the Rights of Woman* (1792). Christine Wilkie-Stubbs has claimed that Wollstonecraft 'was using her writing for children to subvert and interrogate the role of women in society'.[16] But the principal connection between these early moral tales and the new moral tales of the later twentieth century is their commitment to realism and rationalism. Indeed, the classic moral tale developed in conscious opposition to fiction which had included supernatural elements. The warnings of John Locke's *Some Thoughts Concerning Education* (1693) were foundational. He had been adamant that nursemaid's stories used to frighten children into good behaviour did much more harm than good. Sarah Trimmer was paraphrasing him when she argued against fairy stories, claiming that 'the terrific images, which tales of this nature present to the imagination, usually make deep impressions, and injure the tender minds of children, by exciting unreasonable and groundless fears.'[17] Fiction was produced to dramatise this effect. 'The History of Francis Fearful', published in about 1774, explained to its child readers how the stories of Goody Senseless, his nurse, put all sorts of superstitious terrors into Francis' head. When he was sent to school, his fear of bats and scarecrows made him the laughing stock of the other pupils.[18]

This same concern for realism determined what went into the late eighteenth-century moral tales as well as what was left out. Arnaud Berquin, a French children's author whose work became almost immediately popular in translation, and an important influence on many British writers, clearly explained his principles. 'Instead of those wild fictions of the Wonderful, in which their understanding is too commonly bewilder'd,' he wrote, in his books children would:

> see only what occurs or may occur within the limits of their families. The sentiments with which the work abounds, are not above the level of their comprehension. It introduces them, accompanied by none, except their parents, the companions of their pastimes, the domestics [servants] that surround them, or the animals they are accustomed to behold. 'Tis in their own ingenuous language they express themselves: And, interested in the several events the work describes, they are directed by the impulse of their little passions. They are punish'd when they happen to do wrong, and find a recompense resulting from their commendable actions. Every thing concurs to lead them on to virtue, as their happiness, and give them a distaste of vice, by representing it a source of sorrow and humiliation.[19]

The key points here are that readers will meet only those things which they find around them in their own lives, and that it is on these that the didacticism will be based. This is essentially a manifesto for the moral tale.

Key to the reformatory purpose of the British moral tale was the reader's ability to recognise him or herself in the text. Although a few moral tales took poor children as their protagonists, by far the majority were set in affluent, middle-class families in which either leisured parents superintend their children's education or a surrogate, usually a governess, has been appointed. Although some were set in the city, most were located in a bucolic rural environment. These tales mirror, even if they also somewhat idealise, the families of the books' intended consumers. This is naturalistic realism then – striving for an accurate representation of one segment of real life – not the realism of the nineteenth-century novel which attempted to depict the conditions, speech and attitudes of the working classes. It was above all important that readers should be able to identify themselves in the characters they were reading about, their desires and fears, and their errors. Thus Mary Ann Kilner's *Jemima Placid* (c.1783) is really a series of children's everyday faults cast into narrative form. Two sisters fight over the toy furniture for their dolls' houses, smashing their dolls in the process; a boy puts a spider down his sister's neck and she overturns the furniture in her fright; a girl is so excited by the prospect of going to a ball that she vomits in the coach, ruining her own and her companions' dresses. The book's method is clearly explained in its sub-title: *The Advantage of Good-Nature Exemplified in a Variety of Familiar Incidents*. Its aim, though, was not simply to *exemplify*, but to encourage its readers to repent and reform. 'If the characters you meet with in any way resemble your own,' Kilner wrote, 'and if those characters disgust and offend you, instead of throwing the book aside with resentment, you should endeavour to improve the failings of which you are conscious, and then you will no longer meet with your own portrait in that which the Author has described.'[20]

It would be impossible to list all the specific lessons taught by all the moral tales, but they can perhaps be rolled up into one or two basic dicta. First, children must honour and obey adults, especially their parents. Beyond this, they should always be sensible and prudent, planning for the future and assessing their options rationally (unlike Rosamond with her purple jar), and not impetuous, clumsy, temperamental, jealous or selfish. In other words, most classic moral tales urged children not to be childish. This is very clear in *Virtue and Vice: or, the History of Charles Careful, and Harry Heedless* (c.1780). Some children, the narrator declares, 'learn early to act like men and women, while there are other people, who may be said to be boys and girls for the whole course of their lives.' The former, like Charles, are the book's heroes; the latter, like Harry, its villains. It is as a reward for his precocious maturity that Sir Robert becomes Charles' patron, gratifying him by treating him 'rather like a little man, than a child'. In the terms of this book, and most late eighteenth-century moral tales, to be good is to renounce one's childhood, for a 'virtuous child' is almost a contradiction in terms.[21]

One surprise about the lessons of the moral tale are that they are not always especially moral. John Aikin and Anna Laetitia Barbauld's *Evenings at Home* (1792–96), for example, contained many scientific sections, teaching children about botany, say, and manufacturing processes.[22] More frequently, the moral tales seem designed to encourage and enable social and economic advancement rather than any more abstract moral improvement. 'The Purple Jar', for instance, can be read as a fable about the difference between appearance and reality, but it also teaches children more banal lessons such as how to shop successfully. Edgeworth acknowledged that she wrote many tales 'to excite a spirit of industry' and 'to point out that people feel cheerful and happy whilst they are employed.'[23] Overall, the principal drive was to inculcate thrift, honesty, diligence and prudence – what might be termed 'commercial virtues' – and to give a strong sense of the value of things. Even when charitable giving is promoted, as it often is, only a judicious, means-tested philanthropy was countenanced. Charity had become a fiscal transaction rather than moral duty, commendable because it signified a child's economic rationalism rather than any open-hearted benevolence.[24]

The most nakedly commercial of all moral tales were the novels of Barbara Hofland, mostly published in the 1810s and 1820s. Like Edgeworth, she saturates her novels in the financial details of her protagonists' lives. Her two most celebrated novels, *The Son of a Genius* (1812) and *The Daughter of a Genius* (1823), single out for attack those who possess talent but lack financial responsibility. The two 'geniuses' are condemned because they spend extravagantly when they are rich, and make few efforts to earn money when they are poor. Other lessons Hofland urgently teaches are the value of compound interest in *Daughter of a Genius* and the importance of keeping receipts in *Son of a Genius*. When the genius claims that it is beneath his dignity as an artist to ask for a receipt, Hofland's mouthpiece character disagrees: 'a great mind can take in petty cares, an aspiring genius stoop to petty details; since it is impossible to be virtuous and pious without it'. Words like 'virtue' and 'piety' are common in the moral tale, but Hofland's deployment of them here acknowledges that, for her, business rectitude is in itself actually pious and virtuous. It is immoral, and even an affront to God, to despise economic good practice. Piety, morality and commercial probity had become one and the same thing.[25]

Perhaps the principal ambition of the classic moral tale then was to teach children how to prosper. This was a lesson directed at the individual child reader, and perhaps more especially his or her parents who, after all, were likely to making the investment in the child by buying the book. But many moral tale authors also envisaged their books as possessing the power to reform, even perfect, society as a whole. According to some readings, the moral tale was essentially an ideological weapon wielded by the bourgeoisie, used to endorse middle-class principles over both aristocratic and plebeian value systems. When they attacked showiness, languor or economic fecklessness, Andrew O'Malley has argued, they were targeting an aristocratic, dilettante philosophy. When they urged the importance of hard work they were aiming at the putatively lower-class conviction that good fortune came out-of-the-blue, rather than as the result of planning and industry.[26] This supposedly lower-class 'lottery mentality' had been embedded in tales of the supernatural (such as Locke had said servants were fond of telling children). The moral tale was designed to replace such chapbook tales and fairy stories. After all, as one writer put it, they give children 'an erroneous idea of the ways of Providence' by suggesting that God will reward those who are virtuous, even if they do not help themselves.[27] Viewed in another light, though, eighteenth-century moral tales can seem much more conservative, advocating a restrictive acquiescence to things as they are. The concluding moral of Kilner's *Jemima Placid* is 'Unavoidable disasters are beyond remedy, and are only aggravated by complaints. By submitting with a good grace to the disappointments of life, half its vexations may be escaped.'[28]

The moral tale's determination to affect public as well as private morality makes it something of a utopian genre. A useful comparison can be made with the children's literature produced in the heyday of the Soviet Union. This was socialist not bourgeois of course – compulsorily so after the first congress of Soviet writers in 1934 had made socialist realism the only permissible mode for all literary production – but it was similarly unashamed in its ideological agenda. All Soviet children's books had to propagate doctrinally correct thinking, to show the forces of progress triumphing, and to depict all right-minded characters co-operating in the cause of the general good.[29] Children were defined in terms of what they would become – the citizens of the future – not as beings who should be left free from political concerns. 'These principles', it can be said, 'bear a close resemblance to those upon which the English eighteenth-century moral tale was constructed.'[30] In eighteenth-century Britain there was no legislation forcing the moral tale to promote a particular ideological programme, and political and religious differences certainly existed between its ideologically disparate authors. But in their optimistic conviction that children's literature could improve both the individual and society, authors of the moral tale were asserting the right that Maxim Gorky claimed for Soviet writers at the 1934 congress, 'to participate directly in the construction of a new life, in the process of "changing the world"'.[31]

If Gorky's maxim applies to eighteenth-century moral tales, how much more does it fit the realist children's fiction produced from the late twentieth century? Blume's *Forever* was one amongst 'adolescent novels of ideas', as one critics has called them, which sought to make the personal political, trying simultaneously to improve the individual reader and to engineer a better society through the realistic representation of everyday life and its problems.[32] Several books tackled the problem of racism in urban Britain, for example. Bernard Ashley's *The Trouble with Donovan Croft* (1974) wove a story around the adoption of a black boy from a Jamaican background into a white family. Jan Needle's *My Mate Shofiq* (1978) was even more viciously realistic, showing a recession-hit Lancashire mill town as an urban wasteland where racism was endemic. At times it tips over into a sort of hyper-realism, the exaggerated winter weather being designed to emphasise the brutality of life and perhaps, rather awkwardly, the discomfort of the Pakistani families who live there: 'They ought to feel it more, by rights, being as how they came from a hot country', says the book's chief character, Bernard. In both books, the reader is shown the ugliness of children's racism, so vividly, in fact, that Needle in particular was criticised for his accurate representation of his characters' racially offensive language.[33] The passage in which Shofiq explains to his new friends that he does not want to be called a 'Paki' is typical, meant to be shocking in its realism, but ending up rather clumsy because it is so clearly propagandistic:

> 'I can't rightly explain,' he said, 'but it's horrible. I mean I don't call you lot all Whities, or something. There's just something . . . it sounds . . .'
>
> 'Ah rubbish, lad,' said Terry. 'Everyone calls Pakis Pakis. It stands to reason. I mean, my dad calls Pakis Pakis; and blackies. Like West Indian kids gets called niggers and Chinese is Chinkies. I mean, it's just what you get called, it don't mean nowt.'
>
> 'It does, it does!' said Shofiq. 'I'll tell you, it means . . .'
>
> He was helpless. He couldn't explain.
>
> 'I just wish you wouldn't, that's all,' he ended lamely.
>
> 'Rubbish!' said Terry firmly. I'll call you what I like, and you're a Paki, so there.'
>
> Shofiq started to roll up his sleeves.
>
> 'All right then, Smelly White Pig,' he said grimily. 'Take your coat off, lad, 'cause I'm going to batter you.'
>
> Maureen solved it in the end by pointing out that no one was allowed to call Bernard Bernie. Bern was all right, or even Slobberchops. But not Bernie. They discussed as to why, but he couldn't rightly say. But he hated it, and that was that. Terry, who wasn't thick, agreed that he'd not call Shofiq a Paki.
>
> 'It's not just me, though,' said Shofiq. 'Everybody hates it, it's rotten. But thanks, Terry.'

'Well I won't call any of 'em – you – Pakis in future,' said Maureen. 'Pakistanis is good enough for me.'

Shofiq giggled: 'Or Indians, or Bangladeshies, or Bengalis, eh? How about British? It's on me birth certificate!'

But that just got them confused.

What is also evident here is something that differentiates *My Mate Shofiq* from many eighteenth-century moral tales but links it to Soviet propaganda: the idea that the attitudes and values of previous generations should be dispensed with, and the hope that children will be able to make a better world on their own. Terry's father is the villain here as much as the bullies who pick on Shofiq at school. So too is Bernard's father who has to impose redundancies at his mill and has decided to sack the Pakistani workers because, he claims, they are 'always stopping work for religion, some festival do or sommat' and they don't 'try to do it our way'.[34] If there is hope, Needle insists, it lies with the children. This is dramatically restated at the end of *The Trouble with Donovan Croft*. Traumatised by his sense of alienation, Donovan has been entirely mute for the duration of the novel. His friendship with his white foster-brother Keith has been gradually developing though, and he suddenly shouts out to save Keith from an oncoming car. What has overcome society's racism and broken Donovan's silence is not politicians, parents, teachers or social workers, but the friendship of two boys.[35]

Some problem novels can seem more personal than political. Betsy Byars' *The Summer of the Swans* (1970) focused on a boy with learning difficulties; Richard Peck's *Don't Look and It Won't Hurt* (1972) was about unmarried motherhood; Katherine Paterson's *The Great Gilly Hopkins* (1979) was about a fostered girl with behavioural problems who longs to find her real mother but finally learns, when her birth mother rejects her, that it has been this dream that has been preventing her from finding happiness in her life. Others successfully combine both. Shocking as Gail's rape is in Peck's *Are You in the House Alone?* (1976) much of the book's horror derives from the reactions of the snobbish, misogynistic inhabitants of her Connecticut suburb. Her assailant comes from an established, patrician family, while many of her neighbours believe that Gail has been asking for trouble because of her previous sexual relationship with a local boy from a less affluent family. 'Why does the law protect the rapist instead of the victim?', Gail's experiences lead her to demand, to which the only answer the book offers is 'Because the law is wrong'.[36]

Increasingly these modern moral tales have shied away from offering any simple, confident solution to the problems they represent. An excellent example is Berlie Doherty's *Dear Nobody* (1991), a novel with teenage pregnancy at its centre. It reads almost like a deliberate re-writing of Blume's *Forever*, but designed for more cynical times. Like Blume's Katherine and Michael, Doherty's Helen and Chris are in their final year of school, are working towards their places at university, and are experimenting with sex. In *Dear Nobody*, though, the novel's only sex-scene occurs on the second page, is wholly unplanned, and is described in only a single line. Helen becomes pregnant and the rest of the novel takes the form of a complicated narrative, split between Chris's memories of that year, written down on the evening before he leaves for university, and Helen's letters to her unborn child, 'Nobody'. Many of the novel's episodes seem intended to undercut the cosy optimism of *Forever*. Both Helen's and Chris's families are dysfunctional. Chris's mother has left home, and his attempts to find her and build a relationship help set the context for his other concerns. Helen's mother is emotionally distant. She offers Helen no support and almost forces her to have an abortion. Eventually we find that this is because of her guilt and resentment at her own illegitimate birth. Indeed, in *Dear Nobody* there are few if any emotionally stable figures who can dispense wisdom and love in the way that so many of Blume's characters do. In contrast with Katherine's wise and loving grandmother in *Forever*, Helen's has withdrawn from the world to her darkened bedroom. When Helen visits the family planning clinic, she finds not the solicitude and good advice that Katherine had benefited from, but 'young women sitting there, most of them smoking, most of them looking fed up and tired and lonely' and she leaves without seeing anyone.[37]

In fact, despite her emotional confusion, the only composed figure in the book is Helen herself. It is she who knows she must keep her baby and, shockingly, who decides to end her relationship with Chris, much against his wishes, at least partly in order to allow him to take his place at university. She and Chris were 'a pair of kids having fun together', she writes to her unborn child. 'And now we've been catapulted into the world of grown-ups. I'm not ready for forever. I'm not ready for him, and he's not ready for me.' It seems a deliberate rejoinder to Blume's *Forever*, with Helen taking the rational role of Katherine's parents. What Doherty has done is to destabilise the idea of maturity. Gone is the fantasy, so consoling for both young readers and adult authors, that teenagers simply have to learn to accept the wisdom of their elders in order to turn out as happy human beings. It is the younger people – Helen, and even her daughter Amy – from whom we can learn most. The book concludes with the four generations of women in Helen's family sitting together with Amy 'a fine thread being drawn through a garment, mending tears.'[38] *Dear Nobody* could be called a feminist book perhaps, and there may be a suggestion of an anti-abortion agenda. It warns readers about the fragility of relationships and about their social responsibilities. But beyond this, it is difficult to determine precisely what lessons are being taught. Ultimately, Doherty suggests that life is full of emotional complexity but that there is no simple way of dealing with it. People have to deal as best they can with their problems and to welcome rather than fear the richness of life. In a way, this recalls the lessons of some of the eighteenth-century moral tales. 'Unavoidable disasters are beyond remedy, and are only aggravated by complaints', wrote Mary Ann Kilner at the end of *Jemima Placid*. 'By submitting with a good grace to the disappointments of life, half its vexations may be escaped.'[39]

One important question remains: what happened to the moral tale between its early nineteenth-century heyday and what might be thought of as its reincarnation in the problem novels of the 1970s? According to some histories of children's literature moral tales had died out by the Victorian era, superseded by a prolif- eration of new sub-genres: adventure stories, nonsense verse, Carrollian fantasies, family stories, newly re-popular fairy tales, and so on. It is certainly tempting to think of Catherine Sinclair's *Holiday House* (1839) as the moral tale's death-knell. Its preface sav- agely attacked didactic children's literature. The book itself seems calculated to undermine the moral tale. For most of its course it celebrates, rather than castigates, the mischievous behaviour of Harry and Laura, even when they do something as dangerous as setting the house on fire. The disciplinarian Mrs Crabtree can be regarded as a vicious caricature of the sternly rational female teachers who had peopled the late eighteenth-century moral tale, and she is ruthlessly mocked. The book becomes much more pious towards its close, and much darker too when Harry and Laura's brother dies. But this cannot quite banish the memory of the anti-morality of its first half, nor of the way that Sinclair seemed to deride the whole notion of the moral tale by having Uncle David sententiously tell the children that he has 'only one piece of serious, important advice to give', which turns out to be 'never crack nuts with your teeth!' It is, as David Rudd points out, 'an aphorism rarely found stitched into samplers.'[40]

However, it would be more accurate to say that the moral tale evolved than that it become suddenly extinct. Most obviously, it became imbued with an Evangelical Christianity, in which form it thrived at least until the end of the nineteenth century.[41] The process of transition can be observed in the work of Mary Martha Sherwood. Her early works were moral tales in the Edgeworthian manner. Sarah Trimmer commended *The History of Susan Gray* (1802), for example, because 'all the arguments which Reason and Religion can furnish [are] enforced by the most striking examples of *persevering Virtue*'.[42] But thirteen years later, Sherwood reissued her book in a much more Evangelical form, editing out what she had come to consider as the book's doctrinal faults. Her change from rational moralist to Evangelical Christian had happened in India, where she had followed her husband, a soldier. It was her concern at the speed with which British children assimilated into a non-Christian culture that persuaded her of the need for a children's literature which emphasised religious orthodoxy not abstract morality. The result was dozens of tracts and some immensely successful novels, notably *Little Henry and his Bearer* (1814), a neo-Puritan tale describing the boy's pious death after having converted his Indian servant to Christianity, and *The Fairchild Family* (first part, 1818). Perhaps the most appealing today is *The Little Woodman, and His Dog Cæsar* (1818), an extremely enjoyable fusion of fairy tale, animal story and religious tract. It describes how six sinful boys plan to kill their youngest brother William by abandoning him in the forest because only he has heeded their dying father's religious advice. He is saved by a combination of divine intervention and his dog, who fights off wolves and eventually leads him to an isolated cottage which turns out to belong to his pious grandmother. The book ends when his six brothers reappear, their health and fortunes ruined by their wicked lives. William takes them in and puts them on the road to repentance. Sherwood's moral, directed at both children and their parents, explains the importance she ascribed to books that could reach the young: 'Fathers and mothers, you should lead your children to love God while they are little, and while their hearts are tender. And you, little children, lose no time, but give yourselves up to God before you become hard and stubborn, like William's brothers.'[43]

It was both direct authorial interventions like this, which shattered any pretence of realism, and the strict, disciplinary nature of Sherwood's writing, to which the next generation of children's writers objected. Charlotte Yonge and Mary Louisa Stewart (universally known as Mrs Molesworth), for instance, had read Evangelical stories by Sherwood and others when children, and were adamant that, in their own writing, no child should 'be taught the religion of fear', as Mrs Molesworth put it.[44] Yonge was clearly aware of the tradition of didactic fiction, and of her own position within and beyond it. She wanted to provide 'something of a deeper tone than the Edgeworthian style, yet less directly religious than the Sherwood class of books'.[45] It is this careful positioning that has resulted in both Yonge and Molesworth being congratulated for the realism of their characters and settings, and for their role in diminishing the prominence of didacticism. For Roger Lancelyn Green, Mrs Moleworth's writing is characterised by 'the complete absence of any direct moral teaching'. For Marghanita Laski, Yonge's characters, especially Ethel May in *The Daisy Chain* (1856), are drawn with such 'sympathetic realism' that it must have been a huge relief to Victorian children to encounter them. 'To have someone *like ourselves* conquer her faults and reap the reward of her virtues was a conception altogether new in children's literature', Laski writes. This diminishes the achievement of the Edgeworth generation, who also tried to enable readers to recognise themselves in the text, but it stresses again the parallels with twentieth-century didactic fiction.[46]

Yonge and Molesworth are very different authors, the former standing at the forefront of a revised Evangelical tradition, the latter becoming successful with more secular books. Her first hit was *Carrots: Just a Little Boy* (1876), about the youngest of six children, mothered by his older sister Floss when his mother falls ill, who gets into trouble when he unintentionally steals a half-sovereign, so innocent is he about money. It includes the phonetic reproduction of 'baby-talk' which most critics agree makes the books almost unreadable now, although it was one of their most popular features when they were first published. The Evangelical fiction of Yonge and her successors is just as little likely to be popular with modern children and just as easy to mock. Louisa Charlesworth's *Ministering Angels* (1854) recounts at tedious length the good deeds performed by the Clifford family children, a formula inverted by E. Nesbit in *The Wouldbegoods* (1906) in which all the Bastable children's benevolent schemes go horribly awry. Even Margaret Nancy Cutt, who named her study of Victorian children's literature after Charlesworth's book and devoted a chapter to speculating why it was so hugely popular, concludes that 'Judged by the standards of Arthur Ransome, Laura Ingalls Wilder and others of today, this book is hopeless.'[47] Many of its successors were worse, published by various Tract Societies who insisted on the 'basic requirements of a repentance, a conversion, and a Christian death scene'.[48] The description of one of these given by Janey, a twelve-year-old, working-class, Lancashire girl in Frances Hodgson Burnett novel *Haworth's* (1879) is only slightly exaggerated:

> she had th' asthma an' summat wrong wi' her legs, an' she knowed aw th' boible through aside o' th' hymn-book, an' she'd sing aw th' toime when she could breathe fur th' asthma, an' tell foak as if they did na go an' do likewise they'd go to burnin' hell where th' fire is na quenched an' th' worms dyeth not.

'It's a noice book,' Janey adds, 'an' theer's lots more like it in th' skoo' libery – aw about Sunday skoo' scholars as has consumption an' th' loike an' reads th' bible to foak an' dees.'[49]

What is clear is that by prioritising didacticism over realism these Victorian Evangelical children's books were echoing the Puritan books of the seventeenth-century, such as James Janeway's *A Token for Children* (1672). The link is emphasised by the Evangelicals' emphasis on personal amendment and individual salvation rather than general social reform. The good deeds performed by the Clifford children in *Ministering Angels* are important not because they will improve society, but because they will ensure the children's places in heaven. As Gillian Avery has put it, in Charlesworth's moral universe, 'God has created a world where the poor exist to train the consciences and charitable instincts of those better off.'[50] Likewise, Mrs O. F. Walton's *Christie's Old Organ, or Home Sweet Home* (1875) is about life on the streets of Victorian London with the street urchin Christie looking after the ailing street-musician Treffy. But the plot of the novel concerns only Christie's conversion of Treffy to Christianity and Treffy's consequent happy death. This emphasis on individual reform, often with child characters in the role of missionary, is important for two reasons. First it shows how little these later-nineteenth-century didactic texts are concerned with the possibility of social mobility, a substantial shift from the moral tales of a century before. There is never any suggestion that Christie's virtues might enable him to rise from the gutter, nor does he hope to do so. Some of the so-called 'waif-stories' or 'street-arab' tales are different in this regard, Hesba Stretton's *Jessica's First Prayer* (1867) and *Little Meg's Children* (1868), for example, and their American counterparts *Ragged Dick; or, Street Life in New York* (1867) and *Tattered Tom; or, the Story of a Street Arab* (1871) by Horatio Alger. These were written partly to encourage piety and partly to draw attention to the poverty of children in urban slums (both Stretton and Alger were in fact active campaigners against the exploitation of children), but these were exceptions. And the second reason why what might be called the solipsism of the Evangelical texts is important is because it argues that virtue is not to be taught, but is somehow found within oneself, having simply to be wakened. This is evident even in Frances Hodgson Burnett's more secular novels. In *Little Lord Fauntleroy* (1886) the young boy transplanted from the streets of New York to the English aristocracy soon finds himself acting as if he had always belonged there. Sarah Crewe's fortunes change in the opposite way in *A Little Princess* (1905; originally published as *Sara Crewe* in 1887). Having plummeted from affluence on her eleventh birthday when she learns that her father has died after losing all his money in diamond-mine speculation, Sara begins the life of a drudge. Only by imagining herself to be a princess, who must always behave with courage and nobility, does she endure her new life, until she is rescued from poverty by the arrival of her father's business partner with the news that the diamond mines have succeeded.

The point of *The Little Princess* is that Sara found the means of tolerating poverty inside herself. She had not needed to be *taught*. Not only had Hodgson Burnett's novels departed from realism then, but in a sense, they had dispensed with didacticism too. *The Little Princess* seems a moral tale because it tries to show children what virtues are needed to deal with adversity. But it simultaneously undermines the use of didactic literature by showing that these virtues are already within everyone, and even that they can best be wakened by the imagination. This dwindling of faith in the potential and necessity of didactic literature no doubt helped to hasten the decline of the moral tale in the early twentieth century. Coupled with the formulaic severity of Evangelical fiction, the whole idea of realistic, didactic children's literature fell into disrepute. It was not to be revived until the problem novel reinvented the form half a century or more later.

SUMMARY OF KEY POINTS

- Using realism to instruct has been a central aim of children's fiction from the eighteenth-century moral tale to the modern problem novel.
- Overt didacticism became less popular in late nineteenth- and early twentieth-century children's fiction; lessons were supposed to be intuited rather than imposed.
- Early moral tales traditionally aimed to inculcate mature behaviour in children (rationality, forethought, selflessness), but from

the later nineteenth century children's own values (as perceived by adults authors) were often presented as more beneficial than adult attitudes.

- In the later twentieth century the didactic novel for children began to confront political and social questions very directly.
- While early moral tales showed that most problems could be solved by better behaviour or more sensible thinking, the modern 'adolescent novel of ideas' seldom offers simple solutions to the problems it presents.

NOTES

1. Nina Bawden, 'Emotional Realism in Books for Young People', *The Horn Book Magazine*, 56 (1980), 17–33.
2. Catherine Sinclair, *Holiday House: a Series of Tales* (Edinburgh: William Whyte and Co., 1839), p. vi.
3. Charles Lamb to Samuel Taylor Coleridge, 23 October 1802, in *The Letters of Charles and Mary Anne Lamb*, ed. E.W. Marrs Jnr (Ithaca, NY: Cornell University Press, 1976), vol. 2, pp. 81–2.
4. A challenge is a 'formal, written complaint, filed with a library or school requesting that materials be removed because of content or appropriateness'. See the American Library Association, 'Challenged and Banned Books', online at <http://www.ala.org/ala/oif/bannedbooksweek/challengedbanned/challengedbanned.htm> [26 November 2007].
5. Maria Edgeworth, *Rosamond*, 2 vols (London: R. Hunter, 1821), vol. 1, p. v.
6. Mary Wollstonecraft, 'Introductory Address to Parents', *Elements of Morality, For the Use of Children . . . Translated from the German of the Rev. C. G. Salzmann* (London: J. Johnson, 1790), pp. xii–xiii.
7. *Guardian of Education* 2 (1803), 175–82.
8. Maria Edgeworth, 'The Purple Jar', *From Instruction to Delight. An Anthology of Children's Literature to 1850*, ed. Patricia Demers 2nd edn (Don Mills, Ontario: Oxford University Press, 2004), pp. 176–81.

9. F. J. Harvey Darton, *Children's Books in England*, revised by Brian Alderson, 3rd edn (Cambridge: Cambridge University Press, 1982), p. 141; John Rowe Townsend, *Written for Children* (London: Pelican, [1965] 1976), p. 42.

10. Judy Blume, *Forever* (London: Young Picador, [1975] 2005), pp. 93, 100, 128 and 139.

11. Blume, *Forever*, p. 1.

12. Marilyn Butler, *Maria Edgeworth: A Literary Biography* (Oxford: Clarendon Press, 1972), p. 163.

13. P. H. Newby, *Maria Edgeworth* (Denver: Alan Swallow, 1950), p. 24.

14. Mitzi Myers, 'Impeccable Governesses, Rational Dames and Moral Mothers: Mary Wollstonecraft and the Female Tradition in Georgian Children's Books', *Children's Literature*, 14 (1986), 31–59 (p. 34).

15. Blume, *Forever*, p. 124.

16. Christine Wilkie-Stubbs, 'Childhood, didacticism and gendering', in *International Companion Encyclopedia of Children's Literature*, ed. Peter Hunt, 2nd edn, 2 vols (London: Routledge, 2004), vol. 1, p. 355.

17. *Guardian of Education*, 2 (1803), pp. 185–86.

18. *The Lilliputian Magazine; or, Children's Repository*, 6 vols (London: W. Tringham, c.1774), vol. 2, pp. 55–67.

19. Arnaud Berquin, trans. Rev. Anthony Meilan, *The Children's Friend; Consisting of Apt Tales, Short Dialogues, and Moral Dramas*, 8 vols (London: 'Printed for the Translator', 1786), vol. 1, pp. 16–17.

20. Mary Ann Kilner, *Jemima Placid*, 3rd edn (London: J. Marshall & Co., [c.1783] c.1785), pp. 28–9, 63–4, 39 and 89.

21. Anon., *Virtue and Vice* (London: J. Harris, [c.1780] 1815), pp. 28–9 and 24.

22. See Aileen Fyfe, 'Science for young readers' in *Books and the Sciences in History*, ed. M. Frasca-Spada and N. Jardine, (Cambridge: Cambridge University Press, 2000), pp. 276–90.

23. Maria Edgeworth, 'Preface Addressed to Parents', *The Parent's Assistant; or, Stories for Children* (London: MacMillan and Co., [1796] 1897), p. 3.

24. See M. O. Grenby, ' "Real Charity Makes Distinctions":
    Schooling the Charitable Impulse in Early British Children's
    Literature', *British Journal for Eighteenth-Century Studies*, 25
    (2002), 185–202.
25. Barbara Hofland, *The Daughter of a Genius* (London: J. Harris,
    [1823] 1828), p. 111; *The Son of a Genius* (London: John
    Harris, [1812] 1827), pp. 117–18.
26. Andrew O'Malley, *The Making of the Modern Child: Children's
    Literature and Childhood in the Late Eighteenth Century* (New
    York: Routledge, 2003), pp. 1–65.
27. Catharine Macaulay, *Letters on Education* (London and New
    York: Garland Publishing, [1790] 1974), p. 53.
28. Kilner, *Jemima Placid*, p. 90.
29. Ben Hellman, 'Russia', in *International Companion
    Encyclopedia of Children's Literature*, vol. 2, p. 1179.
30. Humphrey Carpenter and Mari Prichard, *The Oxford
    Companion to Children's Literature* (Oxford: Oxford University
    Press, [1984] 1995), p. 464.
31. Maxim Gorky, 'Soviet Literature,' in *Soviet Writers' Congress
    1934: The Debate on Socialist Realism and Modernism in the
    Soviet Union* (London: Lawrence and Wishart, 1977), p. 67.
32. Peter Hollindale, 'The Adolescent Novel of Ideas', *Only
    Connect: Readings on Children's Literature*, ed. Sheila Egoff,
    Gorden Stubbs, Ralph Ashley and Wendy Sutton, 3rd edn
    (Toronto: Oxford University Press, 1996), pp. 315–26.
33. See Elaine Moss, 'The Seventies in British Children's Books',
    The Signal Approach to Children's Books (Harmondsworth:
    Kestrel, 1980), pp. 48–80 (p. 63).
34. Jan Needle, *My Mate Shofiq* (London: Lions, [1978] 1979),
    pp. 10, 88–9 and 98–9.
35. Bernard Ashley, *The Trouble with Donovan Croft*
    (Harmondsworth: Puffin, [1974] 1977), p. 187.
36. Richard Peck, *Are You in the House Alone?* (New York: Laurel-
    Leaf, [1976] 1989), p. 137.
37. Berlie Doherty, *Dear Nobody* (London: Collins, [1991] 1997),
    pp. 1–2 and 47.
38. Doherty, *Dear Nobody*, p. 200.
39. Kilner, *Jemima Placid*, p. 90.

40. Sinclair, *Holiday House*, p. 19; David Rudd, 'The Froebellious Child in Catherine Sinclair's *Holiday House*', *The Lion and the Unicorn*, 28 (2004), 53–69 (p. 61).
41. See Margaret Nancy Cutt, *Ministering Angels. A Study of Nineteenth-century Evangelical Writing for Children* (Wormley: Five Owls Press, 1979) and J. S. Bratton's *The Impact of Victorian Children's Fiction* (London: Croom Helm, 1981).
42. *Guardian of Education*, 1 (1802), 267.
43. Mary Martha Sherwood, *The Little Woodman, and his Dog Cæsar* (Wellington: F. Houlston and Son, [1818] c.1825), pp. 10–11. See M. Nancy Cutt, *Mrs. Sherwood and her Books for Children* (London: Oxford University Press, 1974).
44. Carpenter and Prichard, *Oxford Companion to Children's Literature*, p. 355. See Jane Darcy, ' "Worlds not realized": The work of Louisa Molesworth', in *Popular Victorian Women Writers*, ed. Kay Boardman and Shirley Jones (Manchester: Manchester University Press, 2004), pp. 111–34.
45. Charlotte Yonge, 'Preface', *Scenes and Characters or Eighteen Months at Beechcroft* (London: Macmillan, [1847] 1889), p. viii.
46. Roger Lancelyn Green, *Mrs Molesworth* (London: Bodley Head, 1961), p. 56; Marghanita Laski, *Mrs. Ewing, Mrs. Molesworth and Mrs. Hodgson Burnett* (London: Arthur Baker, 1950), p. 27.
47. Cutt, *Ministering Angels*, p. 68.
48. Ibid., p. 170.
49. Frances Hodgson Burnett, *Haworth's*, 2 vols (London: Macmillan, 1879), vol. 1, pp. 52–3.
50. Gillian Avery, *Nineteenth Century Children: Heroes and Heroines in English Children's Stories 1780–1900* (London: Hodder and Stoughton, 1965), p. 90.

CHAPTER 4

The School Story

W riting in 1940, George Orwell argued that the school story was fundamentally socially and politically conservative and, second, 'a thing peculiar to England.'[1] Both of these judgments are open to question. First, if the genre is inherently conservative, it seems odd that several of the most canonical of its texts were greeted by widespread opprobrium on their first appearance. Rudyard Kipling's *Stalky & Co.* (1899), Robert Cormier's *The Chocolate War* (1974) and Melvyn Burgess' *Doing It* (2003) are all good examples. Second, school stories have existed outside Britain. In Germany *Schulromane* were popular in the nineteenth and twentieth century. Many were being published in the Soviet Union around the time Orwell was writing. And since then, it has been in the United States that many of the most celebrated school stories have appeared – John Knowles' *A Separate Peace* (1960) for example. Indeed, in calling the school story an English genre, Orwell was overlooking many earlier north American classics too, such as Susan Coolidge's *What Katy Did At School* (1873), Louisa May Alcott's *Little Men* (1871) and L. M. Montgomery's *Anne of Avonlea* (1909).

On the other hand, the classic tradition of the school story – narratives in which the school features almost as a character itself, and in which children fit happily into their school, each helping to form the character of the other – does seem to be rooted in British culture. Interestingly, Coolidge's, Alcott's and Montgomery's books were all part of longer series, almost as if these authors had chosen to write about school simply because it was a convenient new theatre for their heroine's operations. As for the German and Russian versions, the former 'appear to be written for an adult rather than a schoolboy audience' one critic has noted, and they usually demonstrate how school adversely affects the development of the individual, rather than how school can be an enjoyable and character-forming experience, whereas many Soviet school stories tended to be written to show how 'an individualistically minded pupil gets corrected by the class collective'.[2] This chapter will reflect the quintessentially British identity of the school story, focusing on texts published first in Britain, although many went on to achieve international popularity. It will be best to point out at the outset that in Britain, a 'public school' actually denotes the most exclusive kind of private school, institutions generally founded in the nineteenth century or earlier and drawing their pupils from the social elite. It should also be noted that most British public schools, as well as other, less prestigious private schools, were single-sex. This resulted in the development of major differences between the traditions of boys' and girls' school stories, differences which will be discussed here as they arise rather than in separate sections. In fact, in recent times, the traditions of boys' and girls' school stories have begun to coalesce, as is evident in the most striking reoccurrence of the form, J. K. Rowling's Harry Potter novels.

Literature designed for children has been set in schools from very early times. Compositions inscribed onto clay in about 2000 BCE have survived which recount school anecdotes amongst the Sumerians of Mesopotamia. One, entitled 'School Days', tells of a boy being late for school because he has overslept and loitered on his way, then getting into further trouble by talking in class and failing to complete his homework. He is beaten, but complains to his father, who invites the headmaster to dinner. Having been treated well and bribed by gifts, the headmaster softens his attitude and praises the boy.[3] This is a remarkable document in itself, but all the more so because of its close similarity to texts being used in medieval England. These *colloquia scholastica*, schoolbooks from which spoken Latin or polite English was to be learned, were produced in substantial numbers from the fifteenth century. They were often composed of dialogues between a master and a pupil, or between fellow schoolboys.[4] A fairly late example is *Pueriles Confabulatiunculae: or Children's Dialogues*, probably written in Latin by Evaldus Gallus in the mid-sixteenth century and which had appeared in English by 1617. Most of its episodes are set in school. Although seriously intentioned, its dialogues are sprightly and even subversive. Somehow the book manages to give a full flavour of a Renaissance schoolroom but also to connect smoothly with the classic school stories of the nineteenth and twentieth centuries. Most of the book's episodes revolve around the laziness of the boys and the perpetual threat of being beaten. But these are pupils who are willing to stand up for themselves, cheekily getting the upper hand over their elders. When the master arrives to beat all the boys who were late to school, for instance, one defends himself by saying that his father had commanded him to check on his crops:

M. [the master] Your father hath command at home, I in the schoole.
A. [Andrew, the pupil] But my father commanded me at home.
M. But I forbad any man to do otherwise, than here I will & command.
A. Will you not, that we obey our parents?
M. Yea, altogether.
A. Why then am I blamed for doing this?

To which the master can only reply, clearly frustrated by the casuistic manoeuvres of his pupil, 'Get thee gone, get thee gone: we spend the time by this strife.' Another boy explains his lateness by pleading that he was forced to help his parents entertain guests who refused to leave until midnight – he escapes the rod, but only if he promises that the master will be invited next time! Beyond such duelling between masters and pupils, there is also much banter and bullying between the boys. They steal one another's property and sneak on each other's wrongdoings: 'Peter hath beaten mee with his fists. . . . He talks of a scurrilous matter. . . . He suffereth me not to study. . . . He hath made water upon my shooes.' And the book ends with a jape straight out of *Billy Bunter* or *The Beano*. When Gisbert is charged by his father to take a sealed letter to the school-master he rightly suspects that it contains instructions for his punishment. Gisbert deftly switches it with one from a school-mate's much more lenient father. The master is thereby instructed never to beat Gisbert but to inflict severe punishment on his innocent but molly-coddled friend.[5]

Although principally a book of instruction, *Pueriles Confabulatiunculae* fulfils what might be thought the three basic criteria of the school story: it is set almost entirely in school; it takes the relationships between the scholars and their teachers as its primary focus; and it contains attitudes and adventures which are unique to school life. These are certainly the hallmarks of the early classics of the genre: Harriet Martineau's *The Crofton Boys* (1841), Thomas Hughes' *Tom Brown's Schooldays* (1857), F. W. Farrar's *Eric, or Little by Little, a Tale of Roslyn School* (1858) and Talbot Baines Reed's *The Fifth Form at St. Dominic's* (first serialised in the *Boy's Own Paper*, 1881–82). The same definition works for the many series which became so popular in the golden age of the girls' story, by L. T. Meade (beginning with *A World of Girls*, 1886), Angela Brazil (from *The Fortunes of Philippa*, 1906), Dorita Fairlie Bruce (from *Dimsie Goes to School*, 1920), Elinor Brent-Dyer (from *The School at the Chalet*, 1925) and Enid Blyton (from *The Twins at St. Clare's*, 1941, and *First Term at Malory Towers*, 1946). Several commentators have felt that this kind of traditional school story was, as Geoffrey Trease put it, 'petering out in the sand' by the mid-twentieth century. Isabel Quigly concurred, calling the final chapter of her study of the genre, *The Heirs of Tom Brown* (1982), 'The decline and fall'.[6] But they were incorrect. Traditional school stories continued to be published, albeit sometimes with a twist. Anne Digby's girls' school stories, from *First Term at Trebizon* in 1978, were conventional in many ways, though, notably, sex was introduced in *Boy Trouble at Trebizon* (1980). The Grange Hill books, based on a British television series, dealt with sex, racism, dyslexia, drugs and many other 'problem issues' from their inception in 1980 with Robert Leeson's *Grange Hill Rules OK?* – but the traditional school story format remained in place. Most remarkably of all, J. K. Rowling's *Harry Potter* series (1997–2007) reused the conventions of the classic school story to great popular acclaim, setting the action at Hogwarts, a school for magicians but in all other respects a reiteration of the traditional British public school.

Many other stories may be set largely in school, but either do not show the school from the pupils' point of view – *The History of Goody Two-Shoes* (1765), for example – or use the school only as a backdrop. Frances Hodgson Burnett's *A Little Princess* (1905) is typical in this regard. Its heroine, Sara Crewe is the victim of her teacher's cruelty, but her retreat into an imaginary world in which she is a princess, takes her well away from the world of school. Louise Fitzhugh's *Harriet the Spy* (1964) similarly relies on a school setting, but its subject is Harriet's personal growth. When the notebooks in which she records her scathing opinions of her schoolfriends are discovered, she realises that she must try to empathise with, rather than condemn, other people. The school setting merely provides the context. Indeed, since the later nineteenth century, almost all Western children have attended school, meaning that writers seeking to represent contemporary children's lives realistically have been more or less forced into one of three courses: to show their protagonists at school, to show them after school or in the school holidays (with the threat of school usually hanging over them), or to somehow remove them from school artificially. This is what the narrator of Roald Dahl's *Danny the Champion of the World* (1975) inadvertently termed 'the problem of school'. 'It was the law that parents must send their children to school at the age of five,' says Danny, 'and my father knew about this.' But Dahl was writing a book about a boy's relationship with his father, so Danny's start at school is delayed for years while he is taught to be a mechanic at home, and then Danny's truancy is connived at by his father when the day of their great poaching adventure comes round. School intrudes occasionally, and we hear of the alcoholism or brutality of the teachers, but Danny always thinks of it in terms of its inferiority to his education at home. Whenever he enters the 'squat ugly red-brick' school, he always imagines that the engraved stone cemented into the brickwork commemorating its foundation in the year of Edward VII's coronation – the symbol of its dignity and authority – would have been put to better use if his father was allowed to vandalise it with a series of daily educational but amusing and subversive adages (for instance, 'I'LL BET YOU DIDN'T KNOW THAT IN SOME BIG ENGLISH COUNTRY HOUSES, THE BUTLER STILL HAS TO IRON THE MORNING NEWSPAPER BEFORE PUTTING IT ON HIS MASTER'S BREAKFAST-TABLE'). Moreover, he obstinately resists his father's suggestion that he should invite schoolmates home, not, he says, 'because I didn't have good friends' but 'because I had such a good time being alone with my father.'[7]

Dahl's fantasy of a son's greater love for his father than his friends flies in the face of most school stories, where fellowship between the pupils is key. Indeed, a great many school stories deal directly with the gradual integration of new pupils into the school community. Angela Brazil's *For the School Colours* (1918), for instance, as well as including an episode with the unmasking of a German spy, centres around the entrance into snobbish Silverside of girls from a less prestigious school. Over the course of the novel, Aveline, with the advice of her friend Mrs Lesbia Carrington, teaches the established Silverside pupils to accept the incomers, and the new girls to fit into Silverside's traditions. However, the majority of school stories focus on the integration of the individual not the group. In Blyton's *First Term at Malory Towers*, the semi-autobiographical Darrell Rivers arrives at the school, worried about fitting in. She chooses badly at first, but ultimately finds the friends who will accompany her for the rest of the series. It is not difficult to see why this process of friend-gathering is so central to many school stories. First, it provides a frame for the narrative. Second, it was often designed to reassure nervous pupils that they would soon find friends. After all, school stories have often been written for the benefit of scared school entrants, from *Tom Brown's Schooldays*, written, as Thomas Hughes said, to convey to his eight-year-old son 'what I should like to say to him before he went to school', to Janet and Allan Ahlberg's more obviously didactic *Starting School* (1988), deliberately designed to help children settle in to this new phase of their lives.[8] And third, the acquisition of friends is central to one of the key themes of the school story, what we might call socialisation, or, to borrow a term from psychoanalysis, individuation. This, according to Carl Jung, is the way in which the wholeness of the self is established by integrating the individual psyche and the collective unconscious of the community, or at least its collective identity. School settings clearly offer a perfect opportunity to depict children learning to balance their sense of self and of community, to mature by integrating themselves into society.

Even some of the very earliest school stories address this theme. *School Occurrences: Supposed to Have Arisen Among a Set of Young Ladies, Under the Tuition of Mrs. Teachwell* (1782), by 'Mrs. Lovechild' (probably Ellinor Fenn), is largely an account of the social negotiations between the four pupils, Miss Sprightly, Miss Pert, Miss Cheat and Miss Pry.[9] Similarly, but about boys, Maria Edgeworth's 'The Barring Out; or, Party Spirit' (1796) is a moral tale with the clear aim of dissuading pupils from forming themselves into gangs. In psychological terms, it is about the boys' *over-*identification with the group, Edgeworth attempting to steer readers back towards a sense of their own individual identity. The story begins conventionally with the arrival of a new boy, Archer. It is he who brings the idea of 'parties' to Dr Middleton's small village school. Seeing another popular boy, De Grey, as a rival, Archer divides the school into two factions, the Archers and the Greybeards. To cement his popularity, he leads his gang in a 'barring-out': an eighteenth-century English schoolboy custom which involves locking themselves into the classroom with enough food and drink to survive a siege by their teacher. Their hope is that they will be able to extract greater privileges from him. In Edgeworth's story, the barring-out goes awry, with food running out and mutiny amongst the conspirators. The situation is saved only when De Grey volunteers as a hostage, and by Archer's belated realisation that De Grey and he should be friends not rivals. Dr Middleton ends the story by commending Archer's decision: 'one such friend is worth two such parties'. In fact, though, as the school story genre developed Edgeworth's warnings against gangs would go unheeded, for close-knit, exclusive friendships would become a frequent feature of school stories. They might be slightly subversive, as with Stalky, Beetle and M'Turk in Rudyard Kipling's *Stalky & Co.* (1899), or mawkishly sanctimonious, as with the 'Secret Society of Fairbank' in L. T. Meade's *The School Favourite* (1908) with its strict four-rule code: 'Love, Obedience, Work, Do a little deed of kindness to some one every day' ('Then, you see, having sworn to love, to obey our teachers, to work, and to do kindnesses, we are formed into a band . . . and I don't think all through our lives this band of fellowship can ever be broken.').[10] But overall, even those school stories which centred on a gang of friends would continue to echo Edgeworth's demand for a balance between individual and community, self-reliance and camaraderie.

It is extraordinary that Edgeworth's eighteenth-century text already contained many of the standard features of the classic boys' school story. As early as 1796, it seems, Edgeworth was operating within a well-defined set of literary conventions, rather than attempting to represent actual school life. The new boy, the stern but kindly master, the midnight feast, the bully, the gluttonous buffoon (named Fisher in 'The Barring-Out', a clear prototype of the famous Billy Bunter who first appeared in 1908 in *The Magnet*) – all these would become very familiar motifs. So too would be the apparent rarity of actual lessons, the sense of school-boy honour, the way in which a chorus of pupils gathers round each protagonist, swayed by their oratory to take one side or another. They play a role much like the mob in Shakespeare's Greco-Roman plays, something recognised by Archer: 'O ye Athenians,' he says to his party, 'how hard do I work to obtain your praise.'[11] Above all, it is Edgeworth's presentation of the power-struggles being waged in the fictional boys' schools that would endure. The rivalry between individual pupils would receive its definitive treatment in the conflict between Tom and the bully Flashman in *Tom Brown's Schooldays*. But it is the continuing struggle for power between pupils and their teachers which is more interesting. 'Masters are regarded as common enemies', the seventeen-year-old Alec Waugh wrote in *The Loom of Youth* (1916), his exposé of life at Fernhurst, a thinly disguised portrait of the English public school which he had just left.[12] This is certainly the impression one gets from Kipling's *Stalky & Co.*, which represents the boys fighting an unremitting guerrilla war, based on mutual detestation, against their housemaster, Mr Prout, and Latin master, Mr King. In Anthony Buckeridge's more decorous school stories of the 1950s and '60s the hostilities have become a little less vindictive, but remain just as central to the narrative, Jennings constantly skirmishing with his teacher Mr Wilkins. Even a modern, jovial story of a co-educational school, Louis Sachar's *Sideways Stories from Wayside School* (1978), opens with Mrs Gorf, 'the meanest teacher in Wayside School', maliciously turning her class one by one into apples until they get their own back by holding a mirror up to her spell.[13]

These hostilities are interesting because they complicate the issues of authority and obedience which lie at the heart of the school story. Superficially, the teachers wield the power and the pupils are required to obey, generally coerced by the threat of severe punishment. But in fact, the children challenge this authority at every turn. In nineteenth-century novels, Gillian Avery points out, this is often because of the class divide, the children, coming from the upper orders, immediately recognising that the teachers are their social inferiors.[14] But the public school boys of children's fiction also seem to break rules on principle. Stalky and his friends seem to regard it as their duty to smoke although they know that if they are discovered they will be expelled. Tom Brown, before his reformation, plans to install 'a bottled-beer cellar under his window' and to slip out from his dormitory every night to fish.[15] Alec Waugh gave clear indications that sodomy was widely practiced and approved of by the boys at Fernhurst, although it was strictly prohibited.[16] In 'The Barring-Out' rebellion is the central theme. Archer's mutiny begins when Dr Middleton forbids the boys to use a building in the school grounds for a theatre. Archer calls this tyranny. Only later do we learn that Dr Middleton knew the building was infected with a dangerous fever. After the siege, Dr Middleton delivers a lesson about the necessary obedience of children to adults acting *in loco parentis*: 'You have rebelled against the just authority which is necessary to conduct and govern yourselves.' But more interesting is his awareness of why Archer rebelled: 'You, sir, think yourself a man . . . and you think it the part of a man not to submit to the will of another.'[17] What 'The Barring-Out' demonstrates, more transparently than most later texts, is that the school story is about children establishing a balance between the obedience of childhood and independence of adulthood. Indeed, the whole structure of the school story, particularly the boarding school story, serves to represent this. They are authoritarian places, with strict rules and harsh discipline, but they are also places of great freedom for their pupils. Teachers are generally absent from their pupils' lives, like Dr Middleton in 'The Barring-Out' or the staff of Rowling's

Hogwarts. So long as the pupils abide by the basic regulations – lesson-times, meal-times, bed-times and so on – they are largely autonomous agents, free to choose their own activities and obey their own rules. Without their decision to break the school rules, there would often be little or no narrative remaining.

Most boys' school stories, then, position their heroes in the paradoxical role of rule-bound rule-breakers. In many nineteenth-century texts this contradiction is resolved by having two levels of teachers: those the boys encounter on a day-to-day basis, regarded as the enemy, and a remote headmaster, who sits in judgment even on his teaching staff. In Kipling's *Stalky & Co.* for example, regular use is made of the pupils' right to appeal to the headmaster if they feel they have been unfairly treated by staff, as when Stalky and his friends are accused of being drunk. The headmaster sides with the boys, refusing to accede to their housemaster's demands for their expulsion. Disregarding the rules, he then administers a beating to show that discipline remains intact. It is a display of arbitrary power which the boys cheerfully accept. Then surprisingly and subversively, he shows his approval of the boys' tormenting of their teachers by allowing them to borrow from his collection of boys' adventure stories. Later, he even confides to an old boy that 'It isn't the boys that make trouble; it's the masters'. This might affirm what most school story pupils think, but to undermine the teachers' authority like this would have been unthinkable in earlier school stories, and would remain so in many later stories, perhaps especially those designed for girls.[18] The morality of such episodes is vexed. In legalistic terms, Kipling and others seem to suggest that boys should respect the judge but deplore the police. But the splitting of authority like this enables the school story to make the argument that boys develop into men by both respecting and testing authority. They mature by a combination of submission and defiance.

This fits neatly into a religious context. Kipling had based his portrait of the 'Head' on Cormell Price, his real-life headmaster at the United Services College. In this, he was following Thomas Hughes, whose *Tom Brown's Schooldays* had featured his headmaster at Rugby School, Thomas Arnold, as the 'Doctor'. Tom Brown comes to idolise him but only in the book's final paragraph, after the

Doctor's death, is the reader told that Tom's 'hero-worship' of the Doctor was a necessary precursor to 'the worship of Him who is the King and Lord of heroes'.[19] In *Stalky & Co.* the Head is literally a saviour, sucking diphtheria mucus from a sick boy's throat and restoring him to life, for which he is worshipped by Stalky and his friends. This connection between the Headmaster and God has become almost a standard feature of the school story, from Dr Middleton in 'The Barring-Out' to Professor Dumbledore in the Harry Potter books. They are loving and benevolent but just and severe, demanding obedience and ready to inflict harsh punishment, or to forgive. Each of their pupils has the free will to choose whether to abide by their teachers' commandments or not. Those who disobey can face physical chastisement, something like the torments of Hell, or worse, face expulsion from the school, their paradise, as befalls Flashman in *Tom Brown's Schooldays* or Fisher, who is 'barred-out' from Edgeworth's educational paradise. But those who sin against their teachers' authority and repent can be welcomed back into the fold – like Archer, who recognises his error and welcomes his punishment, or Tom Brown who is gradually brought away from his early bad behaviour by the subtle intervention of the Doctor. The universe of such school stories, then, is reminiscent of Puritan children's books. Each boy is urged to accept the discipline of the school voluntarily, embracing its authority, in much the same way as Protestant theology insists that each sinner should individually welcome grace into his or her heart. Like Archer before him, Tom Brown is gradually drawn into submission: 'We've always been honourable enemies with the masters', he tells his friend East, trying to convert him to his own new moral views. 'We found a state of war when we came, and went into it of course. Only don't you think things are altered a good deal? I don't feel as I used to the masters.'[20] Learning to accept authority, these boys are really reiterations of the sinners struggling to be pious in Benjamin Keach's *War with the Devil* (1673) or James Janeway's *Token for Children* (1672). In the school story, as in the Puritan world-view, their obedience is never enforced but must be the consequence of their own free-will.

In fact, once one looks for the connections between the Puritan tradition of children's literature and the school story they become increasingly evident. Perhaps the most obvious connection is to be found in the very first of the recognisably modern school stories, Sarah Fielding's *The Governess; or, the Little Female Academy* (1749). Like *Sideways Stories from Wayside School*, *The Governess* opens with apples. Here, the nine girls enrolled at Mrs Teachum's school argue about who should eat the largest apple, a dispute which immediately suggests the disobedience of Adam and Eve and their misuse of free-will. What follows is a description of the way that each of the girls comes to accept her errors and to modify her behaviour. As in so many school stories, Mrs Teachum is largely absent from the narrative. The main body of the book describes the pupils' meetings together after their lessons. Each takes it in turn to tell the story of her life and, almost as if they are on the psychoanalyst's couch, they identify the reason for their behavioural failings, and promise to reform. Mrs Teachum's surrogate is the eldest pupil, Jenny Peace. She speaks kindly to the younger girls, encouraging their introspection, and she acts as a mediator between the pupils and their teacher, asking, for instance, if it is permissible for them to tell fairy tales. In religious terms, and as her surname hints, Jenny Peace can be read as Christ, sent to save the sinners, and a representative of the godlike, remote Mrs Teachum. But Jenny Peace can also seem rather sinister, Mrs Teachum's infiltrating agent. At first, Mrs Teachum herself wanders the school gardens, occasionally dropping in on the arbour where the girls are gathered. But although she 'had a great Inclination to hear the History of the Lives of all her little Scholars . . . she thought, that her presence at those Relations might be a Balk to the Narration, as perhaps they might be ashamed freely to confess their past Faults before her'. To this end, she tells Jenny that 'She would have her get the Lives of her Companions in Writing, and bring them to her', a command which Jenny obeys (the record she keeps, one might suggest, becoming the book that Fielding wrote).[21] Such surveillance would become a feature of many school stories, with informers like Jenny frequently featuring (the role of tale-teller being given more approval in girls' than boys' stories according to Beverly Lyon Clark).[22] But on other occasions it is not quite so clear just how the teachers know what is happening throughout their school. At Rowling's Hogwarts, Professor Dumbledore's ability to be in the right place at the right time suggest an all-seeing eye, and we are left to deduce that all the school's ghosts, sentient portraits and so on act as informants. Certainly Rowling created a world in which all is known to the authorities. Harry's illegal casting of a spell in the school holidays, for example, is followed only moments later by an owl-borne reproof from the Ministry of Magic.[23]

What is significant is not how or even whether the teachers are omniscient, but that the pupils regard themselves as always being under their monitoring gaze. This is the sort of analysis Michel Foucault might have applied to the school story. Writing of prisons, and of society in general, Foucault suggested in his book *Discipline and Punish* (1975), that if someone is aware that they might be under surveillance, they begin to internalise the disciplinary code of those who watch them. In short, they begin to police themselves, meaning that authority no longer has to coerce them into compliance. Foucault's thinking illuminates *The Governess*. Its central theme might be said to be the way that the pupils learn to monitor their own behaviour and to conduct themselves as Mrs Teachum would wish, even when she is not present. They analyse themselves to find out why they disappoint their teacher. The stories they tell also reveal their internalisation of the need for submission. *The Governess* is usually celebrated for including two fairy stories at a time when such tales of the supernatural were reviled as too immoral. But what is not so often noticed is the severe discipline suggested by the longer of these, 'The Princess Hebe'. The main lesson is stated early on by the fairy who saves Hebe's life:

> it was absolutely necessary . . . that she should entirely obey the queen her mother, without ever pretending to examine her commands; for 'true obedience (said she) consists in sub-mission; and when we pretend to choose what commands are proper and fit for us, we don't obey, but set up our own wisdom in opposition to our governors – this, my dear Hebe, you must be very careful of avoiding, if you would be happy.'[24]

The rest of the tale is designed to reinforce the lesson. Certainly, by the time Jenny Peace leaves the school her fellow pupils' habit of self-monitoring is fully installed, Jenny's eye remaining upon them in her absence, as it were, so that 'if any Girl was found to harbour in her Breast a rising Passion, which it was difficult to conquer, the Name and Story of Miss *Jenny Peace* soon gained her Attention, and left her without any other Desire than to emulate Miss *Jenny's* Virtues.'[25] The same pattern frequently recurs, especially in girls' school stories. In Meade's *The School Favourite* (1908), for example, the girls have drawn up their own code of behaviour. But its discipline is far stricter that what their teachers might have imposed. When they transgress, they fine themselves: even the youngest girl, for instance, 'turning scarlet, got off her seat, flew up to Betty' – their president – 'buried her head in her neck and whispered something. Betty took twopence from the hot, chubby little hand and put it in the fundbox', the proceeds of which are given termly to the Society for the Prevention of Cruelty to Children. Because they have internalised the values of the school so thoroughly, they 'are allowed to go without any teachers, because Mrs Temple trusts us so completely.'[26]

One might even go so far as to say that the internalisation of a school's ethos was the central theme of most of the classic school stories of the nineteenth century. *Tom Brown's Schooldays*, for instance, is essentially the story of a boy gradually learning to behave as Dr Arnold would like, even – or especially – when he does not realise that the Doctor is observing his behaviour. Similarly, in Elinor Brent-Dyer's *Exploits of the Chalet Girls* (1933) a proud, aristocratic Prussian girl called Thekla von Stift learns to stifle the snobbishness which goes against the School's egalitarian ethos. This is constructed as a positive thing – 'the atmosphere of the School was doing its duty and she was already a nicer girl than the one who had come in September'.[27] It can also seem like the suppression of individuality. This, notes Debbie Pinfold, was the chief characteristic of the German school story which often 'portrays school life through the eyes of a sensitive, artistic individual who is eventually crushed by the system.'[28] But many classic British and American examples also represent what are essentially totalitarian establishments, each pupil inevitably succumbing, like Winston Smith in Orwell's *1984*, to their 'atmosphere' or 'ethos' or, to use a more loaded term, 'ideology'. Perhaps this was based in reality.

Certainly it was W. H. Auden's opinion that 'at school I lived in a Fascist state'. By deliberately appealing to 'loyalty and honour' ('the only emotion that is fully developed in a boy of fourteen') his teachers, Auden claimed, had been able to create a repressive state policed by self-censorship and informants. The consequence was a community of emotionally stunted boys whose only motivations were fear and competition.[29] Curiously, the character who exhibits this internalisation of the school ethos, and emotional stuntedness, most dramatically is J. M. Barrie's Captain Hook. In *Peter and Wendy* (1911) he agonises about what his Eton College schoolmates would have regarded as good and bad form, and even as he dies, his mind is 'slouching in the playing fields of long ago, or being sent up [for a reward from the headmaster] for good, or watching the wall-game from a famous wall.'[30] Geraldine McCaughrean took up the theme in her sequel, *Peter Pan in Scarlet* (2006), revealing that Hook's longed-for treasure is school trophies, and that the trauma which motivates his misanthropy is that his mother removed him from school before he had a chance to win them.[31]

In fact, totalitarianism has often been very deliberately brought into post-War school stories. Some of the Chalet Schools novels of the 1930s and '40s are set in the shadow of Nazism. In Cormier's *The Chocolate War*, the teacher Brother Leon accuses his pupils of turning 'this classroom into Nazi Germany for a few moments' because they do not intervene as he falsely accuses a student of cheating (a heavy irony, since it is Leon himself who tyrannically bullies his pupils).[32] More comic, but just as menacing, is the school in Gillian Cross's *The Demon Headmaster* (1982). Here the internalisation of the regime is more literal, the power-hungry headmaster hypnotising his school so that they might learn more effectively, win televised quiz competitions, and provide him with national exposure for his sinister ideas ('to have everything sorted out tidily, everything settled for you', to be 'the first properly organized, truly efficient country in the world'). His teachers and prefects are his storm-troopers ('All pupils shall obey the prefects,' they chant. 'The prefects are the voice of the Headmaster.') and those few children who can resist his hypnosis become dissidents, forced into covert operations to destabilise the regime ('I feel like Winston Smith', one of them confides).[33] But the battle for control between school and pupil is personal as well as political. In *The Chalet School and the Lintons* (1934), Thekla becomes the first pupil to be expelled. Ostensibly this is because of her vengeful animosity towards other girls, but it is also a consequence of her determination to remain herself in the face of the school's normalising regime. The same independence is characteristic of the only other girl expelled in the Chalet School novels, Betty Wynne-Davies, described in quasi-political terms as one of 'the worst firebrands the school had ever known'. Notably, Brent-Dyer also characterises both girls as more sexualised than their fellow pupils. Thekla is sixteen years old, but 'in some ways she was a good three or four years older than that', while Betty is found 'using *lipstick*'.[34] They are, it seems, expelled for much the same reason as the nylon-wearing, lipstick-using, invitation-craving Susan Pevensie is banished from Narnia in C. S. Lewis's *The Last Battle* (1956): because they have grown up.[35]

The internalisation of the school ethos is shown most deliberately by Kipling in *Stalky & Co.* His protagonists claim to despise the values which their teachers attempt to instil, especially the ideals of *Tom Brown's Schooldays*: muscular Christianity, fair play, loyalty to the 'house'.[36] But importantly, Stalky and his friends actually devote much of their energy to supporting their house's honour. In response to taunts about their own uncleanliness for example, they place a dead cat under the floorboards of a rival house. Moreover, Stalky and his friends might openly scorn the ethos of the school, but in fact they absorb all its values, turning out to be precisely the kind of army officer whom the school was designed to produce. Kipling represents this inevitable internalisation of ethos clearly in the final story in the collection, 'Slaves of the Lamp Part II'. It recounts the adventures of a grown-up Stalky on the North-West Frontier of India, employing the same tricks to defeat the Khye-Kheen and Malôt tribesmen as he had used to revenge himself on his Latin master. He is still not the gentlemanly, manly hero of *Tom Brown's Schooldays*, always playing fair, but certainly the rebellious boy has been transformed into the willing and devoted agent of empire. Ideological co-option has succeeded where physical coercion had failed.

Fighting at the furthest frontier of empire, if not beyond, Stalky at least remains as unconventional in his tactics as he had been at school. He has formed a strong bond with his Sikh soldiers, who revere him as an almost divine leader, and his old school friends rely on rumour to hear of his exploits. He has much in common with Kurtz in Joseph Conrad's *Heart of Darkness*, published in 1902, three years after the first edition of *Stalky & Co*. The similarity only emphasises the immersion of the classic boys' school story in the discourse of empire. *Tom Brown's Schooldays* can be understood as a preparation for imperial administrators, showing how such schools taught the values necessary for the Empire to be maintained. Tom's father is clear upon this point, admitting that he sends his son to school not 'to make himself a good scholar' but only so he might 'turn out a brave, helpful, truth-telling Englishman, and a gentleman, and a Christian.'[37] Don Randall has argued that Kipling went further. Stalky's school is 'not merely a training ground', but is itself an 'imperial space, a "combat zone" characterised by factional conflicts and territorial struggles.' He is referring to the war Stalky and the other schoolboys wage on the 'natives' of Devonshire, and the way in which 'boys and masters compete for control of various out-of-bounds spaces.' Much the same might be said of many other school stories. The boys of Frank Richards' Greyfriars College, for example, are at war with the local landowner, Sir Hilton Popper. It is not only in Kipling, then, that the school world is presented 'as a valid, and viable space for imperial endeavour'.[38]

It was the enduring popular stories about Greyfriars College by Frank Richards (the favourite pseudonym of Charles Hamilton) that provided the focus for George Orwell's stinging attack on school stories in 1940. Richards' narratives, featuring in weekly magazines like *The Magnet* (1908–40), Orwell thought deeply conservative. They possessed only two 'basic political assumptions', he wrote: 'nothing ever changes, and foreigners are funny.' 'Everything is safe, solid and unquestionable', he continued. 'Everything will be the same for ever and ever.' Orwell also insisted that these stories were read preponderantly by children from the lower-middle and working classes, rather than those who might actually be sent to the sort of expensive boarding school which they featured (attended, after all, by only three per cent of the population). This meant that the stories were 'a perfectly deliberate incitement to wealth-fantasy'. Above, all, they were a product of the English educational system, based more than anything else on status. It was a system, Orwell argued, in which people were segregated according to their schooling: the working classes did not pay for education; their social superiors were divided between those educated at minor private schools, and those who had attended the major public schools.[39] The shadow this demarcation could cast on the later life of a status-conscious adult is indicated by Charles Hamilton's own equivocation about whether or not he had attended a public school. 'He would not say that he had, but he more or less dared me ever to say that he had not', reported one interviewer, adding that 'I came away with the impression that, like so many of his boyish admirers, he had never been to a public school, but he wished that he had.'[40]

Against Orwell, it might be argued that the school story, perhaps particularly the girls' school story, was more often driven by an egalitarian impulse. As already noted, Brazil's *For the School Colours* and Brent-Dyer's *Exploits of the Chalet Girls*, amongst many similar texts, dealt with the successful integration into one school of girls from different social classes. The same might be said of Rowling's Harry Potter books, in which Ron Weasley, from a poor background, mixes on equal terms with Hermione Granger, from a squarely middle-class family (her parent are dentists) and Harry, who is descended from wizarding aristocracy. But what is important is that Orwell's analysis was widely held to be correct, so that after the Second World War school stories began to appear which deliberately challenged the genre's perceived elitism. Geoffrey Trease's *No Boats on Bannermere* (1949) and its sequels were very deliberately set in an average school. Its origin, Trease claimed, was a request from two girls he met when invited to speak at their school, that he should 'write true-to-life stories, about real boys and girls, going to day-schools as nearly everybody did'. In fact, their claim that 'No one seemed to write that sort' was not quite true.[41] Winifred Darch, for one, had written about ordinary schools in the 1920s and '30s.[42] But in any case, the idea of writing school stories which would not be set in exclusive, fee-paying and boarding establishments suited Trease's ideological agenda. He was a communist, and a firm believer that children's books must reflect real social realities. He had corresponded with Orwell, planning the establishment of 'some Leftish juvenile publishing scheme, pink in shade, perhaps backed by the T.U.C. [Trades Union Council] or the Liberal *News Chronicle*'.[43] The scheme never got off the ground, but *No Boats at Bannermere* was not the only book that might have been used as a prototype. *The Old Gang* (1947) by Laurence Maynell (writing as A. Stephen Tring) had already depicted the conflict between the pupils of two neighbouring schools, one a high-status 'grammar school', the other a lowly 'secondary modern'. It was an illustration of the divisions and jealousies established by the Education Act of 1944, which separated British children into three types of school depending on their performance in an examination taken when aged eleven.

Some of the post-War stories set in more realistic school settings have been judged to be just as formulaic as their boarding-school forerunners. E. W. Hildick's *Jim Starling* (1958) and its sequels, for example, are usually discussed in histories of the genre only because of their depiction of the grim Cement Street Secondary Modern School. Mabel Esther Allan's *The School on Cloud-Ridge* (1952) and *Lucia Comes to School* (1953), likewise, are most noteworthy because they are set in progressive schools, where the children impose discipline on themselves (not very different, in fact, from the lawlessness depicted in *Stalky & Co.*, and a theme exploited for its comic value by Gene Kemp in *Dog Days and Cat Naps* (1980) in which a class tries to discipline itself to demonstrate that they should be allowed on a school trip). William Mayne's school stories are also remarkable for their unconventional setting – in a cathedral choir school (presumably based on Canterbury, where Mayne had been a pupil). In some ways they are highly original, full of very subtle expression of the boys' mystification at the school's systems, and depicting a very close relationship between pupils and teachers. This intimacy is emphasised when, at one point in *A Swarm in May* (1955), the first novel in the series, the boys slowly bury their teacher in the sand. Probably because they have never lived outside a institution which provides for all their needs, Mayne's teachers are as dependent and ingenuous as the boys they teach. In other ways, the books are more conventional. Relationships between pupils are a major focus. Owen, the most junior chorister in *A Swarm in*

May, is infatuated with the oldest boy, Trevithic. Mayne also provides some of the standard moral lessons of the school story. The choir should not think of itself as a collection of individuals, but should work together. And the moral of *A Swarm in May* is apparently that 'we must all do our respective duties without argument'.[44] It is a lesson Owen has learned by finally accepting his role as 'Beekeeper', part of a cathedral ritual traditionally undertaken by the youngest pupil. Ultimately, for all its intricate patterning and emotional intelligence, *A Swarm in May* is as optimistic a novel as *Tom Brown's Schooldays*, dealing with a boy's discovery of his own true nature and his proper place in the community.

Mayne's school stories provide a detour from the main road taken by the genre in the post-War years – the gradual inclusion of a greater degree of social realism. Gene Kemp's *Cricklepit Combined School* (1977), set in a run-down school full of rowdy children, was one important contribution to this trend, but it was to reach its zenith in Britain not in books, but in a television programme: *Grange Hill*. This series, devised by Phil Redmond and running from 1978, was part soap opera but still fundamentally a school story. Indeed, it quickly produced a number of spin-off books, some based on the television plotlines, others original, the series beginning with the Marxist writer Robert Leeson's *Grange Hill Rules OK?* (1980). *Grange Hill* was immersed in the school story tradition, but also redefined it. Its attempt at realism was what impressed most early viewers, both positively and negatively. Some critics complained, for instance, about the improbable laxity of the teachers at Grange Hill School. In truth, these ineffective, solipsistic teachers are direct descendants of the masters in *Stalky & Co.*, while Grange Hill's long-time headmistress, Bridget McClusky, stands in a long line of stern but fair headteachers stretching back to Edgeworth's Dr. Middleton. *Grange Hill* was not realistic in its verisimilitude then, but because of its objective depiction of ordinary lives, following in the tradition of realist writers like Henry James. Indeed, it was almost Dickensian, often focusing on lower-class characters. In doing so, it was clearly different from American counterparts like Francine Pascal's *Sweet Valley High* books (from 1984), set in a far more glamorous school world and starring identical twins each of whom the narrator happily describes as 'about the most adorable, most dazzling sixteen-year-old girl imagina-ble'.[45] *Grange Hill*'s insistence of character development also marks a divergence from the classic British tradition, although again, it built on some recent developments. In earlier school stories the characters had often lived in a state of suspended animation. Frank Richards' Greyfriars stories, for instance, followed the academic calendar. But each September, the pupils returned to school no older than they had been a year before. But Geoffrey Trease's *Bannermere* series had already shown its protagonists advancing through their school years, until they ended up at university. *Grange Hill* imitated this (though the aging of the actors perhaps forced the issue). That there was seldom any prospect of the *Grange Hill* pupils graduating to university shows how far Phil Redmond had advanced Trease's attempt to write about real-life working-class schoolchildren.

Overall then, *Grange Hill* was not absolutely innovative, but the ideas Redmond took from contemporary children's books were accentuated so heavily and given such wide currency on television that they did change the direction of the school story. The two areas in which this is particularly true are his depiction of 'problems' and of the relationships between male and female characters. For most of the history of the British school story, schools had been single-sex. Only in the 1970s did fiction begin to catch up with reality of co-education. The moment at the very end of Gene Kemp's *The Turbulent Term of Tyke Tiler* (1977) when Tyke is revealed to be a girl, Theodora, might be taken as symbolic of the full admittance of co-education and its surrounding issues into the school story tradi-tion. Certainly from the 1970s, single-sex establishments have become the exception in fiction. As for sex, it had been almost entirely absent from the British school story, except for some con-troversial references to homosexuality, in Alec Waugh's *The Loom of Youth* (1916) for example. This had not been the case in American texts. Much of Susan Coolidge's *What Katy Did At School* (1873) focused on the infatuation of Kate's school-girl friends with the boys at a neighbouring school. The same theme runs through the *Sweet Valley High* books, which star the flirtatious Jessica and the serially monogamous Elizabeth, although they remain essentially chaste. In Britain, the influence of books like

Judy Blume's *Forever* (1975) and Aidan Chamber's *Breaktime* (1978) was soon felt in school narrative, and sex, or at least relationships, became central.

The issue was treated in a number of contrasting ways. Anne Digby's *Boy Trouble at Trebizon* (1980) remained rather genteel, seeing relationships as an obstacle to be overcome if girls were to achieve academic or sporting success. More graphic are Robert Westall's *Falling into Glory* (1993) and *Doing It* (2003) by Melvyn Burgess, both involving a sexual relationship between a pupil and a teacher. Both these authors, in the manner of *Grange Hill*, did not seek to confine the action of their novels to school, but nevertheless revolved much of the plot around it. Both attempted to capture the authentic feelings of seventeen-year-old schoolboys. In *Doing It*, Dino is so desperate to lose his virginity that he betrays the girlfriend he has for years pursued for someone he thinks 'a bit of a slapper'; Jonathan is confused because the girl he desires is his best friend, and anyway, he 'can't bear the social humiliation of being seen out regularly with a fat girl'; and Ben has to deal with the devastating consequences of 'every schoolboy's dream . . . an affair with an attractive young teacher.'[46] Other important sexualised school stories include the Australian Jenny Pausacker's *What Are Ya?* (1987), which introduced lesbian sexuality into school, a theme already explored less graphically in the American Deborah Hautzig's *Hey, Dollface* (1979). Adèle Geras returned to the traditional boarding-school setting of the British school story for her fairy tale-inspired *Egerton Hall* trilogy (1990–92). In each of these, a girl is traumatised by her sexual encounters. In *The Tower Room* and *Pictures of the Night* the girl has to choose between a boyfriend and college; in *Watching the Roses* she is raped. All these texts demonstrate how radically sex has changed the previously stable patterns of school story life.

But ultimately it is probably the continuities which are more striking than the changes. A comparison of *Doing It* with *Stalky & Co.*, for instance, might at first seem absurd. Immediately highlighted would be the implausibility of Kipling's teenagers who are, apparently, entirely unconcerned with sex (although others have been dubious about Burgess's portrait of boys who are able to think about nothing else: 'God help the publishers and their grubby little lives if they think this tosh is realistic', wrote Anne Fine in one scathing review).[47] Yet Dino, Jonathan and Ben do fit nicely into the roles of Kipling's Stalky, M'Turk and Beetle. The close relationship and separation from the main body of the school are the same for both triumvirates. So too is the sense that school is a preparation for conquests and conflicts to come – at the ends of Empire for Stalky, and for Burgess's characters, in a 'world . . . full of good-looking girls'.[48] Above all, what reading the two books in parallel suggests is that the braggadocio of both sets of boys masks their vulnerability. The sexual swagger of Burgess's characters dissolves when faced with the possibility of actual sexual contact. Their ritualised bragging, it becomes clear, is chiefly intended to bolster their own self-esteem. It is an expression of their anxiety about how they are regarded within the school. So too, we cannot help but suspect, is Stalky's endless need to challenge prefects and teachers, to skip out of school to smoke, and to receive the homage of other boys, even M'Turk and Beetle ('Isn't your Uncle Stalky a great man?' he asks, having Beetle kicked until he concurs).[49] In this sense, both books are about boys desiring to be adults but confined by an environment which regards them as children.

Relationships and sex are not the only 'problem issues' to have featured in recent school stories. *Grange Hill* was celebrated for its plot lines involving, amongst other things, shoplifting, teenage pregnancy, suicide, Asperger's syndrome, child abuse, truancy, racism, disability, AIDS, playground knifings, rape, alcoholism, homophobia, drug-abuse and bereavement. Amongst this procession of problems, the one issue to feature most constantly was that consistent theme of the school story, bullying. Flashman, in *Tom Brown's Schooldays*, is perhaps the archetype, tyrannising smaller boys, stood up to by Tom, and then expelled, in this case for drunkenness. The key elements here are Flashman's confinement of his bullying to general harassment of younger boys, his only tangential relationship to the main plot, and his final punishment by the proper authorities. Each of these elements has been revised. In *Grange Hill*, the most notorious of its succession of bullies, Norman 'Gripper' Stebson (in the programme from 1981–85), excelled Flashman by demanding money with menaces, and then adding racism, to his campaigns of persecution. Likewise, in Aidan

Chambers' *The Present Takers* (1983), one of the first school stories to focus exclusively on bullying, Melanie Prosser used racism to cement her powers of extortion: '*She called me bootpolish and made her gang try to wash me off in the toilet and made some others write stuff on the walls about me which said Go Home*', one victim recalled.[50]

The way to deal with bullies had been re-assessed earlier. In a chapter of *Stalky & Co.*, ironically called 'The Moral Reformers', it was the boys themselves who ended the bullies' careers by luring them into positions of weakness and contriving for them to receive the same physical abuse as they had been inflicting. Again, comparisons with more recent school narratives are illuminating. In *Grange Hill*, 'Gripper' Stebson's career was ended when the pupils he had been terrorising ganged up to inflict retribution. But in a move which confirmed the programme's fundamental conservatism, a teacher stepped in at the last moment to prevent such vigilantism. Instead of being lynched 'Gripper' was expelled: a morally sound message for the audience, but, after *Stalky & Co.*, a re-investment of power, and both real and moral authority, in the adults. On the other hand, Chambers, like Kipling, was apparently convinced that bullying could be defeated only by pupils. Lucy, a victim of Melanie's harassment and extortion, knows that her teachers are 'hopeless', and that if she was to tell them about events in the playground, the teachers would 'make a fuss, but nothing will happen' except that the bullying would get worse. Even when Lucy's parents find out and confront Melanie's mother, they admit that they are powerless. The victims' own ingenious solution is to combine to expose Melanie's cruelty in the class newspaper, a rejection of the violence employed by Stalky and friends, though perhaps reminiscent of Beetle's journalistic attacks on his teachers. Finding herself exposed to ridicule, Melanie is forced to capitulate. It is apparently an optimistic resolution, endorsing the power of pupils but also of print: flattering for all those involved in the production and dissemination of children's literature. But in fact, this utopianism is subtly undermined by Chambers's complicated plot which has Melanie removed from school, ultimately, because of her father's physical abuse, a new kind of bullying that has been exacerbated, Chambers hints, by Lucy's mother's telling Melanie's mother that Melanie was a bully.[51]

The Present Takers was also groundbreaking because of its quiet determination to communicate some of the reasons why Melanie bullies. She is dyslexic, as is revealed by her notes demanding 'PENS REST' (rather than 'PRESENTS'), and she comes from what Chambers means his readers to understand as an uncaring, hostile home. Lucy's father attempts to explain this: 'maybe she's taking out on you something that other people have done to her'. In fact Lucy's insights into the situation are more astute: 'She gets worse if anybody tells. Like it was a competition between her and the grown-ups.'[52] Louis Sachar's *There's a Boy in the Girls' Bathroom* (1987), though designed for younger readers, takes this theme further, exploring the complicated mindset of Bradley Chalkers, a boy with severe behavioural problems (his favourite threat is 'Give me a dollar or I'll spit on you.'). His self-destructive attitudes are patiently unravelled by Carla, a compassionate and unconventional counsellor. Bradley's problem, like several children in the book, is that he is not clear exactly who he is, a confusion symbolically enacted when boys accidentally wander into girls' lavatories and vice versa ('I don't believe in accidents', Carla says). Neither Bradley's teachers, who have given up on him, nor his parents, who at one point want him transferred to military school, realise this. Indeed, it is the Concerned Parents Organization which gets Carla transferred ('Kids have enough *counselling*. What they need is more discipline. If they're bad, they should be punished'). But Carla insists that children must resolve their own difficulties by discovering their own identity and place within the community: 'I never tell them what to do', she says, 'I try to help them to learn to think for themselves.' 'But isn't that what school is for', one parent responds, 'To tell kids what to think?' On the contrary though, the school story schools are most often a neutral site, almost free from prescription and any imposition of identity, in which the process of individuation can work itself out. Carla, a teacher who herself breaks the school rules, is essentially an embodiment of this.[53]

The most compelling representation of school bullying remains, however, Robert Cormier's *The Chocolate War* (1974). Whereas in most school stories, it is the bully who is increasingly isolated, in Cormier's bleak novel it is Jerry Renault, the boy who stands up to bullying, who becomes an outcast. He cannot even turn to his teachers, for they connive in the persecution. At the end of the book, for his refusal to sell chocolates for a fund-raising scheme and for his defiance of the 'Vigils', the school's dominant gang, Jerry is beaten senseless. Even more shocking than the physical violence is what he had gained: the knowledge that that there is no alternative but 'to play ball, to play football, to run, to make the team, to sell the chocolates, to sell whatever they wanted you to, to do whatever they wanted you to do. They tell you to do your thing but they don't mean it. . . . Don't disturb the universe. . . . It's important. Otherwise, they murder you.'[54] It is a brutal, almost Orwellian, education in conformity that contains much wider social relevance. It wholly upsets the reader's expectations, for there is to be no vindication of the stance Jerry took against the bullies. It also overturns the whole school story tradition, of allowing the child to find his or her own identity, and to live independently within the community. It is for all these reasons that Cormier, in *The Chocolate War*, seems to be 'demolishing the school story', as Peter Hunt put it.[55]

But despite Cormier's nihilism, the school story still flourishes. Some remain serious and realistic; many others are more comic, perhaps especially in America. Louis Sachar's whimsical *Wayside School* series (from 1978) and Bruce Coville's *My Teacher is an Alien* (1989) are good examples. Comic school stories are not a new phenomenon. 'The funniest school story ever written', at least according to advertisements appearing in *The Nelson Lee Library* in 1915, was 'Charlie Chaplin's Schooldays', serialised in the weekly *Boy's Realm* magazine.[56] Its existence is testimony to the long-standing cross-media potential of the school story, and of its ability to merge successfully with other genres. Nelson Lee himself, the hero of innumerable magazine adventures, gives further proof of this. He was a second Sherlock Holmes who, forced to seek refuge from a gang of thieves, took up a teaching post at a public school, thereafter combining the roles of schoolmaster and detective. But if one is seeking evidence of the school story's ability to adapt, and to fuse with other genres, the classic example is now J. K. Rowling's *Harry Potter* novels. Like so many authors before her, Rowling has continued the traditions of the British school story while skilfully blending them with fantasy and adventure.[57] This ability to adapt has kept the school story alive for many centuries. The form shows no sign of obsolescence.

SUMMARY OF KEY POINTS

- In the classic school story, the school is not merely a setting for adventure but functions almost as a character itself. Narratives revolve around incidents and attitudes which are implicit in, not extrinsic to, school life.
- School stories tend to focus on socialisation: characters learn how to integrate successfully into a community and to reconcile the demands of self and society.
- A central theme of many school stories is the balance between submission and defiance, authority and autonomy. Pupils are often at war with teachers, but beyond this, a more enduring complicity often exists.
- The British school story can seem a repressive genre since it often endorses the individual's internalisation of school discipline and ethos.
- The great longevity of the school story is largely due to its adaptability: it has successfully combined with other genres, appeared in a range of different media, and has absorbed and responded to changing social conditions.

NOTES

1. George Orwell, 'Boys' Weeklies', in *The Collected Essays, Journalism and Letters of George Orwell*, ed. Sonia Orwell and Ian Angus (London: Penguin, [1968] 1970), vol. 1, pp. 505–31 (p. 511).
2. Debbie Pinfold, *The Child's View of the Third Reich in German Literature* (Oxford: Clarendon Press, 2001), p. 46; Ben Hellman, 'Russia', in *International Companion Encylopedia of Children's Literature*, ed. Peter Hunt, 2nd edn, 2 vols (London: Routledge, 2004), vol. 2, pp. 1174–83 (p. 1180).
3. See Gillian Adams, 'Ancient and medieval children's texts', *International Companion Encyclopedia of Children's Literature*, Hunt (ed.), vol. 1, pp. 225–38 (p. 227).
4. See Jozef Ijsewijn, *Companion to Neo-Latin Studies Part II* (Leuven: Leuven University Press, 1998), pp. 229–31.

5. Evaldus Gallus, trans. John Brinsley, *Pueriles Confabulatiunculae: or Childrens Dialogues, Little Conferences, or Talkings Together* (London: Thomas Man, 1617), pp. 15–16, 17–18, 4 and 29–32.

6. Geoffrey Trease, *Laughter at the Door: A Continued Autobiography* (London: Macmillan, 1974), p. 153; Isabel Quigly, *The Heirs of Tom Brown: The English School Story* (London: Chatto and Windus, 1982).

7. Roald Dahl, *Danny the Champion of the World* (Harmondsworth: Puffin, [1975] 1982), pp. 17, 103, 92–3 and 97.

8. Humphrey Carpenter and Mari Prichard, *The Oxford Companion to Children's Literature* (Oxford: Oxford University Press, [1984] 1995), p. 532.

9. For more on the eighteenth-century school story see Samuel F. Pickering, *Moral Instruction and Fiction for Children 1749–1820* (Athens, GA: University of Georgia Press, 1993), pp. 31–57.

10. L. T. Meade, *The School Favourite* (London: Chambers, 1908), pp. 79 and 99–102.

11. Maria Edgeworth, *The Parent's Assistant Part I*, 2nd edn, 3 vols (London: J. Johnson, 1796), vol. 1, p. 165.

12. Quoted in Quigly, *The Heirs of Tom Brown*, p. 210.

13. Louis Sachar, *Sideways Stories from Wayside School* (London: Bloomsbury, [1978] 2004), pp. 11–15.

14. Gillian Avery, *Nineteenth Century Children* (London: Hodder and Stoughton, 1965), pp. 167–9.

15. Thomas Hughes, *Tom Brown's Schooldays* (London: Parragon Classics, [1857] 1994), p. 139.

16. See Quigly, *The Heirs of Tom Brown*, pp. 208–10.

17. Edgeworth, *The Parent's Assistant*, vol. 1, pp. 220–1.

18. Kipling, *The Complete Stalky & Co.*, ed. Isabel Quigly (Oxford: Oxford World's Classics, [1899] 1999), pp. 52–3 and 196.

19. Hughes, *Tom Brown's Schooldays*, p. 244.

20. Ibid., p. 213.

21. Sarah Fielding, *The Governess; or, the Little Female Academy*, ed. Candace Ward (Peterborough, Ontario: Broadview Press, [1749] 1995), pp. 89–90. See Judith Burdan, 'Girls *Must* Be Seen *and* Heard: Domestic Surveillance in Sarah Fielding's

The Governess', *Children's Literature Association Quarterly*, 19 (1994), 8–14.

22. Beverly Lyon Clark, *Regendering the School Story: Sassy Sissies and Tattling Tomboys* (New York: Garland, 1996), p. 84.

23. J. K. Rowling, *Harry Potter and the Chamber of Secrets* (London: Bloomsbury, 1998), pp. 20–1.

24. Fielding, *The Governess*, p. 123.

25. Ibid., pp. 175–6.

26. Meade, *School Favourite*, p. 103.

27. Quoted in Pat Pinsent, 'Theories of Genre and Gender: Changes and Continuity in the School Story', in *Modern Children's Literature: An Introduction*, ed. Kimberley Reynolds (Basingstoke: Palgrave Macmillan, 2005), pp. 8–22 (p. 11).

28. Pinfold, *The Child's View of the Third Reich*, p. 46.

29. W. H. Auden, 'Honour' from *The Old School* (1934), quoted in *The Oxford Book of School Days*, ed. Patricia Craig (Oxford: Oxford University Press, 1994), p. 317.

30. J. M. Barrie, *Peter and Wendy*, ed. Jack Zipes (London: Penguin, [1911] 2004), pp. 131–2.

31. Geraldine McCaughrean, *Peter Pan in Scarlet* (Oxford: Oxford University Press, 2006), pp. 186–7.

32. Robert Cormier, *The Chocolate War* (London: Penguin, [1974] 2001), p. 36.

33. Gillian Cross, *The Demon Headmaster* (London: Puffin, [1982] 1998), pp. 132–3, 135, 18 and 90.

34. Elinor Brent-Dyer, *The Chalet School Goes To It* (London: Chambers, 1941), later re-titled *The Chalet School at War*, pp. 192 and 142; *The Chalet School and the Lintons* (London: Chambers, 1934), p. 200.

35. C. S. Lewis, *The Last Battle* (London: Grafton, [1956] 2002), p. 128.

36. See Robin Gilmour's '*Stalky & Co.*: Revising the Code', in *Kipling Considered*, ed. Phillip Mallet (Basingstoke: Macmillan, 1989), pp. 19–32.

37. Hughes, *Tom Brown's Schooldays*, p. 47.

38. Don Randall, *Kipling's Imperial Boy: Adolescence and Cultural Hybridity* (Basingstoke: Palgrave, 2000), pp. 91–2.

39. Orwell, 'Boys' Weeklies', in *Collected Essays*, pp. 518 and 511.

40. John Arlott, quoted in Carpenter and Prichard (eds), *Oxford Companion to Children's Literature*, p. 235. In fact, Richards attended private day schools in west London: Mary Cadogan, *Frank Richards: the Chap Behind the Chums* (London: Viking, 1988), p. 12.

41. Trease, *Laughter at the Door*, p. 149.

42. Sheila Ray, 'School Stories', in *The Routledge International Encyclopedia of Children's Literature*, ed. Hunt, vol. 1, p. 472.

43. Trease, *Laughter at the Door*, p. 26.

44. William Mayne, *A Swarm in May* (Haslemere: Jade Publishers, [1955] 1990), pp. 89–90 and 183.

45. Francine Pascal, *Sweet Valley High. Double Love* (London: Bantam Books, [1984] 1995), p. 2.

46. Melvyn Burgess, *Doing It* (London: Penguin Books, [2003] 2004), pp. 134, 153 and 317.

47. *The Guardian*, Saturday 29 March 2003.

48. Burgess, *Doing It*, p. 330.

49. Kipling, *Stalky & Co.*, p. 31.

50. Aidan Chambers, *The Present Takers* (1983), in *The Norton Anthology of Children's Literature*, ed. Jack Zipes *et al.* (New York: Norton, 2005), pp. 1919–87 (p. 1982).

51. Chambers, *Present Takers*, pp. 1969, 1975 and 1986.

52. Ibid., pp. 1940, 1976 and 1970.

53. Louis Sachar, *There's a Boy in the Girls' Bathroom* (London: Bloomsbury, [1987] 2001), pp. 5, 37, 152 and 149.

54. Cormier, *The Chocolate War*, pp. 205–6.

55. Peter Hunt, *An Introduction to Children's Literature* (Oxford: Oxford University Press, 1994), p. 152.

56. *The Nelson Lee Library*, 23 (13 November 1915).

57. See Karen Manners Smith, 'Harry Potter's schooldays: J. K. Rowling and the British Boarding-School Novel', in *Reading Harry Potter: Critical Essays*, ed. Giselle Liza Anatol (Westport, CT: Praeger, 2003), pp. 69–87 and David K. Steege, 'Harry Potter, Tom Brown, and the British School Story: Lost in Transit?' in *The Ivory Tower and Harry Potter: Perspectives on a Literary Phenomenon*, ed. Lana A. Whited (Columbia, MO: Missouri University Press, 2002), pp. 140–56.

CHAPTER 5

The Family Story

Naturally, given the place that children have occupied in society, probably the majority of children's fiction has been set within the family. It could be argued that all these texts are family stories. In James Janeway's *A Token for Children* (1672), for instance, the pious child protagonists typically expire surrounded by a close and supportive unit of siblings, parents and relatives. The eight-year-old Sarah Howley dies 'full of natural affection to her Parents', counselling them how to bear her death so soon after her brother's, and much of the text captures her warnings to her siblings to 'remember the words of a dying Sister'.[1] Even fantasy has frequently been familial. Much of the appeal of C. S. Lewis's *The Lion, the Witch and the Wardrobe* (1950) derives from the relationships between the four siblings. Philip Pullman's *His Dark Materials* trilogy (1995–2000) revolves to a surprisingly large extent around parent-child relationships. Will's bond with his mother and search for his father underlies much of his story. Lyra's gradual discovery that Lord Asriel and Mrs Coulter are her parents forms another important strand, as does the belated realisation of their responsibilities towards her. Even more dominated by ideas of inclusion and exclusion from families is J. M. Barrie's *Peter and Wendy* (1911), though few have called it a family story. The relationships within the Darling family – Wendy, John and Michael, and their parents – are central. The meaning of family, and of its absence, is even more intensely explored with the Lost Boys. They are children who have fallen out of their perambulators in the park who, not having been claimed within a week, have gone to live in the Neverland. Peter himself is another outcast from family. His perpetual boyhood stems from his escape from home on the day he was born, and from his mother barring the nursery window against his return and replacing him with another little boy (so he thinks).[2]

But are these all family stories? Many would favour a narrower definition, admitting only those texts which have been deliberately designed to depict family life and which focus on family relationships. Charlotte Yonge's *The Daisy Chain* (1856) is a good example, describing how the eleven children of the May family cope after a coaching accident kills their mother and injures their father. The remaining siblings constitute the 'daisy-chain' of the title. If this kind of Victorian family story tended to demonstrate the strength and stability of individual families, and of the institution as a whole, more recent variations have explored its weaknesses and collapse. Morris Gleitzman and Anne Fine, to take just two well-known examples, specialise in tragi-comic stories of family rivalries and commotions. Fine's *Madame Doubtfire* (1987; *Alias Madame Doubtfire* in the US) recounts how a divorced father dresses up as a nanny in order to gain access to the children he no longer sees. Gleitzman's *Two Weeks with the Queen* (1989) describes Colin's anger at his parents' favouritism towards his younger brother. Only later does Colin learn that his brother has leukaemia.[3] Yet such stories of family disintegration and reconstruction are not new. A hundred years earlier, Mrs Molesworth's *Sheila's Mystery* (1895) was exploring similar territory. The novel is about two sisters: pretty, sweet and serene Honor, and plain, jealous, querulous Sheila. Sheila thinks she has found the source of her unhappiness when she overhears her parents saying that she had been adopted. She runs away, slowly learns how to be happy, and eventually returns to her family. Only then does she learn that it is Honor, not her, who had been adopted. Sheila's mother's rhetorical question, 'I wonder if parents have often trouble like this', could stand almost as the epigraph for the entire genre, from the eighteenth to the twenty-first century.[4]

As these examples suggest, the paradox of the family story genre is that it probably includes more accounts of family disordering than family coherence. All the texts mentioned so far present families which have been disrupted, removing parents or children from one another by death, divorce, evacuation, flight, abandonment or some other mechanism – Mr March's military service in Louisa May Alcott's *Little Women* (1868), say, or Father's unjust incarceration in E. Nesbit's *The Railway Children* (1906).[5] Jan Mark suggests that the absence of complete families from nineteenth- and twentieth-century family stories is because authors realised 'that children with two harmonious parents were likely to have little to unsettle them'.[6] Gillian Avery agrees, noting that mothers, in particular, 'have a constricting effect on the plot and on the children's activities; their love is so embarrassingly obvious that it can't be overlooked, it stands in the way of that independence that children like to imagine.'[7] But the absence of whole and happy families from family stories is not merely a device to give children freer rein or to allow pathos and adventure into the narrative. Rather, the absence of one or more parents serves to endorse the importance of family. Very many family stories begin with a sundering but proceed to show how the protagonists continually strive to regenerate their family in revised forms. Frederick Marryat's *Children of the New Forest* (1847), for instance, begins when the four Beverley children are orphaned during the English Civil War, and follows their adventures as they learn to live hidden deep in the forest. Having been deprived of their family, the children almost immediately seek to recreate it. The eldest boy and girl, Edward and Alice, become the father and mother, while Humphrey and Edith play the roles of their children, gradually growing to maturity by following their elders' example. They even pretend that their old servant, Jacob, is the grandfather, ostensibly to give them a credible identity when they go to town, but clearly demonstrating their desire to reconstruct a family. Cynthia Voigt's *Homecoming* (1981) is similar. The Tillerman children have already been deserted by their father when they are abandoned by their mother. The novel recounts their long journey to find a new home, from Connecticut to Maryland, led by the thirteen-year-old Dicey. Eventually they arrive at their grandmother's house. But in fact, they have been able to reconstitute themselves as a family before this by themselves, each taking on distinct family roles.

For another author and critic, John Rowe Townsend, it was not so much the physical break-up of the family that was necessary for the family story to flourish, but rather for parents to have their authority diminished. *Little Women*, he argues, could become 'the first great example' of the family story only because it 'marks a relaxation of the stiff and authoritarian stereotype of family life'. 'The family story could not work in an atmosphere of repression or of chilly grandeur', he wrote, for its 'key characteristic is always warmth.'[8] This observation might be challenged on two counts. First, there is no particular reason why all family stories should necessarily be characterised by their warmth. Few would describe the thirteen Lemony Snicket books (1999–2006) as 'warm', but the adventures of Violet, Klaus and Sunny Baudelaire, as their wicked uncle Count Olaf attempts to destroy them, constitute the most popular children's family saga of recent times. Second, it is certainly possible to argue that many children's books featuring families which were published before *Little Women* are less disciplinarian and more affectionate than Townsend allows. Many of the stories comprising *The Children's Friend*, freely translated from the French of Arnaud Berquin in 1786, show this very well. In 'The Little Brother', for example, a young girl called Fanny Warrington is shown her new-born brother for the first time. She is disappointed because he cannot play or talk and seems so weak, and she doubts that she was ever so incapable. Her father carefully explains how tenderly Fanny's mother had cared for her:

> If you did but know, my dearest Fanny, how much trouble you occasion'd her, you'd be astonish'd; for at first, you were so weak, you could not swallow any thing, and every day, we apprehended you would die. . . . and after she had once found means to make you suck, you soon became quite fat, and were the merriest little creature in the world. For two whole years, 'twas necessary every day and every minute of the day, she should attend you with the same degree of care and caution. Often, after she had dropt asleep thro' absolute fatigue, your crying would awake her. She would then get out of bed and hasten to your cradle. Fanny! my sweet Fanny! would she say, no doubt my pretty babe is dry; and put you to the breast.

The account of Fanny's early life is intended to show how devoted parents are to their children, giving up all their own pleasure. The aim of this is didactic, for having learned how good her parents have been to her, Fanny promises 'I will never grieve or disobey you for the time to come'.[9] But it is also as forceful an endorsement of family life as Jo March's much more famous exultation in the second part of *Little Women* (1869; known as *Good Wives* in Britain): 'I do think that families are the most beautiful things in all the world!'[10]

Although it might seem fairly normal today, the kind of family that Berquin depicted in 'The Little Brother' would have been understood as progressive in the late eighteenth century. Many affluent women did not breast-feed but employed wet-nurses for their children. The kind of affectionate, hands-on didacticism shown by Fanny's father might also have been regarded as unusual. Parents inspired to take this kind of direct role in raising their children were probably the primary consumers of the new children's literature that was emerging in the later eighteenth century. Naturally, as well as writing for this kind of family, authors usually wrote about them. John Aikin and Anna Laetitia Barbauld's *Evenings at Home* (1792–96) opens with a description of the happy Fairbourne family, a father and mother and their 'numerous progeny' of children. The reader is told that they all meet together in the evenings, when the boys are home from their boarding schools, to read to one another instructive stories, and it is these stories, in this frame, which fill the book's four volumes. A little less explicitly didactic, and more of a family story in the modern sense, is Dorothy Kilner's *The Holyday Present: Containing Anecdotes of Mr & Mrs Jennett, and Their Little Family* (c.1781). The action of this novel is comprised entirely of the interactions of six siblings and their parents. A typical episode involves Harriet and Charlotte arguing about whether they should keep their feet in the stocks (used to correct their posture) when their mother is out of the room. Charlotte does not, but in her haste to reinsert her feet when her mother returns, she knocks over a table and covers herself in ink. As a result, until 'papa and mamma told them that it was not *good natured*', her brothers tease her by calling her 'sister *Tawney* and Charlotte *Blacky*.'[11]

There is no doubt that these texts were designed primarily to be instructive but they are clearly also family tales. Indeed, they are actually about the institution of family itself as much as anything that would be written by Anne Fine or Morris Gleitzman. Sarah Trimmer's *Fabulous Histories* (1786) is another good example. It presents two interlinked families, one of humans and the other of robins (hence its later and more usual title, *The History of the Robins*). She domesticates her avian family to the very furthest extent of anthropomorphism, making Robin, Dicky, Flapsy, Pecksy, and their mother and father, thoroughly 'human' even if they live in a nest and eat worms. Pecksy is docile and considerate while Robin is rash and conceited. But it is after Dicky has eaten four worms himself without sharing them amongst his siblings that the principal lesson is given: 'In a family every individual ought to consult the welfare of the whole, instead of his own private satisfaction. It is his own truest interest to do so.'[12] Meanwhile, Trimmer has offered advice to parents too. The mother must be the core of the family, nurturing her children, while the father, though also working for its benefit, is allowed a wider ambit. Thus the human Mr Benson is largely absent from the story, leaving his loving if somewhat stern wife to dominate the household. And thus the mother robin, although she looks for food for her brood, confines herself to the immediate vicinity of the nest while her 'husband' scours a much wider area. This kind of moral tale was deliberately reconstructing the family as a close-knit and symbiotic group of two parents and their children, excluding other relatives, shutting out other members of the household such as servants, and increasingly centred around the nurturing mother. 'I view a mother as mistress of the revels among her little people', wrote Ellinor Fenn, the author of many instructive children's books in the late eighteenth-century, often under the pseudonym 'Mrs Lovechild'.[13]

These dedicated and capable women were increasingly cast as the 'mothers of the nation', as one recent study has called them. Their dutiful, nurturing, pious ethos shaped society's self-image, as well as being 'used to justify Britain's colonial imperialism'.[14] This is clearly to be seen in Barbara Hofland's *The Panorama of Europe* (1813), in which the mother of the family plays the role of England in a geographical pageant. She is, says her husband, 'a just representative of a country, which, like her, not only spreads her matronly arms over her own children, to rear them to virtue, and refine them to elegance, but extends the blessings to strangers also, and bids the children of many a distant land rejoice in her protection.'[15] Johann David Wyss's *The Family Robinson Crusoe*, translated from German into English in 1814 and better-known as *The Swiss Family Robinson*, also presents the family as both the practical and moral foundation of empire. Having been wrecked on an uninhabited peninsular, the family, like Daniel Defoe's castaway before them, make a successful life for themselves. It is the family, working together, that tames the wilderness. 'The ten years we have passed', says the father reviewing the progress of what he calls their 'colony', were 'years of conquest and establishment.' It is difficult to imagine a more vigorous endorsement of the family as the most proper and profitable social and political unit.[16]

In another sense too, many of the family stories of the nineteenth century are in the mould of *Robinson Crusoe*. The death of parents leaves the children like castaways, exiled from the world they have known and forced to make a new life on the rocky shore on which they have washed up. Charlotte Yonge's books are the most characteristic of the mid-Victorian family story. *The Pillars of the House* (1873), for example, begins with the death of the father, proceeds to the death of the mother, and then charts how the thirteen children rebuild their family life, with the oldest boy learning to be their new father. Although set firmly in the context of Victorian middle-class society, these children have to fend for themselves, and learn to renounce their childhoods, as much as any desert island castaway. Other good examples of this sort of story include *The Wide, Wide World* (1850) by Susan Warner (writing as Elizabeth Wetherell), with an orphaned girl brought up by a heart-hearted aunt, and Susan Coolidge's *What Katy Did* (1872), with a widowed father left to bring up a large family.

It is Alcott's *Little Women* (1868), however, which has become known as the milestone text in the history of the family story. This is no doubt largely because of its status as the first 'classic' of American children's literature as well as its enduring popularity. But many critics have also seen it as breaking the mould of its genre. Beverly Lyon Clark has claimed that *Little Women* 'marked a departure from the previous moralizing in children's literature'.[17] Ruth K. MacDonald acclaims Alcott's depiction of characters with 'flaws that no writer had previously dared to attribute to fictional characters for children', such as selfishness, vanity, temper.[18] For Shirley Foster and Judy Simons, *Little Women* is 'one of the first fictional texts for children to convey the difficulties and the anxieties of girlhood, and which suggests that becoming a "little woman" is a learned and often fraught process'.[19] All this may be true, but it is perhaps in the ways that Alcott refined the family story as it already existed that the book's success lies, rather than in the ways she transformed it. Most early reviewers commended Alcott not for any great originality, but for 'the thorough reality of her characters'.[20] And Alison Lurie is probably correct to suggest that *Little Women* remains popular fundamentally because 'it is the story of a united and affectionate family living in a small New England town' featuring 'kind, wise, and loving parents, always ready with a warm hug and a moral lesson, and four charming teenage daughters who', she adds, hinting at the book's nostalgic appeal, 'have never heard of punk rock or crack cocaine.'[21] Nikki Gamble agrees, noting that at least at first, *Little Women* provides 'a comforting and warm picture of family life; a celebration of love, duty and loyalty'.[22] The book is, as Gillian Avery has succinctly put it, 'the supreme celebration of family affection'.[23]

And yet Alcott's work can also be read as a much more pessimistic dissection of family life and its limitations. Elizabeth Lennox Keyser has proposed that Alcott's 'view of families in *Little Women* is complex and disturbing'. She notes that the book 'abounds in images of constriction, concealment, and pain'. For instance, having dirtied her own glove, through too close and unladylike an involvement with the real world we infer, Jo must force her hand into her sister's smaller glove if she is to appear like 'a real lady' at a Christmas party.[24] Such episodes are symbolic, says Keyser, of Alcott's interpretation of the family as an institution which enforces strict gender codes and which prevents Jo, and others like her, from achieving independence and fulfilment. Jo's literary instincts have to be curbed so that she learns to write what will serve the family best. And when she has a chance of achieving a kind of personal and artistic freedom with the sympathetic and supportive Laurie, Alcott deliberately destroyed the dream by refusing to allow Jo to marry him, the outcome her narrative had encouraged readers to expect. Professor Bhaer, the man Jo eventually marries at the end of *Good Wives*, is far more overbearing than Laurie, and, says Keyser, he perpetuates the patriarchally centred family from which Jo has been trying to escape and in which, ultimately, she is re-incarcerated.[25] Even if one does not accept that Jo is quite so crushed as all this, it is surely true that in most nineteenth-century children's literature, although families might be 'the most beautiful things in all the world', they are also usually founded on self-abnegation. Both girls and boys give up their individuality in order to support and sustain the family unit.

As we have seen with Voigt's *Homecoming*, stories in which children have been prematurely forced to take on adult roles because of parental absence were still being published in the late twentieth century. However, a century earlier there had been a reaction against narratives in which children were forced to grow up early. Kate Douglas Wiggin's *Rebecca of Sunnybrook Farm* (1903), L. M. Montgomery's *Anne of Green Gables* (1908) and Eleanor Hodgman Porter's *Pollyanna* (1913) are all novels about girls who have lost at least one parent, but these heroines appeal to the reader by virtue of their childishness, not their early-onset adultness. Wiggin's Rebecca does become nurse to her ailing mother; Montgomery's Anne does end the first novel in the series as a carer for Marilla, who had adopted her; and Porter's Pollyanna does learn to cope maturely with the injuries she sustains in a car accident. But even if these girls become exemplary paragons, it is their youthful candour, imagination and *joie de vivre* which are most celebrated, and which have an enormous impact on those around them. Pollyanna brings a new cheerfulness to the dour community into which she has been transplanted, and especially her severe aunt, encouraging them all to play the childish 'glad game' which makes them overlook their problems and focus on their blessings. Anne transforms Matthew and Marilla Cuthbert after they adopt her, bringing love and laughter into their previously strait-laced lives. And even more than the others, Rebecca is carefully constructed as an embodiment of the Romantic child, able to change lives because of a childlike innocence and ingenuousness which Wiggin characterises as semi-divine. The twelve-year-old Rebecca is first introduced in a chapter called 'We Are Seven', after William Wordsworth's poem, and her description makes clear that she is as transcendental and numinous a child as any Wordsworth wrote about:

> Rebecca's eyes were like faith . . . Their glance was eager and full of interest, yet never satisfied; their steadfast gaze was brilliant and mysterious, and had the effect of looking directly through the obvious to something beyond . . . a pair of eyes carrying such messages, such suggestions, such hints of sleeping power and insight, that one never tired of looking into their shining depths . . .[26]

The fascination of Rebecca's childishness is complicated by the obsessive relationship that Wiggin depicts between her and Adam Ladd (nicknamed 'Mr Aladdin'), eighteen years her senior. The novel ends when Rebecca is seventeen and Wiggin was careful to keep Rebecca as a non-sexual being, but Jerry Griswold has offered a convincing Oedipal reading of the text and has gone so far as to call Rebecca 'a *Lolita* without sex'.[27] From the point of view of the development of the family story, though, the important point is that *Rebecca of Sunnybrook Farm*, like other children's books of its time, celebrates not the bridging of the gap between childhood and adulthood but rather the gap itself.

Indeed, it is in family stories that the late nineteenth-century conviction that adults and children were entirely different kinds of creature, living in their own separate worlds, is perhaps most clearly visible. Mary Louisa Molesworth's children's novels were firmly located in middle-class families, generally with both parents alive, but they are set in what Gillian Avery calls the 'nursery world', 'where only the children have any real existence, where adults are kindly, ministering shadows, lacking substance and rarely playing an important part in the action of the story.'[28] *Carrots: Just a Little Boy* (1876) is the classic example, detailing the way that Fabian, always called 'Carrots' because of his red hair, is mothered by his sister Floss, only four years older, even though the children have what Kenneth Grahame called in *The Golden Age* (1895) 'a proper equipment of parents'. Indeed, *The Golden Age* contains the most vigorous deliberation on the gulf between children and adults who live side-by-side in the same house yet do not know each other. It is an account of the games and adventures of five siblings who despair at the dullness of grown-ups. These adults, the 'Olympians', have the freedom to do what they like, marvels the narrator, but inexplicably they spend their time in work, going to church, starting love affairs and other such tedious activities when they could be climbing trees, hunting chickens, pretending to be lions, exploding imaginary mines on the lawn and so on. Worse, the Olympians 'were unaware of Indians, nor recked they anything of bisons or of pirates (with pistols!) though the whole place swarmed with such portents.'[29] While J. M. Barrie, a few years later in *Peter Pan* (1904), would employ such representations of childhood innocence and imagination to entertain children, the effect Grahame hoped to achieve was probably more sentimental, and satirical. *The Golden Age* was intended for adults, designed to instil a nostalgia for vanished childhoods. But by pointing out to adult readers how trivial their concerns must seem to the innocent and open minds of children, Grahame was demanding a reassessment of adult priorities. In this, as in the fact that it was a book for adults that was quickly taken up by children, it is similar to Jonathan Swift's *Gulliver's Travels* (1726) in which the customs and attitudes of both the Lilliputians and Brobdingnagians seem preposterous to Gulliver when he views them from his different perspective.

The same mix of comedy, nostalgia and powerful satire is to be found in another celebrated set of family stories which focused on the unbridgeable gap between adults and children, E. Nesbit's *The Story of the Treasure Seekers* (1899) and its continuations *The Wouldbegoods* (1901) and *The New Treasure Seekers* (1904). These provide an episodic account of the adventures of the six Bastable children. As *The Treasure Seekers* opens, the Bastables' mother has died, and their father is absorbed in his precarious business concerns. It is his poverty which provides the theme for *The Treasure Seekers* as the children try all sorts of strategies to restore the family fortunes. After many miscarrying schemes, they are finally successful when their naivety and good intentions soften the heart of their 'Indian Uncle', whom they wrongly assume to be poor and in need of their charity, and he takes the family under his protection. The

Wouldbegoods begins with the children in disgrace for ruining his garden by acting out Rudyard Kipling's *Jungle Book*. The rest of the book details their attempts to be virtuous, like the children in the moral tales which they have read. Their good intentions almost always backfire.

Nesbit is often seen as another pivotal author in the history of children's literature. This is because her child characters seem free and autonomous. Nesbit clearly advocated the kind of upbringing that allows children to run free of adult supervision, and she derides the sort of coddling child-rearing that has afflicted Denny and Daisy, friends of the Bastables, who have turned out 'little pinky, frightened things, like white mice'.[30] In fact, the 'ideal' adults in Nesbit's books are generally not parents but avuncular older men, with no children of their own, characters like the 'Old Gentlemen' in *The Railway Children* (1906), the 'Indian Uncle' in *The Treasure Seekers* or 'Albert's Uncle', the recluse at whose house the children spend the summer in *The Wouldbegoods*. They are themselves child-like. When given the choice, the 'Indian Uncle' prefers 'play-dinner' to 'grown-up dinner': he lustily joins in with the children in 'hunting' their meal before eating it, and he 'slew the pudding in the dish in the good old-fashioned way.'[31] The same kind of ideal adult had featured in Grahame's *Golden Age*: the curate, 'who would receive, unblenching, the information that the meadow beyond the orchard was a prairie studded with herds of buffalo' and 'was always ready to constitute himself a hostile army or a band of marauding Indians on the shortest possible notice'.[32] It was to reach its apogee with Barrie himself, and his *alter ego*, Peter Pan, both, in different ways, grown-ups who had remained children. What this amounts to is a shifting of the balance in the family story. The relationship between parents and children had become marginal, and those adults who did intrude on the children's lives were no longer the bringers of discipline or wisdom, but themselves learned from, and were liberated by, the children. In a strange way, these novels constructing the child as wiser than the adult are similar to some of the family problem novels of the late twentieth century. In Morris Gleitzman's *Bumface* (1998) for example, Angus looks after his siblings as well as his television star mother. At its close, in order to force his mother to confront her responsibilities,

Angus deliberately spoils his own birthday party by behaving immaturely. It is his attempt to re-impose the breach that Nesbit, Grahame and Barrie had set up between children and their parents.

Much of Nesbit's writing for children is very political. In *The Wouldbegoods*, for instance, the Bastables attempt to force their benevolence on people, and so their plans always fail. Better to investigate the real needs of the poor rather than impose welfare, the book suggests: an endorsement of the position of the Fabian Society, of which Nesbit and her husband were founder members. Equally political, and equally focused on the workings of a single family, are Laura Ingalls Wilder's *Little House* books (1932–71). Each of the seven books is loosely based on the author's own experiences of a late nineteenth-century childhood on the American frontier, but they are not exactly autobiography. Wilder was too young to remember either the home in Wisconsin where *Little House in the Big Woods* (1932), the first novel, takes place, or the year her family spent on the prairie, later part of Kansas but then 'Indian Territory', which features in the second book, *Little House on the Prairie* (1935). Indeed, some of the alterations and absences in the books reveal much about Wilder's purposes in writing these fictionalised memoirs. For instance, she almost entirely omitted from her account the year her family spent in Burr Oak, Iowa, a town far removed from the frontier, where her insolvent parents managed an hotel and Laura and her sister Mary helped out as chamber-maids and waitresses. Omitting this from the books maintained the image that Wilder wanted to project, of a pioneer family living on the edge of the wilderness and always independent and free.

In the *Little House* books, freedom is made possible only by isolation, and isolation necessitates self-sufficiency. These are key themes of the books, and they underpin the idea of family that Wilder endorses. At the beginning of *Little House on the Prairie* Pa decides to move the family into the uncultivated 'Indian Territory', not even part of the United States at that time, because 'there were too many people in the Big Woods now.' They build their new cabin in as remote a spot as they can find. The nearest town, appropriately called Independence, is two days' journey away. Their nearest white neighbour, Mr Edwards, lives two miles away. Having built their cabin, the family faces the challenges of wolves, fire, fever and the native Americans who were already living in the vicinity. Perhaps unsurprisingly the family, and especially Ma, develops something of a bunker mentality, and the book can seem rather claustrophobic. Ma even tries to shut out the other white pioneers from her family. Edwards has helped them build their cabin, but Ma is reluctant to let Pa borrow nails from him. 'I don't like to be beholden, not even to the best of neighbours', she says. Above all, Ma loathes the 'Indians' who intrude (as she sees it) into her house. Pa is less insular, respecting the 'Indians' and cooperating with Edwards, but he is dismayed by the arrival of other colonists in the area and he makes a lock for the stable. 'When neighbours began to come into a country,' Laura recounts, 'it was best to lock up your horses at night, because, where there are deer there will be wolves, and where they are horses, there will be horse-thieves.'[33] The family is constructed as an entirely self-sufficient unit, and as the only social institution in which virtue can thrive. Any larger community – even the handful of settlers who follow the Ingalls family onto the prairie – is understood as necessarily ridden with corruption.

All of the *Little House* books explore the way that the family has, regrettably, to sully itself by a relationship with the larger community. It comes to a head in the fifth book in the series, *The Long Winter* (1942), when severe weather lays siege to the Ingalls. It is the family's self-sufficiency which enables them to survive the shortages, as they resourcefully eke out what little food they have. But it is when grain finally arrives in the local shop, brought by Laura's future husband Almanzo, that Wilder spells out her social credo. The storekeeper says he has the right to sell the grain at a huge profit. Pa, leading a deputation of angry townspeople, just manages to prevent violence but warns that they can boycott the shop. 'If you've got a right to do as you please, we've got a right to do as we please', he says. 'Don't forget every one of us is free and independent.'[34] The idea that the individual and the family is the only virtuous social unit is, of course, a very political point, and Wilder can seem a prophet of the socio-political views that came to dominate Britain and America in the 1980s. One of Margaret Thatcher's most famous pronouncements sums up Wilder's views perfectly: 'there is no such thing as society. There are individual men and women, and there are families. And no government can do anything except through people, and people must look to themselves first.'[35]

The politics of the *Little House* books is linked with the recent controversy about their authorship. Wilder, already 65 when the first book was published, was certainly encouraged in her writing of the books by her daughter Rose Wilder Lane, a professional novelist and journalist. However, in a book called *The Ghost in the Little House* (1993), William Holtz suggested that Rose substantially rewrote her mother's drafts. This conclusion is open to substantial doubt, but it is nonetheless interesting to note Rose's politics and the context in which the first *Little House* books were first published.[36] They appeared during the Great Depression of the 1930s and while Franklin D. Roosevelt was rolling out his New Deal policies of unprecedented social and economic intervention by the federal government. Rose has been described as a 'political crank, with a deep dislike of Roosevelt and the New Deal'.[37] Whether or not she should be considered as a co-author, the *Little House* books can easily be read as a critique of federal government. The Ingalls leave their cabin on the prairie (in Laura's narration at least) not because of their settlement's failure, but because 'some blasted politicians in Washington', in Pa's furious words, have reneged on their promise to 'make the Indians move on again' and open up the land for white settlement.[38] With anti-federal rhetoric like this, it is no wonder that the *Little House* books have become 'an icon of conservative political and family values in America'.[39]

Read more carefully, though, the *Little House* books can begin to seem less confident in their celebration of the independent, self-sufficient and virtuous nuclear family. Laura's narration does idealise her father and mother, and their devotion to their three daughters, but it also subtly reveals surprising tensions between them. Francis Spufford maintains that it is 'one of the quiet excellences of the whole series that they tactfully register, and offer to readers who are able to notice them, far more complication in the picture of the family than they ever comment on explicitly.'[40] The most obvious 'complication' of the happy family is Laura's resentment of her older sister Mary. Occasionally, this bubbles to the surface, as when they find Indian beads and, rather than keep some for herself, Mary gives them to her baby sister, Carrie:

Ma waited to hear what Laura would say. Laura didn't want to say anything. She wanted to keep those pretty beads. Her chest felt all hot inside, and she wished with all her might that Mary wouldn't always be such a good little girl. But she couldn't let Mary be better than she was.

So she said slowly, 'Carrie can have mine, too.' . . .

Perhaps Mary felt sweet and good inside, but Laura didn't. When she looked at Mary she wanted to slap her. So she dared not look at Mary again.[41]

But more deeply buried in the folds of the narration is conflict between Ma and Pa. They never argue, but Wilder allows Laura's narration to reveal Ma's frustration with Pa's wandering spirit. 'This is a country I'll be contented to stay in the rest of my life', Pa says when he has built his cabin on the prairie. But Ma knows him better than he knows himself, asking 'Even when it's settled up?'[42] Such veiled accusations are the only hints of Ma's resentment, but they destabilise the notion of the perfectly unified and contented family.

As for Laura herself, although her childhood is apparently idyllic, she is in a constant state of resistance to the role that has been assigned to her within the family, principally by Ma. She is not an obvious tomboy like Jo in *Little Women*, nor is her discontent ever very loud or explicit. But her mysterious longing to see an Indian baby is suggestive of a desire to escape the confines of her family and the kind of domestic femininity enjoined by her mother. When she actually meets Indian children, her restlessness finds its only open expression:

> She had a naughty wish to be a little Indian girl. Of course she did not really mean it. She only wanted to be bare naked in the wind and the sunshine, and riding one of those gay little ponies.

But even before this, Laura's narration has quietly recorded the tension between her and Ma. 'What do you want to see an Indian baby for?' Ma scolds, adding 'Put on your sun-bonnet, now, and forget such nonsense.' It is the sun-bonnet that works as the most powerful symbol of Laura's incarceration within her mother's values. It stands for the circumscribed role that Ma's family values enforce on women, for 'its sides came past her cheeks' and 'she could see only what was in front of her'.[43] We realise too that it is designed to keep the sun from tanning Laura's face, preventing her from becoming like either the Indians or Pa, both of whom live freer and more natural lives on the prairie. The book, in fact, is suffused by Laura's simmering, though unspoken, desire to escape her internment within Ma's family values.

The *Little House* books compare interestingly with a British family story from the same period, Eve Garnett's *The Family from One End Street* (1937). Like Wilder, Garnett set her novel beyond a frontier, not among the 'Indians' but among the working classes, a setting very seldom previously used for family stories. Mr Ruggles is a dustman; Mrs Ruggles is a washerwoman. They have seven children, each of whom has a separate adventure. This marks a departure from most family stories, in which the siblings tend to stick together. Indeed, *The Family from One End Street* is in some ways not a very convincing family story. Until a final chapter when they are all together, the family can seem more literary 'ballast' than the main focus of the book, providing a context for the children's separate adventures. On the other hand, like the Ingalls, the Ruggles have a strong sense of the family identity and of the differences between them and the other inhabitants of Otwell. They know very well that they are not like the richer people they sometimes meet. More surprisingly, they are just as keen to separate themselves from their neighbours in One End Street as the Ingalls had been on the prairie. They are outraged, for example, at the interference in their affairs by 'Mrs. "Nosey Parker" Smith'.[44]

The Ruggles' attitude to interference in their lives by the state is more complicated. As in the *Little House* books, it is a major theme. It is clear that the 'welfare state' plays a substantial role in the Ruggles' lives. We learn in passing that when Mr Ruggles had broken his leg, national insurance money had supported the family. It is the state which provides a scholarship for Kate, the cleverest of the Ruggles children, to attend a secondary school. After a misunderstanding, the state even pays for Kate's school uniform. The Ruggles often invoke the power of the state to take over responsibility for the children, even if they do so for comic effect. When Mrs Ruggles is being pestered by one of her daughters, for instance, she vows that 'she would support no Government in future that did not promise immediate erection of Nursery Schools to accommodate under-school-age offspring, and relieve harassed mothers.' Garnett subtly indicates that Mrs Ruggles is perilously close to needing the state's childcare help too. In one chapter, young Jo Ruggles positions himself outside a tea shop, hoping to appear so hungry that people will give him money. He plans to spend his gains on seeing the new film at the cinema, and is annoyed when a kind lady buys him buns instead of giving him cash. But Garnett allows the reader to hear the woman wondering 'if she ought to see the Head Teacher about their getting a free meal at school'. Evidently, the local people's perception is that Mr and Mrs Ruggles are on the verge of needing state support. Elsewhere, Garnett seems to express a decided hostility to the welfare state. Mr Ruggles finds a substantial sum of money on his rounds, and honestly hands it in to the police. His friend doubts that he will receive any recompense, telling him of a man who found a pearl necklace worth thousands of pounds, but was rewarded with only a paltry sum of money by its owner. The necklace's owner justified her niggardliness by saying that 'nowadays people was so well-educated by the State they'd no excuse *not* to give back things they found'. The implication is that the institutional charity of the welfare state has caused the decline of genuine, personal gratitude and benevolence. In fact, because of the consistent endorsement of private charity over state support, the Ruggles' world can seem almost feudal. When they deferentially name their son after the vicar they are repaid with a pound note. Then when Mr Ruggles is eventually rewarded with two pounds for handing in the money he has found, tears come to his eyes, and the benefactor is left wondering whether to pity or envy the Ruggles for the simplicity of their lives.[45]

Garnett's preference for private, even feudal, support seems to be based on a conviction that state maintenance is really a challenge to the family. Whereas personal charity, being less comprehensive, simply sustains existing social structures, the welfare state has the potential to replace them. Kimberley Reynolds has made this point with particular reference to the chapter called 'The Baby Show', in which Mrs Ruggles enters her youngest child, William, in the contest to find 'Otwell's Best Baby'. The judges are doctors and nurses, and Mrs Ruggles seems to distrust their scientific talk and secretive ways. Their hospital training and modern techniques are an affront to the role of the mother, and to traditional methods. Reynolds concludes that Garnett recognised 'that many parents resented heavy-handed state intervention, seeing it as questioning their ability to look after their families properly.'[46] It was a theme that would surface more frequently after 1945, when state intervention became more firmly entrenched in Britain and America. The danger that the welfare state posed to the family was powerfully dramatised in John Rowe Townsend's *Gumble's Yard* (1961), for instance, in which four children are so worried that they will be separated from one another and forced into children's homes that they run away to live in a derelict warehouse.

With its concern with the impact of poverty and of the welfare state on families, *The Family from One End Street* should be regarded as an attempt at social realism, even if it is also comic and cute. After the Second World War, the family story would be increasingly dominated by the attempt to depict the sort of lives that children really led, perhaps especially working-class children, and the problems which afflicted real families and the emergence of different patterns of family life. The effects of parental abandonment and of fostering, for example, have been explored in a number of impressive novels including Betsy Byars' *The Pinballs* (1977), Katherine Paterson's *The Great Gilly Hopkins* (1979) and Jacqueline Wilson's *The Story of Tracy Beaker* (1991). Lesbian and gay families have been depicted in Susanne Bösche's *Jenny Lives with Eric and Martin* (translated into English, from Danish, in 1983) and Leslea Newman's *Heather Has Two Mommies* (1989). Divorce and its aftermath are investigated in Anne Fine's *Madame Doubtfire* (1987) and *Goggle-Eyes* (1989). And families in which parents, and especially fathers, are detrimental to their children's well-being include Louise Fitzhugh's *Nobody's Family is Going to Change* (1974) and Gary Kilworth's *The Brontë Girls* (1995). These are both complex family stories. In Fitzhugh's novel, the father is not physically abusive, but tyrannically insists that his son should find a respectable and lucrative profession rather than becoming the dancer that he himself wants to be, and that his daughter should not become a lawyer, but should find fulfilment in 'womanly' domestic duties. Fitzhugh explains his reasons. He has himself worked hard to establish himself as a member of the black middle class, and does not want his children to undo this work. Willie's wish to dance, his father fears, will only reinforce stereotypes of black people. Emma's desire to be a lawyer is interpreted by her father as a challenge to his authority and as a rebellion against the bourgeois family unit which he has striven so hard to create. *The Brontë Girls*, meanwhile, describes a father's attempts to bring up his family as if they were living in the mid-nineteenth century, 'a time when decent and moral behaviour was considered admirable.'[47] Kilworth's book is a satire on those who claim to want a return to traditional family values, for in fact, James Craster, the father, is a sanctimonious, hypocritical bully, and the family disintegrates. Faced with paternal oppression, one of Mr Craster's daughter contemplates suicide, just as Emma in *Nobody's Family is Going to Change* had been pushed into bulimia. Both novels raise the question of children's rights within the family, and whether children should obey their parents even if their authority has been undermined by cruelty or foolishness.

From a partial survey like this it certainly seems that in post-1960 family fiction 'the greatest shift is that the nuclear family itself has come under scrutiny', as Nikki Gamble has put it.[48] In a paradoxical way, though, these accounts of familial diversity and dysfunction do a great deal to reinforce the attractiveness of the kind of 'normal', nuclear family. Gay and lesbian family stories generally simply replicate standard family structures but with two parents of the same sex, their authors understandably seeking to downplay the difference. As we have already seen, in many accounts of absent parents, the children struggle to create a surrogate family out of their siblings or fellow foster-children (as in Byars' *The Pinballs*). Paterson's *The Great Gilly Hopkins* and Wilson's *The Story of Tracy Beaker* may depict girls made angry by their exclusion from traditional families, but both heroines idolise their absent mothers and are convinced that one day they will return. Even if these dreams do not come true, the nuclear family remains in place as the ideal to which they aspire.

Anne Fine's novels are similarly about broken families and derive their narrative momentum from the process of their reconstruction. *Goggle-Eyes* is about a divorced mother Rosie, her two children Kitty and Jude, and her new lover, Gerald. Kitty calls him 'Goggle-Eyes' because of the way she thinks he ogles her mother, and despises him because he disrupts their comfortable lives. For instance, Gerald is amazed that Rosie pays Kitty for gardening, asking whether Kitty pays her mother for her cooking and cleaning. 'I'm her *mother*', protests Rosie, to which Gerald replies 'You are her *family* . . .. You shouldn't be paying her for cooperation. No one should have to bribe their close relations to pull their weight. It is *disgusting*.' Cooperation is the book's central theme. Each family member might have their own talents and roles, but the family succeeds only by working for each other. What is surprising is that Kitty gradually comes to appreciate Gerald for, of all things, his role as the family's authoritarian patriarch. 'Bossing's no problem for Goggle-Eyes', she reluctantly admits, and she admires his 'Because I say so' attitude to problems like her sister's bedtime, especially when compared with Rosie's equivocation. There is a political subtext to all this too, for Gerald is a Thatcherite small businessman while Rosie is a left-wing peace protestor, two hostile positions in 1989 when *Goggle-Eyes* was published. To admire Gerald's authoritarianism and his strict economy is Fine's endorsement of Thatcherism, while her suggestion that split families can, with due care, be reconstructed in a new but still nuclear configuration is a way of reconciling social realities with the Thatcherite belief in family values. It is, therefore, a neat irony, though perhaps not a deliberate pun, that the most amusing parts of the novel depict antinuclear protests – not against nuclear families, but nuclear weapons. At these demonstrations, the police and the protestors collaborate, the former helping the latter to make symbolic cuts in a wire fence so that a point can be made but serious damage and violence avoided. This cooperation does not blur their different roles, but it does serve everyone's interest. What is true of politics, Fine argues, is true for families too.[49]

Not all family stories written since the 1960s are accounts of dysfunction and its repair. One of the most remarkable is Alan Garner's *The Stone Book Quartet* (1976–78), a very different kind of family story to the others discussed here but offering a profound analysis of the meaning of family. With the first of its constituent parts, *The Stone Book*, set in 1864, and the last (though the second to be published), *Tom Fobble's Day*, in 1941, the quartet is a vertical rather than horizontal family story, a sort of family saga. Garner has called it 'the emotional history of one rural family', and the family is clearly his own, although it is as untrustworthy an autobiography as Wilder's *Little House* books or Alcott's *Little Women*.[50] Each of the four books describes the events of a single day. In *The Stone Book*, Mary is shown a deep cave by her father, a stonemason. There she sees a cave painting depicting the hunt of a bison-like creature. Part of the design, an arrow head, is now her father's mason's mark, she realises. As she looks around, she sees on the cave floor innumerable footprints, of 'boots and shoes and clogs, heels, toes, shallow ones and deep ones, clear and sharp as if made altogether, trampling each other, hundreds pressed in the clay where only a dozen could stand.'[51] When her father tells her that each generation of their family has been taken to see this, just once, while they are small enough to fit through the underground passage, we realise that these footprints belong to her ancestors. The idea of ancestral inheritance sets the theme for the series. The second book, *Granny Reardun*, is about Mary's illegitimate son Joseph realising that he does not want to follow in his grandfather's footsteps as a stonemason, but would rather become a blacksmith. The third, *The Aimer Gate* shows him grown up during the First World War, trying to engage his own son in his interests. And the final book is set on the day Joseph dies, but celebrates his last work, an exceptional sledge made for his grandson William.

It is when exultingly flying down the snow-covered hill on his sledge that William comes to terms with the presence of his ancestors, just as Mary had done in the cave. 'He was not alone', he realises. 'There was a line, and he could feel it. It was a line through hand and eye, block, forge and loom to the hill. He owned them all: and they owned him.'[52] Being owned by one's ancestors is not necessarily oppressive, for the books have shown several deliberate breakings from the past, such as Joseph's joyful decision not to become a stonemason. Neil Philip has even gone so far as to say that *Granny Reardun*, and perhaps the quartet as a whole, speaks 'of the need of each generation to escape the shadow of the last'.[53] But the influence of family is inescapable. Indeed, much of the delight of the quartet is to trace the ways in which Garner dramatises this. His characters, though in different generations, behave the same way and do the same things (eat onions, say). They use the same phrases too. Thus the stonemason, Robert, prophesies that his grandson will say of him that 'he was a bazzil-arsed old devil' but a good builder, and, thirty years later, is the very phrase that Joseph uses to describe him. Even things that one character puts down, another will pick up decades later, like a pipe dropped in *The Stone Book* that resurfaces in *Tom Fobble's Day*, where Joseph finds it and blows through it, as if resuscitating the past.[54] In Garner's world, family is as enduring as the landscape in which the saga is set. Just as each generation of children play on the same hills and live in and about the same buildings, they also steer their own way through a cultural landscape slowly shaped by their forebears. In many ways Garner's understanding of the family is quite unique. But in the way that he presents family as a landscape through which the individual has to plot his or her own course, his work fits snugly into the longer tradition of children's family stories that this chapter has considered.

SUMMARY OF KEY POINTS

- The nuclear family has been the standard setting for children's fiction since the seventeenth century, although from the nineteenth century, family stories have just as often been about sibling-to-sibling as parent-child relationships.
- Most classic family stories are about family fracture, disorder or dysfunction, but generally focus on the reconstruction of the family.
- Even the books about non-traditional families that began to appear in the later twentieth century generally take the nuclear family as the ideal to which children should and do aspire.
- Family stories have often been political, exhibiting the family as the best foundation of empire, for instance, or defending the family against attack from the growing power of the state.

- Families have sometimes been represented as constrictive, especially for girls. But the majority of children's literature has endorsed the relationships between siblings, parents and children, and ancestors and descendents, as more liberating than limiting.

NOTES

1. *From Instruction to Delight: An Anthology of Children's Literature to 1850*, ed. Patricia Demers, 2nd edn (Don Mills, Ontario: Oxford University Press, 2004), pp. 56 and 58.
2. J. M. Barrie, *Peter and Wendy*, ed. Jack Zipes (Harmondsworth: Penguin, [1911] 2004), pp. 29, 27 and 98.
3. See *Family Fictions. Anne Fine, Morris Gleitzman, Jacqueline Wilson and others*, ed. Nicholas Tucker and Nikki Gamble (London: Continuum, 2001).
4. Mary Louisa Molesworth, *Sheila's Mystery* (London: Macmillan, [1895] 1896), pp. 75–6.
5. See Chamutal Noimann, ' "Poke Your Finger into the Soft Round Dough": The Absent Father and Political Reform in Edith Nesbit's *The Railway Children*', *Children's Literature Association Quarterly*, 30 (2005), 368–85.
6. Jan Mark, 'Family Stories', *The Cambridge Guide to Children's Books in English*, ed. Victor Watson (Cambridge: Cambridge University Press, 2001), p. 250.
7. Gillian Avery, *Childhood's Pattern: A Study of the Heroes and Heroines of Children's Fiction 1770–1950* (London: Hodder and Stoughton, 1975), p. 224.
8. John Rowe Townsend, *Written for Children* (London: Pelican, [1965] 1976), pp. 79–80.
9. Arnaud Berquin, trans. Rev. Anthony Meilan, *The Children's Friend*, 8 vols (London: 'Printed for the translator', 1786), vol. 1, pp. 38–40 and 45.
10. Louisa M. Alcott, *Good Wives* (London: Puffin, [1869] 1994), p. 339.
11. Dorothy Kilner, *The Holyday Present* (London: J. Marshall and Co., [1781?] c.1783), pp. 38–42.

12. Sarah Trimmer, *Fabulous Histories* (London: T. Longman and G. G. and J. Robinson, [1786] 1798), p. 69.
13. [Ellinor Fenn], *The Art of Teaching in Sport* (London: John Marshall, [1785?] c.1792), p. 6.
14. Anne K. Mellor, *Mothers of the Nation: Women's Political Writing in England, 1780–1830* (Bloomington, IN: Indiana University Press, [2000] 2002), p. 144.
15. Barbara Hofland, *The Panorama of Europe; or, a New Game of Geography* (London: Minerva Press, 1813), pp. 20–1.
16. Johann Wyss, *The Swiss Family Robinson*, ed. John Seelye (Oxford: Oxford University Press, [1814] 1991), pp. 451–2.
17. Beverley Lyon Clark, *Kiddie Lit. The Cultural Construction of Children's Literature in America* (Baltimore, MD: Johns Hopkins University Press, 2003), p. 105.
18. Ruth K. MacDonald, 'Louisa May Alcott', in *Writers for Children*, ed. Jane M. Bingham (New York: Scribners, 1988), p. 3.
19. Shirley Foster and Judy Simons, *What Katy Read: Feminist Re-Readings of 'Classic' Stories for Girls* (Iowa City, IA: University of Iowa Press, 1995), p. 87.
20. See Janet S. Zehr, 'The Response of Nineteenth-Century Audiences to Louisa May Alcott's Fiction', *American Transcendental Quarterly*, n.s. 1 (1987), 323–42 (p. 325).
21. Alison Lurie, *Boys and Girls Forever: Children's Classics from Cinderella to Harry Potter* (Harmondsworth: Penguin, 2003), p. 13.
22. Gamble, 'Introduction', *Family Fictions*, ed. Tucker and Gamble, p. 13.
23. Gillian Avery, 'The family story', *International Companion Encyclopedia of Children's Literature*, ed. Peter Hunt, 2 vols, 2nd edn (London: Routledge, 2004), vol. 1, pp. 454–66 (pp. 460–1).
24. Louisa M. Alcott, *Little Women* (London: Puffin, [1868] 1994), pp. 33 and 36.
25. Elizabeth Lennox Keyser, ' "The Most Beautiful Things in All the World"? Families in *Little Women*', in *Stories and Society. Children's Literature in its Social Context*, ed. Dennis Butts (Basingstoke: Macmillan, 1992), pp. 50–64 (pp. 53 and 62).

26. Kate Douglas Wiggin, *Rebecca of Sunnybrook Farm* (London: Wordsworth, [1903] 1994), p. 13.
27. Jerry Griswold, *Audacious Kids: Coming of Age in America's Classic Children's Books* (Oxford: Oxford University Press, 1992), p. 73.
28. Gillian Avery, *Nineteenth Century Children: Heroes and Heroines in English Children's Stories 1780–1900* (London: Hodder and Stoughton, 1965), p. 160.
29. Kenneth Grahame, *The Golden Age* (Ware: Wordsworth, [1895] 1995), pp. 1 and 2–3.
30. E. Nesbit, *The Wouldbegoods* (Ware: Wordsworth, [1901] 1995), p. 12.
31. E. Nesbit, *The Story of the Treasure Seekers* (London: Puffin, [1899] 1994), p. 222.
32. Grahame, *The Golden Age*, pp. 3–4.
33. Laura Ingalls Wilder, *Little House on the Prairie* (London: Egmont, [1935] 2000), pp. 1, 80 and 66.
34. Laura Ingalls Wilder, *The Long Winter* (New York: Harper Collins, [1940] 1971), p. 304.
35. Margaret Thatcher, in *Woman's Own* (31 October 1987).
36. William Holtz, *The Ghost in the Little House: A Life of Rose Wilder Lane* (Columbia, MO: University of Missouri Press, 1993).
37. Caroline Fraser, 'The Prairie Queen', *New York Review of Books*, 41 (22 December 1994), pp. 38–44 (p. 44).
38. Wilder, *Little House on the Prairie*, pp. 198 and 169.
39. Suzanne Rhan, 'What Really Happens in the Little Town on the Prairie', *Children's Literature*, 24 (1996), 117–26 (p. 125).
40. Francis Spufford, *The Child that Books Built* (London: Faber and Faber, 2002), p. 135.
41. Wilder, *Little House on the Prairie*, p. 112.
42. Ibid., p. 46.
43. Ibid., pp. 192 and 78.
44. Eve Garnett, *The Family from One End Street* (London: Puffin, [1937] 2004), p. 235.
45. Ibid., pp. 215, 170–1, 194, 222, 20 and 242.
46. Garnett, *Family from One End Street*, pp. 176; Kimberley Reynolds, 'Sociology, Politics, the Family: Children and

Families in Anglo-American Children's Fiction, 1920–60', *Modern Children's Literature: An Introduction*, ed. Kimberley Reynolds (Basingstoke: Palgrave Macmillan, 2005), pp. 23–41 (p. 36).

47. Gary Kilworth, *The Brontë Girls* (London: Methuen, 1995), p. 153.

48. Gamble, 'Introduction', *Family Fictions*, p. 26.

49. Anne Fine, *Google-Eyes* (London: Puffin, [1989] 1990), pp. 59, 105, 79–80 and 90–1.

50. Aidan Chambers, 'An interview with Alan Garner' in *The Signal Approach to Children's Literature* (Harmondsworth: Kestrel, 1980), pp. 276–328 (p. 290). See Charles Butler, *Four British Fantasists: Place and Culture in the Children's Fantasies of Penelope Lively, Alan Garner, Diana Wynne Jones, and Susan Cooper* (Lanham, MD: Scarecrow Press, 2006), pp. 205–6.

51. Alan Garner, *The Stone Book Quartet* (London: Harper, [1976–78] 2006), p. 31.

52. Garner, *Stone Book Quartet*, p. 166.

53. Neil Philip, *A Fine Anger: A Critical Introduction to the work of Alan Garner* (London: Collins, 1981), p. 137.

54. Garner, *Stone Book Quartet*, pp. 63, 102, 20 and 152.

CHAPTER 6

Fantasy

Fantasy is an extensive, amorphous and ambiguous genre, resistant to attempts at quick definition. It can incorporate the serious and the comic, the scary and the whimsical, the moral and the anarchic. It can be 'high' – taking place in alternative worlds – or 'low' – set in the world we know. Or it can combine the two. Besides texts set in other worlds, fantasy includes stories of magic, ghosts, talking animals and superhuman heroes, of time travel, hallucinations and dreams. It overlaps with other major genres, notably the fairy tale and the adventure story, but it intersects also with almost any other kind of children's book: the moral tale in the case of Charles Kingsley's *The Water-Babies* (1863), say, or the school story in the case of J. K. Rowling's *Harry Potter* books (1997–2007). The various forms of fantasy are, as Brian Attebery has put it, 'fuzzy sets, meaning that they are defined not by boundaries but by a center' and 'there may be no single quality that links an entire set'.[1]

But as a concept, fantasy is clearly central to any understanding of children's literature. Some have argued that fantasy is the very core of children's literature, and that children's literature did not properly exist until the imagination had been given an entirely free rein to entertain children in unreservedly fantastical books like Lewis Carroll's *Alice's Adventures in Wonderland* (1865) or Edward Lear's *Nonsense Songs, Stories, Botany, and Alphabets* (1870). Indeed, Wonderland, like Neverland, Narnia, Oz or *Tom's Midnight Garden* in Philippa Pearce's 1958 novel, can be regarded as spatial – or perhaps psychological – representations of childhood, places from which one is exiled as soon as one grows up. But it has also been argued that all children's literature is necessarily a fantasy. In the same way that an author writing about Narnia or Neverland is creating a fantasy world which they imagine but cannot actually inhabit, so all adults writing about childhood are describing a world that they can no longer directly experience. According to this view, influentially set out by Jacqueline Rose in *The Case of Peter Pan or The Impossibility of Children's Fiction* (1984), even the most realistic children's story – an eighteenth-century moral tale, say, or a 'problem novel' in the twentieth – is actually an adult's fantasy of what childhood is, or should be.[2] And then in another sense, it might even be claimed that, because it relates that which has not taken place, all fiction should be understood as fantasy – although most critics have preferred to limit the genre to those texts depicting what *could not* (rather than *did not*) happen. Colin Manlove, for instance, argues that fantasy is 'fiction involving the supernatural or impossible'.[3] This is a workable definition that will serve well for this chapter (although it will be possible to consider only a small proportion of children's fantasy literature), but, like a number of common assumptions about fantasy it is far from unproblematic.

For one thing, the supernatural, the impossible and the unreal are not fixed. Is the bible to be regarded as fantasy fiction because it includes miracles? Is *The Divine Comedy* a fantasy because Hell, Purgatory and Heaven do not exist, or because Dante imagined them in a particular way? Are books about witchcraft fantasy? Certainly the two wicked witches in L. Frank Baum's *The Wonderful Wizard of Oz* (1900), or the schools for spells in Jill Murphy's *The Worst Witch* (1974) or J. K. Rowling's *Harry Potter* series, are improbable. But in early modern Europe and America witchcraft was regarded as a reality, so sixteenth- and seventeenth-century books such as Reginald Scott's *Discoverie of Witchcraft* (1584), or Cotton Mather's *The Wonders of the Invisible World* (1693) about the Salem witch trials, surely cannot be considered as fantasy. In the same way, a Victorian author writing about a human walking on the moon would be a fantasist, but a post-1969 writer would not. In other words, fantasy literature depicts things which are contrary to prevailing ideas of reality, rather than which are incontestably supernatural or impossible. But this is only the first of many complications. What of stories which purport to recount dreams, such as Lewis Carroll's *Alice's Adventures in Wonderland* (1865), John Masefield's *The Box of Delights* (1935), or perhaps Maurice Sendak's *Where the Wild Things Are* (1963)? These may be full of impossible things, but it is not defying reality to describe even the most unrealistic dream. Are such texts fantasy any more than, say, the stream-of-consciousness narratives of James Joyce or Virginia Woolf, which tried to show as realistically as possible a character's waking thoughts? Books about children's imaginary friends are curiously placed too. The eponymous heroine of Helen Cresswell's *Lizzie Dripping* stories (1972–75) imagines that she has a witch for a friend, but it is never quite clear whether the witch is simply a product of Lizzie's notorious mendacity, invented to rile her parents. Are the *Lizzie Dripping* books fantasy fiction, or accounts of a teenager's mischief, or insecurity? It is often very unclear where fantasy and realism begin and end. Rather than being a weakness, this ambiguity is one of the strengths of much good fantasy writing.

What seems particularly misguided is to regard fantasy and realism as mutually exclusive categories. It is surely not the case that all literature can be placed somewhere on a scale with pure fantasy at one end, and pure mimesis (the representation of reality) at the other, so that to increase the level of fantasy is to diminish the level of reality (or vice versa). This interpretation can make sense with texts like the *Alice* books, in which the gradual disintegration of the normal life of a genteel Victorian girl is marked by her encounters with progressively curiouser and curiouser creatures and situations. But it does not take sufficient account of fantasy novels which are just as remarkable for their representation of reality as for their supernatural dimension. One good example, already discussed in Chapters 1 and 5, is Sarah Trimmer's *Fabulous Histories* (1786), an account of a human family and a neighbouring brood of polite, thinking, talking robins. This is an anthropomorphic fantasy, not very dissimilar in some ways from Kenneth Grahame's *The Wind in the Willows* (1908) or E. B. White's *Stuart Little* (1945) or *The Trumpet of the Swan* (1970). But *Fabulous Histories* is also determinedly – some would say dispiritingly

– mundane. The robins do not drive motorcars like Grahame's Toad, nor become celebrity musicians like White's swan. Rather, they live in a nest, eat worms and learn to fly. The human characteristics that they do have are prosaic: a childish impetuousness, say, which they can be educated to overcome. This combination of fantasy and reality was not only popular in the early history of fantasy writing. Richard Adams published *Watership Down* in 1972, and its rabbits, like Trimmer's robins, can think and talk, but never wear clothes, go to market, or lose their identity cards – as Beatrix Potter's Peter Rabbit or Pigling Bland have a tendency to do. Fred Inglis has succinctly characterised this form of fantasy by noting that Adams 'gives rabbits consciousness, which they do not have, but keeps them as rabbits.'[4]

Another, rather different example of a text in which reality over-whelms the fantasy is William Mayne's *Earthfasts* (1966). This begins with the emergence from the ground, in the later twentieth century, of a boy called Nellie Jack John who had entered a cave in search of legendary treasure in 1742. He is befriended by the two heroes of the book, David and Keith. The 'explanation' for this time travel is that while underground, Nellie Jack John had picked up one of the candles burning around the sleeping King Arthur and his knights. Awakening Arthur has brought much disruption: standing stones become marauding giants, ancient boggarts (or house ghosts) revive, and finally, terribly, David disappears. Keith eventually realises that he must replace the candle in order to return Arthur to suspended animation and rescue his friends. Clearly *Earthfasts* is, in some respects, a classic time-slip fantasy. But as unlikely as it may seem from this synopsis, the novel is remarkable more for its depiction of life in a quiet Yorkshire village, and of the relationship between the boys, than for its fantastic elements. David and Keith's friendship is the central theme, Mayne subtly suggest-ing the affection, but also dependence and jealousy, that exists between them. Like Nellie Jack John, they are stolidly realistic in their view of events. Indeed, Mayne uses their practicality to demonstrate how unimportant he thinks it is to make the book's fantastical elements entirely credible. 'It was not possible by ordi-nary standards of thought, for a boy to walk for two hundred years underground, and then come out', David thinks. 'Nor was it possi-ble for two more boys to meet him and talk to him, even fight with him for a moment.' But if 'the only explanation was the impossible one' then there are more important things to worry about:

> 'We've had supper and breakfast,' said David. 'But he hasn't. We'd better find him and take him some.'
> 'It's unreal,' said Keith.
> 'Unreal but actual,' said David. 'It was just like it was. If a thing's happened it's happened.'
> 'It isn't reasonable,' said Keith. 'It's an effect without a cause.'
> 'There's plenty of them,' said David. 'But he's the most orphanist person there ever was, and nobody else knows him. So if he exists, whether he's a cause or an effect, we've still got to do something about him.'[5]

Cradlefasts, a sequel published in 1995, continued to subordinate the fantasy to the representation of David's emotional development, using the time-slip mechanism to allow David to come to terms with the death of his mother and baby sister. What one comes to realise with Mayne's novels is that genre can be very unimportant. His fantasy writing focuses on character far more than either plot or the supernatural apparatus. If this is true for Mayne, it is also true, to a greater or lesser extent, of many of the most well-regarded authors of fantasy fiction such as Joan Aiken, Alan Garner, Susan Cooper, Ursula Le Guin and Philip Pullman.

Mayne's somewhat cavalier attitude to sustaining the integrity of his fantasy settings flies in the face of J. R. R. Tolkien's famous dictum that the author should strive to imagine a fully-formed 'Secondary World' into which the reader can enter:

> Inside it, what he [the author] relates is 'true': it accords with the laws of that world. You therefore believe it, while you are, as it were, inside. The moment disbelief arises, the spell is broken; the magic, or rather art, has failed.[6]

There is no doubt that Tolkien's strategy has worked. The phenomenal success of *The Hobbit* (1937) and *The Lord of the Rings* (1954–55), and the sincere flattery of dozens of imitative secondary-world fantasies, amply prove this. This is success achieved even though some critics have found Tolkien's writing so pompous that it is laughable. 'Very seldom does one encounter emotion this fraudulent and writing this bad in any genre', writes John Goldthwaite.[7] But this is perhaps missing the point. The important thing is that even passages of preposterously high-flown heroics do not break the spell that Tolkien has cast. That readers tolerate, and even approve, such overblown writing is the proof of Tolkien's skill in creating the 'truth' of his world.

But Tolkien was surely not quite right about when and why fantasy fails, at least not for all fantasy writing. In his extremely successful 'Discworld' series (from 1983) Terry Pratchett deliberately destabilises the feasibility of his creation. The world is flat and travels through space on the backs of four elephants, who themselves stand on a giant turtle. Although drawing on Indian mythology, this is a cosmology intended to be risible. Similarly, most of his characters and places have absurd names, designed to amuse rather than convince, and he delights in building plots by comically twisting well-known stories. In *The Amazing Maurice and His Educated Rodents* (2001) a troupe of rats works a scam based on the traditional story of the Pied Piper of Hamelin, and it is a rat called 'Dangerous Beans' who eventually saves the town of Bad Blintz from the real danger they uncover. Pratchett's kind of comic, self-ironising and referential fantasy is part of a long tradition. 'Uncle David's Nonsensical Story about Giants and Fairies' in Catherine Sinclair's *Holiday House* (1839) is similar, with the giant Snap-'em-up described as so tall that he 'was obliged to climb up a ladder to comb his own hair', boiling his kettle on Mount Vesuvius, and making tea in a large lake.[8] Just as deliberately absurd is W. M. Thackeray's *The Rose and the Ring* (1854), beginning with Valoroso XXIV, King of Paflagonia, becoming so engrossed in a letter from Prince Bulbo, heir to the throne of Crim Tartary, that he allows his 'eggs to get cold, and leaves his august muffins untasted.'[9] In late twentieth-century children's books, this whimsicality is understood as postmodern irony. Diana Wynne Jones' *Howl's Moving Castle* (1986) is archly set in a land 'where such things as seven-league boots and cloaks of invisibility really exist'. It takes for its heroine Sophie, who complains that she is the eldest of three children because 'Everyone knows you are the one who will fail first, and worst, if the three of you set out to seek your fortunes.'[10] Tolkien's dictum applies even less to what has been called 'low fantasy', in which the magic intrudes into normal life. P. L. Travers, for example, did little to maintain the credibility of *Mary Poppins* (1934), creating a world in which statues and characters from books can come alive, where children can grow and shrink, where the animals in the zoo mysteriously find themselves free and the visitors caged, where gingerbread stars are pasted into the sky. The magic is almost entirely random and, annoyingly to some critics, inconsistent in scale, sometimes affecting only the children, sometimes changing the entire world.

What all these examples suggest is that the supernatural and the normal exist together in fantasy texts, in various proportions and combinations, but that there is no ratio which governs their relationship. To increase one is not to diminish the other. Alison Lurie has noted that William Mayne's writing is often 'in the tradition of [Jorge Luis] Borges or [Gabriel] Garcia Marquez', and their kind of magic realist writing is a case in point, depicting events which are beyond belief but also doggedly realistic.[11] Science fiction operates on a similar principle, but almost exactly the other way around. If magic realists revel in the impossibility of the things they show, goading readers into accepting them in spite of their better judgment, science fiction writers delight in the plausibility of their fantasies, daring their readers to disbelieve things which have been made to seem almost true. Thus, Jules Verne's stories, such as *Journey to the Centre of the Earth* (1864) or *From Earth to the Moon Direct* (1873), are often utterly fantastical, at least in their original nineteenth-century context, but rely for their effect on an underlying viability. Preparations for the journey into the earth are meticulously specified. The voyage to the moon is described in great technical detail (remarkably similar to the actual landings of the late twentieth century). *Twenty Thousand Leagues Under the Sea* (1873) was based on voyages really being undertaken by a French experimental submarine – just as Richard Adams closely based *Watership Down* on R. M. Lockley's scientific study *The Private Life of the Rabbit* (1964). These works offer an endorsement of Tolkien's view, that the reader's conviction must be maintained. The critic Tzvetan Todorov agreed, using the issue of credibility to distinguish between fantasy and the literature of the 'marvellous'. In the latter, he argued, the reader simply accepts that supernatural events are taking place and does nothing to try to explain them. In successful fantasy, Todorov argued, there is almost always some attempt to understand and explain the strangeness and, right up until its conclusion, the reader often cannot quite decide whether the events being described are natural or supernatural.[12]

In children's fantasy writing this uncertainty is often personified in the text by a leading character, who represents the readers and their responses to the strangeness. In Penelope Lively's *The Ghost of Thomas Kempe* (1973), for example, ten-year-old James Harrison only gradually comes to realise and accept that the mysterious occurrences taking place in his new home are caused by a poltergeist. We readers are also initially unsure, despite the book's giveaway title, and we sympathise with James as he tries to find rational explanations for the ghost's interventions in his life. Similarly, in secondary world fantasies, even if child protagonists often display a surprising *sang-froid* when they suddenly arrive in the new world, their willingness to suspend disbelief helps to bridge the gap between misgiving and conviction for the reader too. In C. S. Lewis' *The Lion, the Witch and the Wardrobe* (1950), Lucy Pevensie, then later her other siblings, act as the reader's representatives in Narnia, vicariously exploring and interpreting. They conduct us through this world, mediating our encounters with the fantastic until we become acclimatised to the weirdness. (Lewis's concern that readers would be mystified or shocked by his fantasy world explains his insistence, against all advice, that the recognisable, benign figure of Father Christmas should feature in *The Lion, the Witch and the Wardrobe*.[13]) Tolkien used the same strategy in *The Hobbit*, carefully mediating the reader's reactions to dwarfs, elves, goblins, a wizard and a dragon through the responses of an equally surprised, safe and familiar pseudo-child, Bilbo Baggins. Equally, in his two *Alice* books (1865 and 1871), Lewis Carroll relied on the normality and common sense of Alice to give the reader some kind of perspective on the bizarre creatures he had invented. Without her, Wonderland would surely be not intriguing and amusing, but absurd and tiresome. Her curiosity, concern or impatience, and her struggle to make sense of what she finds, makes what would otherwise be baffling twaddle into captivating nonsense.

However, in some of the best fantasy fiction the protagonist exploring the fantasy world on our behalf is not wholly to be trusted. Alice gives a very partial impression of the people she meets in Wonderland, mediated by her social prejudices and her rather prim and pretentious character. Likewise, it is one of the successes of *The Hobbit* that Bilbo, and through him the reader, is gradually forced to reassess initial character judgments. The dwarfs, for example, begin as jolly scamps in coloured hoods who might have wandered in from Walt Disney's *Snow White and the Seven Dwarfs*, released in the same year as *The Hobbit*. But it is Bilbo's gradual reassessment of their character and motives that transforms them into the much grimmer, almost Wagnerian desperadoes of the novel's close. Those who guide the protagonists can be untrustworthy too. The Cheshire Cat is famously unfathomable, but Peter Pan is actually deliberately misleading as an explainer of the customs of Neverland and the ways of the world. Trying to persuade Wendy about the faithlessness of adults, he lies, unforgivably, about having been forgotten and replaced by his mother.[14] Farah Mendlesohn has commended the work of Dianna Wynne Jones because it 'continually asks us to consider the reliability of whoever is offering to guide us through the dark woods'.[15] This is disorientating for the reader – as if Gandalf, Hagrid or Mrs Doasyouwouldbedoneby had turned out to be self-serving and deceitful impostors.

Some fantasy novels turn all this on its head. In Mayne's *Earthfasts*, or Lively's *Ghost of Thomas Kempe*, it is boys from 'our world' (although still fictional of course) who have to help visitors from the past adapt to their new surroundings. Similarly, in Philip Pullman's *His Dark Materials* trilogy, the 'real' world is introduced only in the second volume, *The Subtle Knife* (1997). When Lyra, the self-assured heroine of the first volume, enters 'our' Oxford she suddenly loses all her savvy and confidence and has to be guided by Will. The first thing that happens to her is that she is knocked down by a car. She finds herself 'a lost little girl in a strange world' and is mystified by all that she sees: 'What could those red and green lights mean at the corner of the road? It was all much harder to read than the alethiometer.'[16] This kind of de-familiarisation can be comic. It is also part of a long tradition of satirical texts (the most famous of which is Montesquieu's *Persian Letters* of 1721) which purport to describe the travels of a foreigner, describing his bemusement at customs and habits which the reader takes for granted, and thus bringing them into question. Transferring this technique to fantasy fiction can be just as comical and just as satirical, but it also helps to draw attention to the arbitrariness of a distinction between fantasy and reality. An excellent example is *Howl's Moving Castle*, in which Diana Wynne Jones takes her characters from the magical land of Ingary to a contemporary, and rainy, Wales. Narrated from Sophie's Ingarrian point of view, Wales is a strange place. People wear tight blue clothes on their legs which force them to walk 'in a kind of tight strut'. In the house they visit, ironically called 'Rivendell' after the 'Last Homely House' in *The Hobbit*, people watch 'magic coloured pictures moving on the front of a big, square box' and can hardly be distracted from what only the reader recognises as computer games. The trip to Wales strengthens Jones' characterisation of the wizard Howl as an ordinary teenage boy. In Wales he is called Howell, a common name, and he is bullied by his sister, which explains his dread of confrontation even in Ingary where he is a powerful wizard. But when he gives his nephews a new computer game that is set 'in an enchanted castle with four doors' each opening on a different dimension – just like his own Moving Castle in Ingary – the reader is forced to consider that one person's fantasy is another's reality, that they are relative terms, not opposites, but different ways of looking at the same thing.[17]

Alan Garner's *Elidor* (1965) provides one of the best examples of a novel in which the divide between reality and fantasy is disintegrating. Four children, a little like the Pevensies, enter a fantasy world and take back with them four 'Treasures'. If these are kept safe, Elidor will be saved from the 'Darkness' that has cursed it. But the rest of the novel is concerned with the attempts of the enemies of Elidor to break through into the Watson children's world to take back the Treasures. Garner's success is in showing how the 'real' and fantasy world lie on top of each other, touching at certain points. The wasteland of Elidor maps precisely onto the derelict Manchester of the Watson children, with its bombed-out buildings and half-demolished slums. There are places where the two worlds touch, explains Malebron, their guide in Elidor, especially those which have been 'battered by war' and where 'the land around quakes with destruction': the slums of Manchester and the war-torn castles of Elidor.[18] In *The Lion, the Witch and the Wardrobe*, the touching point is more mundane: a wardrobe (although made from a Narnian tree, as Lewis explained in his 'prequel', *The Magician's Nephew*). But in another way, the parallelism of the two worlds is even more striking than in *Elidor*. The Pevensie children have been evacuated from London to avoid the air-raids of World War Two, but, as Maria Tatar has pointed out, they 'end up fighting the war by proxy against the armies of the White Witch', until, as Lewis gleefully puts it, 'all that foul brood was stamped out'. They then bring peace and prosperity to post-war Narnia through their wise and benign rule.[19] Five years after the end of the Second World War, Lewis's fantasy was celebrating a victory over tyranny and his hopes for reconstruction. He was also showing how impossible it is to exclude children from conflict, for the Pevensies find their own way to fight. Fantasy, we find, is not an escape from reality but, often, a rewriting of it.

Indeed, even if fantasy writing is, by definition, generally disengaged from reality, it is often easy to discern its entanglement in the ideological controversies of its day. This may be, of course, because fantasy so readily invites symbolic readings. Writing during the political crisis caused by the French Revolution in 1790s Britain, for instance, the radical Thomas Spence argued that 'the stories of enormous and tyrannical giants, dwelling in strong castles, which have been thought fabulous, may reasonably be looked upon as disguised truths, and to have been invented as just satires on great lords'.[20] Some modern critics' exercises in contextualisation can seem even more fanciful, notably attempts to read every detail of the *Alice* books as a comment on late-Victorian politics and society.[21] Yet there can be little doubt that Kingsley's *The Water-Babies* (1863) was a response to on *The Origin of Species* (1859) – an attack on those who unthinkingly denounced Darwin's theories.[22] Equally apparent are the political resonances of the many children's science fiction fantasies published during the Cold War. Robert O'Brien's *Z for Zachariah* (1975), set after a nuclear holocaust, and Jean Ure's *Plague 99* (1989), about an almost equally destructive pandemic, are clearly reflective of anxieties about an imminent apocalypse.

But it is not much more difficult to read the classic 'high fantasies' politically. Both Lewis's *Narniad* and Tolkien's *The Hobbit* advance a particular political economy, fundamentally that developed in the later nineteenth century by proto-socialist thinkers like John Ruskin and William Morris (themselves both authors of fantasy fiction). By the time Tolkien and Lewis were writing, this was a more paradoxical position, conservative in its contempt for the values of industrialised modernity, its casual snobbishness, its traditionalist pietism and its advocacy of autocratic leadership, but hostile to the gross inequalities of unfettered capitalism and concerned with the values of ordinary people, especially the artisan. These contradictions run through *The Hobbit*. The Trolls are mocked and derided for their plebeian names ('Bill Huggins'), Cockney slang ('lumme'), vulgar appetites (beer) and supposedly working-class attitudes (querulousness; an inability to look beyond the present). The Goblins are characterised as a brutal industrial proletariat making 'no beautiful things' but efficiently mass-producing 'Hammers, axes, swords, daggers, pickaxes, tongs' (some of these, one notes, featuring on the Soviet flag). Yet Tolkien equally attacks the rich: not only dragons' pointless and unproductive hoarding ('they hardly know a good bit of work from a bad, though they usually have a good notion of the current market value') but also those leaders who 'have a good head for business' but are 'no good when anything serious happens'. The men of Esgaroth depose these 'old men and the money-counters', crowning the belligerent Bard as their king in place of the non-monarchical 'Master'. In doing so they reveal a reactionary, authoritarian and perhaps even slightly fascistic tendency in Tolkien's fantasy.[23] With its simultaneously anti-socialist and anti-capitalist agenda, it might be said that Tolkien was trying to steer a middle way between the main clashing ideologies of the late 1930s, but it might be noted that the politics of *The Hobbit* are not, in some ways, so very far removed from the rhetoric of Nazism.

The politics of gender in *The Hobbit* are also extremely intriguing. It is very notable that *The Hobbit* contains no living female characters. This might, in itself, be indicative of a desire on the author's part to make Middle Earth a sort of pre-Lapsarian Eden, free, like Narnia, from the complications of sex. But it might also be part of what one critic calls Tolkien's 'subtle contempt and hostility towards women'.[24] Yet it must be clear to any reader with an eye for psychological detail that one of the most important characters in *The Hobbit* is Bilbo's dead mother, Belladonna Took, introduced right at the start of the novel. It is she who has bequeathed to Bilbo 'something not entirely hobbitlike': a thirst for adventure. Once we notice this, it is difficult not to conclude that Bilbo's real quest is to please his absent mother.[25] In any case, the novel is hardly a celebration of machismo. Some of the most influential characters exhibit what might be thought of as 'female' characteristics: Gandalf and Beorn are both nurturing, even maternal figures. And ultimately Bilbo does not triumph because of any 'manly' accomplishment, but because he relinquishes any pretensions to honour or soldierly loyalty, sacrificing his own interests rather than sticking to a destructive desire for profit or prestige. At the novel's close he is congratulated for domestic virtues: 'If more of us valued food and cheer and song above hoarded gold,' says Thorin Oakenshield with the wisdom of one on his deathbed, 'it would be a merrier world.'[26] Of course it would still be a stretch to regard *The Hobbit* as a feminist text, but Tolkien's decision to erase the feminine does raise some interesting questions about the role of gender in high fantasy more generally. Low fantasy fiction written for children in the nineteenth and early twentieth centuries had been written about girls as much as boys: Carroll's Alice, Barrie's Wendy and Baum's Dorothy amongst many others. Tolkien's decision to exile women from Middle Earth seems like a deliberate attempt to masculinise the genre, especially since the sorts of text that he took as a model had included female characters in important roles, the Anglo-Saxon epic *Beowulf* for example. High fantasy of the sort that Tolkien pioneered was cast as a masculine genre right from the start.

It has taken decades for this to change. Female protagonists may have become more common – like Sabriel and Lirael in Garth Nix's 'Old Kingdom' series ('Abhorsen' in the USA, 1995–2003). But what Ursula Le Guin calls 'the intense conservatism of traditional fantasy' based on 'the establishment or validation of manhood' has remained firmly in place. This can be seen from Le Guin's own work, and her reflections on it. In her early fantasy fiction, she came to realise, she 'was writing by the rules', employing an essentially masculinist paradigm. In the first three Earthsea novels (1968–72), she acknowledged, 'the fundamental power, magic, belongs to men; only to men; only to men who have no sexual contact with women.'[27] They follow the story of a male magician Ged, and were, by any standard, extremely successful (as well as being, in some ways, politically radical, for Ged was black). But when Le Guin came to add to the series with *Tehanu* in 1990, followed by *Tales from Earthsea* and *The Other Wind* in 2001, she used the opportunity to recreate her imagined world from a feminist perspective. Not only did she make her central characters female, but she 'reinvented the past', as Perry Nodelman has put it, to show that magic had once been practiced by women, that the forces of patriarchy had later combined to deny them this power, and that Ged's own magic derived from an 'unauthorised' female teacher.[28] Le Guin sought to show how males had appropriated magic in Earthsea, how this had caused social and spiritual corruption, and how the damage could be repaired by the less aggressive behaviour of Tehanu, whose magic aims at reconciliation rather than dominion. But of course this feminised, feminist revision provides another demonstration of the ways in which fantasy has been adapted to suit changing social and cultural values. As Le Guin put it, 'even in Fairyland there is no escape from politics.'[29]

If it is a misapprehension that fantasy is not political, so it is also wrong-headed to imagine that fantasy writing is always liberating in a way that other genres are not. Fantasy does, of course, allow the reader to enter worlds where normal laws and limits do not apply. Harry Potter is clearly liberated by removal from his dreary and disciplined life in Privet Drive to the magical world of Hogwarts. Readers enjoy Rowling's books, it is often said, precisely because they are not like humdrum life. In particular it has been suggested that they have been popular because they offer a change from realistic, issue-based fiction that, some say, is imposed on unwilling children by adults who think they know what is best. But fantasy is seldom actually very anarchic. Hogwarts, like most schools in children's literature, is a very regulated world: disciplined, rule-bound and hierarchically ordered. High fantasy too is generally very structured. It tends to abound in authority figures who impose order, the benign but dictatorial Aslan in the *Narniad* being a classic example. And most authors are careful to ensure that their protagonists (and thereby their readers) always know exactly what they are doing in the fantasy world. In *The Lion, the Witch and the Wardrobe* it is notable that the Pevensie children are not much disorientated by their arrival in Narnia. This is partly because of their trusting nature, but also because they so obviously have a purpose there. The prophesy explained to them by Mr Beaver, but alluded to by Mr Tumnus almost as soon as Lucy first steps into Narnia, leaves little room to doubt the children's trajectory:

> 'Down at Cair Paravel – that's the castle on the sea coast down at the mouth of this river which ought to be the capital of the whole country if all was as it should be – down at Cair Paravel there are four thrones and it's a saying in Narnia time out of mind that when two Sons of Adam and two Daughters of Eve sit in those four thrones, then it will be the end not only of the White Witch's reign but of her life, and that is why we had to be so cautious as we came along, for if she knew about you four, your lives wouldn't be worth a shake of my whiskers!'[30]

This use of a prophecy that must be fulfilled is a common motif in fantasy writing. In *Edidor* the Watsons are even shown a book by Malabron which contains a picture of them, as well as the usual prophetic verses.[31] It is, perhaps, a hangover from the medieval quest narratives which influenced much fantasy fiction. But it is also a means by which the fantasy world can be ordered. In Russell Hoban's *The Mouse and His Child* (1969) there is both a quest and a prophecy. The Child, welded to his father because together they form a clockwork toy, wants to find a home and a mother, as well as to become 'self-winding'. Hoban emphasises the quest element by introducing a frog toward the beginning who pretends to read the mice's fortune. He is as surprised as anyone when a true spirit of prophecy mysteriously overcomes him and he divines that 'The enemy you flee at the beginning awaits you at the end.' 'That isn't much to look forward to', says the Mouse, rightly, but his Child, and the reader, take a sense of direction from the prediction.[32] Prophecy and quest mean that readers are likely to be less bewildered by the weird fantasy world Hoban has created. Alice's progress along the chessboard, culminating in her inevitable coronation as a queen, imposes the same kind of order in Carroll's *Through the Looking Glass*. Some authors deliberately play with this prophesy motif. In *Howl's Moving Castle*, Diana Wynne Jones introduces a witch's curse in Ingary which orders the fate of the novel's lead characters, but turns out actually to be a photocopied homework exercise which has somehow been carried through from 'our' world. A prophesised narrative structure can be constricting. In *The Lion, the Witch and the Wardrobe* the Pevensies' destiny is set out for them, and the only anxiety is whether Edmund will be brought round to join his siblings on the four thrones. In *His Dark Materials*, Philip Pullman seems to be reacting against the lack of free-will in Narnia. Lyra and Will (his name is far from insignificant) are continually having to make their own choices. It is noticeable that, unlike the Pevensies, Harry Potter, or the return of the king in *The Lord of the Rings*, their coming is not foretold, although the fate of the world hangs on it.

We get the impression that Narnia has been waiting for the Pevensie children, as Sleeping Beauty's palace has been waiting for the Prince. If Narnia has not quite been in a state of suspended animation, then it has certainly been gripped by an endless winter, with all the unnatural stasis and sterility this implies, until the children's arrival brings renewal. Indeed, in the majority of parallel-world writing we find that the world revolves around the protagonists. This is not to say that they remain stationary while the world around them is transformed, although this does sometimes seem to be the case, as in Catherine Storr's *Marianne Dreams* (1958), an account of the adventures in a dream-world created by the heroine's doodles with a magic pencil while she is confined in a sick-bed. Rather, in books like *The Lion, the Witch and the Wardrobe*, we get the impression that the fantasy world lacks an independent existence, that it has only been created for the benefit of the central characters. Carroll's *Alice* books provide another example. The Mad Hatter's tea party might have been going on before Alice arrives, and the tarts might have been stolen out of her sight, but we nevertheless get the impression that Wonderland and the Looking-Glass world exist for Alice's benefit, and almost that the inhabitants are on standby until Alice appears to interview them. We might call this 'Ptolemaic' fantasy, the world revolving around the protagonist as Ptolemy thought the sun, stars and planets revolved around the

Earth. But some fantasies are more 'Copernican', with the protagonist often disoriented, travelling through a fixed universe, as Copernicus realised the Earth revolved around the sun.

Lucy Boston's *The Children of Green Knowe* (1954) is one such text. The past inhabitants of a house called Green Knowe blithely continue to live their unchanging lives, as ghosts of a sort, while the at first mystified protagonist, Tolly, slowly learns about their history and is occasionally able to see them and join in with their games. Kingsley's *The Water-Babies* is similar. Tom, a chimney-sweep, is transformed – into an 'Eft' – which means that he can begin a new, clean life in an aquatic world which was always there, but hidden (though what Kingsley does not make immediately clear is that Tom has in fact drowned, and that his existence as a Water-Baby is his afterlife). In this kind of 'Copernican' fantasy, the protagonists are generally powerless and shy in the fantasy world. In 'Ptolemaic' fantasies, child characters become powerful and important figures, although in their real worlds they have been weak. In Garner's *Elidor*, Roland is the youngest and feeblest of the siblings, but 'Here, in Elidor,' he is told by Malebron, 'you are stronger', and discovering this, he leads his siblings in their quest.[33] For Roland, as for Harry Potter, Lyra Silvertongue, Bilbo Baggins and the Pevensies (especially Lucy), all of whom are subordinate in their home worlds, no less than the fate of the world rests on their shoulders once they enter the fantasy.

Another common assumption about fantasy writing is that it represents the antithesis of the didactic tradition in children's literature. Many histories of children's books make this case, arguing that in the late eighteenth and early nineteenth centuries, delight and instruction were at war within children's texts, fantasy eventually, and inevitably, triumphing.[34] This paradigm can be collapsed in at least two ways. First, many early didactic texts were often couched as fantasies. Sarah Trimmer's *Fabulous Histories* (1786) and Dorothy Kilner's *The Life and Perambulations of a Mouse* (1784) are good examples. Eighteenth-century secondary world fantasies exist too, most famously Swift's *Gulliver's Travels* (1726), which came to be read by children soon after its publication. Alternative worlds are also to be found in some very early texts that were always intended for the young, such as *The Prettiest Book for Children; Being the*

History of the Enchanted Castle; Situated in One of the Fortunate Isles, and Governed by Giant Instruction (1770). The description provided by 'Don Stephen Bunyano' focuses almost entirely on the educational opportunities that the Giant Instruction wisely provides there, but the Fortunate Isles are part of the tradition that would lead to Charles Kingsley's St. Brendan's Isle in *The Water-Babies*, J. M. Barrie's Neverland or the archipelago of islands in Le Guin's Earthsea series.

Second, didacticism has consistently remained at the heart of children's fantasy writing. The ground-breaking fantasies of the 1860s and 1870s certainly had not lost their determination to teach. It is difficult to imagine a more preachy text than *The Water-Babies*, which uses the medium of fantasy to attack spiritual corruption as well as the more worldly scandal of child chimney-sweeps. Mrs Bedonebyasyoudid represents the spirit of the Old Testament, and Mrs Doasyouwouldbedoneby the New. Mother Carey and the little girl Ellie play other parts in this theological masquerade, allowing Tom, eventually, to find his way to Heaven by going to the Other-end-of-Nowhere – that is to say, Hell – to save his old master, Grimes. The novel reads rather like a medieval morality play. George MacDonald's novels expound similar social and spiritual teachings. *At the Back of the North Wind* (1871) combines accounts of the harsh lives of the poor, like Nanny, a destitute crossing-sweeper, with an allegorical representation of salvation. In *The Lion, the Witch and the Wardrobe* the didacticism is even clearer. Edmund transgresses, giving way to greed, selfishness and spite, and is punished by the cruelty of the White Witch and being denied a Christmas present. This, it has been pointed out, is the sort of morality that a child can easily understand and might wish for: no tedious moral lectures nor long drawn-out process of repentance, but clear punishment, quick confession, and a swift readmission to the good graces of those he has wronged. His sins are completely forgotten by the time he takes up his place as one of the monarchs of Narnia.[35]

Other fantasy novels teach more sophisticated lessons. In Anne Barrett's *Caterpillar Hall* (1950), for instance, a magic umbrella allows Penelope to see the moments from other people's childhoods when they wanted something as badly as she wanted the umbrella. Their frustrated desires explain why they have become the adults they are – strict, sad, wistful, angry – and Penelope cannot help but empathise. The didacticism of *The Hobbit* is less ostentatious but equally central to the story. Suddenly taking a more serious turn, the novel ends with Bilbo stealing the prized Arkenstone from his dwarf companions, or rather appropriating it as his share of the treasure, and passing it to the dwarfs' enemies so that it can be used as a bargaining chip in the brokering of a treaty. Read as a fable, the moral is about the importance of overcoming avarice and selfishness, perhaps even selfhood. This goes some way to answering the question archly raised by the narrator at the very start of the novel: Bilbo 'may have lost the neighbours' respect, but he gained – well, you will see'. He gains much from the adventure, including the ring that would feature so prominently in the Tolkien's further account of Middle Earth's history, but it is how he changes as a person that the narrator was surely referring to. 'You are not the hobbit that you once were', Gandalf tells him at the end of the novel.[36] What Bilbo has acquired is a stronger sense of his identity, the knowledge that he can survive outside the comfort of his home, and a life of creativity and fulfilment instead of timidity and torpor. Ultimately, *The Hobbit* is more a novel of personal development, or *Bildungsroman*, than a straightforward fantasy quest narrative. Even Carroll's *Alice* books, often regarded as the books in which unhampered fantasy finally triumphed over the instructive tendency, can be regarded as didactic in this way. There may be no religious allegory, nor social realism, and it would be reductive to suggest that Carroll had intended only to write a *Bildungsroman*, but Alice does return from Wonderland wiser, and more aware of her own identity, than she was. At the start of her adventure she is downright insensitive. Meeting a mouse, the first thing that comes into Alice's mind as a fit subject for conversation is her cat, Dinah, 'such a capital one for catching mice'. She repeats the same mistake several times, but slowly learns to be more empathetic. By the time she is being told by the Mock Turtle about whiting (a kind of fish), she has at least come to realise that she must watch what she says: 'I've often seen them at dinn—', she says, checking herself just in time (leaving the Mock Turtle to wonder where Dinn actually is).[37]

More obvious is Carroll's representation of his heroine's psychological development. From the fall down the rabbit-hole, which might easily be understood as a kind of birth, Alice grows steadily in Wonderland, her adventures paralleling a child's gradual maturation. Her first encounters are with small, cute creatures – rabbits and mice – but progressively she meets more frightening adults: the Duchess, the Hatter, the Queen. These are not the safe, pleasant interactions of the nursery. Nor do these new acquaintances help Alice much, but rather challenge her. They are competitive, capricious, selfish and deceitful. Increasingly, she is confronted with all sorts of 'adult' concerns too: anger, fear, nostalgia, death, judgment. These encounters shape Alice's sense of self, which she had wrongly thought of as set and stable. She comes to doubt herself, and to develop – in size, but also psychologically. Indeed, the books can be understood as a quest for identity. In *Through the Looking Glass*, Alice advances until she reaches psychic fulfilment as a queen. In Wonderland, she keeps growing and shrinking until she finds out what her right size is. The text is dominated by questions of identity. Having grown enormously, she loses the certainty that she and her body are one, considering sending a letter to 'Alice's Right Foot, Esq.' – a male form of address, we note. Later, she seriously wonders if she is actually Ada or Mabel. It is the Caterpillar who confronts her most bluntly about this. 'Who are *you?*' he quizzes. Alice cannot answer, saying that she was one thing when she got up, but 'I think I must have been changed several times since then'. For the caterpillar, presumably later to metamorphose into a moth or butterfly, such transformation is natural. For Alice it is a source of great anxiety, manifested when the Wood Pigeon asks why it should matter whether she is a little girl or a serpent: ' "It matters a good deal to me," said Alice hastily'.[38]

If Alice is gaining a sense of self, she is also learning other vital lessons about the rules of life, and more particularly, their dismaying inconstancy. The Queen's croquet game (or the Caucus Race, or Lobster Quadrille) is incomprehensible to Alice, apparently without rules. But everyone else seems to understand. As is often pointed out, this replicates the way that many aspects of the adult world might appear to a child encountering them for the first time. Alice longs for rules, but is constantly disappointed. She believes she knows how tea parties should be conducted, but the Mad Hatter shows she cannot be so sure. She is proud of knowing how judicial trials work, but the Wonderland court works on principles that she cannot fathom. Only the Cheshire Cat seems to acknowledge that there are no rules and one can never fully make sense of what is happening. The Alice books are not didactic in a conventional sense, but like other *Bildungsromans*, by dramatising some of the difficulties of interacting with the adult world, they do offer the reader an oblique education, and comment on, if they do not quite help with, the construction of a stable identity.

Fantasy is extremely well suited to consideration of questions of identity. The journey to another world, or another time, de-contextualises the protagonists, removing them from the structures that locate and bind them into a particular role within the family, the school, or the larger society. They then have to discover afresh who they are, and, usually, can return to their reality at the end of the novel with a stronger sense of themselves. Perhaps this helps to explain why children's fantasy has become increasingly prevalent. Quite apart from the many satisfactions it offers to the readers, authors find the form eminently suitable for the transmission of lessons on selfhood, these being regarded now as the best kind of instruction that good children's literature can and should teach. Identity exchange fantasies, such as F. Anstey's *Vice Versa; or, A Lesson to Fathers* (1882) or Mary Rogers' *Freaky Friday* (1972), show this clearly. In the former a haughty businessman and his schoolboy son find themselves inhabiting one another's bodies; in the latter, a teenager is metamorphosed into her mother. By the end of the novels, the characters have gained a cross-generational empathy and a stronger sense of their own identity. The same questions of selfhood are explored more directly in Penelope Farmer's *Charlotte Sometimes* (1969), in which a 1960s schoolgirl is somehow transported back and forth between her own time and the period of the First World War, where everybody knows her as a girl called Clare. Unsurprisingly, Charlotte finds it increasingly difficult to cling to her own identity. She has to discover what it is that makes her Charlotte, and not Clare. Less schizophrenic, but no less disconcerting, is Jones's *Howl's Moving Castle*, in which the young heroine Sophie is magically aged. She prematurely learns a great deal about life as an old woman, but she also comes to accept that, even as a girl, she possesses many of the characteristics that she will have when old. The reader finds, from Sophie's experience, that the child is already the adult that he or she will become. The search for one's mature identity is central to Philip Pullman's *His Dark Materials* too. Children's demons change shape, but settle into a fixed form when they reach adulthood. The trilogy concludes when Lyra and Will's demons finally settle, symbolising the same realisation of identity that forms the denouement of many other children's fantasy novels.

The relationship between childhood and adulthood is a related theme, often central to fantasy fiction and particularly time-slip novels. Philippa Pearce wrote that she 'wanted to explore that almost unimaginable concept of adults having once been children', and to do so devised *Tom's Midnight Garden* (1958).[39] Its eponymous hero is a lonely child on the verge of adulthood who has been sent away to live with his strict aunt and uncle. He finds that, every night, he can visit a garden that no longer exists. There, he finds solace in the friendship of a Victorian girl called Hattie. Only right at the end of the novel does he discover that the old woman who lives upstairs from his aunt and uncle is in fact Hattie, now grown up. *Tom's Midnight Garden* is an entrancing and gripping novel and it would be quite unfair to call it a didactic text, but it was clearly constructed to tutor its readers. Each time Tom returns to the garden he finds Hattie at a different age. When, finally, he returns to find that Hattie has grown up, he is devastated, but slowly he learns to reconcile himself to the loss, or rather to accept that people develop and change. The lesson applies directly to Tom too, for we understand that his unhappiness was the result of an unwillingness to accept change in his own life. As well as showing that the old were once young, Pearce teaches young readers that they cannot hold onto childhood forever. The book serves equally well to teach adult readers that they cannot forever treat their sons and daughters as children. All things change, Pearce shows, but just as Hattie, however old, will always be Hattie, and just as the house to which Tom has moved will always retain traces of its former inhabitants, so identity remains secure despite external alteration.

Perry Nodelman has noted that 'children's literature is frequently about coming to terms with a world one does not understand – the world as defined and governed by grownups and not totally familiar or comprehensible to children'.[40] Good fantasy literature dramatises this experience, transporting its characters into a past time or new world where all is strange and perplexing. Perhaps this mirroring of their own daily experience helps to explain why children relish fantasy so much. Or perhaps it is because in a new world where nobody knows the rules, children are not placed at a competitive disadvantage, and consequently feel the equal of adults in a way that they do not in their real lives. In certain time-slip novels, when a figure from the past is propelled into their lives, these children become, relatively speaking, figures of knowledge and authority. This is certainly the case in Lively's *The Ghost of Thomas Kempe* or Mayne's *Earthfasts*. In other fantasies, where the children are sent into the past, or another dimension, they are equally significant, fêted because of their exoticism, or honoured and empowered because, like the Pevensies in Narnia, they find themselves to be somehow vital to the well-being of the world. This fantasy of empowerment is central to the appeal of fantasy writing to children. But the genre has appealed to the adults who write it surely at least in part because it can so easily be adapted to provide lessons of all kinds, moral, political, practical and psychological.

SUMMARY OF KEY POINTS

- No children's books are pure fantasy, but combine fanciful and realistic elements. To increase the amount of fantasy is not to diminish the reality, nor vice versa. Fantasy has often been used to satirise or rewrite reality.
- Most fantasy writing is not completely anarchic, but presents carefully structured alterative realities which are usually controlled by strict rules.
- Fantasy can be both empowering or disorientating for protagonists and readers.
- The process of self-discovery, and questions about how identity remains fixed despite external change, are central to much good fantasy writing.
- Fantasy has always included, and continues to include, didactic elements.

NOTES

1. Brian Attebery, *Strategies of Fantasy* (Bloomington, IN: Indiana University Press, 1992), pp. 12–13.
2. Jacqueline Rose, *The Case of Peter Pan or The Impossibility of Children's Fiction* (London: Macmillan, 1984).
3. Colin Manlove, *The Fantasy Literature of England* (Basingstoke: Macmillan, 1999), p. 3. For wider discussions see Eric S. Rabkin, *The Fantastic in Literature* (Princeton: Princeton University Press, 1976), Rosemary Jackson, *Fantasy: The Literature of Subversion* (London: Methuen, 1984), Kathryn Hume, *Fantasy and Mimesis: Responses to Reality in Western Literature* (New York: Methuen, 1984), Lucie Armitt, *Theorising the Fantastic* (London: Arnold, 1996) and Peter Hunt and Millicent Lenz, *Alternative Worlds in Fantasy Fiction* (London: Continuum, 2001), pp. 1–41.
4. Fred Inglis, *The Promise of Happiness: Value and Meaning in Children's Fiction* (Cambridge: Cambridge University Press, 1981), p. 208.
5. William Mayne, *Earthfasts* (London: Hodder, [1966] 1995), pp. 25 and 27–8.
6. J. R. R. Tolkien, 'On Fairy-stories', *The Tolkien Reader* (New York: Balantine, [1947] 1966), p. 37.
7. John Goldthwaite, *The Natural History of Make-Believe: A Guide to the Principal Works of Britain, Europe, and America* (New York: Oxford University Press, 1996), p. 218.
8. Catherine Sinclair, *Holiday House* (London: Hamish Hamilton, [1839] 1972), p. 127.
9. W. M. Thackeray, *The Rose and the Ring or the History of Prince Giglio and Prince Bulbo* (London: John Murray, [1854] 1909), p. 1.
10. Diana Wynne Jones, *Howl's Moving Castle* (London: Harper Collins, [1986] 2005), p. 9.
11. Alison Lurie, 'William Mayne', in *Children and their Books: A Celebration of the Work of Iona and Peter Opie*, ed. Gillian Avery and Julia Briggs (Oxford: Clarendon Press, 1989), pp. 368–79 (p. 375).
12. Tzvetan Todorov, *The Fantastic: A Structural Approach to a Literary Genre*, trans. Richard Howard (Ithaca, NY: Cornell University Press, [1970] 1975), pp. 41–2.

13. A. N. Wilson, *C. S. Lewis: A Biography* (London: Collins, 1990), p. 221.
14. J. M. Barrie, *Peter and Wendy*, ed. Jack Zipes (London: Penguin, [1911] 2004), p. 98.
15. Farah Mendlesohn, *Diana Wynne Jones: Children's Literature and the Fantastic Tradition* (New York: Routledge, 2005), p. 90.
16. Philip Pullman, *The Subtle Knife* (London: Scholastic, [1997] 1998), pp. 68, 73 and 77.
17. Jones, *Howl's Moving Castle*, pp. 146–7, 148–9 and 151; J. R. R. Tolkien, *The Hobbit* (London: Collins, [1937] 1998), p. 64.
18. Alan Garner, *Elidor* (London: HarperCollins, [1965] 2002), p. 54.
19. C. S. Lewis, *The Magician's Nephew* (London: Collins, [1955] 1980), p. 219, and *The Lion, the Witch and the Wardrobe* (London: Grafton, [1950] 2002), p. 166. Maria Tatar, ' "Appointed Journeys": Growing Up with War Stories', in *Under Fire: Childhood in the Shadow of War*, ed. Elizabeth Goodenough and Andrea Immel (Detroit, MI: Wayne State University Press, 2008), pp. 237–50 (p. 243).
20. Thomas Spence, *Pigs' Meat; or, Lessons for the Swinish Multitude*, 2 vols (London: T. Spence, c.1795), vol. 2, p. 209.
21. See Jo Elwyn Jones and J. Francis Gladstone, *The Red King's Dream, or Lewis Carroll in Wonderland* (London: Jonathan Cape, 1995).
22. See also Rose Lovell-Smith, 'Eggs and Serpents: Natural History Reference in Lewis Carroll's Scene of Alice and the Pigeon', *Children's Literature*, 35 (2007), 27–53.
23. Tolkien, *The Hobbit*, pp. 51–4, 84, 37–8 and 302–3.
24. In Tolkien's work, Catharine R. Stimpson argues, women 'are either beautiful and distant, simply distant, or simply simple' and in *The Lord of the Rings*, she adds, there is outright misogyny, as when a 'jubilant, exultant Tolkien tells how Sam forces Shelob [a monstrous spider that Stimpson identifies as a 'bitch-castrator'] . . . to impale herself, somewhere in the region of the womb, on his little knife.' *J. R. R. Tolkien* (New York: Columbia University Press, 1969), pp. 18–19.
25. Tolkien, *The Hobbit*, p. 13. See William H. Green, ' "Where's mama?" The construction of the feminine in *The Hobbit*', *The Lion and the Unicorn*, 22 (1998), 188–95.

26. Tolkien, *The Hobbit*, p. 346.
27. Le Guin, *Earthsea Revisioned* (Cambridge: Green Bay, 1993), pp. 8, 5, 7 and 9.
28. Perry Nodelman, 'Reinventing the Past: Gender in Ursula K. Le Guin's *Tehanu* and the Earthsea "Trilogy"', *Children's Literature in Education*, 23 (1995), 179–201. See also Laura B. Comoletti and Michael D. C. Prout, 'How They Do Things with Words: Language, Power, Gender, and the Priestly Wizards of Ursula K. Le Guin's Earthsea Books,' *Children's Literature*, 29 (2001), 113–41.
29. Le Guin, *Earthsea Revisioned*, p. 7.
30. Lewis, *The Lion, the Witch and the Wardrobe*, p. 77.
31. Garner, *Elidor*, p. 56.
32. Russell Hoban, *The Mouse and His Child* (London: Faber & Faber, [1969] 2005), p. 26.
33. Garner, *Elidor*, p. 48.
34. See Geoffrey Summerfield's *Fantasy and Reason: Children's Literature in the Eighteenth Century* (London: Methuen, 1984).
35. Doris T. Myers, *C. S. Lewis in Context* (Kent, OH: Kent State University Press, 1994), p. 132.
36. Tolkien, *The Hobbit*, pp. 12 and 361.
37. Lewis Carroll, *Alice in Wonderland*, ed. Donald J. Grey (New York: W. W. Norton, [1865 and 1871] 1992), pp. 18, 26 and 80.
38. Carroll, *Alice in Wonderland*, pp. 14, 15, 35 and 43.
39. Obituary of Phillipa Pearce, *The Daily Telegraph*, 27 December 2006.
40. Nodelman, 'Some Presumptuous Generalizations About Fantasy', in *Only Connect: Readings on Children's Literature*, ed. Sheila Egoff *et al.*, 3rd edn (Toronto: Oxford University Press, 1996), pp. 175–8 (p. 178).

CHAPTER 7

The Adventure Story

It is hard to pin down precisely what distinguishes the adventure story from other kinds of writing for children. There are many classic texts which seem straightforwardly to fit the description. Daniel Defoe's *Robinson Crusoe* (1719) and Jonathan Swift's *Gulliver's Travels* (1726) are often seen as forerunners. Historical novels in the vein of Sir Walter Scott became popular with children in the nineteenth century – Frederick Marryat's *Children of the New Forest* (1847), for instance, or, in America, the 'Leather-Stocking Tales' by James Fenimore Cooper, culminating in *The Last of the Mohicans* (1826). High Victorian tales of quests and hazards like Jules Verne's *Twenty Thousand Leagues Under the Sea* (1873) or Henry Rider Haggard's *King Solomon's Mines* (1885) might be regarded as characteristic of the genre. Or perhaps only those novels placing children, not adults, at the centre of events can be regarded as truly archetypical: Robert Louis Stevenson's *Treasure Island* (1883), say. Some adventures seem playful, other deadly serious. Arthur Ransome's *Swallows and Amazons* (1930), however exciting, is essentially an elaborate game. At around the same time the Hardy Boys (from 1927), Nancy Drew (from 1930) and Enid Blyton's Famous Five and Secret Seven (from 1942 and 1949) were unmasking hardened villains and solving serious crimes – although these are hardly 'hard-boiled' thrillers. In novels like Ian Serraillier's *The Silver Sword* (1956) or Anne Holm's *I Am David* (1963), with their protagonists on the run from persecution, the stakes are much higher and the tension much more taut. More recent adventure stories vary in tone in complex ways. Anthony Horowitz's *Stormbreaker* (2000) and Charlie Higson's *Silverfin* (2005) may be all-action thrillers set in the world of international espionage, but they are as fantastical, if not quite as comic or camp, as the James Bond films that inspired them. There is very little to joke about in Robert Cormier's *After the First Death* (1979) or Peter Dickinson's *The Seventh Raven* (1981), in which international terrorism provides the adventure. Often in children's books the narrators provide retrospective accounts of events, so the excitement does not come from knowing whether they live or die, but from discovering how they have coped with their traumatic experiences.

What even this short list demonstrates is that the boundaries of the children's adventure story are very blurred. Many of these books were first intended for an adult audience. Some deliberately sought a cross-over readership of adults and children: *King Solomon's Mines*, for example, was dedicated 'to all the big and little boys who read it'.[1] Others were abridged for younger readers. *Robinson Crusoe*, for instance, has been one of the most frequently rewritten of all books, pirated abridged editions appearing within the year of its first publication. Editions designed especially for children were being produced by the 1760s, although children had no doubt been reading chapbook versions much earlier. The thousand-plus pages of its three volumes were sometimes reduced to as few as eight pages.[2] As for *Gulliver's Travels*, the versions designed for children, whether by publishers or film-makers, have easily supplanted Swift's original: the cute and comical Lilliputians remain in the public imagination, sometimes with the gross and oafish Brobdingnagians, but the absurdism of book three, and the misanthropy of the Yahoo and Houyhnhnm section, together with the satirical intent of the whole, have routinely been discarded.[3] Another blurred boundary is the line between fiction and reality. If Defoe and Swift provided ersatz travellers' tales, other adventures stories were (more or less) true. In the nineteenth century, descriptions of the expeditions of James Cook and Mungo Park, and later David Livingstone and Henry Stanley, were marketed for children. These accounts could be extremely exciting, especially once they were abridged. Adventure novels like *King Solomon's Mines* and

Verne's *Journey to the Centre of the Earth* (1864), based around the fragmentary maps left by previous explorers and describing expeditions across *terra incognita*, clearly owed a great deal to these non-fictional texts. The line between adventure stories and history books is similarly indistinct. Even without any blatant fictionalisation, biographical accounts of Alexander the Great, William Tell, Dick Turpin, Admiral Nelson, Florence Nightingale or Anne Frank could provide as much adventure as any wholly imagined narrative. Biblical stories and classical myths were also doubtless read as adventures, and continue to be so: Hercules, Odysseus, Samson, David and Goliath.

In fact, it is open to question whether adventure is a distinct and demarcated literary genre at all. Few texts can be regarded as *only* adventure. The adventure in *Swallows and Amazons* animates a fairly traditional family story for instance. Likewise, Serraillier's *The Silver Sword*, Holm's *I Am David* and Beverley Naidoo's *The Other Side of Truth* (2000) are first and foremost refugee stories, dealing with the horror of war and repressive states and concomitant issues of fear, freedom and identity. The adventure, it might be said, simply provides the frame. Adventure enlivens most children's historical novels too, but in the best examples, it remains subordinate to the skilful recreation of the historical period, and the other concerns of the author. In early children's historical novels, authors used adventure to teach history, as is made clear by the title of Barbara Hofland's *Adelaide; or, the Intrepid Daughter: a Tale, Including Historical Anecdotes of Henry the Great and the Massacre of St. Bartholomew* (1822). Isaac Taylor's *Scenes in Africa* (1821) was more overtly didactic in intent, much of the text taking the form of conversations between a child and an instructor, just as if they are in the classroom. But the lessons are inserted in an exciting narrative in which the child and his teacher are captured by pirates, sold into slavery and then freed by the Emperor of Morocco to continue their educational journey around Africa.[4] This didactic dimension of children's adventure stories has never entirely faded. G. A. Henty claimed that 'any one who has read with care the story of *The Young Buglers*', his novel of 1880, 'could pass an examination as to the leading events of the Peninsular war.'[5] The historical accuracy of his novels was always promoted by his publishers as a major selling point.[6] In the twentieth century authors were making similar claims about the veracity, and therefore educational potential, of their novels. In a postscript to her novel describing the birth of printing in England, *The Load of Unicorn* (1959), Cynthia Harnett admitted her account was '*only* a story', but, pointing out her meticulous research, hoped that there was not 'too much "fiction" '.[7]

Historical fiction has also been tailored to fit other agendas. In Mark Twain's *The Prince and the Pauper* (1882), the young King Edward VI learns how the poor live when he is mistakenly driven from the royal court, although it is the story of how he reclaims the throne that probably interests the reader more. In *Bows Against the Barons* (1934), Geoffrey Trease used the Robin Hood stories to preach a sort of chivalric communism. 'We're comrades in Sherwood, all equal', Robin tells the sixteen-year-old hero, Dickon, recruiting him join a rebellion against the rich and powerful oppressors.[8] 'It is a constantly shifting and changing story that holds one all the way, with its adventures and strange peoples and places', the distinguished historical novelist Rosemary Sutcliff has noted, writing of Henry Treece's experimental novel of life in Neolithic Europe, *The Dream-Time* (1967). But the adventure is generally the vehicle for the novel's other concerns, in this case 'a plea for people to get to know each other and care about each other more; for peace instead of war, making instead of breaking.'[9] The adventure story, it might be argued, is not really a genre at all, but rather a sort of flavour or colouring, used to give an appealing taste or appearance to works with other agendas.

One other very blurred boundary is between adventure stories and fantasy fiction. J. R. R. Tolkien's *The Hobbit* (1937), C. S. Lewis's Narnia books (1950–56), Philip Pullman's *His Dark Materials* (1995–2000), not to mention many fairy stories, both traditional and modern, are all tales of adventure. But in another sense too, almost all adventure stories are fantasies. The children's adventure story typically takes for its protagonists figures who are unimportant in their normal lives. They are usually on the margins of the community, neglected and often victimised – like Cinderella, or the waif-like Lyra in *His Dark Materials*, or the fatherless boys of Stevenson's *Kidnapped* or *Treasure Island*. Even if it is only because they are children (or simply small, as in the case of Bilbo Baggins), these protagonists, before they begin their adventures, are identified as powerless and dependent. The narrative then suddenly places these characters right at the centre of important events. They have to encounter great dangers and to make momentous choices. A great deal often hinges on their success or failure, not only for them themselves, but for those around them, and sometimes society as a whole. Essentially, the adventure story is a fantasy of empowerment. It makes the marginal and insignificant character central and crucial. The reader vicariously shares this thrill of aggrandisement. Subordinate and dependent in their real lives, children reading these books are invited to imagine themselves as influential and important. The adventure story is the imaginary fulfilment of the wish to be significant.

A classic example of this is the widely popular child detective sub-genre, exemplified in the American *Nancy Drew* and *Hardy Boys* books, the *Tintin* comic strips by the Belgian 'Hergé' (from 1930) and Erich Kästner's *Emil and the Detectives*, published in Germany in 1929. In Britain, the most popular examples are probably the twenty-one novels of Enid Blyton's *Famous Five* series, although others, such as C. Day Lewis's *The Otterbury Incident* (1949), are much more critically well-regarded. Blyton's five – Julian, Dick, Anne and Georgina ('George'), and a dog, Timmy – are ordinary enough, and holiday in ordinary enough places. In each of the books, though, they are catapulted into importance by their discovery of sinister plots which only they can foil. In triumphing over the criminals they assert their equality with, or actually superiority to, adults. They often become the dominant figures in their own families, frequently rescuing Quentin (George's father, the uncle of the other children). This fantasy of empowerment takes on a national dimension too. The left-wing Erich Kästner had certainly understood the collaboration of righteous children against depraved adults as political. In his account of the formation of a gang of twenty-four Berlin children, some rich, some poor, to recover the money stolen from him, Kästner created an optimistic parable about the power of youth to regenerate a corrupt society. Due to its immense popularity the book was not burned by the Nazis, as were some others Kästner had written, but nor was it reprinted, and attentive readers in Germany and abroad might well have understood it as an anti-Nazi document.[10] For their part, just like Emil's 'detectives' or many a superhero, the Famous Five are also the defenders of society, engaged in a continual fight against injustice. More specifically, it should be noted that Blyton's series began in 1942, during the darkest days of the Second World War. With its chief character sharing the name of England's patron saint, it is easy to see how the series appealed to child readers by providing them with a fantasy of their own centrality to the fight against the nation's enemies. The books could give children a sense that, metaphorically, they too were joining the war effort.

The detective story is just one classification of adventure, but most others, in different ways, can also be said to appeal to the child's desire for consequentiality.[11] 'Hunted Man' adventures, such as Stevenson's *Kidnapped* and Holm's *I Am David*, or, for an older audience, John Buchan's *The Thirty-Nine Steps* (1915), dramatise this desire most clearly. The hunted children may often be unwitting and powerless victims, but the relentlessness of their pursuers shows just how significant these children actually are. Likewise, in children's historical novels, the young protagonists frequently find themselves playing pivotal roles in great events. In Susan Cooper's *Victory* (2006), the fictional Samuel Robbins is pressed into naval service as a ship's boy and finds himself being rescued by Admiral Nelson and later present at Nelson's death at the Battle of Trafalgar. In 'Wanderer' stories, such as Verne's novels, the central protagonists establish their significance by visiting places and witnessing events that few, if any, have seen before.

Similarly, in what are often called 'Robinsonnades', the species of adventure novels derived from *Robinson Crusoe*, the castaways are of necessity at the centre of all the action. In most early examples, like *The Swiss Family Robinson* (1812–13) begun by Johann David Wyss, or Marryat's *Masterman Ready* (1841–42), children were marooned along with their parents. But by the mid-nineteenth century, child characters found themselves alone on their desert islands. Here, through heroic acts and tremendous feats of endurance, they were able to assert their credentials as worthy and preternaturally mature heroes. R. M. Ballantyne's *The Coral Island* (1858), for instance, closes with a 'native' chief telling Jack Martin, 'Young friend, you have seen few years but your head is old. Your heart also is large and brave' – an affirmation of maturity and importance that Jack (and the reader) would have valued highly. Indeed, when the chief continues that 'We, who live in these islands of the sea, know that Christians always act thus' and 'we hope many more will come', Jack becomes not only a child capable of survival away from civilisation, and not merely a missionary (like the rather dull ones he encounters on the island), but a kind of apostle, personifying both the religion that will enlighten the world and the righteousness of empire.[12]

In some fantasy adventures this wish-fulfilment of significance is taken to even greater lengths. The child protagonist becomes not merely an evangelist, but a Messiah. At the beginning of C. S. Lewis's *The Lion, the Witch and the Wardrobe*, for example, the four Pevensie children are neglected and frequently admonished, but once through the wardrobe, they find that Narnia revolves around them. Four thrones wait for them there, and it is the success or failure of their actions which will determine the fate of the entire kingdom. Only they can end the eternal winter and redeem creation. Lyra and Will in Philip Pullman's *His Dark Materials* have equal cosmic significance, becoming the new Adam and new Eve. But what is fascinating is the way in which the imbalance between children's everyday powerlessness and the power that they obtain in these adventures is represented and resolved. In Susan Cooper's *The Dark is Rising* series, for instance, her heroes are young boys, but paradoxically they are also amongst the 'Old Ones', destined to lead the eternal fight against the forces of Darkness. Cooper's depiction of the impossible duality of their situation, having to behave like children in front of their parents but simultaneously defeat the rising Dark, can be almost comical. In *The Dark is Rising* (1973) the eleven-year-old Will Stanton knows he must get to the Manor, but his parents are unwilling to brave the blizzard to get there. Despite being the only one who can break the power of the Dark, Will is compelled to resort to childish pleading and sulking to persuade his father to let him go. Only when this fails does he reveal his power to the mysterious 'Walker' who is sheltering with the family, frightening him into convulsions so that Will's parents have to consent to taking him to the Manor for treatment.[13] At all costs, it seems, he must retain his childish powerlessness in front of his parents, while simultaneously fulfilling his Messianic destiny. From the reader's point of view, this two-facedness is important in maintaining their fantasy of empowerment. Like Will, they need to reconcile the comforts of childish dependence with the desire to imagine themselves more important and endangered than they seem. Cooper is very successful at depicting this tension. In the first novel in the series, *Over Sea, Under Stone* (1965), just as he is about to find the Grail which will help to keep the Dark at bay, Barney Drew hears voices inside his head:

> Who are you to intrude here, the voice seemed to whisper; one small boy, prying into something that is so much bigger than he can understand, that has remained undisturbed for so many years? Go away, go back where you are safe, leave such ancient things alone . . .[14]

Cooper is dramatising Barney's longing for the insignificance and childishness which he had formerly resented. She shows her protagonists coming to terms with unaccustomed power, caught between their longing to control events, and their doubts that, after all, they are only children. Tolkien's Frodo, Pullman's Lyra and Stevenson's Jim Hawkins experience the same doubts.

The preservation of the ordinary childishness of heroes and heroines engaged on really very remarkable adventures is important for another reason too: it helps to allow readers to envision themselves as possible participants in the adventure. Nina Bawden began her novel *On the Run* (1964) by trying to establish the ordinariness of the origins of her adventure, and in doing so provides what might be read as an adventure-writer's manifesto:

> There are two things to remember about adventures. They always happen when you are not expecting anything to happen and the beginning is usually quite unexciting and ordinary so that you seldom realize that something important has begun. Adventure always creeps up on you from behind.[15]

Many authors have gone to great lengths to establish the possibility, or even likelihood, of adventure. C. Day Lewis began *The*

Otterbury Incident, for example, by having George, the narrator, muse on the beginnings of the story that would end with him and his friends bringing a gang of crooks to justice. 'Suppose I say it all began when Nick broke the classroom window with his football', he starts, but quickly wonders if this only happened because they were fighting against another gang of boys, or because they had been playing at being soldiers before that. This discussion of the mundane origins of the adventure, and of the impossibility of saying when it started, is supposed to show that it might have happened to anyone. When he concludes that the adventure could not have happened 'if there hadn't been a real war and a stray bomb hadn't fallen in the middle of Otterbury' the intention is surely to universalise the events even further, to make George and his friends the representatives of any and all children who had lived through the Blitz, and to establish the War itself as the ultimate adventure, the Otterbury incident being merely an outcrop of something that had united the nation in one great escapade.[16] In a way, Peter Pan's announcement that 'To die would be an awfully big adventure' makes the same point: that adventure does not happen only to a few lucky characters in novels, but to all.[17] Peter has it the wrong way round though, for ultimately everyone is part of the same great adventure: life.

Children's authors and publishers had not always sought to give the impression that ordinary children could easily find themselves embroiled in adventure. Even if the popular literature that children sometimes read in the eighteenth century was full of daring deeds, the books published especially for them then seem designed to minimise the appeal and likelihood of adventure. Chapbook versions of *Robinson Crusoe* portrayed him as a lone figure active and armed against the perils of his hostile island, for instance, but versions especially for children focused much more on the domestic elements of his story. Their illustrations tend to show Crusoe sitting at his table, with his pots neatly arranged around him, his garden cleared and separated from the jungle, and his guns hung up unused on the wall of his hut. The ending of these children's editions was often rewritten so that Crusoe regretted deserting his parents and causing them grief.[18] Similarly, despite the fact that Britain was at war for much of the eighteenth century and that many children were actively engaged in these conflicts at home and even in the military, children's books dealing with warfare tended to emphasise its horrors, not its excitement. Even during the age of Nelson and Napoleon, books like William Francis Sullivan's *Pleasant Stories; or, The Histories of Ben, the Sailor, and Ned, the Soldier* (c.1818) were carefully designed to dampen boys' martial ardour. It begins with the return to his family of an ex-serviceman who warns his nephews not be to be so foolish as to enter the armed forces. They ignore his advice, but their own hardships, punishments and wounds soon convince them that he was right.[19]

By the nineteenth century, the age of the classic adventure story, any reluctance to embrace adventure was generally held to be cowardly, or 'muffish'. 'There are three distinct classes of boys', says Ralph, authoritatively, in Ballantyne's *The Gorilla Hunters* (1861), 'namely, muffs, sensible fellows, and boasters'. In order to become a 'sensible fellow', Ralph explains, it is important for boys to be 'inured from childhood to trifling risks and light dangers of every possible description, such as tumbling into ponds and off trees'. Boys 'ought never to hesitate to cross a stream on a narrow unsafe plank *for fear of a ducking*' nor 'to decline to climb up a tree to pull fruit merely because there is a *possibility* of their falling off and breaking their necks.' This reasoning 'applies to some extent to girls as well', Ralph concludes, for all children should 'encounter all kinds of risks, in order to prepare them to meet and grapple with the risks and dangers incident to man's career with cool, cautious self-possession', whether it be fighting off a furious leopard or 'being set on fire by means of crinoline'.[20] Ballantyne's philosophy of adventure stands in stark contrast to the ethos of the cautionary and moral tales of eighteenth and early nineteenth centuries. Many of these had been designed specifically to dissuade children from climbing trees or crossing streams on narrow, unsafe planks.

Yet the dominance of the moral tale form had never removed all adventure from children's literature. Despite being pilloried by some as the very antithesis of excitement, morality could certainly co-exist with adventure. A good example is the story of Thomas Two-Shoes. In *The History of Goody Two-Shoes* (1765), perhaps the most famous of the eighteenth-century moral tales, Margery (nicknamed 'Goody') is a poor orphan who learns to read, becomes a teacher, brings harmony to her village, and ends happy and rich having married the local magnate. Early on in the book Goody is separated from her brother Tommy who is sent off to sea. He returns at the end of the story, having made his fortune. Most eighteenth-century editions of *Goody Two-Shoes* contained a short appendix, outlining how Tommy had become so wealthy. His story had the tone of a chapbook tale. He was castaway 'on that part of the coast of *Africa* inhabited by the *Hottentots*', where he found a mysterious book 'which the *Hottentots* did not understand, and which gave him some Account of *Prester John's* Country'. He tames a lion and sets out to explore, ending up in the Land of Utopia. Here he finds a statue, with an inscription revealing that on May Day morning the statue's head will turn to gold. Finding it does not do so, he solves the riddle by digging where the shadow of the statue's head falls, and finds the hidden treasure of an ancient philosopher.[21]

Several writers took this rather scanty account as an invitation to write a fuller sequel, but in it is an 1818 version that most interestingly puts flesh on the bare bones of the original story. The author, Mary Belson Elliott, was concerned with the continuity of her sequel, taking pains to account for Thomas being called 'Two-Shoes' and scrupulously explaining why Goody and Tommy could not correspond during their adventures. She expanded the story substantially too, sending Tommy to the West Indies, where he becomes involved in a slave insurrection, and only then describing how Tommy himself becomes enslaved in Africa. Tommy earns his freedom by exposing a plot being hatched by other slaves to assassinate their owner. This echoes events in Jamaica earlier in the novel, when his life had been preserved only because a slave called 'Black George' had betrayed a plot to murder the island's white population. Both Black George and Tommy triumph over what Elliott suggests is their self-interest in wanting to be free, preferring at all costs to preserve peace and prevent bloodshed, and to trust in God for their delivery from slavery. The biggest change, though, is in the way Tommy acquires his fortune. For Elliott, solving a riddle and discovering hidden treasure was either too preposterous or insufficiently edifying. Her Tommy becomes rich by honest trade, as well as receiving a legacy from the friend whose life he had saved by betraying the conspiracy. Elliott, in a word, has moralised the tale. She even ends the book with 'a slight account of the places named in this history' for those readers who 'may not have studied Geography'. Yet this has by no means eliminated the adventure. Her 67-page narrative encompasses, amongst much else, the persecution of its hero by a cruel sea captain, a slave rebellion, a night of terror being held prisoner at gun-point, a ship-wreck, capture by Algerine pirates, six years in slavery in Tunis, and a comic interlude during which Thomas cures a canary's broken leg by attaching a prosthetic limb.[22] Predating all of James Fenimore Cooper's and Frederick Marryat's novels, Elliott's *Adventures of Thomas Two-Shoes* has a claim to be considered one of the very first modern children's adventure novels, even if it also clearly displays the author's didactic, Quaker impulses.

Certainly *The Adventures of Thomas Two-Shoes* fulfils many of the criteria of the genre as it was to develop during its nineteenth-century heyday. It has a characteristic setting, a characteristic hero, and a characteristic plot. These elements can be quite straightforwardly elaborated, even though the best adventure stories are generally those which interestingly and provocatively diverge from the usual formula. For one thing, most classic adventure stories share an exotic setting. Elliott's *The Adventures of Thomas Two-Shoes* took the reader from Britain to the Caribbean and Africa then back again. Desert islands and polar wastes would prove popular, as would subterranean and, later, extraterrestrial destinations. If set in Britain, the adventures often take place on the margins – Cornwall, Wales, the Highlands of Scotland. If set in America, the adventures most often occur just beyond the western frontier, as in Barbara Hofland's early Texan story *The Stolen Boy* (1830), or innumerable Westerns, or Laura Ingalls Wilder's *Little House* books (from 1932). Equally, the exoticism could be provided by historical remoteness. At first, Henty tended to set his adventures during the military campaigns of the eighteenth and early nineteenth centuries: *The Young Buglers: a Tale of the Peninsular War* (1880) or *The Cornet of Horse: a Tale of Marlborough's Wars* (1881). Increasingly he began to delve further into ancient history to find more alien locations: *The Young Carthaginian: a Story of the Times of Hannibal* (1887), *For the Temple: a Tale of the Fall of Jerusalem* (1888) and *The Cat of Bubastes: a Tale of Ancient Egypt* (1889). He exposed his readers to the exoticism of working-class life too in books such as *Facing Death: The Hero of the Vaughan Pit – A Tale of the Coal Mines* (1882) and *Through the Fray: A Tale of the Luddite Riots* (1886). The same 'historical remove' tactic has since been endlessly employed. In many cases it is fair to say, as Kirsten Drotner has alleged of S. Bracebridge Hemyng's 'Penny Dreadful' adventure stories about Jack Harkaway, that these changes of historical or geographical locations are simply changes of scenery, while the central characters, and the author's preoccupations, remain largely unchanged.[23] Henty for one is guilty as charged, his unpretentious, plucky, honourable boy heroes remaining very much alike wherever they are to be found, and his concern to advance a particular idea of Britishness consistently being in view. His preface to *Beric the Briton: a Story of the Roman Invasion* (1893), for instance, reminded his readers that they were descended from 'the valiant warriors who fought so bravely against Caesar' that he was depicting, and linked Boadicea's revolt against 'the oppressive rule of Rome' with Britain's nineteenth-century imperial mission.[24] Rosemary Sutcliff's more sophisticated historical adventure *Outcast* (1955) also features a boy called Beric, but Sutcliff took great pains to describe life in Roman Britain and fastidiously emphasised its differences from her own era. Her story is concerned primarily with Beric's ostracism. Born a Roman, but orphaned in a shipwreck, Beric is taken in by a Celtic tribe, but is later expelled and ends up as a slave on a Roman galley. His personal tragedy becomes an emblem of the destructiveness of tribal groupings, quite opposite from the happy story of ethnic assimilation and nation-building presented by Henty.

The most accomplished historical novelists are true to their period in another way too, developing a style which matches their subject. Leon Garfield's novels depicting the adventures of children in the mid-eighteenth century seem stylistically to be very like the picaresque novels first published then. The opening of Garfield's *Jack Holborn* (1964) clearly shows the debt to Tobias Smollett's *Roderick Random* (1748) or Henry Fielding's *The History of Tom Jones, A Foundling* (1749):

My story must begin when I boarded the *Charming Molly* at Bristol. Before that there's little to tell. My name is Jack, surnamed 'Holborn' after the parish where I was found: for I had neither father nor mother who'd cared enough to leave me a name of my own.[25]

Henry Treece's novel of the Neolithic era, *The Dream-Time* (1967), was more experimental, written in 'very short and simple words' since his characters 'were so near the beginning that they can have had only the fewest and simplest of words with which to talk to each other and share their thoughts and feelings and ideas'.[26] This was taking the exoticism of the adventure story to new heights, defamiliarising the language of the novel, as well as its location.

The characteristic plots of the adventure story are as conventional as the exoticism of its settings, and can be taxonomised in much the same way that Vladimir Propp set out the fundamental narrative units of fairy tales in *Morphology of the Folktale* (1928). Most stories start with a domestic crisis of some kind which means that the protagonists have to leave the security of their home. This is generally followed by a minor adventure, during which they prove their worth, and then the opening up of the quest which will provide the main excitement for the rest of the novel. This quest is generally structured as a series of more minor crises which culminate in the completion of the mission: finding the treasure, solving the crime, freeing the hostage, returning home, and so on. Protagonists are usually either born with, or come into possession of, a special asset which helps them: a special skill, a clever pet, a weapon. Sometimes it is this asset which establishes the quest, like Jim Hawkins' map in *Treasure Island*. Generally the protagonists are not quite alone, being accompanied by a faithful companion. This figure can be a surrogate parent, like Jacob Armitage in Marryat's *Children of the New Forest*, who helps the orphaned children to become self-sufficient once they have been 'marooned' in their secret hideaway deep in the forest. More interesting are ambiguous figures who both teach and terrorise the children at the centre of the adventure, guarding and threatening in equal measure. One classic example is J. M. Barrie's Peter Pan; another is Long John Silver in Robert Louis Stevenson's *Treasure Island*. According to the conventional adventure tale structure Silver should be the villain of the novel, whom Jim Hawkins must overcome if he is to succeed in his quest. Certainly Silver terrifies Jim, and is murderous, treacherous and selfish. But, in what Dennis Butts calls 'the greatest irony in the book' they also become like father and son, Silver looking after Jim, and Jim ardently admiring Silver.[27] In this respect *Treasure Island* causes readers more confusion, but is perhaps ultimately more satisfying, than another of Stevenson's split-personality novels, *The Strange Case of Dr Jekyll and Mr Hyde* (1886), for Silver is both Jekyll and Hyde at once, needing no potion to transform him. Jim recognises both sides to himself too, and as Stevenson's narrative shuttles him backwards and forwards between the mutineers and the loyalists, he finds himself wanting to remain faithful to his respectable friends Squire Trelawney and Captain Smollett but also strongly drawn to the pirate life.

In modern and contemporary adventure stories this classic plot structure has been amended in some interesting ways. Robert Cormier's *After the First Death* (1979), for instance, is a gripping and complex account of a terrorist hijacking of a bus full of school-children which pits its three focalising characters in conflict with one another. Sixteen-year-old Miro is elated with the prospect of making his first kill – the bus-driver – and thereby announcing his manhood to Artkin, the leader of the terrorist cell. The plan is con-fused when it turns out that the bus is being driven by Kate, a young woman, unexpectedly substituting for her uncle. She is taken hostage along with the children, and it is through her eyes that we view much of the 'operation'. Much the same age as Miro and, as he notices, 'almost a mirror to himself', is Ben, the son of the army officer in charge of the attempt to rescue the children. He enters the story when he is recruited to act as a go-between during nego-tiations with the terrorists. This is an adventure story then, but distinctively modern in its subject-matter and also in its rearrange-ment of the plot structure. Kate's quest, insofar as she has one, is to stay alive. She fails, for Miro eventually succeeds in the mission he had originally set himself: killing the bus-driver. Indeed, in one way at least Miro does succeed as any Henty hero might, sacrificing himself for the greater glory of his homeland's freedom: 'It does not matter whether or not I get away', he tells Kate before he murders her, 'Whether I live or die. Whether anyone else lives or dies. I have served my purpose.' Ben's adventure is more complicated still. When he delivers his message to the terrorists they torture him to reveal the time at which the army will launch their attack. He surrenders to the pain and divulges the plan, only to find out later that his father had deliberately fed him misinformation, knowing that Ben would be tortured and that he would 'betray' him. Unable to forgive his father's deception, but guilty also at his own weakness and credulity, Ben commits suicide. Miro, meanwhile, overcomes any doubt or remorse about murdering Kate, kills again, and ventures onwards 'into the world that was waiting for him.'[28]

Cormier's ending takes up elements of the classic adventure tale but distorts them horribly. Miro's resolution is a chilling reiteration of the rejection of 'sivilization' and decision to 'light out for the Territory' with which Mark Twain ended *The Adventures of Huckleberry Finn* (1884). *After the First Death* is also dominated by relationships between fathers and sons. Miro reverences Artkin as Jim Hawkins admires Long John Silver, always seeking to impress him. Just as Jim betrays Silver's plot, and Ben 'lets down' his father, Miro is responsible for Artkin's death, failing to warn him of the soldiers' attack in his own eagerness to escape. He is driven to shoot Kate only when she makes him realise that Artkin was probably his actual father, her murder a result of the self-loathing he feels at his probable patricide. This is the same self-loathing that drives Ben to suicide, and that torments Ben's father, whose haunted narration takes over from Ben's at the end of the novel. This is pessimism without hope of redemption, characteristic of Cormier's rejection of any need in children's literature for happy endings.[29] He is also apparently arguing that in the modern, post-Vietnam War world, the old, straightforward adventure is no longer possible. Ben's father seems to realise this, talking of his enlistment, with a friend called Jack Harkness, on the very day after the Pearl Harbour attack, and their ardent patriotism, 'pure and sweet and unquestioning'. Ben's generation, his father knows, is not so trusting. It 'looks at itself in a mirror as it performs its duties. And wonders Who are the good guys? Is it possible we are the bad guys?'[30] Only murderous terrorists have the old faith and desire for heroism. Jack Harkness (whose very name links him with an outdated literary tradition, reminding us of Jack Harkaway, the hero of S. Bracebridge

Hemyng's classic Victorian adventure tales) died at Iwo Jima, and with him died the age of adventure.

Yet, since Cormier, many writers have endeavoured to rehabilitate the children's adventure novel. For some, this has meant finding new contexts for adventures, and sometimes adding a political dimension. For instance, Beverley Naidoo's *Journey to Jo'burg*, published in 1985, was set in contemporary South Africa (where it was banned until 1991), and used the classic quest/journey theme to expose the injustice and cruelty of the apartheid regime. Others have more stubbornly attempted to reintroduce old adventures to new audiences. One American firm has republished all of G. A. Henty's books in paper and electronic format for a twenty-first century readership because, their advertisements assert, 'the examples set by Henty's heroes of honesty, integrity, hard work, courage, diligence, perseverance, personal honor, and strong Christian faith are unsurpassed.'[31] In Britain, two publishers announced in 2003 that they were 'so fed up with feminism and political correctness' that they would republish 'great buccaneering, derring-do, true-life adventures' under the 'Young Spitfire' imprint, since, they said, boys needed books demonstrating 'masculine principles and masculine emotions.'[32]

Authors such as Charlie Higson, with *Silverfin: A James Bond Adventure* (2005), and David Gilman, with *Danger Zone: The Devil's Breath* (2007), have also tried to lure boys into reading with exciting adventures, but they take themselves less seriously than Henty, writing with a degree of irony and much postmodern self-referentiality. These books are the equivalents of the *Star Wars* and *Indiana Jones* films (from 1977 and 1981 respectively) which revitalised the adventure film genre after its post-Vietnam fall from fashion. Like the films, the books delight in cliché, picking up familiar motifs from the classic adventure tradition and employing them with a knowing nod to the audience, or giving them a new twist. This tendency to pastiche, though not undermine, the classic adventure genre is immediately evident with Joshua Mowill's *Operation Red Jericho* (2005). It is set in 1920s Shanghai and follows Becca and Doug's investigation of their parents' sudden disappearance, leading to the discovery of an ancient secret society. The book purports to be the account of these adventures passed down by

Becca to her great-nephew, the author, and it includes her letters and diaries, her fold-out maps, sketches and photographs. The book even comes bound with an elastic cord, such as an adventurer might use to keep her book tight shut while she is being chased by ruthless, but slightly hapless, villains. The improbability of these adventures is emphasised. One might even think that the authors invite their readers to conclude that the adventures of Great-Aunt Becca, or Higson's young James Bond or Horowitz's Alex Rider, are actually taking place in these characters' imaginations.

Despite these rehabilitation strategies, the adventure genre remains tainted for many modern readers because of two things: its association with empire, and its perceived misogyny. These are certainly the two areas that most critical debate has focused on. In its representation of gender, for instance, the classic adventure story can seem extremely conservative. Kimberly Reynolds has suggested that by the late Victorian period, children's literature had bifurcated into separate canons for girls and for boys. 'Girls' stories' such as those appearing in *The Girl's Own Paper*, and by L. T. Meade and Evelyn Everett-Green, endorsed the values of domesticity. Meanwhile adventure tales by Henty, and those that appeared in *The Boy's Own Paper*, were designed to encourage what John Ruskin identified as the specifically male talent for 'speculation and invention . . . adventures . . . war . . . conquest.' These separate boys' and girls' literatures 'rejected modifications to attitudes towards sexual difference', Reynolds argued, while at the same time these same attitudes were being challenged in fiction for adults. Worse still, the values of the Victorian age stayed in place in children's literature long after the age that spawned them had passed. 'Today's juvenile fiction', Reynolds wrote in 1990, 'carries within it images, structures, attitudes and value systems which are at least partially shaped by their earlier counterparts.'[33] According to this analysis, the adventure story is almost irredeemably sexist.

The same might be said of the imperialism of the adventure story. The genre's genesis and apotheosis in the early and late nineteenth century respectively should be seen, Dennis Butts states, 'both as an expression and a result of popular interest in the rise of the British Empire'.[34] Henty is the classic example, the writer who, according to Kathryn Castle, 'exemplified the ethos of the new imperialism, and glorified its military successes.'[35] His novels exhibit a thoroughgoing racism. The 'natives' of the Empire, and especially sub-Saharan Africans, 'are just children', his characters are wont to proclaim:

> They are always laughing or quarreling. They are good-natured and passionate, indolent, but will work hard for a time; clever up to a certain point, densely stupid beyond. The intelligence of an average negro is about equal to that of a European child of ten years old.[36]

These people are not children in the same sense as his heroes are still children. For Henty's Europeans, childhood is a state of potentiality; for his Africans it is a state of incapacity. His heroes exhibit natural abilities but can also be schooled, both before and during their adventures, to make them civilised adults. The 'natives' cannot be educated. As Lord Kitchener observes in one novel, there may be 'a lot of good in these black fellows if one could but get at it.' The only means to 'get at it', of course, was to impose the yoke of Empire.[37]

But the encoding of imperialist ambition in the adventure story was not unique to the Victorian period. *Robinson Crusoe*, Edward Said pointed out, 'is about a European who creates a fiefdom for himself on a distant, non-European island'. This is important not only because it shows the colonial impulse was embedded in adventure fiction long before the idea of a British Empire had reached maturity, but also because Defoe's novel can be seen as the 'prototypical modern realistic novel'.[38] As such, Said argued, it reveals how almost all modern fiction is in some ways concerned with the imperial project. Certainly, the adventure novel in particular seems structurally imperialist, no matter where or when it is set, or indeed whether or not it emerged from a nation which had established or retained a formal empire. In the typical 'imperial romance', as Claudia Marquis calls it, a boy is thrown into a struggle for which his background has not specifically prepared him, but in which he triumphs, against lesser people, by virtue of the values that his society has imbued him with (resourcefulness, honour, perseverance, pluck). When he triumphs, he affirms his home culture, legitimising its dominion over inferior peoples and uncivilised lands.[39]

As Claudia Nelson puts it, 'The struggle between stereotypical hero and equally stereotypical villain becomes emblematic of Britain's noble quest to civilize non-Western societies.'[40] A similar point can be made for American children's literature. The United States may have lacked an empire on the European model, but its adventure stories generally affirmed 'civilised' America's right to dominate 'inferior peoples' – slaves, Native Americans, the poor – both within and beyond its borders. It can be argued that the recurrent descriptions in children's literature of white children's attainment of dominion over foreign lands and indigenous people is a sort of symbolic re-telling of the imperial enterprise. One might even go so far as to say that it represents a sort of fantasy of colonialism, and that the need constantly to re-stage the colonial act reveals a lack of confidence in its legitimacy and sustainability, rather than any self-assured sense of mission. Certainly, neither direct nor oblique representations of colonial adventure suddenly vanished from children's literature after the loss of Empire. As M. Daphne Kutzer puts it, 'the desire for empire does not go away' in British children's literature, or if it does, it is 'replaced by its close cousin, nostalgia for a lost and more powerful Britain and a more perfect British past.'[41]

Yet it is possible to dispute both the inherent anti-feminism and imperialism of the adventure story. Certainly girls happily read what we might think of as boys' books. Sally Mitchell draws on memoirs and surveys to show that many late Victorian and early Edwardian girls avidly consumed adventures stories and identified with their heroes.[42] Equally, even in the Victorian period, many adventure stories featured girls as central characters. *The Girl's Own Paper* feminised some adventure classics, serialising Elizabeth Whittaker's 'Robina Crusoe, and her Lonely Island Home' (1882–83) for example. Original adventure novels for and about girls were hardly unknown either. Bessie Marchant, sometimes called 'the female Henty', wrote many, including *Three Girls on a Ranch: A Tale of New Mexico* (1901) and *Molly Angel's Adventures* (1915), the story of a fourteen-year-old girl left to fend for herself on the Western Front of the First World War.[43] From here, it was only a short distance to Captain W. E. Johns' novels about 'Worrals of the WAAF' (1941–50). As a Flight Officer in the Women's Auxiliary Air Force, Joan Worralson's official job was to deliver aircraft to the men who would fly them into battle, but she often found herself drawn into actual combat, though always by chance rather than intention, becoming in effect the female 'Biggles'. This rather clumsy compromise between wanting to make the adventures of heroines as exciting as those of heroes, yet not being prepared entirely to efface the 'proper' divide between men's and women's lives, was commonplace. In *Little Miss Robinson Crusoe* (1898), by 'Mrs. George Corbett', the castaway's life is full of adventure. She fights with 'an awful enemy' (a giant crab) and 'a fearful-looking beast' (an octopus), and must confront a 'hideous-looking snake' and 'death-dealing flowers', not to mention overcoming all the usual problems attendant on being marooned on a desert island (hers is starkly called the 'Land of Death', because of its frequent earthquakes and eruptions). But Leona Robinson, though announced as a tomboy from the start, must also exhibit her feminine qualities: making her own clothes, describing herself as a 'born cook' who 'fairly revelled in the concoction of all sorts of wonderful things', thinking of her desperate search for food as a trip 'to market', and making herself a doll to mother, because, although she had a pet monkey, 'how much more comforting a baby would be'.[44]

However awkwardly achieved, this kind of merging of gender roles has become very significant for some critics. Martha Vicinus has found that Victorian biographies of eminent women often encouraged readers to emulate their more 'masculine' traits, such as courage, initiative and independence.[45] Claudia Nelson notes that supposedly 'feminine' virtues like patience, self-effacement and chastity, and the nurturing and domestic instinct, were at the heart of much Victorian children's literature, even the ostensibly masculine adventure story. At least before the last years of the nineteenth century, they exhibit a 'complex mythology', she argues, 'in which the desire to reject the feminine ethic combats the desire to embrace it.'[46] Megan Norcia has gone further, arguing that this hybridity was designed to enable girls to 'join and surpass their male counterparts in the imperial project.' Norcia notes that Isabel Fraser, the central character in L. T. Meade's 1892 novel *Four on an Island: A Story of Adventure*, is simultaneously a female Crusoe and an 'Angel of the House'. It is her domestic skills which keep her and her companions alive on their desert island, and which enable them to maintain their English identity in these most difficult and foreign of circumstances. '*Four on an Island* not only posits that girls be allowed to participate in adventure,' Norcia concludes, 'but it demonstrates that they are *more fit* than boys to do so, because they, like Crusoe, are the preservers of nation through the establishment and maintenance of the domestic space.'[47]

It is books like *Four on an Island* that show how deeply enmeshed so much Victorian adventure writing was in the colonial project. But just as Norcia, Nelson and other critics have detected a certain blurring of gender roles in the classic adventure story, so it is also sometimes possible to identify a more vexed relationship with empire. Most of the 'westerns' that proliferated in the dime novels and magazines of the late nineteenth century were clear that the white hero was manifestly destined to exert dominion over the entire continent, no matter how many 'Indians' he had to kill in the process. But some also endorsed, either directly or indirectly, the values of the American wilderness and its 'noble savage' inhabitants. It is possible to read James Fenimore Cooper's series of *Leather-Stocking Tales* (1823–41), John Cawelti has concluded, in two apparently contradictory ways: 'From one angle, it appears to be an affirmation of the benevolent progress of American civilisation; from another, it is an attack on the same civilization as measured against the natural nobility of a pastoral hero.'[48] The same duality persisted in many later Westerns, and is certainly to be found in Laura Ingalls Wilder's half-frightened, half-admiring treatment of the 'Indians' in her *Little House* novels (from 1932). Ma might be continually telling Laura to be more civilised and less like the 'Indians', but Laura's sense of adventure inspires her fascination with their lives, and she comes to share Pa's grudging respect for their dignity, self-sufficiency and oneness with nature.

Other kinds of frontier novel exhibit the same tensions. In Stevenson's *Kidnapped* (1885), for instance, the Scottish Lowlander David Balfour at first derides the more 'primitive' Highland culture represented by Alan Breck. By the end of the novel, though, David has come to respect the generosity, stubbornness and nobility of the Highlanders, and to forget what he had formerly thought their foolish devotion to a former king and their 'childish' vanity and rages (just as Alan has come to accept David's thrift, rationality and his status as one of colonisers of the still wild Highlands). A confused relationship between colonised and coloniser is also at the heart of much of Rudyard Kipling's writing. On one level, *Kim* (1901) validates the 'Great Game' of empire, its orphaned hero discovering his identity, and his duty, as a member of the white ruling class who can perform great deeds in the British secret service. But the novel is all about cultural hybridity. More fluent in vernacular languages than English, and more at home on the streets than in the institutions of the Raj, Kim is as much Indian as he is British (if British at all: his father was a Catholic Irishman). Don Randall's book *Kipling's Imperial Boy* (2000) has taken this case furthest, arguing that Kipling uses adolescent heroes wrestling with their own identities – Kim, Mowgli in *The Jungle Books* (1894–95) and Stalky in *Stalky & Co.* (1899) – to explore the possible futures of the Empire after the shock of the Indian Rebellion of 1857. Their amalgamation of cultures, and perhaps even races, and their reconciliation of imperial duty with respect for the civilisation of the colonised, might be Kipling's answer to the contradiction of Britain's position in India.[49]

Nevertheless, most critics continue to explore the ways in which the classic adventure story helped to recruit boys into the ranks of those who would support, administer or fight for the Empire.[50] One fictional boy deeply affected by the adventure stories to which he is devoted is Oswald Bastable in E. Nesbit's *The Wouldbegoods*, published in 1901, towards the end of the Second Boer War. 'I should like to be a soldier', 'to go to South Africa for a bugler', Oswald declares following his reading of S. R. Crockett's *The Surprising Adventures of Sir Toady Lion* (1897), in which two young boys play at being military heroes. When soldiers pass by his house, Oswald and the rest of the Bastable children cheer them lustily. 'It was glorious', Oswald comments. All this, though, is a prelude to the real subject of the chapter. News arrives from the South African war that a local man, Bill, has been killed. Trying to alleviate the grief of Bill's mother, the Bastables characteristically succeed only in making things worse when they construct a fake tombstone for the fallen hero. Although the chapter ends happily when Bill returns home, wounded rather than dead, what Nesbit provides is a sophisticated satire on the unthinking patriotism engendered by the sort of adventure books that the Bastables have been reading. There are hints of this right from the start. When the soldiers pass by, the Bastables deck themselves out with ancient swords and bayonets borrowed from the house in which they are staying. Oswald's offhand comment that 'They are very bright when you get them bright, but the sheaths are hard to polish' provides a metaphor for the easiness of militarism (the bright swords) and the difficulty of maintaining peace (the dull scabbards). Likewise, when the soldiers depart for the war, their officer's comment to the children that his troops will have to change out of their ceremonial uniforms and wear 'mud-colour' foretells their likely fate, to fall on the field of battle, without even a grave like that which the Bastables enthusiastically construct for Bill. The fiasco of the erroneous telegram bearing the news of Bill's death adds to the critique of war, a critique made more pathetic by the dismal comedy of the children's attempts to memorialise the soldier. After all this, Oswald's final ruminations must be read as deeply ironic. 'I am very glad *some* soldiers' mothers get their boys home again', he says, once Bill has returned:

> But if they have to die, it is a glorious death; and I hope mine will be that. And three cheers for the Queen, and the mothers who let their boys go, and the mother's son who fight and die for old England. Hip, hip, hurrah![51]

Nesbit, whose book appeared in the same year as the notorious 'Khaki election' of 1901, was evidently satirising the power of the adventure story to inspire thoughtless patriotism and militarism in young boys. What is extraordinary is that this closing passage of the chapter has routinely been omitted from modern editions of the novel. This must presumably be because the abridgers have missed Nesbit's irony, or because they deem readers likely to take Oswald's sentiments at face value – and such an enthusiastic endorsement of militarism (*if* taken at face value) would be unacceptable in children's books published after the World Wars. But whichever way we interpret it, the decision of later abridgers to omit the chapter's original ending is also testimony to the power of the adventure story to captivate, and even indoctrinate, by offering children a heroism that their routine real-life subordination makes especially appealing.

SUMMARY OF KEY POINTS

- Adventure stories provide a fantasy of empowerment for children, describing a heroism that their real-life powerlessness makes especially appealing.
- Many of the best adventure stories depict a conflict between children's yearning for consequentiality and their residual desire for protection and supervision.
- Early children's books often portrayed adventure as something to be avoided, but from the mid-nineteenth century adventure was represented as something that might happen to anyone and ought often to be welcomed.
- Classic nineteenth-century adventure stories were often less sexist, racist and imperialist that modern critics sometimes suggest, one of their common themes being an endorsement of ethnic, gender and generational empathy and hybridity.

NOTES

1. H. Rider Haggard, *King Solomon's Mines* (London: Puffin, [1885] 1994), p. i.
2. See Pat Rogers, 'Classics and Chapbooks', in *Books and their Readers in Eighteenth-Century England*, ed. Isabel Rivers (Leicester: Leicester University Press, 1982), pp. 27–45 and Martin Green, *The Robinson Crusoe Story* (University Park, PA: Pennsylvania State University Press, 1990).
3. See M. Sarah Smedman, 'Like Me, Like Me Not: *Gulliver's Travels* as Children's Book', in *The Genres of Gulliver's Travels*, ed. Frederick N. Smith (Newark, DE: University of Delaware Press, 1990), pp. 75–100.
4. Isaac Taylor, *Scenes in Africa, For the Amusement and Instruction of Little Tarry-at-Home Travellers* (London: Harris and Son, 1821), pp. 2–3.

5. G. A. Henty, *The Young Buglers, A Tale of the Peninsular War* (London: Blackie, [1880] 1887), p. iii.

6. See Leonard R. N. Ashley's *George Alfred Henty and the Victorian Mind* (San Francisco, CA: International Scholars, 1999).

7. Cynthia Harnett, *The Load of Unicorn* (London: Egmont Books, [1959] 2001), p. 244.

8. Geoffrey Trease, *Bows Against the Barons* (London: Elliott and Thompson, [1934] 2004), p. 27.

9. Rosemary Sutcliff, 'Postscript' to Henry Treece, *The Dream-Time* (London: Heinemann Educational Books, [1967] 1974), p. 96.

10. See Gerda Faerber, '*Emil and the Detectives*: a Publishing Story', *Signal*, 89 (1999), 100–14.

11. The classifications that follow are partly based on the taxonomy of adult adventure stories developed by Martin Green in *Seven Types of Adventure Tale: An Etiology of a Major Genre* (University Park, PA: Pennsylvania State University Press, 1991).

12. R. M. Ballantyne, *The Coral Island* (Ware: Wordsworth, [1858] 1993), p. 264.

13. Susan Cooper, *The Dark is Rising* (London: Puffin, [1973] 1976), pp. 185–8. See M. Daphne Kutzer, 'Thatchers and Thatcherites: Lost and Found Empires in Three British Fantasies', *The Lion and the Unicorn*, 22 (1998), 196–210 (p. 198).

14. Susan Cooper, *Over Sea, Under Stone* (London: Puffin, [1965] 1968), p. 194.

15. Nina Bawden, *On the Run* (London: Puffin, 1964), p. 7.

16. C. Day Lewis, *The Otterbury Incident* (London: Puffin, [1948] 1961), p. 11.

17. J. M. Barrie, *Peter and Wendy*, ed. Jack Zipes (London: Penguin, [1911] 2004), p. 84.

18. Andrew O'Malley, 'Crusoe at Home: Coding Domesticity in Children's Editions of *Robinson Crusoe*', *British Journal for Eighteenth-Century Studies*, 29 (2006), 337–52.

19. See M. O. Grenby ' "Surely there is no British boy or girl who has not heard of the battle of Waterloo!": War and Children's Literature in the Age of Napoleon', in *Under Fire: Childhood in the Shadow of War*, ed. Andrea Immel and Elizabeth

Goodenough (Detroit, MI: Wayne State University Press, 2008), pp. 39–57.

20. Crinolines were stiff petticoats worn under women's dresses. Ballantyne, *The Gorilla Hunters* (London: T. Nelson, [1861] 1874), pp. 64–5.

21. Anon., *The History of Little Goody Two-Shoes* (London: T. Carnan and F. Newbery, [1765] 1772), pp. 144–54.

22. Mary Belson Elliott, *The Adventures of Thomas Two-Shoes* (London: W. Darton, 1818), p. 63.

23. Kirsten Drotner, *English Children and their Magazines 1751–1945* (New Haven, CT and London: Yale University Press, 1998), p. 105.

24. G. A. Henty, *Beric the Briton: a Story of the Roman Invasion* (London: Blackie, [1893] no date), 'Preface', p. 6.

25. Leon Garfield, *Jack Holborn* (Harmondsworth: Kestrel, [1964] 1984), p. 7.

26. Sutcliff, 'Postscript', in Treece, *Dream-Time*, p. 95.

27. Dennis Butts, 'The Adventure Story', in *Stories and Society: Children's Literature in its Social Context*, ed. Butts (Basingstoke: Macmillan, 1992), pp. 65–83 (p. 75). See pp. 70–3 for a concise analysis of the formal characteristics of the children's adventure story.

28. Robert Cormier, *After the First Death* (London: Puffin, [1979] 1998), pp. 199, 217 and 233.

29. See Judith Elkin *et al.*, 'Cormier Talking', *Books for Keeps*, 54 (1989), 12–13 and Judith Plotz, 'The Disappearance of Childhood: Parent-Child Role Reversals in *After the First Death* and *A Solitary Blue*', *Children's Literature in Education*, 19 (1988), 67–79.

30. Cormier, *After the First Death*, p. 134.

31. Robinson Books website <http://www.robinsonbooks.com/> [accessed 26 November 2007].

32. Nigel Reynolds, 'Forget the namby-pamby girly stuff, here are ripping yarns for real chaps', *The Daily Telegraph*, 9 October 2003.

33. John Ruskin, *Sesame and Lillies* (1871), in Reynolds, *Girls Only? Gender and Popular Children's Fiction in Britain, 1880–1910* (Hemel Hempstead: Harvester Wheatsheaf, 1990), pp. 50 and 152–4.

34. Butts, 'The Adventure Story', p. 66.
35. Kathryn Castle, *Britannia's Children: Reading Colonialism Through Children's Books and Magazines* (Manchester: Manchester University Press, 1996), p. 55.
36. G. A. Henty, *By Sheer Pluck* (London: Blackie, 1884), p. 118.
37. G. A. Henty, *With Kitchener in the Soudan* (London: Blackie, 1903), p. 206.
38. Edward Said, *Culture and Imperialism* (London: Chatto and Windus, 1993), pp. xii–xiii.
39. Claudia Marquis, 'Romancing the Home: Gender, Empire, and the South Pacific', in *Girls, Boys, Books, Toys: Gender in Children's Literature and Culture*, ed. Beverley Lyon Clark and Margaret R. Higgonet (Baltimore, MD: Johns Hopkins University Press, 1999), pp. 53–67 (p. 54).
40. Claudia Nelson, *Boys Will Be Girls: The Feminine Ethic and British Children's Fiction, 1857–1917* (New Brunswick, NJ: Rutgers University Press, 1991), p. 119.
41. M. Daphne Kutzer, *Empire's Children: Empire and Imperialism in Classic British Children's Books* (New York: Garland, 2000), p. 129.
42. Sally Mitchell, *The New Girl: Girls' Culture in England, 1880–1915* (New York: Columbia University Press, 1995), especially pp. 111–13.
43. See Michael Paris, *Warrior Nation: Images of War in British Popular Culture, 1850–2000* (London: Reaktion, 2000), p. 23, and Krista Cowman, '"There are kind Germans as well as brutal ones": The Foreigner in Children's Literature of the First World War', *The Lion and the Unicorn*, 31 (2007), 103–15.
44. Mrs. George [Elizabeth Burgoyne] Corbett, *Little Miss Robinson Crusoe* (London: C. Arthur Pearson, 1898), pp. 78, 194, 150, 172, 221, 146, 125 and 127.
45. Martha Vicinus, 'Models for Public Life: Biographies of "Noble Women" for Girls', pp. 52–70 in *The Girl's Own: Cultural Histories of the Anglo-American Girl, 1830–1915*, ed. Claudia Nelson and Lynne Vallone (Athens, GA: University of Georgia Press, 1994).
46. Nelson, *Boys Will Be Girls*, p. 118.

47. Megan Norcia, 'Angel of the Island: L. T. Meade's New Girl as the Heir of a Nation-Making Robinson Crusoe', *The Lion and the Unicorn*, 28 (2004), 345–62 (pp. 358, 348).

48. John G. Cawelti, *Adventure, Mystery, and Romance: Formula Stories as Art and Popular Culture* (Chicago, IL: University of Chicago Press, 1976), p. 207.

49. Don Randall, *Kipling's Imperial Boy: Adolescence and Cultural Hybridity* (New York: Palgrave, 2000).

50. See J. A. Mangan, 'Noble Specimens of Manhood: schoolboy literature and the creation of a colonial chivalric code', in *Imperialism and Juvenile Literature*, ed. Jeffrey Richards (Manchester: Manchester University Press, 1989), pp. 173–94 and Christopher Parkes, '*Treasure Island* and the Romance of the British Civil Service', *Children's Literature Association Quarterly*, 31 (2006), 332–45.

51. E. Nesbit, *The Wouldbegoods* (Ware: Wordsworth, [1901] 1995), pp. 43–4, 48 and 57.

Conclusion

Several things make children's literature unique among the many branches of academic literary study. First, as is often pointed out, it is the only category of literature that is defined in terms of its intended readership. Canadian literature, for instance, does not consist of all, or only, books read by Canadians. And crime fiction, to take another example, is not defined as those novels read by criminals. But children's literature is not children's literature because it is written *by* children, nor because it is *about* children, but only because of who it was ostensibly written *for*. This is connected with a second peculiar characteristic of children's books: that the intended audience is seldom actively involved in studying it academically. If we attempt to view books through children's eyes, or try to analyse texts on their behalf, we must remain aware that this is at best a kind of ventriloquism. Perhaps, as some critics suggest, we should acknowledge that children's books never really become the cultural property of children at all: they are written by adults, to suit adult purposes, and for kinds of children that adults construct to be the perfect readers of their books. If this is the case, there is no inconsistency whatsoever in adult critics discussing children's books, on their own terms, and without the least reference to any real children.

Another important difference between children's literature and the main body of literary studies is the condescension, even disdain, with which it has sometimes been greeted. Sustained study of children's literature in universities began only in the 1960s, a product of political shifts that led to distrust of the traditional canon and perhaps to a less formalist approach to literature that laid more stress on texts in context, rather than studying books simply for the sake of their stand-alone literary accomplishment. Nevertheless, this first entry of children's literature into the academy was often met with suspicion. Teaching, studying and researching children's literature could be characterised as beneath the dignity of serious students and academics. It was regarded as being too easy or, perhaps worse, too much fun. Or the whole undertaking could be presented as regrettable since it shattered the fondly remembered 'magic' of children's books, or even the 'innocence' of childhood. In 1992, Beverly Lyon Clark taxonomised 'Thirteen Ways of Thumbing Your Nose at Children's Literature' and other critics, both before and since, have also tried to pinpoint exactly why and how children's literature had been marginalised.[1] Was it due to turf wars between departments of education and departments of literature? Was sexism at its root, because children's literature had become associated predominantly with female teachers and students? Was it due to an unshakeable perception that studying children's literature was undemanding? When I was appointed to a job in children's literature in the School of English at Newcastle University in 2005, the *Guardian* newspaper, generally supportive of educational innovation, reported 'That's not going to be very hard, is it? The writing's big and there are lots of pictures.'[2]

But such condescension is on the wane, both generally and in almost all academic establishments. This might be for a variety of reasons. An increase in the attention paid to children's literature is probably tied up with its new-found centrality in culture: the *Harry Potter* effect as it might succinctly be called. Children's books – and not only J.K. Rowling's – have become the bestsellers of the late twentieth and early twenty-first century. They have crossed over into the reading lives of adults, and into cinema, theatre, computer games and many other media. This phenomenon demands scholarly attention. Meanwhile, trends within universities have also continued to advance the study of children's literature. For one thing, undermining literary canons, in some cases as soon as they begin to form, has become almost *de rigueur*. For another, new critical work on children's literature, perhaps especially theoretical and historical, has shown that teaching and research in children's literature cannot reasonably be regarded as in any way less sophisticated than work in more established fields. Indeed, many teachers have now recognised that one of the most effective ways to introduce recondite subjects and concepts to students – eighteenth-century cultural history, say, or the idea of the postcolonial – is through children's literature. After all, children's books often seem to invite readings that focus on historical context or that expose theoretical problems. And then the sheer popularity with students of courses in children's literature has been difficult to ignore. With British students now joining their North American counterparts in paying tuition fees, and so being increasingly regarded as the paying customers of universities, academics are becoming aware that their curricula must reflect what students want as well as what they are supposed to need. The commissioning of books like this *Edinburgh Critical Guide to Children's Literature* is testament to both the increased respectability and a new perceived saleability of children's literature studies.

What all this means is that children's literature studies, having achieved a certain maturity as a discipline, now stands at a fork in the road. One path leads towards the full integration of the study of children's books into the wider study of literature in general. The other option is to protect its separateness. Both alternatives have their rewards and their hazards. The erasure of the divide between the study of adult and children's literature might be taken as an indication that an equality, long sought and long resisted, has finally been reached. It could also open up new ways of exploring children's books. If academic books on Canadian literature, or crime fiction, or poetry (to take some arbitrary examples) were to include books designed for children alongside books for adults, not even hiving them off to a separate chapter, then a new kind of analysis would have to evolve, based perhaps more on formal qualities and generic continuities than issues of readership and reception. But the risks of such an approach are obvious. Writing for children has its own distinct genres, and although fantasy novels, say, or school stories, have sometimes been written for adults, it might be argued that these specialised forms of children's literature require independent consideration. Similarly, it might be argued that the more frequent presence of illustration in children's books, or the need to write for consumers with certain reading and comprehension competencies, or certain age-related needs, boundaries and desires, demands special teaching strategies and critical machinery. One might go further, arguing that the integration of the study of children's books into the study of literature in general risks institutionalisation. We might remember that one of Beverly Lyon Clark's 'Thirteen Ways of Thumbing Your Nose at Children's Literature' was for critics to refuse to acknowledge a divide between literature for children and for adults, thus, she worried, keeping the idea of a literature especially for children out of the intellectual limelight. Perhaps what makes children's literature studies so vital is its position on the outside, its practitioners imagining themselves as a sort of guerrilla force fighting against outdated, repressive literary orthodoxies. And some critics and teachers might be anxious to retain their position outside mainstream literary studies for more pragmatic reasons. Complete integration would mean renouncing a separate infrastructure for children's literature studies – its separate sub-departments within literature or education programmes, its discrete conferences, societies, awards and publishing outlets.

Yet the loss of a discrete academic community and identity is surely not to be regretted when weighed against a higher esteem for the subject and the practical advantages of integration. Certainly, it would be ludicrous to suggest that it should become a point of principle that children's literature should never be considered as a separate entity. And it would be very regrettable if the student, teacher or critic ever lost sight of the age of the intended (and actual) readership when discussing children's books. But to investigate writing for children and adults together must benefit both. Any appreciation of postcolonial children's literature, for example, will be impoverished if it is not placed in its wider literary and cultural contexts, and this will require it to be read collectively, not even only in parallel, with works originally intended for adults. Equally, any understanding of the postcolonial will be diminished if books produced for children are not evaluated as an important part of that discourse. To ignore children's literature in thinking about cultural responses to the Enlightenment, for instance, or to Darwinism, or to the Cold War, would not only render the research incomplete, but would be missing out on some crucial and immensely revealing data.

Of course much admirable work that considers adult and children's writing together has already been done, both by those who would consider themselves specialists in children's literature and those who would not. Now that the study of children's literature has become securely established, this work can provide the foundation for a new, less circumscribed approach to children's books, with writing for adults and writing for children read together and within the same contexts. Such criticism should blur the boundaries of children's literature, not define and police them. If this is how the future of children's literature studies does develop, then a critical guide to children's books might soon become obsolete. But one of the advantages of working in an area of literary studies that is still rapidly developing is that the directions it will take are entirely unpredictable. However much academic sense it might make to see the borders of children's literature studies overrun, from both sides, perhaps its students, teachers and researchers will respond to their subject's hard-won acceptance by protecting their gains and defending their territory. Academic protectionism or free-trade: it will be fascinating to find out which approach, if either, prevails.

NOTES

1. Beverly Lyon Clark, 'Thirteen Ways of Thumbing Your Nose at Children's Literature', *The Lion and the Unicorn*, 16 (1992), 240–44.
2. Alice Wignall, 'Harry Potter studies', *Guardian Education Supplement*, February 15 2005. The article did add 'Oh, don't be facile. It's a perfectly respectable academic discipline.'

Student Resources

GLOSSARY

Abridgement

A shortened version of a text, often produced in the belief that it will make an adult book more suitable for children. Cuts may be made to reduce the length of the work, to make its style more accessible, or to exclude material that is perceived to be unsuitable. Books designed originally for children are also sometimes abridged for new generations of readers, often without any acknowledgment that cuts have been made. See also **adaptation** and **bowdlerisation**.

Adaptation

A text not simply **abridged** but largely or wholly re-written. This may be for presentation to a different audience (children rather than adults; very young children rather than older children) or for presentation in a different format (children's poem rather than folk ballad; film rather than book). See **recontextualisation** and **remediation**.

Annual

A publication appearing at the same time each year, often at the end of the year for the Christmas market. Annuals became established in the early nineteenth century, and were increasingly compilations of pre-existing weekly or monthly publications bound together in new covers.

Anthropomorphism

Attribution of human attributes or personality to non-human things – often animals, but also inanimate objects such as dolls. Stories about them, and even narrated by them, have formed a staple of children's literature since the eighteenth century.

Ballad

A poem that recounts a story, often set out in 'ballad stanzas' of four lines rhyming *abcb*, and, strictly speaking, designed to be sung.

Battledore

Originally, a **hornbook** but lacking the horn covering. From the mid-eighteenth century, the term usually refers to the hornbook's replacement, an oblong card, folded into three, on which the alphabet and other text and images were cheaply printed.

Bibliotherapy

The production and use of books representing specific social, psychological or physiological problems as therapy for readers concerned by, or suffering from, these same dilemmas or conditions.

Bowdlerisation

The editing of a text to omit any material considered offensive or unsuitable, usually used in a pejorative sense. The term is derived from Thomas Bowdler's *Family Shakespeare*, published in 1818 for use by children with their parents.

Catechism

A series of questions and answers designed originally to educate and enforce religious orthodoxy. At first an oral process, catechisms were printed for children from the sixteenth century, and by the eighteenth century were being used for secular education, particularly mathematics and geography.

Chapbook

Although strictly speaking texts sold by travelling pedlars called 'chapmen', the term is often used loosely to describe various forms of short and cheap pamphlets common from the sixteenth to the nineteenth centuries. Usually containing popular and plebeian material, they were designed for a cross-generational audience, but in the early 1800s chapbooks designed especially for children were produced in large numbers.

Chromolithography

See **Lithography**.

Copperplate engraving

An illustration technique adopted for some children's books from the mid-eighteenth to the early nineteenth centuries. Lines are cut into the smooth metal plate which is then inked. The ink is wiped from the plate so that it remains only in the grooves. When printed this can produce precise, high-quality images, and engraved text and image can be combined on a single plate.

Counter-factual history

An account of a course of events which has not, but might have, happened. Such 'virtual histories' are not uncommon in children's literature, for instance Michael Cronin's *Against the Day* (2003) about Britain under Nazi occupation or Joan Aiken's *The Wolves of Willoughby Chase* sequence (from 1962), in which the Hanoverian

Succession of 1714 did not take place. Philip Pullman presents a similar alternative reality in the **secondary world** of his *His Dark Materials* (1995–2005), in which the Protestant Reformation, and certain key inventions, have not occurred.

Crossover literature

Texts originally marketed for either children or adults but adopted, without **abridgement** or **adaptation**, by a mixed-aged readership. J.K. Rowling's *Harry Potter* novels provide a good example, but the phenomenon has existed for many years, as for instance with Rudyard Kipling's *Kim* (1901).

Dime novel

Cheaply produced **series fiction** produced in America from the 1860s for a mixed-aged readership, often containing sensationalist material and similar to the British **penny dreadful**.

Disneyfication

A usually pejorative term for the ways in which children's literature and world folklore have been adapted, and commodified, by the films, theme parks and other products of the Walt Disney Company.

Emblem

A picture with a symbolic meaning, accompanied by text that explains the symbolism and sometimes adds a moral. Religious emblem-books were produced for children from the seventeenth century.

Engraving

See **Copperplate engraving**, **Process engraving** and **Wood engraving**.

Evangelical literature

Writing that stresses the literal truth of the Christian Scriptures, the personal responsibility of all individuals for their own salvation (even children) and the need for social reform on religious principles. Evangelical children's literature was common in the later seventeenth century (see **Puritan literature**), and was revived in the early nineteenth century.

Filmsetting or photocomposition

A printing process, in use for children's books since the 1950s, that involves projecting the material to be printed onto photographic film and then making printing plates from the film.

Folktale

Stories of great antiquity, with no known author and originating in an oral tradition, and told by, or about, ordinary working people. Many **adaptations**, both direct or indirect, have been produced for children. See **Legend** and **Myth**.

Frontispiece

An illustration facing the title-page of a book, common in eighteenth- and nineteenth-century children's literature.

Gesta Romanorum

'Acts of the Romans': a compendium of legends, biographies and stories popular with children in Latin and English, and in manuscript and print forms, from the fourteenth to the eighteenth century.

Golden Age

A term sometimes applied to the period from the publication of *Alice's Adventures in Wonderland* (1865) to the 1910s or 1920s during which much innovative, successful and enduring children's literature was published in Britain. The existence of a second Golden Age in the 1950s and 1960s is sometimes posited.

Harlequinade

Picturebooks originally based on pantomime performances, allowing the reader to reproduce stage effects by lifting flaps to reveal new scenes underneath. Produced from 1770 until the early nineteenth century, these represent an early example of **remediation**.

Hornbook

The alphabet and other simple educational and devotional material printed on paper attached to a piece of wood shaped like a small paddle or bat, and often covered with a protective translucent sheet of horn. Used throughout the early modern period and evolving into the **battledore**.

Imprint

Details of a book's publisher, place of publication and date, usually printed on the title-page or elsewhere in the book's front-matter. By extension, also used for the series brand names used by publishers (for example, **Ladybird**).

Intertextuality

The incorporation or referencing of other already existing writing in a text, a common phenomenon in children's literature. This can be explicit, as when E. Nesbit's Bastable children in *The Treasure Seekers* (1899) deliberately model their own lives on the characters they have read about in nineteenth-century fiction, or more allusive, as when Will Parry in Philip Pullman's *Northern Lights* (1995) almost gives up his quest so that he can return to help his ailing mother, just as Digory had almost broken an oath for his sick mother in C.S. Lewis' *The Magician's Nephew* (1955).

Jest book

Collections of comic anecdotes, stories, jokes and verses, cheaply published for a mixed-age audience, often in the form of a **chapbook**, from the sixteenth to the early nineteenth century.

Ladybird books

A publisher's **imprint** in use from 1915 (and surviving a takeover of the original company by Penguin Books in 1999). The books adopted their distinctive standard size and use of full colour on every page in the 1940s, and were organised into a Key Words Reading Scheme from 1964.

Legend

Like the **folktale**, legends have no known author and derive from an oral tradition, but they usually concern great heroes and (less often) heroines, possibly actual historical figures, and may originally have been told by specialised story-tellers. See also **Myth**.

Letterpress

Printed text, as opposed to illustration. Also used to distinguish material printed from raised type or blocks from that printed from **lithographic** plates.

Limerick

Five-line comic verse form, with rhyme structure **aabba,** used for children's poetry since the early nineteenth century. Edward Lear used the form extensively in his nonsense verse, but the term itself was not current until the 1890s.

Lithography and Chromolithography

A process of printing in which the artist draws directly onto a stone or metal plate with a crayon that repels water. When the plate is wetted and then inked, the ink adheres only to those areas drawn in by the artist, producing bold and effective images when printed. If this is done successively with several inks a multi-coloured image can be cheaply produced ('chromolithograhy'). The process became widespread from the mid-nineteenth century.

Myth

Stories that explain natural, cosmic and spiritual phenomena, such as floods or the creation of the world, and that are notionally believed to be true. A collection – or mythology – can form the basis of a particular society, but some very similar myths are found in distant and diverse cultures.

Nonsense

Verse or prose that distorts or inverts reality, or employs made-up language, but usually remains within rigid formal structures. It has been used, for comic or satirical effect, for several centuries, but was most influentially adopted for use in children's books by Edward Lear and Lewis Carroll in the mid-nineteenth century.

Penny dreadful

Name given, usually by its critics, to a cheap pamphlet, designed for a mixed-aged audience, containing crime, supernatural or other sensational stories. Often written in parts, and popular in the mid-nineteenth century. See **dime novel**.

Picturebook

A text in which pictures and words are equally significant (so that the pictures do not merely function as illustrations of the text), and in which the interaction between them produces gratification and meaning for readers. Although they pre-date printing, picturebooks in the modern sense became popular only in the early nineteenth century.

Postcolonial literature and criticism

Work both deriving from, and written about, countries and cultures that have formerly been under the control of European colonial powers is called postcolonial. Postcolonial critics may study the many children's texts written about imperialism, Daniel Defoe's *Robinson Crusoe* (1719) or Rudyard Kipling's *Kim* (1901) for instance, as well as looking at more strictly postcolonial work such as Anita Desai's *The Peacock Garden* (1979) or Ken Kalonde's *Smiles Around Africa* (1997).

Primer

Originally a prayer book, usually in Latin, but from the Reformation, used to describe books of simple instruction, in letters, religion or secular subjects.

Problem novel

Fiction designed to represent and offer indirect advice on particular physiological, psychological and social issues, such as obesity, learning disability, divorce or racism. Usually, but not always, for older children and young adults, and common from the 1970s. See **young adult literature**.

Process engraving

A means of transferring a drawing to a printing block photographically, so that the artist's design can be engraved, then printed, precisely as drawn. Before this process was perfected in the late nineteenth century it had been customary for engravers to modify artists' designs.

Puritans

English Protestants who were convinced that the Church of England needed further reform after the Reformation. They believed in the absolute truth of the scriptures and that all carried the stain of

Original Sin, regardless of age. Puritanism, and Puritan children's literature, flourished in England in the later seventeenth century.

Realism

The accurate depiction of real life in a literary work, but also sometimes the portrayal of lower-class life.

Recontextualisation

The **adaptation** of a written text in a new medium, for instance as television programme, film, stage-play or computer game, rather than as another written text. See also **remediation**.

Religious Tract Society (RTS)

Founded in 1799 to produce **Evangelical literature**, and by the 1810s specifically targeting children. During the nineteenth century, its publications became less overtly religious, including *The Boy's Own Paper* and *Girl's Own Paper* from 1879 and 1880 respectively.

Remediation

The representation of one medium in another, as when a website imitates a newspaper. In children's literature, this process often works in reverse, as when a novel attempts to imitate a website or animated film. See also **harlequinade**.

Robinsonnade

A literary descendent of Daniel Defoe's *Robinson Crusoe* (1719) in which the protagonists struggle to survive in an isolated and hostile environment and, in doing so, learn more about themselves.

Romances

Adventure narratives, most often in verse, circulating orally and in written form in the Middle Ages, for instance *Guy of Warwick*.

Always popular with children, they were printed as **abridgements** especially for them, often as **chapbooks**, from the late eighteenth century.

Second golden age

See **Golden Age**.

Secondary world

A term, first used by J. R. R. Tolkien, for the complete alternative realities used in much fantasy fiction. Although travel between these alternative universes and our own may be possible in some fantasy literature, Tolkien held that, if full credibility is to be retained, secondary worlds ought to be an alternative not an addition to our primary universe.

Series fiction

Novels designed from their inception to be part of a potentially infinite series, united by the same characters, narrative patterns or settings, thus not, at least strictly speaking, a limited set, such as J. K. Rowling's *Harry Potter* novels. Derived from the **dime novel** and **penny dreadful**, series fiction has been increasingly common since the early twentieth century.

Society for Promotion of Christian Knowledge (SPCK)

Founded in 1698 to distribute religious publications, it published many books for children in the eighteenth and nineteenth centuries, including fiction and natural history.

Time-slip fantasy

A text in which protagonists find themselves transported to a different time, either accidentally, through their own agency or by the intervention of others, or in which a character from the past or future appears in the main characters' present. In some books, more than one time period is present simultaneously, and characters can wander between them. A frequently used device in children's literature since the early twentieth century.

Urchin verse

Children's poetry that aims to capture the ordinary voice and attitudes of real, usually urban, children, and popular especially in Britain since the 1970s.

Vignette

A small, separate illustration, either pictorial or purely ornamental, used to decorate a book, often found at the start or end of a section.

Wood engraving

A finer-lined and more subtly shaded **woodcut,** made on the more durable end-grain of wood, not the planed plank, and by tools used for **copperplate engraving**. The technique was pioneered and perfected by Thomas Bewick in the late eighteenth century, and remained the primary form of children's book illustration for a century.

Woodcut

A picture produced by cutting away parts of a wooden block around the lines to be inked and printed. These blocks could be set along with type to print illustration and **letterpress** on the same page. Because it was simple and cheap, most pre-nineteenth century children's books were illustrated in this way.

Young adult literature

Texts, mostly fiction, designed to be suitable for teenagers. In print from the 1950s, most 'YA' literature has sought to dramatise real-life events and concerns, especially sex, selfhood, and the quest for autonomy. See **problem novel**.

GUIDE TO FURTHER READING

This section is intended as a concise guide to the books, websites and journals (but not individual articles) currently available that will help with general aspects of children's literature studies. It should be used in conjunction with the references to more specifically relevant critical material that are to be found in the notes to the main chapters of this book.

Children's literature journals

Canadian Children's Literature/Littérature canadienne pour la jeunesse (University of Winnipeg)
Children's Literature (Modern Language Association Division on Children's Literature and Children's Literature Association, Johns Hopkins University Press)
The Children's Literature Association Quarterly (Children's Literature Association, Johns Hopkins University Press)
Children's Literature in Education (Springer)
Horn Book Magazine (The Horn Book Inc.)
International Research in Children's Literature (Edinburgh University Press)
The Journal of Children's Literature Studies (Pied Piper Publishing)
The Lion and the Unicorn (Johns Hopkins University Press)
The Looking Glass: an Online Children's Literature Journal (www.the-looking-glass.net)
New Review of Children's Literature and Librarianship (Taylor and Francis)

Theory of children's literature

Beckett, Sandra L. (ed.), *Reflections of Change: Children's Literature Since 1945* (Westport, CT: Greenwood, 1997).
Dusinberre, Juliet, *Alice to the Lighthouse: Children's Books and Radical Experiments in Art* (London: Macmillan, 1987).
Hollindale, Peter, *Ideology and the Children's Book* (Stroud: Thimble Press, 1988).

Hollindale, Peter, *Signs of Childness in Children's Books* (Stroud: Thimble Press, 1997).

Hourihan, Margery, *Deconstructing the Hero: Literary Theory and Children's Literature* (London: Routledge, 1997).

Hunt, Peter, *Criticism, Theory and Children's Literature* (Oxford: Blackwell, 1991).

Lesnik-Oberstein, Karín, *Children's Literature: Criticism and the Fictional Child* (Oxford: Clarendon Press, 1994).

Lesnik-Oberstein, Karín, *Children's Literature: New Approaches* (Basingstoke: Palgrave, 2004).

Lurie, Alison, *Not in Front of the Grown-Ups: The Subversive Power of Children's Literature* (London: Bloomsbury, 1990).

McGillis, Rod, *The Nimble Reader: Literary Theory and Children's Literature* (New York: Twayne, 1996).

Nikolajeva, Maria, *Children's Literature Comes of Age: Towards a New Aesthetic* (New York: Garland, 1996).

Nodelman, Perry, *Words About Pictures: The Narrative Art of Picture Books* (Athens, GA: University of Georgia Press, 1988).

Rose, Jacqueline, *The Case Against Peter Pan, or the Impossibility of Children's Literature* (London: Macmillan, 1984).

Stephens, John, *Language and Ideology in Children's Fiction* (London: Longman, 1992).

Early history of children's literature (pre-1860)

Alderson, Brian and Felix De Marez Oyens, *Be Merry and Wise: The Origins of Children's Book Publishing in England, 1650–1850* (New Castle, DE: Oak Knoll Press, 2006).

Darton, F. J. Harvey, *Children's Books in England*, 3rd edn, revised by Brian Alderson (Cambridge: Cambridge University Press, 1982).

Hilton, Mary, Morag Styles and Victor Watson (eds), *Opening the Nursery Door: Reading, Writing and Childhood, 1600–1900* (London: Routledge, 1997).

Immel, Andrea and Michael Witmore (eds), *Childhood and Children's Books in Early Modern Europe, 1550–1800* (New York: Routledge, 2006).

Jackson, Mary J., *Engines of Instruction, Mischief and Magic: Children's Literature in England from its Beginnings to 1839* (Lincoln, NB: University of Nebraska Press, 1989).

McGavran, James (ed.), *Romanticism and Children's Literature in the Nineteenth Century* (Athens, GA: University of Georgia Press, 1991).

Marks, Sylvia Kasey, *Writing for the Rising Generation: British Fiction for Young People, 1672–1839* (Victoria, BC: University of Victoria, 2003).

O'Malley, Andrew, *The Making of the Modern Child: Children's Literature and Childhood in the Late Eighteenth Century* (New York: Routledge, 2003).

Pickering, Samuel F., *John Locke and Children's Books in Eighteenth-Century England* (Knoxville, TN: The University of Tennessee Press, 1981).

Pickering, Samuel F., *Moral Instruction and Fiction for Children, 1749–1820* (Athens, GA: University of Georgia Press, 1993).

Richardson, Alan, *Literature, Education, and Romanticism: Reading as Social Practice, 1780–1832* (Cambridge: Cambridge University Press, 1994).

Vallone, Lynne, *Disciplines of Virtue: Girls' Culture in the Eighteenth and Nineteenth Centuries* (New Haven, CT: Yale University Press, 1995).

Modern and contemporary children's literature (post-1860)

Carpenter, Humphrey, *Secret Gardens: A Study of the Golden Age of Children's Literature* (London: Unwin, 1985).

Clark, Beverley Lyon, *Kiddie Lit: The Cultural Construction of Children's Literature in America* (Baltimore, MD: Johns Hopkins University Press, 2003).

Edwards, Owen Dudley, *British Children's Fiction in the Second World War* (Edinburgh: Edinburgh University Press, 2007).

Foster, Shirley and Judy Simons, *What Katy Read: Feminist Re-Readings of 'Classic' Stories for Girls* (Iowa City, IA: University of Iowa Press, 1995).

Hunt, Peter, and Millicent Lenz, *Alternative Worlds in Fantasy Fiction* (London: Continuum, 2001).

Knoepflmacher, U. C., *Ventures into Childhood: Victorians, Fairy Tales and Femininity* (Chicago, IL: University of Chicago Press, 1998).

Natov, Roni, *The Poetics of Childhood* (New York: Routledge, 2003).

Nelson, Claudia, *Boys Will Be Girls: The Feminine Ethic and British Children's Fiction, 1857–1917* (New Brunswick, NJ: Rutgers University Press, 1991).

Reynolds, Kimberley, *Radical Children's Literature: Future Visions and Aesthetic Transformations in Juvenile Fiction* (Basingstoke: Palgrave, 2007).

Reynolds, Kimberley (ed.), *Modern Children's Literature: An Introduction* (Basingstoke: Palgrave Macmillan, 2005).

Miscellanies and general histories

Avery, Gillian and Julia Briggs (eds), *Children and their Books: A Celebration of the Work of Iona and Peter Opie* (Oxford: Clarendon, 1989).

Clark, Beverley Lyon and Margaret Higgonet (eds), *Girls, Boys, Books, Toys: Gender in Children's Literature and Culture* (Baltimore, MD: Johns Hopkins University Press, 1999).

Egoff, Sheila, Gordon Stubbs, Ralph Ashley and Wendy Sutton (eds), *Only Connect: Readings on Children's Literature*, rev. edn (New York: Oxford University Press, 1996).

Hunt, Peter, *An Introduction to Children's Literature* (Oxford: Oxford University Press, 1994).

Styles, Morag, *From the Garden to the Street: Three Hundred Years of Poetry for Children* (London: Cassell, 1998).

Thacker, Deborah Cogan and Jean Webb, *Introducing Children's Literature: From Romanticism to Postmodernism* (London: Routledge, 2002).

Reference and anthologies

Carpenter, Humphrey and Mari Prichard, *The Oxford Companion to Children's Literature* (Oxford: Oxford University Press, 1984).

Demers, Patricia (ed.), *From Instruction to Delight: An Anthology of Children's Literature to 1815*, 2nd edn (Don Mills, Ontario: Oxford University Press Canada, 2004).

Hunt, Peter (ed.), *International Companion Encyclopedia of Children's Literature* 2nd edn, 2 vols (London: Routledge, 2004).

Hunt, Peter, *Children's Literature* (Oxford: Blackwell Guides to Literature, 2001).

Kline, Daniel, *Medieval Literature for Children* (New York: Routledge, 2003).

Watson, Victor (ed.), *The Cambridge Guide to Children's Books in English* (Cambridge: Cambridge University Press, 2001).

Zipes, Jack (ed.), *The Oxford Encyclopedia of Children's Literature*, 4 vols (New York: Oxford University Press, 2006).

Zipes, Jack, Lissa Paul, Lynne Vallone, Peter Hunt and Gillian Avery (eds), *The Norton Anthology of Children's Literature: The Traditions in English* (New York: Norton, 2005).

Websites

Perry Nodelman's bibliography of children's literature: http://www.uwinnipeg.ca/~nodelman/resources/allbib.htm

Hockliffe Project (British children's books 1700–1840): http://www.cts.dmu.ac.uk/hockliffe

Jane Johnson's manuscript nursery library: http://www.dlib.indiana.edu/collections/janejohnson

Baldwin Collection of Children's Books: http://palmm.fcla.edu/juv/juvAuthorList.html

International Children's Digital Library: http://www.icdlbooks.org/

Seven Stories: the Centre for Children's Books: http://www.sevenstories.org.uk

Index

TOURISM ESSENTIALS: 1

Tourism and Oil

Preparing for the Challenge

Susanne Becken

CHANNEL VIEW PUBLICATIONS
Bristol • Buffalo • Toronto

Library of Congress Cataloging in Publication Data
Becken, Susanne
Tourism and Oil: Preparing for the Challenge/Susanne Becken.
Tourism Essentials: 1.
Includes bibliographical references and index.
1. Tourism–Environmental aspects. 2. Sustainable tourism. 3. Climatic changes.
4. Petroleum industry and trade. 5. Fuel consumption. 6. Energy consumption. I. Title.
G156.5.E58B434 2015
338.4'79104–dc23 2014033164

British Library Cataloguing in Publication Data
A catalogue entry for this book is available from the British Library.

ISBN-13: 978-1-84541-488-7 (hbk)
ISBN-13: 978-1-84541-487-0 (pbk)

Channel View Publications
UK: St Nicholas House, 31–34 High Street, Bristol BS1 2AW, UK.
USA: UTP, 2250 Military Road, Tonawanda, NY 14150, USA.
Canada: UTP, 5201 Dufferin Street, North York, Ontario M3H 5T8, Canada.

The policy of Multilingual Matters/Channel View Publications is to use papers that are natural, renewable and recyclable products, made from wood grown in sustainable forests. In the manufacturing process of our books, and to further support our policy, preference is given to printers that have FSC and PEFC Chain of Custody certification. The FSC and/or PEFC logos will appear on those books where full certification has been granted to the printer concerned.

Typeset by Techset Composition India (P) Ltd., Bangalore and Chennai, India.
Printed and bound in Great Britain by Short Run Press Ltd.

Contents

Figures

Tables

Boxes

1 Introduction

> *The failure today to bring the potential reality and implications of peak oil,*
> *indeed of peak everything, into scientific discourse and teaching is a grave*
> *threat to industrial society.*
> (Hall & Day, 2009: 237)

1.1 Context

This has been called the Century of Declines (Heinberg, 2007). The planet now holds a population of over 7 billion people, and this number is expected to increase to 11 billion by the end of the 21st century. Along with population growth, economic activity and wealth have increased. Global gross domestic product (GDP) per capita has grown tremendously: more than 13 times as fast as the population (Cox, 2012). This growth is amazing and to some even astonishing. In fact, the last century has defied Malthusian predictions of mass starvation and disease as a consequence of accelerated population growth. The reason is that not only has the population grown exponentially, but so has our use of fossil fuels. In the last 100 years cheap fossil fuels have enabled a massive increase in agricultural productivity, evidenced in the heavy use of machinery, fertilisers and pesticides. In conjunction, mobility has increased to an extent that over 1 billion people are now travelling across borders every year.

The use of oil, coal and gas has increased, but also that of other natural resources, for example water, copper, phosphate, biomass, grain and meat. Global energy consumption continues to increase, despite the global financial crisis in 2009. As can be seen in Table 1.1, global energy demand in 2012 amounted to 12,730 million tonnes of oil-equivalent (toe) per day. Oil is the most important primary energy source, making up 33% of all use. In 2013, oil consumption amounted to 4185 toe, the equivalent of 91,331 oil barrels per day. The largest increase between 2011 and 2013, however, was observed for coal, with a 5.4% growth. Oil consumption increased by 2.5% between

Table 1.1 Recent global energy consumption: 2011, 2012 and 2013

	2011 million tonnes of oil-equivalent per day	% share	2012 million tonnes of oil-equivalent per day	% share	2013 million tonnes of oil-equivalent per day	% share
Oil	4081	33	4139	33	4185	33
Natural gas	2914	24	2986	24	3020	24
Coal	3629	30	3724	30	3827	30
Nuclear	600	5	560	4	563	4
Hydroelectric	795	7	834	7	856	7
Renewables	266	2	241	2	279	2
Total	12,225		12,483		12,730	

Note: This table does not include energy extracted from small-scale biomass use, e.g. wood-fired cooking.
Source: British Petroleum (BP) (2014).

those years – with much of this being met by unconventional oil resources such as tar sands. Natural gas and renewable energy sources have increased by 3.6% and 5.0%, respectively. Renewable energy sources still make up only 2% of all global energy use, and are far from 'replacing' fossil fuels.

In the 1970s, there was a strong interest in population growth and resource constraints, evidenced in a range of scientific publications including the well-known book *The Limits to Growth*, commissioned by the Club of Rome (Meadows *et al.*, 1974). The oil crises in 1974 and 1979 further highlighted the importance of considering planetary constraints on development. Ecologists were interested in concepts such as carrying capacity, and this was also reflected in tourism and leisure research, where academics focused on growth limitations related to recreational visitation to natural areas. In response to the thinking of that era, a new scientific discipline emerged – ecological economics – that was interested in developing metrics for understanding human environmental footprints and the role of natural capital in economic production. However, as argued by Hall and Day (2009), this focus has changed dramatically, with critical discussions about finite resources and planetary capacities having almost completely vanished from the public and scientific debates.

Instead the focus has moved on to more specific environmental problems, including the impacts of fossil fuel consumption, particularly global climate change. For the last decade (at least), climate change has been central to scientific and political debates on humans' influence of natural systems.

Solutions for reducing greenhouse gas emissions and policy frameworks both for climate change mitigation and adaptation are being discussed intensely by scientists, leading businesses and policymakers. Further, climate change is institutionalised in various formats, including the United Nations Framework Convention on Climate Change and the Intergovernmental Panel on Climate Change. Climate change is a highly prominent issue, and different to resource depletion, of great public interest (Friedrichs, 2011).

More recently, there is increasing evidence of addressing climate change and Peak Oil as joint problems (e.g. Curtis, 2009; Rozenberg *et al.*, 2010). Clearly, both are related to the (excessive) use of fossil fuels. Stoft's (2008) book *Carbonomics. How to Fix the Climate and Charge it to OPEC*, for example, highlights the close relationship between climate change and oil security, and seeks to develop effective policy mechanisms to address both. Some have argued that climate change will automatically be solved by shrinking oil resources. Others have pointed to the fact that Peak Oil will only increase climate change risks as we are gradually consuming more carbon-intensive and 'dirty' sources of energy. So, while climate chance and Peak Oil seem to be a highly related problem, their solutions often differ – to the extent that climate change mitigation policies could be completely opposite to measures that promote energy security.

In a recent study, McGlade and Ekins (2014) undertook detailed modelling to understand the climate impacts of burning all the fossil fuel that could be exploited. They concluded that the political goal of keeping global warming under the 'dangerous' level of 2 degrees Celsius is incompatible with the exploration of carbon-intensive oil resources, such as tar sands or deepwater resources. They argued that if we were serious about climate change, we should not waste economic resources on exploratory drilling of resources that should never be exploited. While discussions of this type are emerging, at this present point they are largely confined to a limited number of academic specialists or advocates. It is not uncommon that 'anti-oil' campaigns bring together a number of activists that are either concerned about climate change, Peak Oil, threats to wildlife and the marine life in particular, and other societal issues related to 'consumption' (see Figure 1.1).

In the mainstream literature, including elite magazines such as *The Economist* (Becken, 2014), issues surrounding oil supply and demand are largely addressed by economists and by institutions such as the International Energy Agency (IEA). Mainstream neo-classical economists' views are built on the premise that 'something will turn up, when the price of oil is high enough, because something always does', even though it is known that 'there isn't anything conceivable that could replace conventional oil, in the same quantities or energy densities, at any meaningful price' (BP Exploration

Figure 1.1 Advertisement for a summit to discuss (and protest against) deep oil exploration in the southern waters of New Zealand, organised by Oil-Free-Otago
Source: http://oilfreeotago.com/links/#

Manager Richer Miller, in Newman, 2006: 2). Only a few scientists have pointed to the critical role of energy and the problems associated with its 'finite' substitutability (e.g. Daly, 1978, 2008). As a result, Peak Oil is not widely debated as a global economic and environmental risk (Wicker & Becken, 2013). The limited discourse and attention means that many decision-makers (including those related to tourism) may have difficulties conceptualising the idea of Peak Oil.

At the same time as the world worries about global financial systems, climate change, and maybe biodiversity loss, many of the resources that we are depending on are reaching capacity – or peak. The peak in oil production is probably the most widely discussed resource peak – and it is the focus of this book. However, other peaks have been identified as well, including peak coal and uranium (Höök, 2010), peak water (Bell, 2009), peak phosphate and minerals (Prior *et al.*, 2012), peak globalisation (Curtis, 2009), and even peak wireless space (Commonwealth Scientific and Industrial Organisation (CSIRO), 2014). Sometimes the imminence of several peaks requires difficult and precarious trade-offs. For example, the water–energy nexus is increasingly discussed as a challenge, where energy supply depends on water (e.g. for cooling in power plants) and water supply depends on energy (epitomised in desalination plants). It will become increasingly challenging to meet both demands for water and energy.

Thus, numerous challenges for maintaining growth and development – including tourism development – are manifesting themselves. Decoupling growth from resource use has been heralded as the approach to overcome physical constraints (see Figure 1.2). Thus, thanks to ever-increasing resource efficiencies, it is argued, continuous growth can be achieved. That means that less resource input is required to achieve the same, or growing, levels of output. The United Nations Environment Programme (UNEP) defines decoupling as a critical step towards a Green Economy in which well-being and equity can be improved while reducing environmental risks and scarcities.

One challenge of decoupling is that increasing efficiencies are usually more than compensated for by increases in economic activity, thus leading to overall growth (Tienhaara, 2010). This rebound effect is well-established in the field of energy efficiency, where more efficient devices lead to greater usage and an overall increase in energy use. Should the world not achieve a decoupling and continue business-as-usual, then global resource extraction would triple by 2050 (UNEP, 2011). Others have argued that the 2009

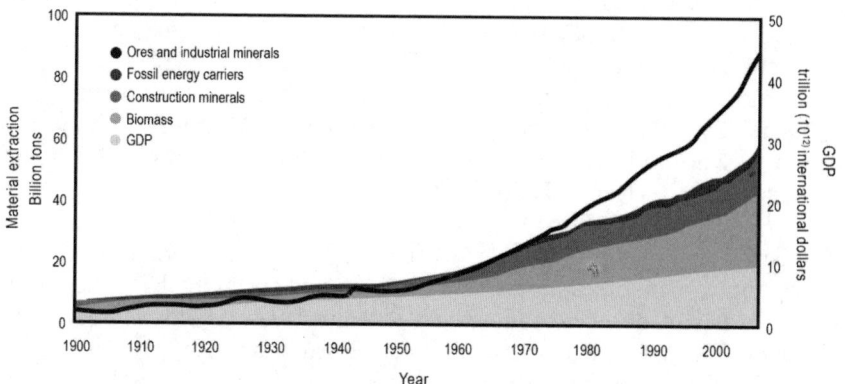

Figure 1.2 Global GDP, biomass and resource extraction in billion tonnes from 1900–2005 – is decoupling possible?
Source: After Krausmann *et al.* (2009), in UNEP (2011).

financial crisis highlighted that the current growth model is unsustainable and requires a fundamental change (in Tiernhaara, 2010). Such change is not predicated in the concept of the Green Economy, which has to be seen as a 'paradigm nudge' as opposed to a much needed 'paradigm shift' (Weaver, 2009).

Peak Oil is one of the most imminent and pervasive challenges to humankind and its existing economies and societies (Hall & Day, 2009). Ninety-five percent of all goods produced around the world depend on the input of oil. Oil is not only used directly as an energy source, but often as the base material of lubricants, plastics, pharmaceuticals, textiles and paints (Zentrum für Transformation der Bundeswehr, 2010). Heinberg (2011: 112) noted 'Quibbling over the exact meaning of the word "peak", or the exact timing of the event, or what constitutes "oil" is fairly pointless. The oil world has changed.'

Most people take energy for granted and have little appreciation for the uniqueness and usefulness we extract from fossil fuels. Colin Campbell, one of the leading scientists in the Peak Oil debate, summarised this point as follows:

> It was as if oil provided us with an army of unpaid and unfed slaves to do our work for us. It has been calculated that a drop of oil, weighing one gram, yields 10,000 calories of energy, which is the equivalent of one day's hard human labour. In other words, today's oil production is equivalent in energy terms to the work of 22 billion slaves. Financial control of the world has led to a certain polarisation between the wealthy West and the other countries which find themselves burdened by foreign debt as they export resources, product and profit. Many people have come to think that it is money that makes the world go round, when in reality it is the underlying supply of cheap, and largely oil-based, energy, that has turned the wheels of industry, fuelled the airliners and the bombers, and generally acted as the world's blood stream. Midas-like wealth flowed to those who find themselves having a controlling position in the System. (Campbell & Heapes, 2008: 7)

Tourism is very energy-intensive (Scott *et al.*, 2008), and as will be discussed in this book, consumes about 10% of oil-equivalent globally. Thus, as an example, a large number of imaginary 'energy slaves' would be required to transport people to and from their holiday destinations. As we will see later in this book, the average tourist who travels by air uses 0.57 barrels of oil per flight. One barrel of oil alone contains the energy of about 23,000 hours of human labour (Heinberg, 2013). Campbell and Heapes' quote above not only highlights the magnitude of energy supplied by oil, but it also points to the intricate relationship between energy wealth, political power, military conflict and terrorism (*The Economist*, 2004). Thus, Peak Oil – and the global distribution of supply and demand – is a precarious issue, potentially much more so than global climate change. While tourism is often heralded as a force of good (e.g. as in the 2014 World Travel and Tourism Council Global Summit) and an ambassador for peace, its thirst for the black gold is indirectly adding to geopolitical conflicts over access to oil resources.

1.2 Purpose and Structure of This Book

The introduction above highlights the pervasive and grave risks associated with Peak Oil, both for society broadly and for tourism specifically. Despite the alarming trends outlined above, there is no discussion about Peak Oil in tourism. This book aims to address this important gap. The book acknowledges the relevance of the existing tourism discourse on resource consumption and environmental risks, in particular previous work on tourism and climate change (e.g. Becken, 2013b; Becken & Hay, 2007, 2012; Gössling, 2010; Peeters *et al.*, 2007; Scott *et al.*, 2012). However, by specifically unpacking the threat of Peak Oil and its implications for tourism, this book discusses absolute physical limits to tourism, rather than environmental risks and consumer choices. It therefore also responds to Hall and Day's (2009) call to bring peak resources back into the academic debate. In the views of this author this is of critical importance to tourism.

This book cannot provide a full analysis of Peak Oil implications for tourism, nor will it be within the scope of analysis to deliver an exhaustive analysis of different stakeholder views, actions and vulnerabilities. However, the book aims to provide a first basis for discussing these important dynamics relevant to the phenomenon of Peak Oil. Substantial knowledge gaps that became apparent while writing this book will be pointed out where relevant.

As this book will show, the consequences of Peak Oil are likely to require a reconceptualisation of tourism. The rationale of this book is therefore to provide essential information on the current status of oil use in tourism, its growth expectations and alternative development pathways in the face of decreasing availability of cheap oil. It is hoped that this book is not only informative to those interested in tourism theory and practice, but that it serves as an eye opener to those interested in sustainable tourism (in the true sense of the word). It is also hoped that the book will stimulate more critical examinations of the future of tourism and encourage global dialogue in support of tourism resilience.

The objectives of this book are:

(1) to provide an estimate of tourism's contribution to global energy demand;
(2) to critically assess growth forecasts that determine the common discourse of tourism development;
(3) to provide comprehensive information on the current understanding of oil resources, and also investigate issues of data availability, credibility and vested interests;
(4) to provide a theoretically informed assessment of the impacts of growing oil prices on tourism economies, destinations and businesses; and
(5) to explore alternative energy sources and new forms of tourism in a post-Peak Oil era.

Several scientific disciplines underpin this book. Predominantly, the impacts of Peak Oil on tourism can be approached through economics and geography, including transport geography. These two intersect through key theories, for example about price elasticities and economic decision-making by tourists. However, as will be apparent throughout the book, other disciplinary understanding is also required, for example from social psychology or the political sciences. Similar to research on climate change mitigation behaviour, theories around environmentally friendly or ethical behaviour are relevant to understanding why people will or will not act on Peak Oil-related risks. The relevant theories will be referred to within the individual chapters.

The book is structured into eight chapters (Figure 1.3). First, it seems important to provide an understanding of just how energy – and more specifically oil – dependent tourism is. Chapter 2 therefore builds on earlier tourism carbon footprint analyses (most notably Scott *et al.*, 2008) and investigates energy use of global tourism and sub-sectors. Tourist transportation is clearly the most fuel-thirsty component of tourism, contributing 8% to global oil demand. A destination perspective highlights the oil-intensity of some destinations, especially islands that primarily depend on international aviation for their tourism activity.

Tourism has been growing faster than many other economic sectors. In fact, tourism forecasts build on the historic relationship between GDP and tourist activity (e.g. measured in expenditure), whereby the latter usually increases by between 20 and 40% more than GDP (Chapter 3). If growth trends witnessed in the past – and especially occurring right now in relation to Chinese tourism – continue, tourism's role in global oil demand will increase substantially. Alternatively, there is a possibility that the majority of forecasts (i.e. the mainstream) will not eventuate because of rapidly rising oil prices. Calls for a steady-state-economy and slow growth, or even

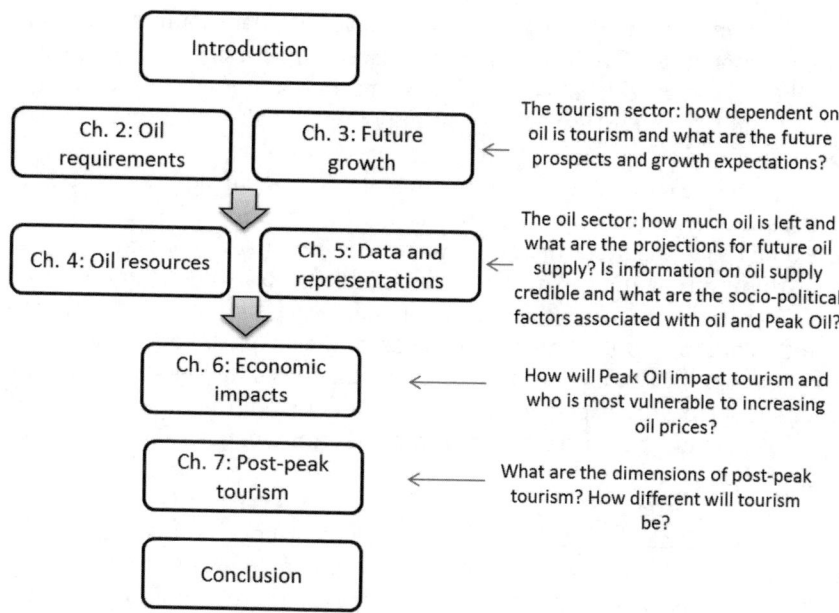

Figure 1.3 Structure of this book and key questions addressed in the different chapters

de-growth, are explored by a small number of experts, but remain marginal to the dominant discourse.

Whether one believes in traditional forecasts or alternative future scenarios depends probably on the extent to which one sees oil as a limiting factor to growth. Chapter 4 therefore explores the latest literature on oil resources, production trends and decline rates. It also provides some information on unconventional resources, including shale gas. These are included not only because they have indeed become increasingly important in the supply of liquid fuels, but also because the surge in shale gas production in the United States has shifted the discourse from one of doom to one of euphoria (Becken, 2014). Technology has once again prevailed and overcome physical barriers – so the proponents of the 'shale revolution' argue. Chapter 4 shows that this boom may be relatively short-lived and not likely to be repeated elsewhere in the world.

Rhetoric and manipulated discourse are critical elements of the global oil debate (Chapter 5). Oil firms, oil exporting countries and even oil importing countries all have reasons for maintaining positive messages around global oil supply. Partly this is related to business interests, but also to geopolitics or concerns over national security. For these reasons, and in combination with extremely limited access to robust and verified data sources, the public discourse on Peak Oil is almost non-existent (Friedrichs, 2011). A small number of so-called 'peakists' is the exception – and due to limited high-calibre support and little involvement in political affairs, their wider impact is small.

It therefore remains to wait for rising oil prices, as already experienced in 2008, and assess their impacts on tourism as they happen. Chapter 6 synthesises the economic literature on oil prices and key macroeconomic parameters, finding that increasing oil prices are likely to be detrimental for all countries in the long run, even oil exporting ones. Using concepts of elasticity of income and price elasticity of demand, the chapter shows how higher oil prices are likely to reduce tourism activity, especially long-haul tourism. Tourism businesses display different vulnerabilities depending on a range of factors, including their customer mix, distance from markets and the uniqueness of their product.

Chapter 7 attempts to explore several avenues for reducing tourism's vulnerability to Peak Oil. Four key elements of 'post-peak' tourism are identified: (i) renewable energy sources; (ii) low-carbon transportation systems; (iii) new forms of tourism demand and behaviour; and (iv) localised travel and destinations. The chapter shows that Peak Oil will not be the end of tourism – but significant changes are to be expected. Changes may be negative, but Peak Oil also bears some opportunities. Regardless, and as for Peak Oil mitigation more generally (e.g. Hirsch et al., 2005), the sooner the tourism sector understands the challenges, the less disruptive will be the impacts.

The conclusion – Chapter 8 – summarises the key points made in this book and indicates areas for future essential research to support the tourism transformation. It will also touch on the notion that Peak Oil could provide an opportunity for much needed change. I would like to close the introduction with Edison's famous quote from 1931 that still seems so valid over 80 years later.

> I'd put my money on the sun and solar energy. What a source of power! I hope we don't have to wait until oil and coal run out before we tackle that. (Thomas Edison, 1931, in Newton, 1987, p. 31)

2 A Thirsty Sector: Oil Requirements of Tourism

2.1 Introduction

This chapter begins with the big picture of how much oil tourism uses. Subsequently, the oil requirements of tourism sub-sectors or individual businesses will be analysed in more detail. The transport sector will be examined first, followed by tourist accommodation and other tourism-related sectors. Then, a destination perspective is explored. The reason for this macro-to-micro scale approach is to gain an appreciation of just how much oil tourism consumes. This is important for two reasons. First it highlights the vulnerability of the tourism sector, should oil prices continue to rise, and second it shows that any measures or agreements (e.g. following similar lines of global climate change frameworks) put into place to address Peak Oil must consider the role tourism and global travel play in this challenge.

Before we begin, it is important to understand the different units of energy that can be used for measuring fuel use. Typically, oil is measured in barrels (bbl) or British Thermal Units (Btu). The latter can easily be converted into barrels and this has been done in this chapter where necessary. Second, it is very common to measure fuel and other energy use in joules, or more specifically in megajoules (MJ) (1 million joules). One barrel of oil contains about 5562 MJ of energy. This amount of energy would fuel an average car for a journey of about 2700 km.

Because MJ is the standard measure for comparing different types of energy (e.g. oil, gas and coal) this chapter mainly presents energy information in MJ or larger versions of it (e.g. GJ = gigajoules or a thousand MJ). Where useful, MJ are converted into barrels of oil (or oil-equivalent to be more specific). This allows us to illustrate and compare oil usage relative to oil production, for example as discussed in Chapter 4. Energy conversions of this kind do not consider the different quality associated with different energy sources (for more detail, see Patterson, 1996).

It is important to distinguish electricity from other energy sources, because electricity – at least in theory – is easier to substitute than fossil fuels. For example, a hotel has the option to install solar hot water to reduce its electricity use for heating water (see Chapter 7). It could also invest in photovoltaic cells or wind turbines, and – most importantly – it can improve its efficiency of use. This has great business relevance given that energy costs can constitute in the order of 8% of gross operating revenue (Becken & Carboni, 2008). The greater the share of electricity, the less exposed a business is to global oil prices or Peak Oil (see Chapter 6).

However, all energy systems are coupled and shortages or price fluctuations in one energy system will inevitably affect the other systems. This has been most prominent for the relationship between oil and gas, but is also evident for electricity, which to a large extent is produced based on the combustion of fossil fuels. For this reason, electricity use is only a partial shelter to global oil prices. Electricity systems are under increasing pressure, just like global oil production (see Chapter 4), because of environmental restrictions on gas or coal-fired power plants (that collide with climate change targets), limited potential for expanding hydro-power, social opposition to wind-farms, and a range of issues associated with nuclear power.

2.2 Estimate of Tourism's Total Oil Use

There are no official estimates of the total oil consumption of tourism. Instead, tourism's contribution to global carbon dioxide emissions can be used as a proxy for liquid fuel use, or 'oil' for simplicity (for more detail on liquid fuels and oil, see Chapter 4). In 2008, a global team of experts provided a comprehensive estimate of the carbon footprint of global tourism as part of a state-of-the-art tourism and climate change report for the United Nations World Tourism Organisation (UNWTO) (Scott *et al.*, 2008). The data available from this study are used to estimate oil use from tourism.

As a first approximation for tourism's oil use, Scott *et al.*'s estimates of transport carbon footprints are employed. These transport emissions data include both international and domestic tourism. For the purpose of the estimate of oil use presented in this chapter, only emissions from overnight visitors – both international and domestic – are considered. Day-trippers are excluded. The UNWTO report distinguishes between different types of air travel, rail, car and coach transport. Each transport mode is characterised by

Table 2.1 Estimate of fuel intensity of tourist transport modes

Transport mode	CO_2 (kg/pkm)	L/pkm	MJ/pkm*	Assumptions made for the oil estimate
Air < 500 km	0.206	0.082	2.990	All planes use jet kerosene
Air 500–1000 km	0.154	0.064	2.235	
Air 1001–1500 km	0.130	0.054	1.887	
Air 1501–2000 km	0.121	0.050	1.756	
Air > 2000 km	0.111	0.046	1.611	
Bus/coach	0.022	0.008	0.313	All buses use diesel
Car	0.133	0.059	2.020	All cars use petrol
Rail	0.027	0.010	0.384	All rail uses diesel, even though it is noted that some railways use electricity or coal

Note: *Energy use has been derived by using calorific values provided by the Intergovernmental Panel on Climate Change (IPCC, 2006).
Source: Calculated from carbon intensities in Scott et al. (2008), pp. 124 and 127–128.

specific carbon dioxide (CO_2) emission factors, measured in kg CO_2 per passenger-kilometre (kg/pkm) (Table 2.1, first column).

It is possible to calculate backwards from emissions to estimate fuel burn in litres per passenger-kilometre (L/pkm) and energy intensity in megajoules (MJ/pkm). As is well established in transport energy studies, the energy intensity is highest for short-haul flights due to the impact of the energy-intensive take-off phase, relative to a short flight time at cruise altitude. As shown in Table 2.1, several assumptions on the fuel type had to be made to derive the estimates presented below.

Importantly, the UNWTO study (Scott et al., 2008) provides unique data on global tourist transport volumes in 2005. In total, domestic and international tourists travelled almost 8000 billion passenger-kilometres (Table 2.2). This is a number too large to imagine, but it is about the same distance as travelling 200 million times around the Earth's equator or 10 million times to the moon and back. The largest share of this distance was by air (49.6%). These data are now eight years old, and given the increasing popularity of air travel (Figure 2.1), it is likely that the proportion of air travel has grown to well over half of all tourist travel. In total, tourist transport consumed in the order of 372,000 million litres of fuel in 2005, or the equivalent of about 2346 million barrels (Mbbl).

Table 2.2 Estimated oil use for global tourist transport

Travel volume in 2005	Pkm (billion)	Estimated litres of fuel (million)	Converted into million barrels (Mbbl)**
Total air	3,924	211,718	1,334
Total car	2,462	145,420	916
Other (assume rail)*	1,524	15,314	96
Grand total	7,910	372,452	2,346

Notes: *The Scott et al. (2008) data provide transport volumes for air, car and other. The energy intensity of rail travel is assumed for 'other', although other could also include water-based transport or buses.
**Using a conversion factor of 0.0063 barrels per litre.
Source: Calculated from carbon intensities in Scott et al. (2008), pp. 124 and 127–128.

Figure 2.1 Passengers going through security control at Barcelona (Spain) airport
Notes: The new Terminal 1 at Barcelona Airport has increased maximum capacity to 55 million passengers per year. Currently, the airport counts about 34 million passengers.

Transport is not the only tourist activity that requires oil. In fact, transport makes up only 75% of tourism's carbon footprint (Scott et al., 2008). Other key components of the tourism product are accommodation, tourist activities and services. There are no global data on the oil demand of these elements, and as we will see further below, it is very difficult to estimate the global oil use in hotels and other establishments. One reason is that accommodation businesses use a wide range of energy sources, with the most important source being electricity (in the order of 65% of total energy demand, see further below). Second, the data available on energy use in tourist accommodation are considerably less detailed than those on tourist transport.

For these reasons, the UNWTO estimates of accommodation and recreational activities' share of the total carbon footprint of tourism are used as basic approximations of oil use for non-transport tourist activities. According to Scott et al. (2008), commercial tourist accommodation used by international and domestic tourists contributed 21% of tourism's total emissions in 2005. An additional 4% was added by leisure-related activities. The conversion of carbon dioxide emissions from tourist accommodation and activities into oil is complex, because of a much more diverse energy mix in those tourism sub-sectors (see also further below).

For this reason, we simply extrapolate from the above estimate of 2346 Mbbl of oil for tourist transport. Adding 25% to this figure, results in a total amount of 2933 Mbbl for global tourism in 2005. Thus, tourist accommodation and other activities would approximately use 587 Mbbl of oil per year. According to the British Petroleum (BP) Statistical Review of World Energy (BP, 2013), global oil consumption in 2005 was about 84.1 Mbbl per day, or 31,000 Mbbl per year. This means that tourism's oil requirements made up about 9.5% of global oil consumption in 2005. Relative to the present, this is a conservative estimate, as tourism is likely to have grown more than other industries over the last eight years. It is probably safe to state that tourism contributes in the order of 10% of global oil use. Future research should explore in more detail how much oil is consumed by tourism. This could then not only be stratified by end use (e.g. transport and accommodation) but also by tourist type or country of consumption.

2.3 Oil Intensity of Tourist Transport

Global transportation is driving the current overall demand for oil (International Energy Agency (IEA), 2013b). Transportation is also responsible for most of the increase between the present use and the IEA's energy demand scenarios for the future. In the New Policies Scenario (see Chapter 4), the contribution of transport to total oil demand will grow from 53% in 2009 to 60% in 2035. The growth in global tourism is, no doubt, contributing to this trend. In the following, different types of tourist transport will be examined in terms of their oil intensity.

2.3.1 Air transport

> ...Jet fuel and the issues surrounding it are among our top priorities and biggest challenges. (Tony Tyler, CEO of the International Air Transport Association (IATA) at the Aviation Fuel Forum in Berlin, May 2013)

As evident in the above analysis, air travel has become the most prolific form of transport for tourism when measured in passenger-kilometres and fuel consumption (Tables 2.1 and 2.2). In 2012, the total number of passengers in that year amounted to 2977 million. In the same year, the global aviation industry consumed about 273,000 million litres of jet kerosene, or 1714 Mbbl (IATA, 2013a). In 2005, according to the IATA, there were 2157 million passengers who consumed about 257,000 million litres of fuel, or 1616 Mbbl. The difference of about 280 Mbbl between the IATA figure and the tourism estimate of 1334 Mbbl shown in Table 2.2 could be explained by diplomatic travel, migration and other non-tourism travel.

In a separate study, Nygren *et al.* (2009) estimated that the aviation industry consumed about 1811 Mbbl of jet kerosene in 2006. This represented about 6.3% of world refinery production. Not all aviation fuel is related to passenger transport. An indication of relative importance of passenger versus freight traffic can be gained from a comparison of revenue. IATA (2013b) statistics show that revenue is heavily biased towards passenger transport (US$538 billion in 2012) compared with cargo (US$62 billion). In reality, many airplanes carry both freight and passengers and it is difficult to allocate fuel use. If all fuel is allocated to passengers, the average passenger consumes about 92 litres of fuel or the equivalent of 0.57 barrels per flight.

The aviation industry spent about US$214 billion on fuel in 2013 (IATA, 2013a) at a cost of US$108 per barrel of Brent oil (or US$124 for jet kerosene in 2013). The fuel costs translated into an average of 31% of operating costs in 2013; thus the fuel requirements of air travel constitute an important, if not the most critical factor, for airlines' operations management. The 2013 fuel bill was about $4 billion more than the 2012 one and about five times as high as the sector's fuel cost in 2003 (US$44 billion, IATA, 2013a), when Brent oil traded at an average of US$28.8 per barrel. As will be discussed in more detail in Chapter 6, fuel prices significantly affect the airlines' profitably. During 2008, when oil prices reached record high levels, aviation demand decreased and profits were negative. This continued into 2009 in response to the global financial crisis, despite lower fuel prices. Since then, fuel prices – and the airlines' fuel bill – have increased again, but so has profitability (Figure 2.2).

The dependence on oil is aviation's 'Achilles heel'. Accordingly, the industry has invested substantially in improving fuel efficiency over the last

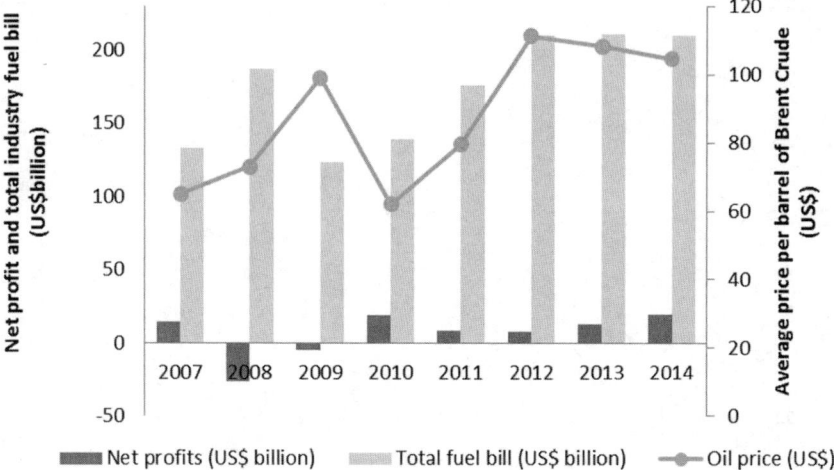

Figure 2.2 Airline profit and average fuel price between 2001 and 2014
Source: Based on data from IATA (2013a and 2013b).

decades. The actual improvement rate is highly contested. A 1997 report by Rolls-Royce that was cited in the IPCC Special Report on Aviation (Penner *et al.*, 1999) claimed that the fuel use of new jet aircraft was 70% lower in 1997 compared with 1960. Peeters *et al.* (2005) rejected this high rate of improvement and provided an alternative estimate of 55%. More recently, and based on data of 26,331 aircraft, Rutherford and Zeinali (2009) estimated that the increase in efficiency of fuel burn between 1960 and 2008 amounts to 51%.

More specifically, Rutherford and Zeinali (2009) showed that efficiency improvements were most prominent in the 1960s, due to the introduction of wide-body aircraft such as the Boeing 747-400. Annual increases in fuel efficiency per seat-kilometre reached 2.3% in those years. Further gains were achieved in the 1980s (3.5% per annum), when mid-range aircraft were introduced that were powered by new high bypass ratio turbofans (e.g. Boeing's 757 and 767). Since 2000 the average fuel efficiency per seat-kilometre has stagnated. Similar assumptions about fuel efficiency trends underlay an analysis of fuel demand undertaken by Chèze *et al.* (2011) (Figure 2.3).

The two main aircraft manufacturers, Airbus and Boeing, are both working on more fuel-efficient models. The most efficient aircraft at the time of writing is the Airbus 380 family (Figure 2.4). It uses about 20% less fuel per seat than other comparable aircraft, and when fully loaded, it reaches fuel consumptions of less than three litres per 100 km. This compares favourably with the global fleet average use as shown in Table 2.1 above (e.g. 4.6 L/100 km

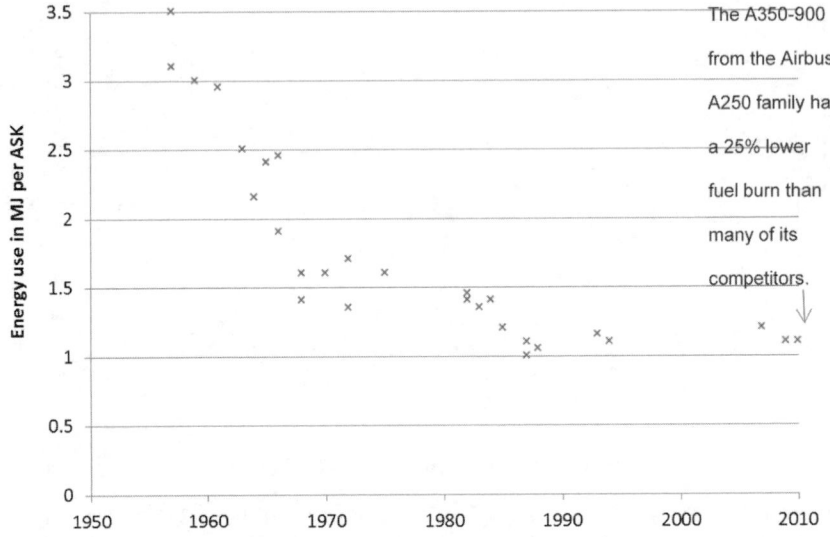

Figure 2.3 Fuel consumption by aircraft
Notes: Measured in megajoules per available seat-kilometre (ASK), beginning with the Comet 4
   aircraft model from 1958 to the average fuel use of the Airbus A350-900 in 2011.
Source: Chèze *et al.* (2011).

Figure 2.4 Singapore Airlines A380 preparing for an inter-continental flight from Zurich
to Singapore

for travel over 2000 km). Currently, there are 57 Airbus A380s in operation and only seven airlines use them: Singapore Airlines, Qantas, Emirates, Lufthansa, Air France, Korean Air and China Southern. Not all airports can accommodate the double-decker style A380.

The IATA (2013b) projected that revenue passenger-kilometres will increase by 6% in 2014, 5.9% in 2015, 5.0% in 2016 and 4.5% in 2017. Not all of this growth will result in increased fuel demand as airlines seek to maximise efficiency. As a result, the IEA (2012) estimated that oil demand from aviation will continue to grow at a rate of only 2.6% per annum between current demand and 2035. Chèze et al. (2011) estimated an annual growth rate of aviation fuel consumption of only 1.9% between 2008 and 2025; resulting in an overall increase in demand of 38%. They too predicted that traffic volumes will grow relatively faster, namely by 100% between 2008 and 2025. Thus, they concluded that while improvements in efficiency will be realised, these do not fully compensate for air traffic growth. According to both the IEA and Chèze et al. (2011), much of this growth will be fuelled by demand from the Chinese aviation market (Figure 2.5). China's contribution to global air traffic has already doubled from 4.7% in 1996 to 8.6% in 2006 (see also Chapter 3 for more details on tourism growth out of China).

Figure 2.5 Passengers boarding a domestic flight from Chengdu to the Tibetan plateau

2.3.2 Land transport

While increasing volumes of fuel are used for air travel, land transport (and most prominently car travel) is still the dominant form of transport in terms of journeys made, especially for domestic tourism. Fuel use varies considerably between different types of land transport. Transport manufacturers provide information on how much fuel a vehicle requires per 100 km of travel; however these reflect laboratory data, based on ideal conditions. Real-world fuel consumption can differ substantially from these factory estimates.

Estimating total fuel use for land-based tourist transport is challenging and the above UNWTO (Scott *et al.*, 2008) figures are probably the best available. The key issues are (Becken, 2000a, 2000b):

- Vehicle fuel efficiencies differ substantially between countries. For example the average car in Europe is more fuel efficient than the average car in Australia or the USA;
- The calorific values of fuel, most prominently diesel and petrol, are not the same around the world;
- Individual driver behaviour and road conditions greatly effect fuel efficiency;
- Fuel use data are often only available in the form of megajoules per vehicle-kilometre (MJ/vkm), ignoring load factors typical (and not always known) of tourist transport;
- Country-specific traffic congestions (e.g. frequent congestion in Japan, Lipscy & Schipper, 2013) is difficult to account for; and
- The vehicle fleet composition of rental vehicle companies is an important factor, as for example, the introduction of modern cars, or a change in the ratio of diesel to petrol cars, alters the average fuel consumption. Some rental vehicles use biofuel blends or have liquefied natural gas powered or electric vehicles in their fleet.

Therefore, the fuel consumption of a particular type of tourist transport in MJ/pkm can only be estimated by assuming average fleet compositions and average fuel efficiencies (Becken & Hay, 2007). Most countries maintain detailed statistics on transportation, including traffic volumes and average energy use. For example, the European Union through its statistical division Eurostat provides data on passenger transport for all member countries. In addition, many countries or states provide data on energy use per passenger-kilometre. These can be used as first approximations for tourist transport wherever available, but caution needs to be exercised as estimates vary widely. Table 2.3 illustrates how different fuel efficiencies are for a number

Table 2.3 Energy use per passenger-kilometre: Examples from different studies around the world for a range of land transport modes, including air travel for comparison

Transport mode	Energy per passenger-kilometre (MJ/pkm)	Country	Source
Bus	1.41	Australia	Rail CRC (2006)
Bus	1.32	South Australia	Apelbaum Consulting Group (2007)
Bus	0.70	Japan	Lipscy and Schipper (2013)
Bus	0.40	Spain	Sanyé-Mengual *et al.* (2014)
Car	2.73	South Australia	Apelbaum Consulting Group (2007)
Car/Passenger road vehicles	2.78	Australia	Rail CRC (2006)
Car Toyota Prius	1.05	Global	Strickland (2009)
Domestic air	2.50	Australia	Rail CRC (2006)
Domestic air	2.00	Japan	Lipscy and Schipper (2013)
Domestic air <500 km	2.99	Global average	Scott *et al.* (2008), see Table 2.1
Light rail (2004–2005)	1.92	Australia	Rail CRC (2006)
Urban rail (2004–2005)	1.47	Australia	Rail CRC (2006)
Non-urban rail (2004–2005)	1.20	Australia	Rail CRC (2006)
Motorcycle	2.01	South Australia	Apelbaum Consulting Group (2007)
Rail/train	1.60	South Australia	Apelbaum Consulting Group (2007)
Rail/train	0.40	Japan	Lipscy and Schipper (2013)
Rail/train	0.34	Denmark	Strickland (2009)
TGV rail	0.16	France	Strickland (2009)
London Underground	0.54	UK	Strickland (2009)
Shikansen High Speed Rail (2005)	0.35	Japan	Rail CRC (2006)
Tram	1.74	South Australia	Apelbaum Consulting Group (2007)

of countries. The table also gives an indication of the relative difference between different types of transport.

The information presented in Table 2.3 does not take into account the carbon intensity of different energy sources. Trains, for example, increasingly use electricity as an energy carrier. High-speed trains, in particular, rely on electricity. This means that in addition to being more energy efficient, they also contribute less to the Peak Oil challenge. At the same time, it matters where the electricity comes from. In France for example, nuclear power plants with no input of fossil fuels typically generate electricity, whereas in China, electricity is coal-based. Coal is to some extent a substitute for oil or gas.

One way to compare the 'fossil fuel intensity' is to examine carbon emissions (as already illustrated in the above estimate of tourism's oil demand). Figure 2.6 shows the CO_2 intensity for different segments of High Speed Rail (HSR) in comparison to car and air travel. Baron et al. (2011) show that HSR in France (LGV Mediterranée) emits 11.0 grams of CO_2/pkm, compared with 151.6 grams of CO_2/pkm for the car and 164.0 grams of CO_2/pkm for air travel. The same study also reveals the relatively high carbon costs for track construction of HSR (especially when viaducts and tunnels are required), but

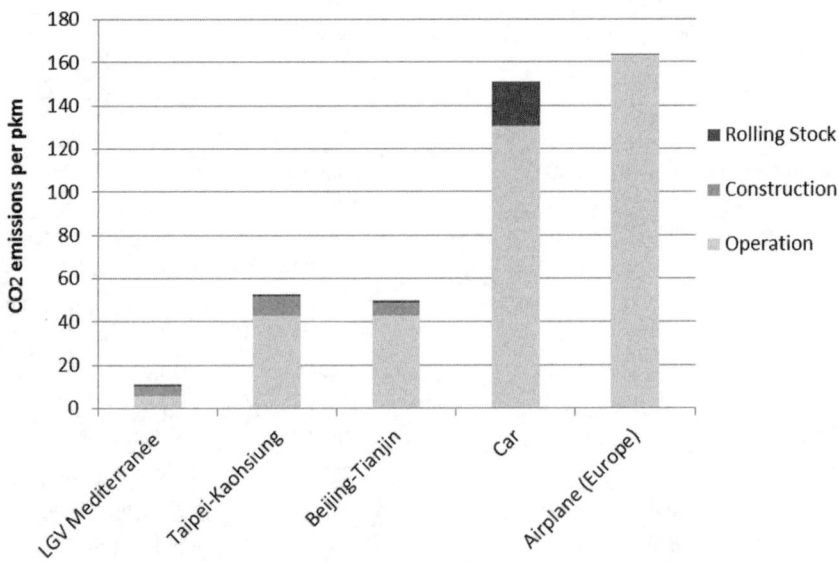

Figure 2.6 Comparison of the carbon intensity of different rotes of High Speed Rail
Note: The CO_2 emission figures depend on the country-specific electricity mix and carbon intensity.
Source: After Baron et al. (2011).

Table 2.4 Energy consumption for different types of tourist transport in New Zealand

Transport mode	Energy use per vehicle kilometre (MJ/vkm)	Average load factor (pax)	Energy use per passenger-kilometre (MJ/pkm)
Backpacker bus	23.10	39.8	0.58
Camper van	4.54	2.20	2.06
Coach (tour bus)	23.10	22.9	1.01
Hitch-hiking	3.25	3.16	1.03
Motorcycle	1.22	1.40	0.87
Private car	3.25	3.16	1.03
Recreational boat	9.62	5.49	1.75
Rental car	2.35	2.50	0.94
Scheduled coach	NA	NA	0.75
Shuttle bus/van	3.22	5.46	0.59
Train	NA	NA	1.44

Source: Becken (2002a, 2002b).

low intensity for production of stock (i.e. carriages) and maintenance. For example the carbon costs of constructing a car are 20 times as high as those of HSR per passenger-kilometre.

Only a few sources are available that specifically report tourist transport energy use. Tourist behaviour is sometimes different from 'average transport behaviour' represented in transport statistics, for example because tourists choose different types of vehicles or travel with larger groups. Families going on holiday, for example, would have a higher vehicle occupancy rate than single driver commuters. Becken's (2002a, 2002b) research of transport energy use by tourists in New Zealand provided some information on tourism-specific fuel intensities that were derived from national data in combination with tourist surveys (Table 2.4). It emerged that fuel use depends significantly on vehicle occupancy. So-called backpacker buses enjoy high load factors, resulting in a relatively small per-passenger fuel use of only 0.58 MJ/pkm.

2.3.3 Water transport

The International Maritime Organisation (IMO), in their publication *International Shipping Facts and Figures* (IMO, 2012), distinguishes passenger ships that transport people for 'fun' from those that provide transport as a 'function'. Functional passenger water transport includes ferries that follow regular schedules, or other shipping services that are designed to take people from one place to another as quickly and cheaply as possible. Ferries can be small, but can also accommodate up to 3000 passengers and include car transport (e.g. those crossing the English Channel). In contrast, fun-related water transport refers to cruise ships that offer leisure activities during travel and therefore constitute much more than just transportation. The largest cruise ship is the Oasis of the Seas, carrying up to 6360 passengers and 2100 shipping crew. It has been afloat since 2009 and is run by Royal Caribbean International.

Since most studies focus on freight shipping or passenger transport more broadly, it is difficult to get a complete picture of how oil-intensive tourist water transport is. Globally, passenger water transport (i.e. ferries and cruise ships) consumed about 229 million barrels of fuel in 2007 (based on IMO, 2007, in Walnum, 2011). Not all of this fuel is related to tourism, as passenger transport may also include other travel purposes (e.g. commuting or 'functional' water transport). The earlier mentioned UNWTO (Scott et al., 2008) study did not give consideration to cruise ship tourists, and adding the oil requirements of passenger water transport related to tourism would increase oil demand substantially.

In addition to difficulties of limited data disaggregation in relation to water transport (i.e. freight versus passenger, and classification of passengers), most studies focus on CO_2 emissions, rather than fuel consumption. However, as discussed earlier, emissions are a reflection of fuel use, and analyses such as the one shown in Figure 2.7 are informative. For example, it can be seen that both shipping and aviation emissions are largely related to international transportation, although aviation has a more significant domestic travel component. Emissions from maritime shipping are dominated by freight, whereas aviation emissions are driven by passenger travel.

There are only a very few studies that have attempted to analyse the fuel intensity of tourism water transport. As can be seen in Table 2.5, passenger travel by ship is comparatively energy-intensive. In fact, in a detailed study on energy use and greenhouse gas emissions from cruise ships travelling to New Zealand, Howitt et al. (2010) reported that cruise ships are about three times as fuel intensive as aeroplanes. Since cruise ship holidays are sold on the basis of number of days, it is useful to consider energy demand per day rather than per kilometre travelled (Atmosfair, 2010).

As already discussed by Becken and Hay (2007), from a climate change mitigation perspective, cruise ships have thus far escaped the global scrutiny of energy use and 'carbon footprinting'. There are a number of reasons (Becken, 2002a). First, cruise ship companies are large and powerful and a challenge to approach. They typically operate on a global scale and are less likely to be 'captured' in standard energy surveys. In addition, there is a great

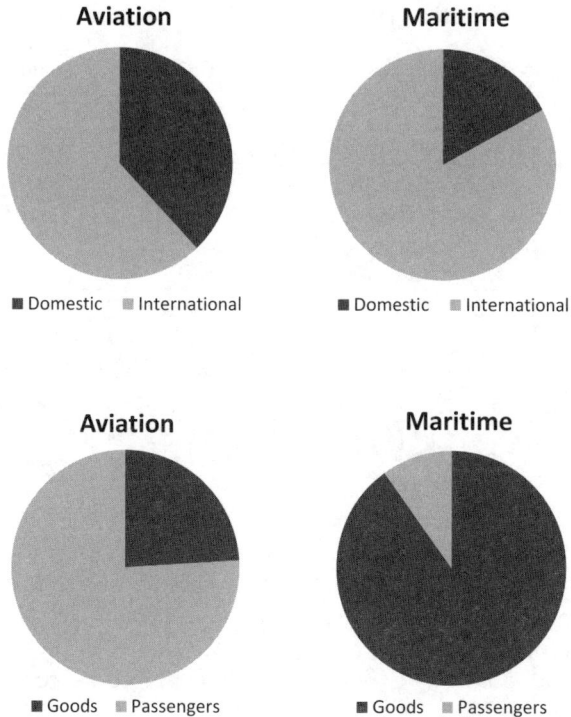

Figure 2.7 Comparison of emissions from aviation and maritime transport for 2007
Source: International Monetary Fund (IMF) (2011).

variety in cruise ships, both in terms of size and services offered. Even cruise ships of the same build can be fitted out quite differently (e.g. cabins and recreational opportunities) and therefore have different energy demands. Accordingly, fuel consumption differs substantially. To date, it has been very difficult to derive average values of energy efficiency and fuel use.

Just like some island resorts (Becken, 2005a), cruise ships are like 'mini cities' that need to be self-sufficient in terms of water use, wastewater treatment, waste management and all other services. In addition, cruise ships accommodate substantial numbers of staff. All of these factors add to fuel consumption that need to be accounted for. There is no agreed methodology if and how this fuel use is apportioned to passengers.

Cruise ships often have several engines (i.e. main and ancillary) as they fulfil several different functions. The main engine typically burns heavy fuel oil, which is considered a relatively 'dirty' fuel compared with diesel and petrol. The main engine is used for propulsion and the ancillary ones are

Table 2.5 Energy consumption for different types of water transport

Type of water transport	Energy use	Country	Source
Cook Strait Ferry	2.4 (MJ/pkm)	New Zealand	Becken (2002b)
Cruise ships	2,000–10,000 MJ/day	Global	Peeters *et al.* (2004)
Cruise ships	1,500–4,000 MJ/day	Global	Becken (2002a)
Cruise ships	1,600 MJ/night for the hotel function of a ship	Global	Howitt *et al.* (2010)
Cruise ship (weighted average)	3.7 (MJ/pkm)	Norway	Walnum (2011)
Ferries	3.5 (MJ/pkm)	New Zealand	Becken (2002b)
Norwegian 'Hurtigruten'	7.2 (MJ/pkm)	Norway	Gössling (2002)
Ship	1.87 (MJ/pkm)	Spain	Sanyé-Mengual *et al.* (2014)

generally employed for electricity generation. Ancillary engines typically use diesel oil. Howitt *et al.* (2010) estimate that about two-thirds of cruise ship fuel consumption is for transportation and one-third is for accommodation and entertainment. Atmosfair (2010) estimate that the hotel function consumes about 30–50% of all energy, mostly related to air-conditioning and ventilation (Figure 2.8).

On 1 January 2014, a new regulation on reducing emissions from international shipping came into force. More specifically, a new chapter was added to the MARPOL Annex VI Regulations for the prevention of air pollution from ships. Marpol 73/78 refers to the International Convention for the Prevention of Pollution From Ships, which was developed in 1973 and modified by the Protocol of 1978 (Marpol stands for marine pollution). The regulation requires that new ships comply with the Energy Efficiency Design Index (EEDI), and all other ships need to develop a Ship Energy Efficiency Management Plan (SEEMP). The regulations apply to all ships of 400 gross tonnages or more. Information on the impact of this new policy is not available yet.

In response to increasing public pressure, growing expectations around corporate social responsibility, and increasing fuel costs, cruise ship companies have begun to produce formal environmental reports in which they present energy efficiency measures, amongst others. The American-owned cruise line, Princess Cruises (2009) for example, reported the following activities:

- monitoring of leaks;
- cruising at slower speed and planning of fuel efficient routes;

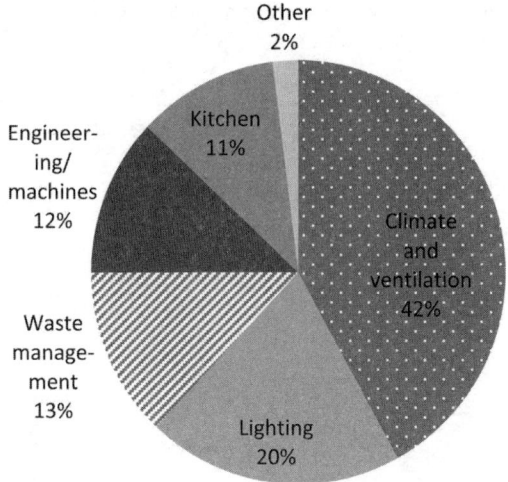

Figure 2.8 Electricity consumption on board of a cruise ship broken down by end use
Source: Based on Atmosfair (2010).

- educating ship captains and other officers/crew about fuel efficiency;
- evaluating engineering designs and implementing advanced designs for propulsion systems for new ships;
- implementing hull and propeller cleaning programmes to reduce marine growth and friction;
- evaluating weather patterns to identify fuel efficient routes; and
- optimising diesel generators and using engine heat for hot water systems.

2.4 Accommodation Energy Use

Tourist accommodation is diverse: it includes hotels of all types of quality, motels, hosted accommodation, apartments, camping grounds, youth hostels and backpacker accommodation. Accordingly, the energy profiles are very different, both in terms of energy sources and areas of energy end use. The most common form of energy used in tourist accommodation is electricity. Table 2.6 provides a summary of international studies on hotel energy use and the estimated share of electricity as part of the total energy demand. The range is from as low as 48% to 86%, with an approximate average of 65%.

A small number of studies provide more detail on energy use in tourist accommodation by fuel type. For the case of a hotel in Cyprus, Simmons and Lewis (2001) reported that electricity accounted for 70% of total energy

Table 2.6 Research on energy use in tourist accommodation and contribution of electricity to total energy consumption

Country/region and year of data	Energy intensity (MJ/m²/year)*	Share of electricity (%)	Source
Europe (2004)	Average 364 (Hilton) Average 285 (Scandic)	49 48	Bohdanowicz and Martinac (2007)
Hainan, China (2010)	Average 474	83	Lu et al. (2013)
New Zealand (1998–2000)	571 (hotel)	75	Becken et al. (2001)
Greece (2002)	485	68	Xydis et al. (2009)
Turkey Antalya (2005)	Average 1,558	86	Onut and Soner (2006)
Singapore (2008)	Average 1,537	77	Rajagopalan et al. (2009)
Spain (2003)	318 (seasonal hotels, 3*)[+] 439 (seasonal hotels, 4*)[+] 647 (annual hotels, 3*) 719 (annual hotels, 4*)	45 62 57 56	Rossello-Batle et al. (2010)
Taiwan (2010)	Average 1,008	83	Wang (2012)
Measured in energy per guest night			
Cyprus (2001)	87 MJ/guest night	70	Gössling (2002)
Majorca (2001)	51 MJ/guest night	57	Gössling (2002)

Notes: *Converted from kWh by applying a factor of 3.6.
[+]Seasonal hotels are those that are not open year-round.
Source: Based on Lu et al. (2013).

demand, oil made up 29%, and gas 1%. For another hotel in Majorca the mix was approximately: 57% grid-supplied electricity, 8% gas, 2% oil and 34% electricity from renewable sources. For the case of Singapore, hotels that relied on both electricity and gas had an average breakdown of 91% for electricity and 9% for gas. Those Singaporean hotels that also used diesel boilers, had a mix of 77% electricity, 8% gas and 15% diesel (Rajagopalan et al., 2009).

Hotels with their own electricity generation (i.e. using diesel generators) are more dependent on oil. Gössling (2000) estimated that oil consumption per guest night in Zanzibar, Tanzania was 267 MJ for smaller hotels and up to 1555 MJ for new resorts that are still characterised by low occupancy rates. High energy demand by island hotels due to diesel-generated electricity was also found in the South Pacific (Becken, 2005a).

The fuel mix of tourist accommodation in New Zealand was 75% electricity, 12% coal, 9% liquefied petroleum gas (LPG), 3% fuel and 1% wood (Becken *et al.*, 2001). A detailed breakdown by accommodation type is provided in Figure 2.9. Motels rely almost exclusively on electricity, whereas hosted accommodation, such as Bed & Breakfast (B&B) businesses, show a broader mix of fuel sources. The reason is that smaller businesses maintain various systems for heating and cooking, for example open fireplaces, diesel boilers for hot water and gas cooking stoves. Similarly, campgrounds in New Zealand were found to use diesel fuel for water heating. This has possibly changed since the 2001 study.

The role of different types of energy in hotel operations was illustrated in a study of Jordanian hotels, where electricity and diesel consumption were analysed for different hotel departments. Based on a sample of 80 hotels, stratified into five categories (one star to five star quality), Ali *et al.* (2008) found that diesel was the main energy source in laundries, where boilers are used to produce hot water and steam (Figure 2.10 and Figure 2.11).

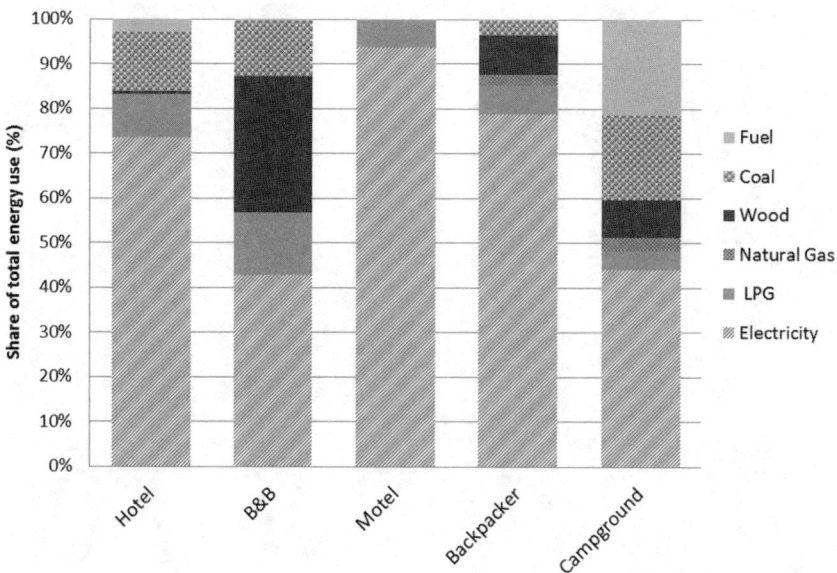

Figure 2.9 Energy use in tourist accommodation in New Zealand by fuel type and accommodation category
Source: Becken *et al.* (2001).

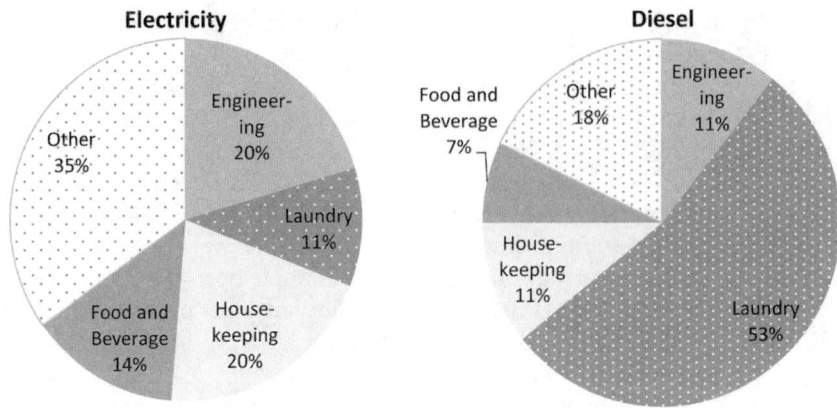

Figure 2.10 Electricity and diesel consumption in hotels in Jordan
Source: Based on Ali *et al.* (2008).

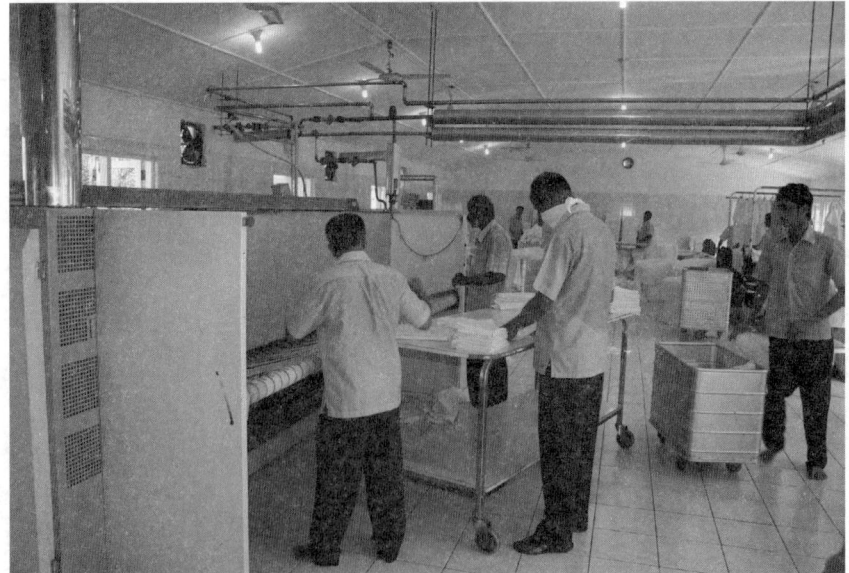

Figure 2.11 Laundry operation in a tourist resort
Note: Laundries are energy-intensive components of a hotel and often use diesel or gas to generate heat.

2.5 Other Tourist Activities

When tourists travel they engage in a broad range of leisure activities. Many of these consume energy. Sightseeing tours in cities or safaris in Africa (Figure 2.12), for example, are popular tourist activities that involve considerable transportation, and as a result consume fuel. Very little has been published, however, on the energy demand of tourist recreation or leisure more broadly. A Norwegian study, for example, established that leisure activities contributed around 23% of the total private and public sector energy use in Norway (Aall, 2010). In terms of energy use, the key activities identified by Aall were holidays, outdoor recreation and second homes.

A number of studies are available that have focused on the energy use of a particular leisure activity, typically in a broader non-tourism context. The Carbon Trust (2005) in the United Kingdom, for example, developed best practice guidelines for energy use in public swimming pools. The report states that 25-metre swimming pool centres use between 2063 (best practice) and 4810 (average practice) MJ/m^2 of fossil fuels per year. In addition, pools consume between 547 and 853 $MJ/m^2/year$ of electricity. At an average

Figure 2.12 Safari tourism in a National Park in Zambia
Note: Tourists are transported in (often early model) buses over rugged terrain and at slow speeds, and the fuel consumption is likely to be high.

centre size of 1000 square metres, the fossil fuel use of a swimming pool therefore amounts to between 352 and 820 barrels of oil per year. These figures are similar to those reported by Sydney Water (2011) for 42 aquatic centres in Sydney, Australia.

The energy intensity of selected recreational activities is shown in Table 2.7. These figures present the direct energy use only, but it is important to remember that the indirect energy demand for some activities is substantial. For example, plates served in Hilton and Scandic hotels require between 14 and 22 MJ of energy for preparation and cooking (Bohdanowicz & Martinac, 2007), but Strahan (2007) reminds us that for every joule we eat (in terms of nutritional value) it takes about ten times the energy to produce the food. The energy intensity of food production is particularly high for meat-based diets.

The energy profiles of recreational tourist activities are extremely diverse, and accordingly the breakdown into different fuel sources differs vastly. It is therefore particularly challenging to estimate oil requirements across all tourist activities and on a global scale. Becken and Simmons (2002) provide

Table 2.7 Energy intensities for different leisure activities

Activity	Energy use per visit (MJ)	Based on source	Country
Day at Disneyland	403	Ng (2009) (rough estimate)	USA
Experience centres	29	Becken and Simmons (2002)	New Zealand
Golf	12	Becken and Simmons (2002)	New Zealand
Heli-skiing	1,300	Becken and Simmons (2002)	New Zealand
Indoor ice skating	29	Müller (1999)	Switzerland
Museums, art galleries	10	Becken and Simmons (2002)	New Zealand
Rafting	36	Becken and Simmons (2002)	New Zealand
Restaurant meal	14–22	Bohdanowicz and Martinac (2007)	Europe
Restaurant meal	18	Müller (1999)	Switzerland
Scenic boat cruises	165	Becken and Simmons (2002)	New Zealand
Swimming in public pool	20	Sydney Water (2011)	Australia
Swimming in public pool	47	Müller (1999)	Switzerland
Watching TV (3.8 hours/day)	1.8	Müller (1999)	Switzerland

Source: Expanded from Becken and Hay (2007).

some insight into the energy use of different activities commonly undertaken by tourists in New Zealand. Aviation fuel, for example, is used by airborne activities (e.g. scenic flights, skydiving, sky jumping), but also by some motorised water activities such as jet boats. Indoor activities are more likely to rely on electricity. Other destinations and other activity portfolios are likely to differ substantially from the New Zealand example.

2.6 Destination-Based Energy Demand

The functioning of tourist destinations depends on a reliable supply of affordable energy. This is not always guaranteed. Island destinations, for example, rely on complex supply chains that typically bring different types of refined fuel products into the country (Figure 2.13). The risks associated with such fuel imports have been recognised early on, for example for the case of Hawaii. Tabatchnaia-Tamirisa *et al.* (1997) examined the energy use of tourism in Hawaii and found that tourists were responsible for 60% of the total fuel use in the island state. This was particularly concerning given that 92% of Hawaii's energy is generated from imported oil. Using a

Figure 2.13 One of two petrol stations in Male
Note: Fuel supply in the Maldives depends on a multi-stage supply chain from oil-producing countries, via refineries, the Maldives' fuel island to the point of sale.

Table 2.8 Tourism in Hawaii: Direct and indirect energy use by tourism in 1987

Energy use	Electricity (Mbbl)	Petrol (Mbbl)	Aviation fuel (Mbbl)	Other (diesel, LPG, bagasse, residual, etc.) (Mbbl)
Direct tourist use	–	2.15	–	–
Indirect tourist use	1.03	0.66	14.26	4.93
Total use	1.03	2.81	14.26	4.93

Source: Converted into barrels based on Tabatchnaia-Tamirisa *et al.* (1997).

scenario approach the authors also concluded that the growing trend of international tourists, who are associated with a higher energy intensity compared with domestic tourists, is leading to an overall increase in energy demand in the future.

Table 2.8 shows the energy demand of Hawaii tourism in 1987. Aviation fuel was the most prevalent fuel type with 14.26 Mbbl. The consumption of aviation fuel was considered 'indirect' as tourists purchase the service from the airline, rather than the fuel directly. Petrol was the only fuel consumed by tourists directly as a result of rental car usage. The Hawaii Tourism Authority (2013) provides historical data on tourist arrivals. In 1987, there were 5,770,585 arrivals. This has grown to 7,867,143 in 2012, representing a growth rate of over 36%. Assuming that energy consumption has increased at the same rate (assuming no gains in efficiency), the total fuel use of tourism in Hawaii today amounts to 31.4 Mbbl per year. This is more than the total use of countries such as Venezuela, Egypt, Turkey or Malaysia.

In the following section, the concept of a destination energy metabolism is explored through several examples. This is followed by a brief discussion on the energy demands of different types of tourism.

2.6.1 Destination energy metabolism

When examining energy use, or more specifically the use of different types of energy, it is useful to think of a tourist destination as a system. A system is characterised by different elements that interact with each other, amongst others through the exchange of energy. Sanyé-Mengual *et al.* (2014) used an industrial ecology approach and referred to these energy flows as 'energy metabolism'. Figure 2.14 shows the energy metabolism associated with tourists' travel from home to the destination, and with their activities at the destination. These include internal mobility, accommodation, and other activities. Part of the metabolism is the destination's ability to supply its own energy, for example from renewable sources (see also Chapter 7).

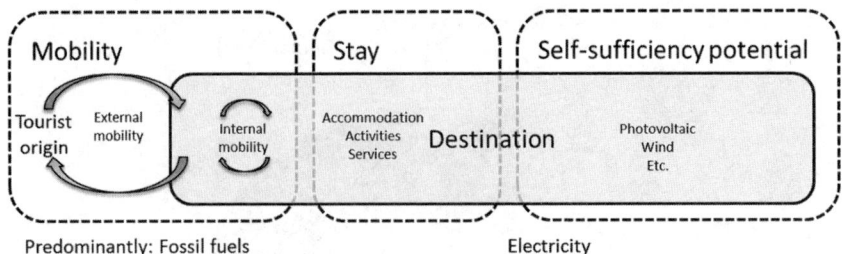

Predominantly: Fossil fuels   Electricity

Figure 2.14 Energy metabolism of tourist destinations, including tourists' external mobility to get from their origin to the destination and self-sufficiency potential
Source: Based on Sanyé-Mengual *et al.* (2014).

Analyses of tourist energy metabolisms have been performed at various levels of detail. Kelly and Williams (2007) examined the case of Whistler, Canada. Their results highlighted that commercial activities comprised 39% of the total energy use of 2.9 GJ in 2000. Similarly, Becken and Cavanagh (2003) undertook a comparative energy use analysis of tourism for the years 1999 and 2001 in New Zealand. Due to reductions in domestic travel, the overall energy use decreased by over 7.46% over these three years, despite an increase in international tourism. The energy use of origin-destination transportation was not included in this New Zealand analysis, nor was energy use related to recreational activities and food consumption (Table 2.9).

The breakdown of direct energy use by the New Zealand tourism sector into different fuel sources is presented in Figure 2.15. The high demand for petrol, diesel and aviation fuel reflects the significant transport component of tourism in New Zealand – a country that is characterised by a number of

Table 2.9 Energy use of tourist transport and accommodation in New Zealand in 1999 and 2001 (transport and accommodation sub-sectors only)

Tourists	Trips 1999	Trips 2001	Change trips (%)	Energy use 1999 (PJ)	Energy use 2001 (PJ)	Change energy use (%)
International arrivals	1,437,552	1,694,537	17.88	4.87	5.22	7.33
Domestic overnight trips	16,889,000	16,557,000	−1.97	17.78	15.72	−11.56
Total	18,326,552	18,251,537	−0.41	22.64	20.95	−7.46

Source: Becken and Cavanagh (2003).

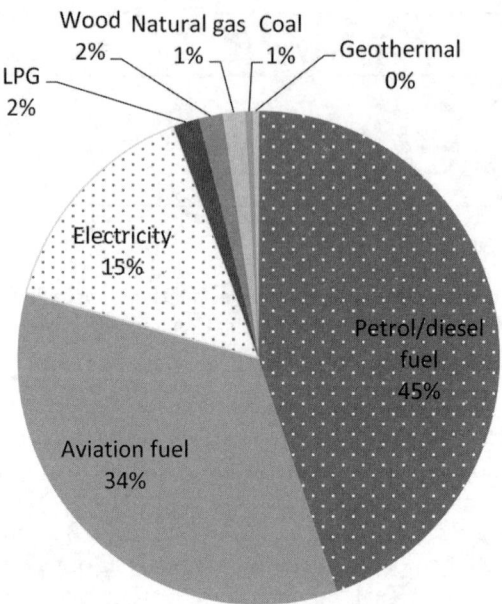

Figure 2.15 Different types of energy consumed by tourism in New Zealand for domestic transport and accommodation in 2001
Source: Becken and Cavanagh (2003).

iconic tourist attractions spread out over two islands and a distance of 2000 kilometres (e.g. Milford Sound, Mt Cook and Rotorua) (Becken, 2005b).

In a related analysis, Becken and Patterson (2006) presented the findings of an input-output (I-O) model-based analysis on the environmental foot-print of tourism. They found that in the years 1997–1998 the direct energy use by the tourism sector amounted to 27.53 PJ – a figure similar to Becken and Cavanagh's (2003) total of 20.95 PJ. In addition, I-O models can provide data on indirect energy use, for example, associated with the delivery of goods and services to tourism operators. This indirect energy use of tourism in New Zealand amounted to 19.83 PJ in 1997–1998. Converted into million barrels of oil, the New Zealand tourism sector consumed 4.7 Mbbl directly and 3.4 Mbbl indirectly in those years. Since then, international arrivals have increased to 2,564,618 million and domestic tourism has levelled out at 16,559,428 overnight trips (New Zealand Ministry of Business, Industry & Innovation, 2013). Therefore the total direct energy demand for domestic transport and accommodation in 2012 would be in the order of 23.6 PJ or 4.0 Mbbl (a similar magnitude to tourism in Hawaii). This figure does not include energy use related to other tourist activities, indirect effects or international aviation. If international aviation was included, the total fuel use would increase by about 90% (Becken, 2002a).

Walz *et al.* (2008) presented a more detailed and micro-scale analysis of an energy metabolism and carbon footprint for the popular alpine resort of Davos in Switzerland. The system was defined as the Davos region. This means that all energy use within the Davos geographic boundaries was included, but consumption occurring outside the region (e.g. tourist transport) was not considered. A wide range of data sources was required to estimate the Davos energy metabolism, including, for example, heating fuel imports into the region from key suppliers, data on central heating boilers from chimney sweeps, and traffic data from within the region.

The key energy findings are presented in Table 2.10. Heating was the largest contributor to tourism energy demand (65.5%). Most of the heating depends on fossil fuels, although some accommodation providers also use electricity. The total energy use of heating, mobility and machinery added up to 1,838,030 GJ of energy in 2005. This translates into 1.84 PJ or 0.31 Mbbl of oil-equivalent.

Table 2.10 Energy demand of tourism in Davos, Switzerland in 2005

End use	Energy consumption (GJ)	Breakdown into sources (GJ)
Heating	1,185,516	
Fossil fuel		1,012,859
Electricity		114,117
Thermal heating and power plant		13,777
Wood		26,184
Geothermal		15,927
Natural gas		2,653
Mobility	257,631	
Road traffic		225,525
Railway		28,122
Air traffic		3,984
Machines	394,882	
Electricity		369,203
Off-road machines		25,678

Source: Based on Walz *et al.* (2008); kWh converted into GJ.

2.6.2 Types of tourism

Not all tourists use the same amount of energy. Different types of holidays require different inputs of energy, and individual behaviours shape each trip's energy profile. Analysis of different energy or carbon footprints has mainly been driven by the desire to communicate the impacts of particular behavioural decisions to tourists. Scott *et al.* (2008) have argued that energy and emission estimates are complex and abstract and need to be translated into meaningful information for individual tourists, tour operators and other stakeholders.

The UNWTO has communicated the carbon intensity of different holiday types by presenting the carbon footprint of different types of holiday packages. They have also compared the amount of CO_2 emissions to the average emissions by World, European Union, and American citizens (Scott *et al.*, 2008). A 14-day trip from Europe to Thailand, for example, emits 2.8 tonnes of CO_2, whereas a fly-cruise from the Netherlands to Antarctica produces nine tonnes of CO_2. Diving holidays were discussed as often being energy-intensive as they typically involve tourists from Northern countries travelling to tropical regions (i.e. long-haul travel), and once at the destination require substantial boat transportation (Figure 2.16). Taking a holiday

Figure 2.16 Tourists boarding a small-scale cruise boat in Fiji

closer to home reduces emissions and the consumption of fossil fuel. Efforts to communicate carbon footprints to tourists or customers have been discussed in more detail by Becken and Hay (2012).

Differences exist even at the micro-scale. Sanyé-Mengual *et al.* (2014) compared the energy flows of 10 core tourist hubs on the island of Menorca, Spain. The selected hubs were representative of different types of tourism in the Mediterranean, for example in relation to their tourist–resident population mix, occupied land surface and occupancy rates of buildings. All of these differences were reflected in the tourist profile of the different hubs, and accordingly, energy use patterns varied.

The energy use per tourist and trip ranged from 3418 MJ in Platges de Fornells to 6800 MJ in Son Bou. Hotel hubs typically had higher energy demands, as many of their visitors arrive by plane, whereas residential areas were less energy intense. Spanish tourists who have lower external mobility needs frequent these latter hubs. However, since residential areas offer fewer services, the internal mobility (mostly car-based) is higher. Tourist energy use also differed when compared on a daily basis. On average, tourists in Menorca consumed 248 MJ per day, but this ranged from 180 to 400 MJ. Partly, this was driven by different lengths of stay, but also by different energy intensities per day. Similar 'daily energy budgets' were found for tourists in Taiwan (118–502 MJ/tourist-day) (Kuo *et al.*, 2012) and New Zealand (341 MJ/tourist-day) (Becken *et al.*, 2003).

2.7 Conclusion

Energy efficient upgrades to aircraft, the shift to renewable fuel for aviation and cruise liners, energy technology solutions in hotels, as well as countless other initiatives are placing tourism at the forefront of the clean energy transformation. (Talib Rifai, Secretary General, launching the World Tourism Day campaign, 27 September 2012)

Tourism is energy-intensive, but progress is being made towards a more energy-efficient tourism sector. This chapter examined the oil requirements of tourism. Based on the global carbon footprint of tourism (Scott *et al.*, 2008), it is estimated that global tourism is responsible for about 10% of annual oil demand. This is a substantial figure; especially considering that not all tourism activities are included in this estimate, for example cruise ship travel. Also, the indirect energy demands are not accounted for. This is an important task for further research, in particular because the communication of the economic benefits of tourism usually accounts for *direct* and *indirect* effects.

Clearly, transportation is the most 'fuel thirsty' element of tourism. In total, it makes up around 75% of tourism's total oil demand. Aviation is the most significant component – and one likely to grow in the years to come. Accommodation and other tourist activities also depend to some extent on oil or other fossil fuels. A reliable estimate is much more difficult to obtain because of a lack of data and a more complex energy profile. Electricity is the most commonly used form of energy in tourist accommodation, and some of this could be supplied from renewable energy sources. Understanding tourism's energy – and more specifically oil – demand is critical when planning for the future, particularly when considering tourism growth as predicted by key organisations (see Chapter 3).

A destination perspective to oil demand is useful, because this is where the 'rubber hits the road'. Tourists have to travel to destinations (example Hawaii) and they want to travel within their holiday destination. If a destination is exposed to unreliable – and increasingly expensive – oil supply chains, the delivery of a tourism product will be difficult. The Maldives are an example of a country highly dependent on a complex global and national oil supply chain that not only facilitates transport of tourists to their resorts, but also – almost exclusively – is the source of electricity and potable water generation at these resorts. Thus, accounting for oil requirements and identifying opportunities for decreasing vulnerability should be a key priority for such destinations.

3 The Sky is the Limit: Growth Expectations for Tourism

Tourism has grown at an impressive rate, and an increasing number of regions around the world have established themselves as major tourist destinations. As a result, tourism has performed a critical role in the economic development of many countries. At the same time, dependencies on the arrival of ever-increasing numbers of tourists have increased. In 2013, the United Nations World Tourism Organisation (UNWTO) stated that tourism has become the largest and fastest growing economic sector in the world (see also Figure 3.1). This growth – from 25 million international tourist arrivals in 1950 to 1035 million in 2012 – has continued despite a number of crises, including the terrorist attacks of 9 September 2011 and the outbreak of Severe Acute Respiratory Syndrome (SARS) in Asia.

An abundant number of tourism forecasts, either at national or global levels, are available. Most countries try to 'predict' their tourist arrivals at least for the next five to 10 years. Typically, these predictions are based on econometric models using information on key macroeconomic variables (e.g. gross domestic product (GDP)). Some countries add a more qualitative expert or Delphi panel analysis (referred to as 'industry sentiment' in Australia, for example) to fine-tune the econometric model and its assumptions. Projections are slightly less certain than forecasts and focus on likely trends or scenarios (Yeoman et al., 2009). In scenario-based projections, users are encouraged to develop their own views on which scenarios are likely to eventuate. Only a few analyses explore scenarios for tourism (e.g. Draper et al., 2009; Urry, 2010), and mostly these are undertaken by academics. Such alternative approaches may also include backcasting or normative forecasting (Dubois et al., 2011; Peeters & Dubois, 2010).

This chapter discusses mainstream forecasts that are used for the planning and development of tourism. It is important to critically examine mainstream assumptions, as these are likely to be most influential. Tourism

Figure 3.1 Why tourism matters: Infographic developed by the UNWTO to communicate the benefits of tourism
Source: UNWTO (2013).

growth forecasts are explored first, followed by future trends reported for aviation. Particular attention will be paid to the Boeing and Airbus forecasts and implications for airport developments. This is followed by a brief discussion of tourism growth within and from China, as well as cruise ship tourism, as one of the fastest growing niche markets globally. This chapter concludes with a discussion of alternative perspectives for the future of tourism that differ in their assessment of growth from the conventional representations.

3.1 Tourism Growth Forecasts

The Leaders' Declaration from the G20 world leaders' meeting in Los Cabos, Mexico (18–19 June 2012), recognizes: 'the role of travel and tourism as a vehicle for job creation, economic growth and development', and the need to 'work towards developing travel facilitation initiatives in support of job creation, quality work, poverty reduction and global growth'.

Most tourism forecasts provide an analysis of trends that are firmly anchored in the values attached to growth. Chapter 5 provides further discussion on how future projections inevitably reflect the value held by those who develop them. Most of the tourism forecasts reflect Western worldviews, are short-term in nature and base their assumptions on an analysis of historic data. The following sections outline the main trends that are usually included in these analyses, namely change in the economy, demographics, technology and/or geopolitics (Becken, 2012).

Many – if not all – trend analyses assume ongoing economic growth and rising incomes (Dwyer *et al.*, 2008) that create large volumes of people that are willing to spend their discretionary income on travel. In particular, a growing middle class is expected in the BRIC countries, i.e. Brazil, Russia, India and China (Dwyer *et al.*, 2008). In 2020, it is believed that almost half of the Chinese population will be middle class with an annual income between US$18,137 and US$36,275 (Amadeus, 2009). Similarly, due to increasing globalisation and liberalization, business travel is expected to grow rapidly (Dwyer *et al.*, 2008). Most of the future analyses acknowledge that there are risks associated with downturns in the global economy, but only a few include these in their model development.

The world population is not only growing, but also getting older, at least in the wealthier countries (Dwyer *et al.*, 2008). Moreover, the population is generally getting healthier (especially the elderly) and older people are predicted to undertake more travel. An opposing trend that has been noted is one of increasing obesity and lifestyle related diseases. The search for health and well-being is an important consumer trend that provides new business opportunities (Amadeus, 2009). Most detailed future analyses also consider changing family compositions (e.g. more single households), new travel patterns (e.g. shorter holidays) (European Travel Commission, 2004), and the desire for a more balanced lifestyle (Tourism Victoria, no date). Yeoman *et al.* (2009) project a greater demand for authenticity of tourism products.

Technological advancements are expected to change the tourism sector. Key changes are already observed in the information technology sector, facilitating new forms of communication and virtual travel (Bosshart & Frick, 2006). Another important trend relates to potential breakthroughs in the production of biofuel (e.g. from algae, Draper *et al.*, 2009), and other improvements in transportation efficiency. The increasing competitiveness of high-speed trains has been noted (European Travel Commission, 2004) (see Chapter 7). Reductions in the carbon intensity of travel are not only important in terms of operational costs, but also in relation to environmental values and attitudes held by travellers (Becken, 2007).

Political prognoses consider questions of geopolitical change. China and India are generally seen as key forces emerging in the geopolitical landscape. Already, global tourism is distinctly changing due to growth of Chinese outbound tourism (see further below). In addition to changing world orders, there is also a trend towards greater risks of terrorism (including cyber terrorism, Dwyer *et al.*, 2008). Finally, travel is a key factor in the spread of infectious diseases and the risk of global pandemics. A resulting 'climate of fear' may restrain people's propensity to travel in the future (Amadeus, 2009).

At a global level, the most commonly cited and used tourism forecast is the one provided by the UNWTO. This is not surprising given that the UNWTO is the UN agency responsible for tourism. UNWTO collects country tourism statistics and, based on these, develops global forecasts. The World Tourism Barometer is an assessment of short-term trends, whereas the Tourism Highlights publication and Tourism Towards 2030 (UNWTO, 2011) provide long-term forecasts (UNWTO, 2013). In its most recent Highlights report, the UNWTO (2013) summarised the key trends of international tourism in 2012. These were:

- The number of international overnight tourist arrivals globally exceeded 1000 million for the first time.
- The strongest growth occurred in the Asia Pacific region, with a 7% increase in international arrivals compared with the previous year (see Figure 3.2).
- Africa saw strong growth at a rate of 6%.

Figure 3.2 Major growth in tourism infrastructure and assets can be observed in the Asia Pacific region
Note: This photo shows the Marina Bay Sands hotel and convention centre – marketed as the most spectacular hotel in Singapore.

- Tourism growth in the Middle East was negative (–5%); mainly attributed to political tensions and crises.
- The income from international tourism reached US$1075 billion worldwide; representing an increase of 3.1%.
- China became the most prevalent source market in the world.

The most important tourism countries in the world can be measured, for example, in terms of arrivals or receipts. As in previous years, France was the top-ranking country in terms of international tourist arrivals with 83 million visitors in 2012. In terms of receipts (US$54 billion), France ranked third. The United States (US) ranked first in terms of tourism receipts (US$126 billion) and second in terms of arrivals (67 million). China has established itself as one of the top destinations, ranking third in arrivals (58 million) and fourth in receipts (US$50 billion). In its most recent barometer publication, the UNWTO predicts global growth in international tourist arrivals for 2013 in the order of 3% to 4% (UNWTO, 2014).

The long-term outlook for tourism, according to UNWTO's Tourism Towards 2030 (UNWTO, 2011), is that international arrivals will increase by 3.3% per annum between 2010 and 2030. In 2030, there will be 1.8 billion international tourists. Emerging destinations will grow faster than advanced ones, namely at a rate of 4.4% per annum, compared with 2.2%. As a result, the market share of emerging economies will have increased from a base of 30% in 1980 to 47% in 2012, and 57% by 2030. The most important emerging destinations are in Asia, Latin America, Central and Eastern Europe, Eastern Mediterranean Europe, the Middle East and Africa. The forecast assumes that growth will then slow somewhat, namely to 2.9% after 2030.

The UNWTO forecast is based on a causal model in which the key predictor is GDP. Thus the model does not attempt to simulate the more detailed trends discussed earlier in this chapter. GDP is commonly used as a proxy for income (more specifically potential travellers' discretionary income), and the potential for business travel. The GDP is measured in purchasing power parity (PPP) to account for effects related to currency exchange rates. The UNWTO uses estimates of GDP growth rates provided by Oxford Economics. In a somewhat circular argument it is important to note that GDP itself is strongly influenced by tourism activity. For the case of the European Union, Wan Lee and Brahmasrene (2013) established that a 1% growth in tourism receipts leads to economic growth in the order of 0.5%. In addition to GDP, the UNWTO considers the (predicted) cost of transport, both for aviation and surface transportation. In their central model, the cost of air transport is assumed to grow by 1.1% per year from 2010 and 2030. Third, the model includes 'wild cards' in the form of one-off events (e.g. SARS).

National forecasts are generally in line with the global picture provided by UNWTO, but they provide a more refined understanding of specific circumstances and trends. The Australian forecast from 2013, for example, predicted that international visitor arrivals to the country would grow by 5.8% in 2014 (to 6.6 million) and 5.6% in 2015 (to 7 million) (Tourism Research Australia, 2013). The growth of Australian tourism is largely due to the expansion of the Chinese market. Importantly, national forecasts also often include domestic tourism. The domestic market in Australia is forecast to grow at a lower level of 2% in 2014 (to 293 million visitor nights) and from then on 1.1% per annum by 2023.

3.2 Aviation Forecasts

The development of air travel has always been highly relevant to tourism and analyses of tourism growth. Over the last 20 years, aircraft capacity has grown by more than 25% (measured in available seat-kilometre (ASK)), the global air route network has expanded, and the average distance travelled has increased (Figure 3.3). Air travel has doubled every 15 years and is forecast to continue to do so (Airbus, 2013).

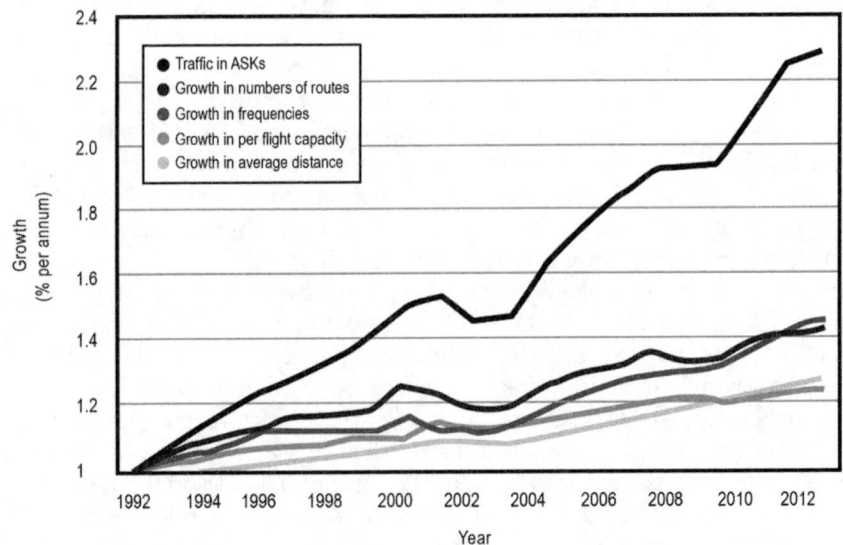

Figure 3.3 Evolution of the aviation industry (base year 1992 = 1)
Source: After Airbus (2013).

The main aircraft manufacturers, Boeing and Airbus, both provide future outlooks of the aviation market. Both are used widely as a basis for tourism development and infrastructure planning. Boeing (2013), in their Current Market Outlook, aims to forecast long-term air traffic volumes and airplane demand. Integrating top-down and bottom-up analyses develops the forecast. The former uses aggregated variables (e.g. economic growth) to project demand, whereas the latter estimates traffic between and within individual countries, based on economic predictions, growth momentum, trends, travel attractiveness and projections of airline regulations (e.g. openness). Other factors, such as new air services, are considered in the fine-tuning of the model. In its most basic form, Boeing (2013) finds that the relationship between revenue passenger-kilometres (RPK) and other factors is:

$$\text{RPK } (growth) = \text{GDP } (growth) + f(t),$$

with $f(t)$ being a time-varying function that typically accounts for 20–40% of growth in air travel. As a result, air traffic generally grows faster than GDP. This can be seen in Figure 3.4 where cargo traffic (in revenue-tonne kilometre) and passenger traffic (revenue-passenger kilometre) display higher growth rates than GDP.

Both Boeing and Airbus predict that air travel will continue to be resilient to crises and external events, including increases in global oil prices. Passenger volumes increased by 5.3% in 2012 compared with 2011 (Boeing, 2013), and this trend is expected to continue for the next 20 years (about 5%

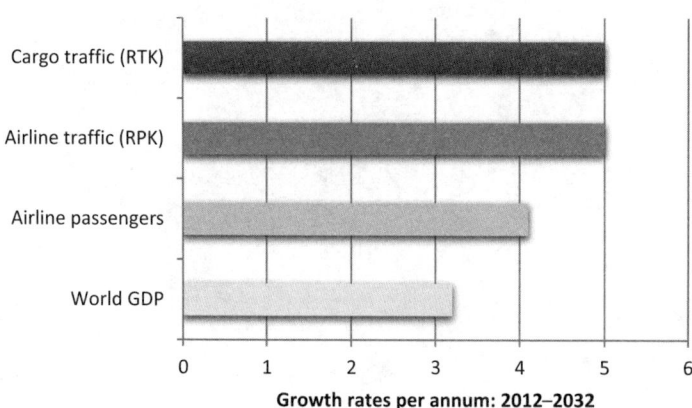

Growth rates per annum: 2012–2032

Figure 3.4 Expected annual growth in percent in cargo and passenger traffic, and GDP
Source: After Boeing (2013).

per annum). Airbus expects growth in the order of 4.7% between 2012 and 2032 (Airbus, 2013), especially driven by growth in emerging markets. More specifically, Airbus notes that, by 2032, 10.4% of world air traffic will be domestically in China. Domestic air travel in India will be the sixth largest market in the world. Airlines in the Asia Pacific region will fly 34% of all traffic in the world.

Today over 900 airlines operate more than 20,000 aircraft, and the forecast growth in demand necessitates investment into more aircraft. Boeing (2013) sees a long-term demand for 35,280 new airplanes at a cost of US$4.8 trillion. Forty-one percent of these new aircraft will replace older planes, and 59% of deliveries will add to an expansion of the global fleet. Thus, the global fleet will grow by 20,930 airplanes in 2032. Most of these will be single-aisle (24,670 airplanes); driven by the substantial growth in low-cost carriers (LCC) (Figure 3.5). The share of LCCs will grow from 17% of RPKs in 2012 to 21% in 2032 (Airbus, 2013).

Considering substantial growth in demand and route networks, many airports around the world are planning further extensions (Figure 3.6). The Middle East, in particular, is positioning itself as a major hub for global air travel (O'Connell, 2011; Figure 3.7). Table 3.1 highlights the size of and expansion plans for major Middle Eastern airports. Dubai in particular is planning to host the largest airport in the world, the 'Dubai World Central'.

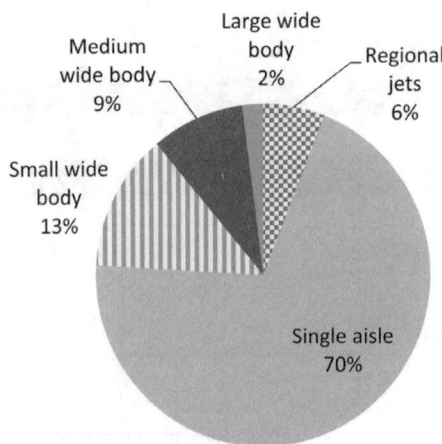

Airplane deliveries

Figure 3.5 Deliveries of aircraft by 2032 by different types of planes
Source: Boeing (2013).

Figure 3.6 Construction works at Munich Airport. Munich is currently building a Satellite Terminal to extend Terminal 2 by an additional capacity of 11 million passengers per annum

Figure 3.7 Tourism services in Abu Dhabi – one of the growth hubs of tourism in the Middle East

Table 3.1 Airport development plans for the Middle East based on 2007 data

City	Airline operating base	Cost (US$ billions)	Capacity (million pax)	Details
Dubai	Emirates	4.5	70	Expansion: Terminal 3
Dubai	Emirates	10.0	160	Dubai World Central
Doha	Qatar Airways	0.3	16	Expansion and upgrades
Doha	Qatar Airways	11.0	50	New airport
Abu Dhabi	Etihad Airways	6.8	20	Expansion: Runway, New Terminal,
Jeddah	Saudi Arabia	4.8	25	2 new terminals and upgrade
Saudi Arabia	Saudi Arabia	5.3	na	5 new regional airports
Ajman UAE	na	3.3	na	New airport
Kuwait	Kuwait Airways	2.1	12	Double current capacity
Oman	Oman Air	2.0	na	3 new airports
Muscat, Oman	Oman Air	1.0	12	Upgrades and new terminal
Bahrain	Gulf Air	0.5	12	Upgrades and expansion
Sharjah UAE	Air Arabia	0.2	8	Upgrades and expansion
Baghdad	Iraqi Airways	2.0	na	3 new terminals and upgrades

Note: na = not applicable.
Source: O'Connell (2011).

Aircraft manufacturers, airlines, and airports not only seek to understand growth rates, but they also need to 'predict' other changes in this very dynamic industry. Boeing (2013) summarises these factors as: fuel prices, economic development, environmental regulations, infrastructure, market liberalisation, airplane capabilities, trends in other modes of transport, business models and emerging markets. Fuel is clearly one of the major challenges, having doubled in price in the past 10 years. Airlines are responding to increasing fuel prices by investing substantially in improving the energy efficiency of their fleets. Thus, while airfares have effectively decreased by 43% between 1980 and 2012 in real terms (Airbus, 2013), the future predictions are for continuous increases.

3.3 China: The Growth Engine?

The growth of tourism in China is nothing short of phenomenal. Not surprisingly, China is widely seen as the world's growth engine and the key source of tourist arrivals all around the world (e.g. Henderson *et al.*, 2011). With ongoing economic growth – Chinese GDP is forecast to increase by 6.4% per year over the next 20 years – China's share of global GDP will grow from presently 8.5% to 16% by 2032 (Boeing, 2013). An analysis of GDP at 700 locations around the world highlighted that the 'centre of gravity' of global economic activity has shifted from the mid-Atlantic Ocean towards the East and, by 2030, will be located somewhere between India and China (CSIRO, 2013).

As a result of economic growth, disposable incomes have increased substantially in China, for example by 14% between 2011 and 2012 alone (in CSIRO, 2013). As will be discussed in more detail in Chapter 6, disposable income is the key determinant of travel propensity. Already the increase in outbound tourism from China is staggering. In 2012, China, for the first time, overtook both long-time top spenders Germany (US$84 billion) and the US (US$83 billion) and took rank number one in terms of being the most prolific spender on international tourism (US$102 billion). The increase in international tourism from China between 2011 and 2012 was a whopping 37%.

A major trend in China, and other emerging economies, is an increase in urbanisation. Megacities, in particular, will dominate the Chinese landscape. Seven out of the top 10 largest cities in the world will be in Asia (Airbus, 2013). Shanghai will be the third largest city in the world with 28 million people (Figure 3.8). This urbanisation is interpreted as further facilitating air travel, as the majority of people live in close proximity to an (international) airport.

Air traffic out of China is already significant and expected to continue to grow. Boeing and Airbus estimate that over the next 20 years, airlines based in China will require about 6000 new airplanes. The Asia Pacific region will receive over 10,000 new aircraft deliveries (Airbus, 2013; Boeing, 2013). Out of these, 61% constitute growth rather than replacement (Airbus, 2013). Trends in air travel in the Asia Pacific region, including China, differ from elsewhere in the world in that route capacities are much larger. Thus, the use of large Airbus A380 planes, for example, is common to link Asian hubs (e.g. Shanghai to Hong Kong). Using such large aircraft would not be viable on regional routes in Europe or North America due to lower passenger numbers.

Not surprisingly, airports in China are climbing up the ranks of the world's largest airports in terms of capacity (Figure 3.9). When measured on current traffic volumes, four Chinese airports feature in the top 20. Beijing is now ranked number two of the world's busiest airports, and Hong Kong and Guangzhou are ranked at nine and 15, respectively. Shanghai Pudong International Airport is the 18th busiest airport globally.

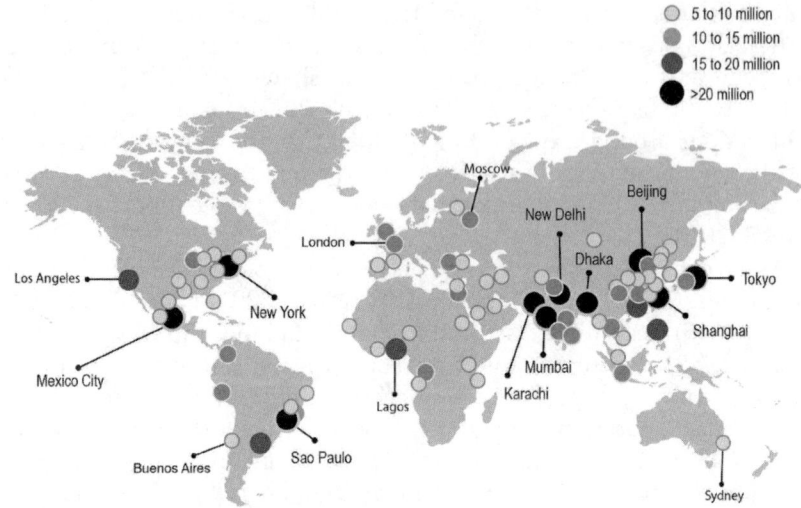

Figure 3.8 Global urbanisation and large urban populations
Source: After United Nations Department of Economic and Social Affairs, in Airbus (2013).

Figure 3.9 The largest airports by seats available in the week starting 31 March 2013
Source: Based on Centre for Aviation (2013).

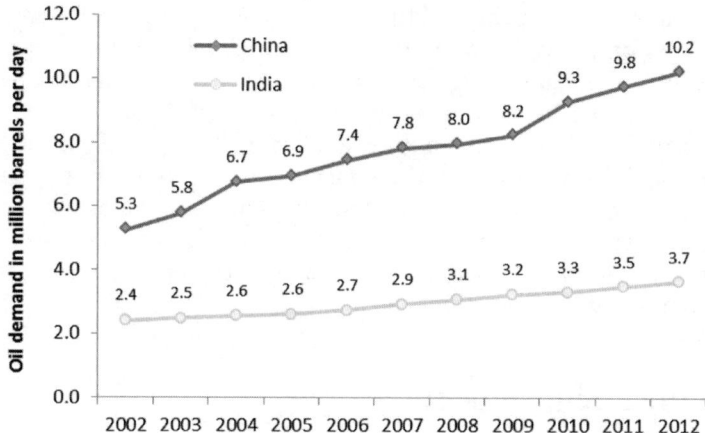

Figure 3.10 Comparison of oil demand trends in China and India
Source: Using data from BP (2012).

Economic growth of the magnitude witnessed in China is inextricably linked to an increase in energy consumption. Oil demand data by BP (2012) highlight the rapid increase in demand in China (Figure 3.10). Consumption has more than doubled between 2002 and 2012. For comparison, it can be seen that oil demand in India is growing at a much slower rate.

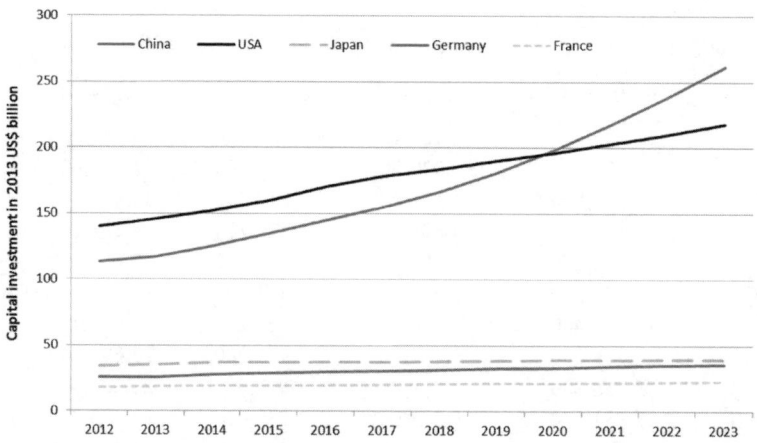

Figure 3.11 Forecast capital investment in travel and tourism – growth between 2012 and 2023
Source: Based on data from WTTC (2013).

An important component of future growth is investment. Recent analysis by the World Travel and Tourism Council (WTTC, 2013) showed that Asian countries are investing substantially in tourism. China in particular shows the largest increase in capital investment for the forecast period between 2012 and 2023. As can be seen in Figure 3.11, China has the largest absolute *and* relative growth in investments. Almost all major international hotel groups are not only represented in China, but expanding massively. In comparison, the US is also investing substantially in its tourism sector, but the relative growth rate between current investment in 2012 and future investment in 2023 is much smaller.

3.4 Cruise Ship Tourism

Tourism growth cannot be discussed without mentioning the cruise ship industry. It is often said that the global cruise industry is the fastest growing segment of tourism. Over 20 million passengers went on a cruise in 2012 globally (Table 3.2). More than half of these were US citizens, but growth in 'other' markets is also strong (notably driven by Asian demand). Statistics on the number of ships globally differ dependent on the source, but it is in the order of 300 to 400 cruise ships. Collectively, these can accommodate over 250,000 passengers on any given day (Cruise Market Watch, 2013). According to the Cruise Lines International Association (CLIA, 2013), in 2012 the US

Table 3.2 Cruise ship passengers between 2008 and 2018 (forecast)

Year	North America	Europe	Other	Worldwide passengers
2008	10,870,400	4,124,100	1,784,500	15,779,000
2009	10,887,100	4,338,900	1,990,100	17,216,000
2010	11,748,700	4,452,900	2,219,500	18,421,000
2011	12,176,700	4,683,600	2,316,700	19,177,000
2012	12,582,200	5,053,400	2,499,600	20,135,000
2013	12,972,300	5,260,600	2,627,100	20,859,900
2014 (f)	13,374,400	5,476,200	2,761,100	21,611,700
2015 (f)	13,789,000	5,700,800	2,901,900	22,391,700
2016 (f)	13,758,300	6,192,000	3,073,000	23,023,300
2017 (f)	13,881,000	6,377,000	3,230,000	23,488,000
2018 (f)	14,186,000	6,568,000	3,392,000	24,146,000

Note: (f) = forecast.
Source: Based on Cruise Market Watch (2013).

cruise industry contributed more than US$42 billion to the American economy, measured in total economic activity. Clearly, cruise ship tourism is an increasing economic force, at least in some parts of the world.

Cruise ship tourism is a relatively new phenomenon, although ocean passages date back to as early as May 1819, when Black Ball Lines, operating out of New York, became the first shipping company to offer a scheduled passenger service from the US to England. In the second half of the 20th century cruise holidays grew in popularity, yet remained with the affluent and late middle-aged demographic groups. The sector then saw unprecedented growth from the 1970s and 1980s, but leveled to an estimated annual growth rate of 8% in the 1990s.

In more recent decades, growth in cruise ship tourism has remained, but the product has diversified. Entertainment on board is much more large-scale and includes education and cultural offerings, interactive entertainment supported by technology (e.g. iPhone applications), food themed cruises, signature restaurants and celebrity chefs, and major events (e.g. Dancing with the Stars). Diversification has also led to the development of fly-cruise options, increase in cruise ship capacities, including superliners that host up to 6000 passengers, and a wide range of cruise durations, price options and itineraries. New destinations have been added to the global routes, especially in Asia where more and more exotic ports are offered as part of new itineraries.

Shanghai, for example, hosts a specialty port for luxury ships, which accommodated 62 vessels in 2012, but is expected to welcome over 150 in 2013 (CLIA, 2013) (Figure 3.12). At the same time, cruise companies are building their networks in Asia. Costa Cruises, for example, is expanding its product to depart from Hong Kong, Shanghai and Tianjin for short cruises to Taiwan or South Korea, Japan and Vietnam. In Beijing, a company called Azamara Club Cruises included 40 new ports in their product range, for example Beijing (Xingang), Shanghai (Haitong) and Jinhae, and South Korea.

The cruise industry predicts substantial growth for the future. In 2013, there will be six new ships added to the global fleet. This will increase passenger capacity by 14,074. By the end of 2015, the industry plans to operate 13 more cruise ships, adding a further 8.9% to passenger capacity. The CLIA (2013) reports an investment of over US$10.3 billion into cruise ships between 2013 and 2016, towards 29 new ships and one refurbishment. The overall trends are: more and larger ships and greater economies of scale. At the same time market segmentation will continue, with offerings targeted to traditional cruise ship passengers, but also to families (e.g. Disney cruise) and the youth market.

Australia is one of the fastest growing cruise ship markets. In the world market, there has been an increase of 27% in Australian cruise ship passengers

Figure 3.12 Cruise ship terminal in Shanghai (with permission from Peter Ye, Deputy General Manager of the Terminal Corporation)

in 2010 compared with the previous year (International Cruise Council Australia, 2010). A recent report by Deloitte Access Economics (2012) shows that the cruise industry's economic contribution to Australia in 2010–2011 increased by 44% relative to an earlier assessment undertaken in 2007–2008. For the future, up to 2019–2020, Deloitte Access Economics estimate an annual growth rate for Australian cruise ship passengers of about 7%.

3.5 Alternative Scenarios

> Anyone who believes that exponential growth can go on forever in a finite world is either a madman or an economist. (Kenneth E. Boulding, British economist and writer 1910–1993 in United States Congress House (1973))

The trends and forecasts discussed above are commonly reported by tourism organisations and constitute an almost universal view of the future. However, the methodologies presented above are firmly anchored in the growth paradigm that assumes (and expects!) ongoing growth in GDP – as authoritatively provided by Oxford Economics – and a continuation of historic development patterns. Very rarely are different development pathways considered, including so-called 'black swans' or one-off unpredictable events (e.g. Centre for Aviation, 2013).

It is important to avoid 'wishful' predictions, especially in the light of tourisms' promise to promote economic (and sustainable) development, stability, peace and poverty reduction (Cole & Razak, 2009). This section discusses two 'versions' of alternative growth scenarios. One relates to sensitivity analyses that are undertaken by those who provide mainstream forecasts. These types of approaches maintain the key assumptions (e.g. ongoing economic growth) but also test the effect of minor deviations from what is considered to be the most likely course of events. On the other hand, a number of analysts provide a radically different view of the system or the world we live in – arriving at very different conclusions for how economic growth and as a result tourism activity – might unfold.

3.5.1 Sensitivity analysis

> The long-term has become a luxury few airlines can afford. (Centre for Aviation, 2013: 5)

The Centre for Aviation (2013) provides some commentary on the increasing uncertainty that airlines face. In fact, it is argued that 'uncertainty is the new normal'. Uncertainty in the aviation sector relates to the way the Gulf carriers are changing the aviation world, the rapid growth from China, and increasing fuel prices. As a result, airlines today focus merely on short-term survival, rather than taking longer-term strategic views. Most airlines are already actively engaging in risk management strategies such as capacity control (i.e. avoiding oversupply of capacity), leasing planes (rather than purchasing), hedge fuel and currency (to avoid surprises in the future as a result of sudden change), and fuel surcharges.

According to the Centre for Aviation (2013) there is very little room for any further risk management. In their review they warn that price increases in the order of a further US$30 per barrel could result in severe reductions in air travel; for example up to 15% or 20% of long-haul seat capacity. Routes that are least profitable would be cut first. The global nature of aviation makes it particularly susceptible to any event, anywhere in the world. Examples include volcanic ash clouds, terrorist threats or attacks, and snowstorms. The Centre for Aviation concludes that we can expect many more of these 'black swans' in the years to come.

Similar to the aviation sector, the UNWTO also considers some deviations from the pure growth scenario. In their sensitivity analysis for Tourism Towards 2030 they modify the underlying assumptions about growth rates and transport costs (UNWTO, 2011). As will be seen in Chapter 6, both of these factors are heavily influenced by global oil prices. If the growth rate in global GDP was 2.8% instead of 4.0%, as assumed in the central scenario, global international tourism would generate 1.4 billion visitors by 2030 instead of 1.8 billion (note that this scenario still assumes overall positive growth). Increases in transport costs of 1.4% per year (instead of 1%) would result in 1.66 billion international arrivals in 2030 (instead of 1.8 billion). Figure 3.13 visualises the central UNWTO scenario and alternatives resulting from the sensitivity analysis. Not surprisingly, changes to the growth rate have the largest impact.

Only a few analyses aim to categorise different factors by their degree of uncertainty. The Tourism 2023 study from the United Kingdom (Draper *et al.*, 2009) is a good example of a 'future thinking' exercise that explicitly distinguishes drivers of change that are more certain than others. Climate change impacts, water scarcity, cost of resources (including oil), growth in visitor numbers, an ageing population, and political instability were the more certain factors in Draper *et al.*'s scenario analysis. How environmental attitudes affect mobility, future legislation and the price of oil were perceived as less certain (among others). The Tourism 2023 study moves towards a different paradigm where past trends are not taken as the best predictor of future

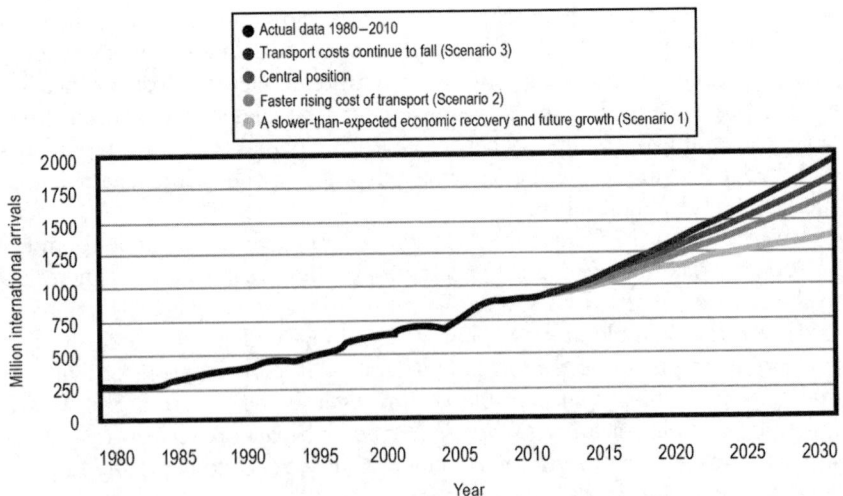

Figure 3.13 Tourism Towards 2030: UNWTO projections for tourism growth (in million international arrivals) and sensitivity analysis
Source: UNWTO (2011).

trends. The following section discusses some of the radically different perspectives that have been put forward.

3.5.2 Breaking with hegemonic views of eternal growth

Economic growth as we know it is over and done with. (Heinberg, 2011: 1)

There is a risk that analysts focus on those aspects that appear more certain, failing to recognise the less certain events as potentially equally plausible factors of change (Becken, 2012). In fact, some would argue that unexpected or non-linear changes are more likely in the complex tourism system, than the simple continuation of linear trends during times of equilibrium (Becken, 2013a; Farrell & Twining-Ward, 2004). Some of these unexpected changes could manifest in the form of rapid shifts and irreversible change, which would mean breaking 'ossified political structures in which more is better, and more of the same is also safer' (Patzek, 2007: 9).

Opposing views to the mainstream forecasts and scenarios are rare, but they exist. In 2010, Auckland Airport in New Zealand contracted the consulting firm Market Economics (2010) to assess the future economic impacts of the airport for the wider Auckland region and the New Zealand economy. The report triggered an angry blogger to write the following:

An Auckland airport report estimates the airport corridor's contribution to the economy for the next 20 years, but outrageously fails to even mention the future risks to the airline and tourism industries of higher oil prices and/or fuel shortages.

The report by Market Economics simplistically takes tourism and freight growth figures for past decades and projects these into the future. Based on these historic patterns it suggests a business as usual scenario where international and domestic travel will generate NZ$17–24 billion by 2031, with a cumulative difference in growth between 2006 and 2031 of 19%.

But nowhere in the report – I repeat nowhere – is there any mention, let alone discussion, of the risks to the airline and tourism industries of rises in global oil prices in the next 20 years. As for the possibility of aviation fuel shortages, this is also completely beyond the pale for the report's authors. (Denis Tegg, 27 January 2011)

Heinberg (2011), in his book *The End of Growth* makes a compelling argument why absolute growth is over, and – if anything – only relative growth is achievable. Relative growth allows for growth in some regions, but at the expense of other regions. It also means that there could be periods of growth; but these are likely to be followed by contraction. Building on the same underlying principles as the 1972 bestseller *Limits to Growth* (Meadows *et al.*, 1972), Heinberg discusses the flaws of the current financial systems, the denial of physical capacities in economic theories, and the role of energy in the rapid growth of the last century. One shortcoming that Heinberg notes is particularly significant: the failure to recognise the importance of fossil fuels – and more specifically the availability of cheap and easily transportable oil – as a key ingredient that facilitated industrialisation and economic growth. This unique opportunity, he argues, cannot be repeated in future times as we near the peak of global oil production (Chapter 4).

Economic theories allow for eternal growth through two key mechanisms; namely substitution and efficiency. Substitution relates to the ability to substitute one material (or capital) for another. In theory, natural capital can be replaced by human capital and technological inventions. If one resource becomes scarce and expensive, the market (and its 'invisible hand') will ensure that human ingenuity will find ways for the development of alternatives. Efficiency, on the other hand, means that more production can be achieved with the same or less input. Typically, in our modern economies, this refers to labour productivity where greater outputs per unit of employee can be generated. Less commonly, efficiency is interpreted to maximise productivity in terms of natural resources such as energy. This latter pursuit of energy productivity falls under the banner of environmental management or corporate social responsibility (CSR) and is often considered a business cost rather than a mainstream activity.

Heinberg (2011) also spends some time explaining why China's growth will not last forever. One of the key risks to the Chinese economy is its dependence on coal. Seventy percent of China's total energy is coal based, and while China possesses substantial resources on its own, it has become a net importer of coal. Coal production, just like oil, will peak one day. Analyses of peak coal are even more contested than those for oil (see Chapter 5), and estimates of the Chinese coal peak range from as soon as 2015 or 2025, to a maximum of 62 years of production at current levels. In addition to looming energy constraints, the structure of the Chinese economy as an export-dependent country makes it vulnerable to fluctuations in the economies of its trading partners, and to competition by countries that can produce cheaper (e.g. Indonesia or Pakistan). Finally, problems of a potential real estate bubble and demographic structures (e.g. an ageing population and one child policy) mean that China is facing severe challenges in supporting ongoing growth for the long-term future.

Messages that convey these trends are messages that people do not wish to hear. As a result these views are often overheard or marginalised. The call for a steady-state economy that recognises that development – including that of tourism – depends on the limited availability of natural capital is rarely discussed and left to scientists and activists. Hall (2010) explores how such steady-state tourism might look like. Building on Daly (2008), he defines a steady-state destination as one that has a throughput at a sustainably low level that considers depletion as well as pollution, and to which population and capital stock adjust as demanded by the environmental conditions. Overall, Hall argues, consumption can be reduced by efficiency (as in the neo-classical paradigm above) and sufficiency. Sufficiency relates to behavioural changes in the sense of 'degrowth' or 'decroissance'. Importantly, Hall notes that 'degrowth' is less about downsizing, but *right* sizing the economy in environmental terms. Slow travel, as discussed in Chapter 7, is therefore an antithesis to the common way of excess consumption and travel (Urry, 2010). Thoughts about degrowth of tourism may sound blasphemy to those involved in the tourism industry, but are certainly relevant to our discussion about Peak Oil and tourism.

3.6 Conclusion

This chapter presented some of the most important tourism forecasts produced globally. The UNWTO and aircraft manufacturers provide detailed assessments of future tourism growth and demand of air travel. Methodologically, these forecasts are based on econometric models that include GDP as one of their core variables. Since forecasts of global GDP are generally predicting overall growth, it is not surprising that the tourism sector also expects growth. In fact, the underlying assumption – based on past experience – is that tourism grows at a faster rate than GDP, namely in the order of 20–40% more. Tourism growth in and out of China is a key factor in this development; and the global tourism industry does not expect this to change in a while. In addition to China's presently healthy tourism market, significant growth in niche markets, such as cruise ship tourism, adds to the overall sentiment of optimism and level of investment.

A critical examination of the growth paradigm is almost absent from the tourism debate, both at global and national levels. Only a small number of analysts and 'critical voices' provide evidence and reasoning why economic growth cannot be eternal – at the very least dictated by simple physics of a fixed pool of resources. There are several reasons for the disregard of such 'limits to growth'. These include the widely believed economic theories that simply deny physical constraints, but are adopted almost universally by leading economists, politicians, business people and other decision-makers. Further, the absence of a critical discussion lies in collective denial (Cohen, 2001), lack of understanding and wishful thinking of those who are simply not able to imagine a society so different to the one we live in today (Becken, 2012).

It is strongly suggested that future studies of tourism trends are approached with greater scepticism and criticality, for example by using a risk management framework that allows for inclusion of low probability–high impact events. Future forecasts should also reflect on the realities of economic growth globally, and from 'engines' such as China. More 'realistic' scenarios for the future will generate greater long-term benefit for tourism as they will allow decision-makers to undertake their own risk management and make informed investment decisions. This chapter refrained from making judgements on the probabilities of different 'futures', nor did it outright reject the mainstream approach to tourism forecasting. However, in a carbon-constrained world it will be increasingly important to understand possible shifts in development, and tourism would benefit greatly from more research in this area, including research that uses novel techniques for forecasting and scenario analysis (Lempert et al., 2003).

4 The End of Plenty: Physical Constraints

4.1 Overview: What is Oil?

What is oil? Black liquid energy. The answer may seem simple, but definitions of what is included in oil statistics, and what is not, are complicated. The Energy Information Administration (EIA, 2006) defines crude oil as: '...a mixture of hydrocarbons that exist in liquid phase in natural underground reservoirs and which remain liquid at atmospheric temperature and pressure'.

Crude oil is the dominant liquid fuel that is reported by energy agencies, but not the only one. Crude oil (as it comes out of the well) is typically not the liquid fuel we use – it has to be refined into the different types of fuel, including petrol, diesel or kerosene. Crude oil is less in volume than the refined product, due to so-called refinery gains. The refining process of crude oil into usable hydrocarbons results in an increased volume of final liquid fuels (even though energy has been lost in the process of making these end products, Heinberg, 2013). Energy organisations, such as the EIA and International Energy Agency (IEA), therefore typically add refinery gains to their production figures – including those associated with imported crude oil (i.e. making American production, for example, look bigger than it is).

Statistics of 'conventional oil', as for example the ones provided in the IEA's annual World Energy Outlook (WEO), also include natural gas liquids (NGLs), even though they are typically gaseous and not liquid. However, they can be blended with crude oil. In addition, condensates are included in energy statistics (Figure 4.1). Condensates refer to light oil which condenses from natural gas when it is exposed to surface temperatures and

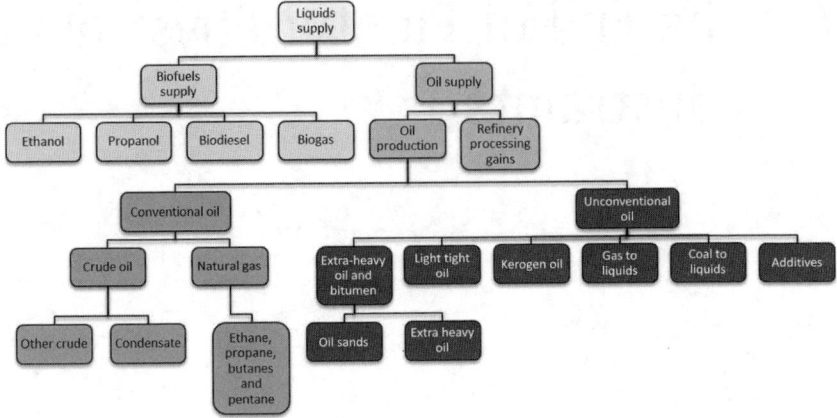

Figure 4.1 Classification of liquid hydrocarbons and other fuels
Source: Based on IEA (2012).

pressures. It is produced at natural gas wells as well as gas processing plants (UK Energy Research Centre (UKERC), 2009). More recently, energy statistics started to include biofuel or non-conventional oils, which leads to an overall growth of liquid fuels, even though conventional fuels are stagnating or declining. Further, both the IEA and the EIA include coal-to-liquids (CTL) and gas-to-liquids (GTL) as unconventional fuel sources in their statistics. The IEA (2012) suggested a classification of liquid fuels as shown in Figure 4.1. This chapter focuses on conventional fuel, but also includes a brief discussion on unconventional fuels at the end of the chapter.

Global annual production curves often include all types of liquid fossil fuel and show a trend of a steep increase, since the 1950s, with several shorter periods of reduction, most notably in the 1970s, during the oil crises. The annual production of oil in 2010 based on an inclusive definition was 28,031 million barrels of oil-equivalent or 28 billion barrels (IEA, 2012: 62).

More often, production is discussed as barrels produced per day, rather than on an annual basis. According to the BP *Statistical Review of World Energy* (2013), which includes crude oil, shale (tight) oil, oil sands and NGLs, daily production in 2012 was 86.15 million barrels (Mbbl). Estimates of global daily production differ widely, depending on the primary data and definitions used. Figure 4.2 shows different estimates of global oil production trends (UKERC, 2009), with all trends showing a flattening curve from the mid-2000s onwards.

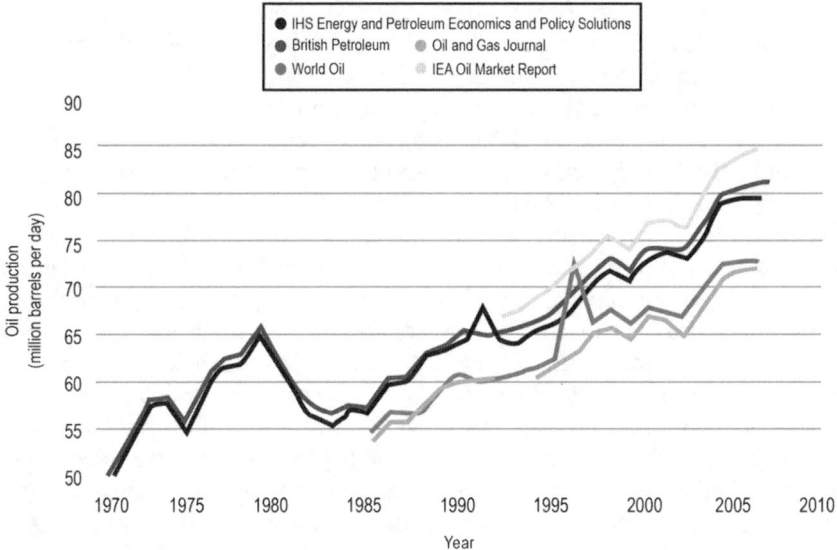

Figure 4.2 Global oil production trends compiled from different data sources
Original note: *OGJ* (*Oil & Gas Journal*) and *World Oil* only include crude oil, condensate and syncrude. BP Statistical Review and IHS Energy also include NGLs. IEA and EIA also include refinery gains, CTL, GTL and biofuels.
Source: After UKERC (2009).

4.2 Future Projections

Future production rates are highly uncertain, but the IEA's WEO with its three different scenarios is used by most commentators as a starting point for debate. The projections are adjusted annually, but have only changed marginally between, say, 2012 and 2010. Further, projections are derived from the World Energy Model, which is largely driven by energy demand rather than supply. The demand focus is a common problem of oil forecasting models, as it reflects a predict-and-demand mentality that may not meet physical realities.

In addition, forecasts typically include short-term supply shocks, but they fail to include more persistent or permanent constraints such as physical limits (Benes *et al.*, 2012). It is also not clear if and how important feedback effects are accounted for in energy projections. For example, the IEA energy model assumes an average growth in gross domestic product (GDP) of 3.2% per annum between now and 2035 (i.e. GDP is seen as driving demand for energy as a dependent variable), but – as seen in Chapter 6 – higher oil prices can have significantly negative impacts on GDP. This represents a negative feedback loop. Higher oil prices can also have significant impacts on investments in oil exploration and technology. Again, this is a negative feedback loop. It is unlikely that such effects are captured.

In their projections, the IEA is using three scenarios: the Current Policies Scenario; the New Policies Scenario, and the very ambitious 450 Scenario – alluding to a target of 450 parts per million of carbon dioxide in the atmosphere target. Since the 450 Scenario demands stringent climate and energy policies, it is not discussed further here (it is deemed unrealistic considering the present emission path). The current trend of energy demand is probably most aligned to the Current Policies Scenario (i.e. some but not many energy policies are implemented), but the IEA focuses most of their discussions on the New Policies Scenario. The New Policies Scenario assumes an implementation of energy policies over and above the status quo. This has to be seen as an optimistic scenario in which demand for fossil energy would be somewhat curbed by widespread policies relating to energy efficiency and alternative energy sources. In the New Policies Scenario of 2010 the projected demand of oil (i.e. any liquid fuel other than biofuel) in 2035 will be 99 million barrels per day (mb/d), at a cost of US$113 per barrel. The 2012 WEO adjusted this to 100 mb/d with a projected cost of US$125 per barrel in 2035. The American EIA predicts energy demand to be 108 mb/d in 2030 (in Cobb, 2012).

In the past, future production curves of ongoing growth typically relied on the fact that the oil producing and exporting countries (OPEC), and specifically Saudi Arabia, could keep producing more. This argument has disappeared more recently, and instead substantial growth in non-conventional resources across the globe is assumed. In their latest WEO, the IEA (2012: 81) stated:

> Oil production, net of processing gains, is projected to rise from 84 mb/d in 2011 to 97 mb/d in 2035, the increase coming entirely from natural gas liquids and unconventional sources. Output of crude oil (excluding light tight oil) fluctuates between 65 mb/d and 69 mb/d, never quite reaching the historic peak of 70 mb/d in 2008 and falling by 3 mb/d between 2011 and 2035.

Several points are interesting about this quote. The first is that the increase in unconventional – that is much more expensive forms of oil (see further below) – is critical for meeting energy demand. The second is that the IEA explicitly states that there has been a peak in conventional oil production, namely in 2008. An earlier WEO report put the peak date at 2006 (IEA,

2010: 101). Third, the statement of decline in production of conventional oil in the order of 3 mb/d is highly optimistic when considering the growth chart shown in Figure 4.3 where most of the conventional crude oil to be produced in 2035 is from fields yet to be developed or yet to be found. As can be seen from Figure 4.3, it is very important to understand which types of oil are discussed when people advocate for or against the notion of 'Peak Oil'.

In an alternative approach to forecasting oil production and prices, Benes *et al.* (2012) in their International Monetary Fund (IMF) Working Paper, for the first time, developed a model that includes both drivers of demand and long-term geological constraints on supply. The authors found that they were able to better model oil prices and that the price-insensitive geological component of supply (i.e. physical constraint) is mostly responsible for recent increases in price. The model also showed that further increases in world oil production were associated with a near doubling of oil prices over the next decade. The doubling of prices is a permanent effect; something that has rarely been incorporated in policy discussions about future energy supply.

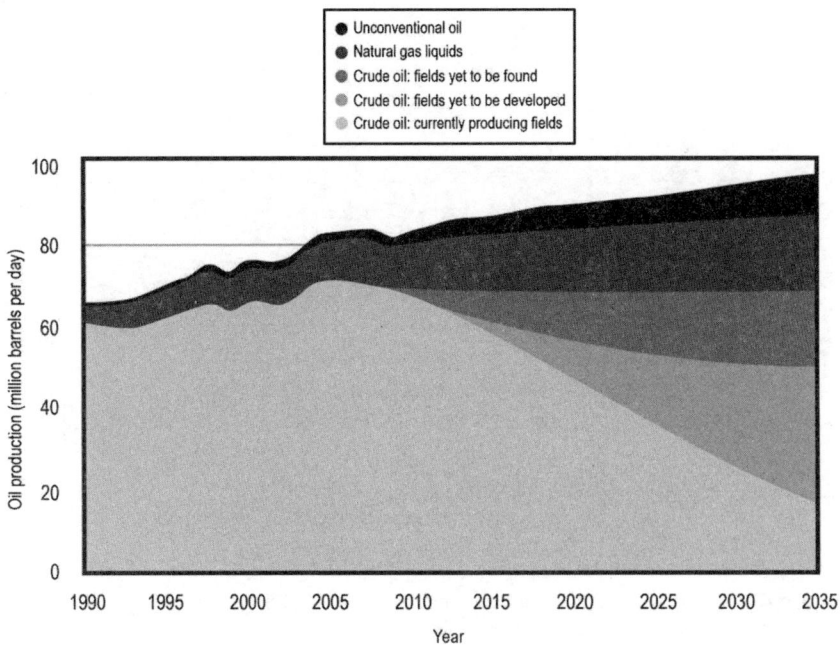

Figure 4.3 Future world oil production in the IEA's New Policies Scenario
Source: IEA (2010).

4.3 Peak Oil: A Contested Space

4.3.1 What does 'Peak Oil' mean and when is it?

The fact that oil is a finite resource is not being disputed, but the proposition that its production might reach a maximum in the *near future*, after which it declines, is highly contested. The idea of a peak in oil production goes back to King Hubbert in 1956. Back then, Hubbert estimated that American oil production would roughly follow a bell-shaped production curve and peak around 1970. Over the following years he came up with several quite different methods to estimate the peak (including a global peak which he predicted to be around 2000) (Deffeyes, 2005). While Hubbert's scientific predictions caused great objection and personal animosity, Hubbert was proven right. America's oil production peaked in 1971.

Most oil producing countries have reached their maximum conventional oil production (Figure 4.4). In some cases, the peak might be temporary due to above-ground constraints. Iraq, for example, is generally believed to hold substantial reserves, with production being constrained mainly as a result of

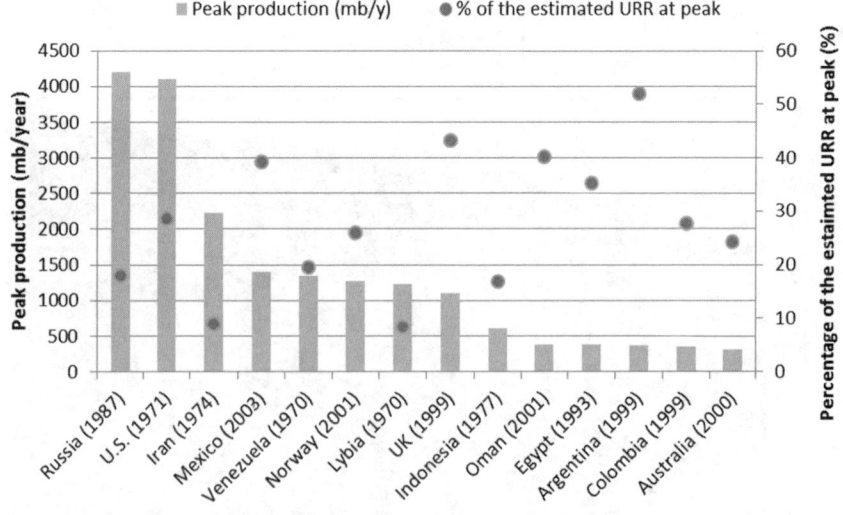

Figure 4.4 Countries that have moved past their Peak Oil production
Original note: Shows year of peak production in brackets and estimated percentage of the United States Geological Service (2000) estimate of ultimately recoverable resource (URR) that was produced by the date of peak.
Source: Based on UKERC (2009).

political conflict and lack of foreign investment. Most prominently, however, countries such as Russia, the United States (US), Libya and the United Kingdom (UK) peaked many years ago. Venezuela is an interesting example, as its conventional production is believed to have peaked in 1970, but large resources of about 270 billion barrels of extra-heavy oil, mostly from the Orinoco Belt, have improved its outlook (Chapman, 2013). The proportion of oil left in the field at peak production is provided as well (see Figure 4.9; and also further below).

Since Hubbert, many scientists have attempted to predict a global peak in oil production, using Hubbert's methods and new techniques. Approaches include fitting a parametric oil production curve to an existing production profile or estimating supply through a bottom-up or field-by-field analysis (de Almeida & Silva, 2009). In their authoritative meta-analysis on oil depletion, the UKERC (2009) provided a detailed review of the different methods, their strengths and weaknesses, and an overall assessment of what period of time is the most likely for a global peak.

Another recent example is de Almeida and Silva's study (2009) that involved a bottom-up approach that scaled estimates up from individual countries, based on countries' production information published through both the IEA and the EIA. In addition, this study used data from Skrebowski's (2004) new 'megaprojects'. De Almeida and Silva included conventional crude oil, condensate, natural gas liquids, and unconventional liquids from tar sands (or bitumen) and arrived at an estimated timing for a global peak in liquid oil production between 2008 and 2012. Not surprisingly, the production peak – or a plateau, rather – in de Almeida and Silva's study was mostly influenced by assumptions on the future production in Saudi Arabia. A recent revision of their data confirmed the timing of their earlier estimate, with the decline of global production starting in 2012.

Table 4.1 shows a range of Peak Oil forecasts over time. The range is vast – which is rather astonishing, considering the central role that oil plays in our economies and lives. It is noticeable, though, that those authors or agencies that initially put the peak into the very distant future, for example Shell and Cambridge Energy Research Associates (CERA), have gradually adjusted their timing downwards towards earlier peaking. Likewise, initially pessimistic estimates have been revised upwards. Deffeyes, Koppelaar and Skrebowski are examples. This indicates a converging trend with a peak somewhere between 2010 and 2020.

Projections of future oil supply depend on many assumptions, for example URR, reserve growth, decline rates and depletion. These will be discussed in more detail below. Because of different assumptions (many of which might be equally legitimate) about key parameters it is almost impossible to produce one single curve that provides a universally accepted 'best

Table 4.1 Estimates for the global peak of oil production

Date of forecast	Timing of peak	Reference
2000	2004–2014	Bartlett (2000)
2000	2021–2112	Wood and Long (2000) for EIA
2000	Beyond 2020	IEA (2000)
2001	2003–2008	Deffeyes (2001)
2003	2007–2009	Simmons (2003)
2003	Around 2010	Campbell (2003)
2003	After 2010	World Energy Council (2003)
2003	2010–2020	Laherrere (2003)
2003	2025 or later	Davis (2003) for Shell
2004	2006-2007	Bakhtiari (2004)
2004	After 2007	Skrebowski (2004)
2004	Before 2010	Goodstein (2004)
2004	After 2020	Jackson and Esser (2004) for CERA
2005	Before 2009	Deffeyes (2005)
2006	After 2012	Koppelaar (2006)
2006	After 2030	IEA (2006)
2006	After 2035	Jackson (2006) for CERA
2007	2008-2018	Robelius (2007)
2007	2015	Koppelaar (2007)
2007	About 2015	Laherrere (2007)
2008	After 2017	CERA (2008)
2008	2020 or later	Shell (2008)
2009	2008–2012	De Almeida and Silva (2009)
2010	After 2035	EIA (2010)
2010	2010	Aleklett *et al.* (2010)
2010	2014	Nashawi *et al.* (2010)
2012	No peak	Maugeri (2012)

Source: Compiled based on de Almeida and Silva (2009) and Chapman (2013).

estimate'. Instead, an alternative approach is to present future projections in the form of probabilistic curves. Krumdieck *et al.* (2010) used a wide range of existing oil supply projections to develop such a probability assessment (Figure 4.5). So, rather than representing a hypothetical scenario, the supply probability approach can be interpreted as expert consensus. The lowest

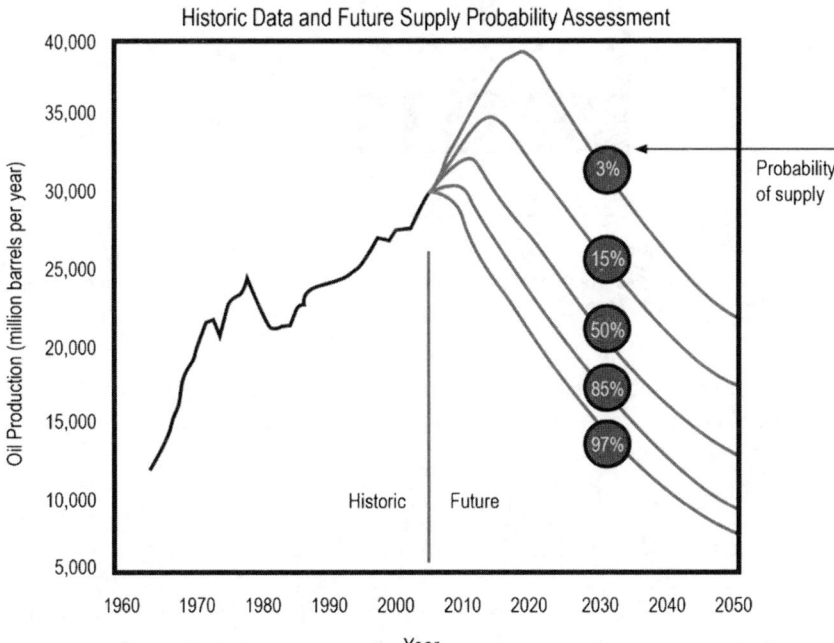

Figure 4.5 Oil production data up to 2050, and probabilistic future supply projections
Note: Based on Monte Carlo simulations using data on future oil supply from petroleum geology and energy experts)
Source: Krumdieck *et al.* (2010).

(most pessimistic) of the curves, for example, indicates that there is a 97% probability that global oil supply would be at least at this level, if not higher. The most optimistic curve, that is the 3% probability curve at the top, indicates that there is only a 3% probability that future supply will be at this or a higher level.

4.3.2 How much oil is there: 'Ultimately recoverable resources'

One of the key questions is how much oil there is and how do we know about it? How big is the URR? The URR includes all the resources that will be exploited over time (Figure 4.6). They are composed of the cumulative production, reserves (what we know today), future reserve growth (see below) and yet-to-find resources. The cumulative production to date is known relatively well. The size of reserves, as we will see later,

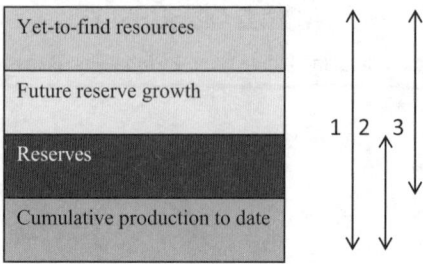

Figure 4.6 Ultimately recoverable resources and what they are composed of
Notes: 1 = ultimately recoverable resource; 2 = cumulative discoveries; 3 = remaining resources.
Source: Based on UKERC (2009).

is less transparent; as is the extent of future reserve growth. Estimates of yet-to-find resources are anyone's guess (see also Chapter 5 on the political nature of oil projections).

Deffeyes (2005), a geologist who worked at the Shell research lab in Houston alongside King Hubbert in the 1950s and 1960s, explained in his book *Beyond Oil* that very few places on Earth have all the right ingredients for the formation of oil. Geological structures (basins) needed to capture organic material (e.g. in the Cretaceous 100 million years ago), which then needed to be buried sufficiently deep to reach temperatures of around 100 degrees Celsius to break down the organic matter into smaller molecules (those with five to 20 carbon atoms are liquid oil, those with less than five carbon atoms are gas) (Aleklett, 2012). Oil then has to migrate upwards until it is trapped in so-called source rock, with sufficiently large pores to hold the oil. The source rock needs so sit underneath an impermeable layer or cap rock to stop the oil from migrating upwards and disappearing to the surface. San Joaquin Valley Geological Services in California provides an excellent education resource on the history of its oil industry, including a number of easily readable graphics and illustrations of oil formation, exploration and exploitation (Figure 4.7).

Most oil resources are concentrated in a small number of large fields that were discovered relatively early, many of them between the 1940s and 1960s. No more than 100 fields worldwide make up about half of the global oil production and about 500 fields account for three-quarters of production. There are only two fields that have an estimated URR of over 50,000 million barrels (or 50 billion barrels). These are Ghawar in Saudi Arabia, with an estimated URR of between 66 and 150 billion barrels, and Greater Burgan in Kuwait, with 32 to 75 billion barrels (Aleklett, 2012). Table 4.2 shows Ivanhoe and Leckie's 10 categories of oil fields, classified into megagiant,

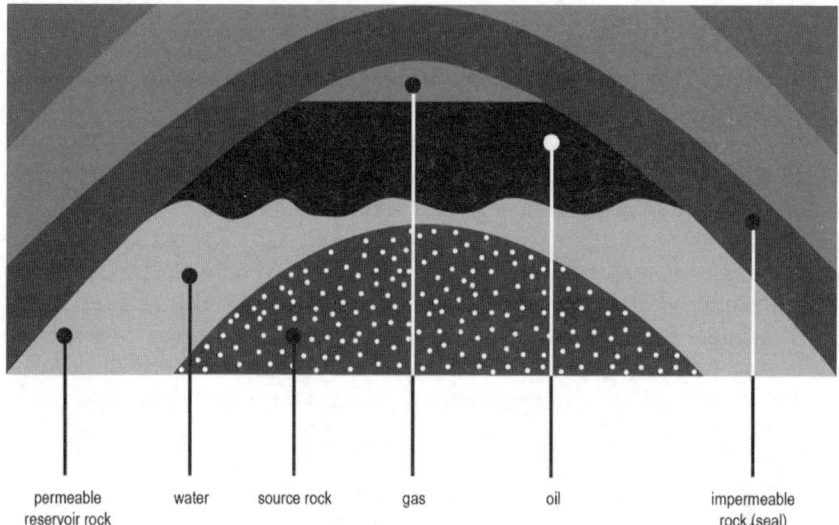

permeable
reservoir rock

water

source rock

gas

oil

impermeable
rock (seal)

Figure 4.7 Geological structure for oil and gas fields
Source: Joaquin Valley Geological Services (2013).

Table 4.2 Ivanhoe and Leckie's estimate of the size distribution of the world's oil fields

Category	Estimated URR (million barrels)	Numbers in the world
Megagiant	>50,000	2
Supergiant	5000–50,000	40
Giant	500–5000	328
Major	100–500	961
Large	50–100	895
Medium	25–50	1109
Small	10–25	2128
Very small	1–10	7112
Tiny	0.1–1	10,849
Insignificant	<0.1	17,740
Total		41,164

Source: In Sorrell *et al.* (2012: 710).

supergiant, giant and others. It can be seen that other fields are numerous; however, their contribution to overall production is relatively small. So it is the top ones that have the greatest importance for future supplies (Sorrell *et al.*, 2012).

The estimates of the URR differ substantially, ranging between 2000 and 4300 billion barrels – a factor of over two (Sorrell *et al.*, 2010). Aleklett (2012) reported that humans have consumed about 1100 billion barrels of oil. So, depending on the estimate we have used up about half or a quarter. The most detailed assessment was made by the US Geological Service (USGS, 2000), which produced an estimate of 3345 billion barrels of ultimate resources. This estimate has been criticised heavily by some, but is nevertheless used by key agencies such as the IEA. Depending on the URR, the peak in oil production has either been passed or might be as far out as 2034 (Figure 4.8).

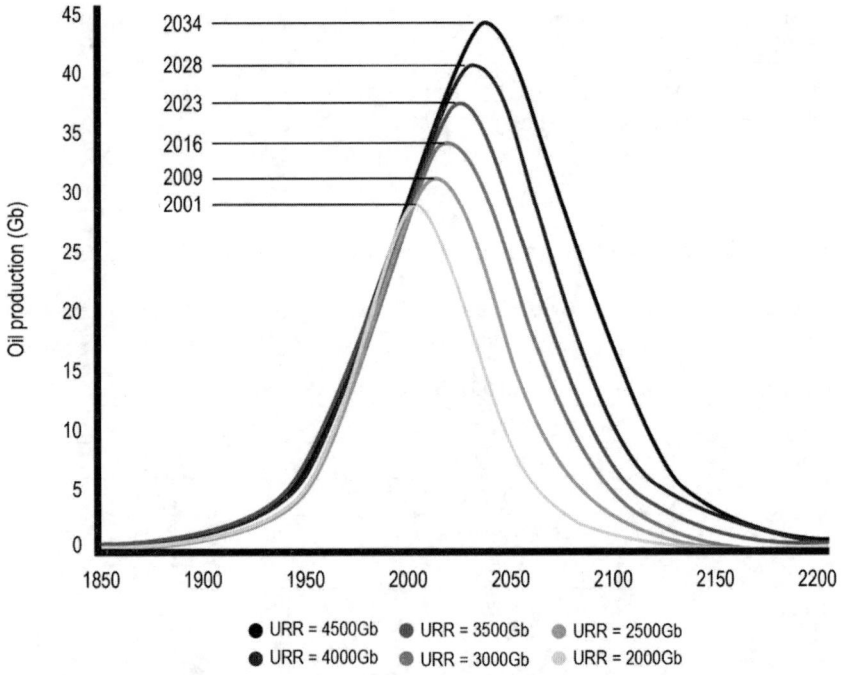

Figure 4.8 Peaking of global conventional oil production under different assumptions about the global URR using a simple 'bell-shaped' model of global production
Notes: With an assumed URR of 4000 Gb, the global peak would be in 2028. Increasing the global URR by 1 billion barrels delays the peak by less than five days.
Source: Sorrell *et al.* (2010).

Regardless, the UKERC (2009) concluded that only very optimistic assumptions would imply a peak beyond 2023.

4.3.3 Reserve growth

Most of today's growth is a result of the revision of existing fields. To understand statements about oil reserves, it is essential to distinguish proved (1P) and probable (2P) reserves (Figure 4.9). Proved reserves basically relates to the amount of oil that can be extracted with today's technology and economic viability. The probability attached to this is 90%. Probable reserves have a likelihood of being exploited of 50%. Some also report 3P reserves, which include possible resources. 1P reserve estimates are usually very conservative and cautious. However neither 1P nor 2P are typically audited or verified. Especially in the OPEC countries, which are most important in terms of global oil supply, the quality or integrity of the estimates is highly uncertain.

David Strahan (2007: 69), author of the book *The Last Oil Shock*, illustrates how estimates of oil reserves are produced. When a field is discovered, and oil engineers have not only mapped the area and its geological structures, but also measured the porosity of the rock, they will be able to estimate how much oil there is. This is the *original oil in place* or OOIP. Not all of this oil will be developed: it is only an estimate of the total resource. To estimate the reserve, engineers need to estimate a recovery factor. For example if the OOIP is 100 million barrels and the recovery factor is 35%, the proved and probable reserve is 35 million barrels. This is very rough, but serves as first guidance. To provide 1P reserves, the company needs to be much more conservative, as they need to be almost certain that this number will be produced or even exceeded. This figure can be as small as 10% of the initial

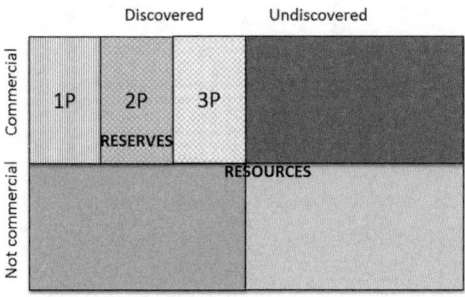

Figure 4.9 Illustration of oil resources (all of the oil on Earth) and those reserves that are commercially exploitable and either discovered (1P, 2P, 3P) or undiscovered (yet-to-find)
Source: UKERC (2009).

proved and probable estimate; so in the above example that might be 3.5 million barrels. Over time, estimates improve and the 1P reserves almost inevitably grow. Sometimes also 2P estimates increase over time.

Reserve estimates are often revised and typically grow. This is simply because advanced technology (e.g. 3D and 4D seismology) for understanding the field or recovering the resource enables improving the estimate of the reserve over time. Increases in global oil price may also lead to a revision of reserves, as previously uneconomical areas might now become viable. Typically additions are positive, although sometimes fields can be revised downward, resulting in reserve growth. One key element of reserve growth has been enhanced recovery methods. Typically, recovery factors are in the order of 34%; however, factors of up to 80% are possible (Sorrell *et al.*, 2012). Techniques such as injection of carbon dioxide can enhance recovery substantially, maybe in the order of several percent.

Estimates of reserve growth vary widely by region. This may also depend on definitions and stringency in reporting. There is some indication that larger fields tend to have greater reserve growth. Also, onshore fields were found more likely to be revised upwards than offshore fields. Since production is moving more towards smaller fields, as well as offshore ones, it is possible that future reserve growth rates will be less than those experienced in the past.

4.3.4 Decline rates and depletion

To make up for falling production, new resources need to be discovered and made available as reserves are being depleted. Herein lays the key challenge: new discoveries are insufficient to cover future needs for production. Discoveries have long peaked: in the early 1960s. Colin Campbell (2003) – and other experts – has produced a 'growing gap' graph. The graph (Figure 4.10) shows oil production relative to discoveries and highlights the fact that today's production is based on very early discoveries. Heinberg (2013) brings the challenge to the point, noting that for every four to five barrels consumed today, the industry only finds one new barrel. Many of these new barrels are found in challenging environments, for example deep-sea oil fields.

The situation can be summarised as a big tank (the proved reserves) from which we draw oil for various uses. The discovery rate ensures that the tank is continuously topped up with new resources. The rate of filling up the tank is slow and does not match withdrawal. Reserve growth also makes the tank bigger. Most of the oil 'in the tank' is coming from Organisation for Economic Co-operation and Development (OECD) countries (see also Chapter 5). Canadian tar sands also make up a significant proportion of the 'potential

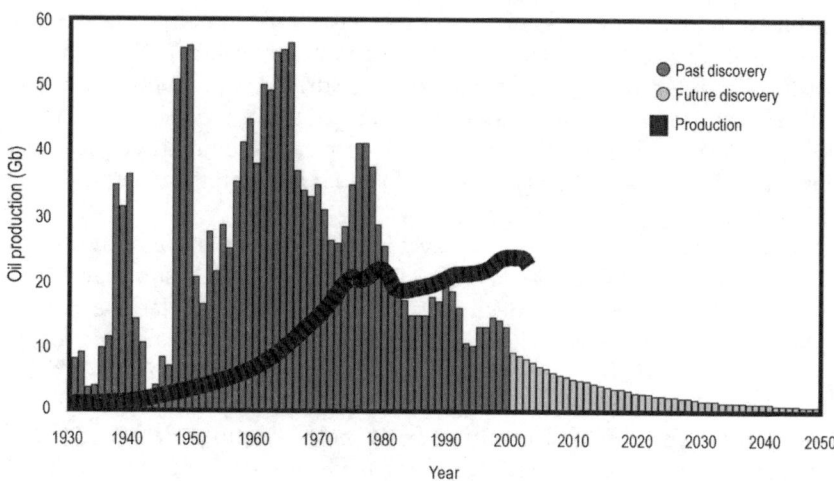

Figure 4.10 Cumulative (conventional) discoveries and production
Source: Campbell (2003).

tank', as discussed further below, but their current exploitation – that is output – is miniscule.

According to the UK Industry Taskforce on Peak Oil & Energy Security (2010), the current total consumption out of the global oil tank is about 84.5 million barrels (Mbbl) per day; but the discovery rate is only 30 Mbbl per day. This is not quite as dire as Heinberg's assessment, but still only represents about one-third when comparing discovery with production. Thus, the World Energy Council (2011) warns that 'time is running out to prove that newly discovered fields and new technology can more than compensate for flagging production from the rapidly aging fields beyond OPEC' (WEC, 2011: 18, in Chapman, 2013).

The trend of global oil production can be better comprehended when the development of one individual oil field is understood. Aleklett (2012) compares conventional oil fields to cola bottles, whereby the liquid coke is tied up in a sponge. When the bottle is turned upside down, some of the cola will pour out under pressure, but soon the flow will slow down and eventually stop – even if most of the liquid is still in the bottle. The pores of the sponge hold the cola tight. Only additional measures will help to get some more of the liquid out. The same applies to an oil field. Enhanced recovery is necessary.

When a field is discovered and production starts, recovery usually grows substantially in the early phases. The oil flows to the surface because it has been kept under great pressure (under a cap rock). Eventually, however, the pressure in the reservoir will decrease (or water will break through) and production will decline. If additional wells are drilled or production purposefully slowed down, a sharp peak can be avoided and a production plateau is observed instead. Eventually the decline is terminal and rapid. The so-called post-peak decline rate differs for each field and is higher for smaller fields (e.g. 12% per annum) than large fields (e.g. 4%).

Several estimates for a globally averaged decline rate have been put forward. Sorrell *et al.* (2012), based on calculations by the IEA, summarise that for all post-peak fields, the decline is 6.7% per year. Calculated across all fields operating in the world, that is including those that have not yet peaked as well as those that have peaked, the estimated yearly decline is 4.1% per year. This means that over 3 million barrels per day need to be added to make up for the shortfall resulting from global decline. Heinberg (2013) translates this into the need to discover new oil sources the size of Saudi Arabia every three years – a prospect that is highly unlikely.

An important point relates to the extent of depletion of an oil field. Once production starts and oil is produced from a field, the available reserve inevitable reduces. Analysts are particularly interested in what proportion of the original reserve is still in place when production reaches its maximum output (i.e. peak). Several analyses have been put forward, and Sorrell *et al.* (2012) summarise that, globally, the production-weighted depletion at peak is 37%. However, depletion varies a lot, with some fields being as low as 22%, and others managing to be close to or even over 50% (Sorrell *et al.*, 2012).

4.4 Unconventional Resources

4.4.1 It's the energy return, stupid!

Peak Oil sceptics, such as Maugeri (2012), purport that technological advances will incrementally allow us to access new resources, making up for the depletion of existing reserves. Ignoring technological progress, they argue, is the main flaw of the Peak Oil theory (Chapman, 2013). New technologies will enhance production of existing resources and make accessible new sources such as unconventional oils. Others argue that new sources might all but soften the decline; they will not compensate for reductions in conventional oil and thereby not avert a global peak.

When focusing the discussion on volumes of oil produced it is easy to forget the actual *net energy* that we gain from exploitation efforts. Thus, we need to consider very carefully how much energy is required to produce a certain amount of energy. This leads us to the resource pyramid and the very important topic of energy return (Figure 4.11). Bardi (2009, in Bridge, 2010) candidly points out that producing oil is not the same as getting beer from the fridge – a barrel is not necessarily a barrel.

The energy return on energy invested (EROEI) is absolutely crucial for assumptions about future available net energy as well as prices. EROEI also comes back to the point that we are not 'running out of oil', but running out of *cheap* oil. Heinberg (2013) put it simply: it takes energy to get energy. Every stage of energy production requires energy input (e.g. pumping water, transporting and maintaining technology, refining, etc.). The EROEI – sometimes referred to as energy return on investment (EROI) – measures how much the gain is in energy over and above investment. In the early days of oil production, the EROEI was very high – in the order of about 100:1 (Heinberg, 2013; UKERC, 2009). However, this has dropped to 20:1 for US oil fields in the 1990s (Cleveland 1992, 1995, in UKERC, 2009) or 18:1 for all fields globally in 2006 (Gagnon et al., 2009).

Unconventional oil resources have an even lower EROEI. Heinberg (2013) noted that tar sands, tight oil and biofuels have a ratio of 5:1, or maybe even

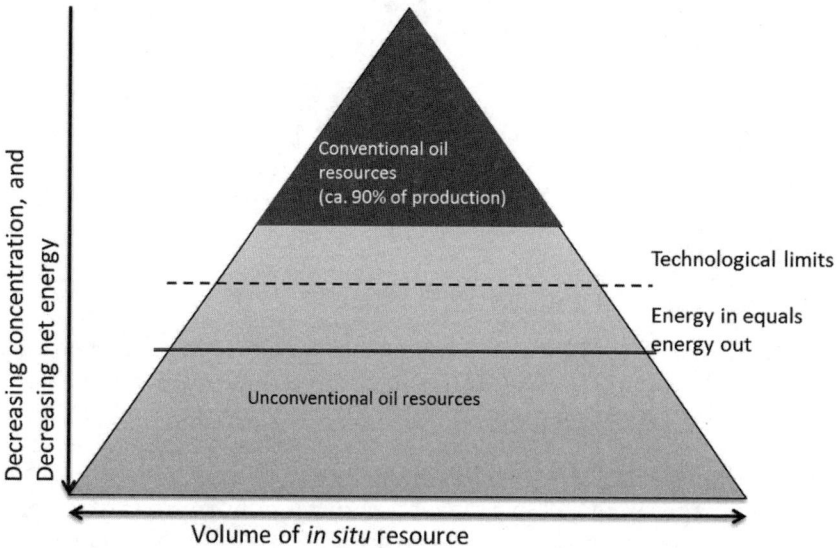

Figure 4.11 The resource pyramid – highlighting the diminishing concentration and net energy of unconventional oil resources
Source: Hughes (2013).

Table 4.3 Production costs for different sources of liquid fuel

Type of liquid fuel	Estimated production cost in US$ (based on year 2000)	Approximate proportion already consumed (%)
Conventional oil	1–15	55
Enhanced oil recovery	15–22	50
Tar sands	20–25	25
Gas-to-liquid synfuels	20–32	20
Coal-to-liquid synfuels	35–38	20
Oil shale	22–90	10

Source: After Brandt and Farrell (2006).

less. This is also reflected in the high production costs that make most unconventional resources only economically viable with high oil prices. Production of conventional oil in Abu Dhabi (United Arab Emirates), for example, might only be in the order of $1 per barrel (Aleklett, 2012), whereas the production of oil shale could be up to $80 per barrel (Table 4.3).

Heinberg (2013: 31) pointed out that the fact that we are increasingly producing from less concentrated sources with lower net energy gains is evidence that conventional oil production has peaked and we are moving down the resource pyramid:

> The relentless decline in EROEI of oil is one of the biggest underreported economic stories of our times. Available net energy – what makes society work – is dwindling away even as production statistics *seem to show* a North American oil and gas production boom (original emphasis).

4.4.2 Panacea to the oil crisis: Fracking?

Nothing has caused as much excitement in the global energy scene as the upsurge in fracking. The US is at the forefront of fracking; mainly for gas production but increasingly oil as well. For example, between 1998 and 2008, US gas reserves grew by a whopping 44.7% (UK Industry Taskforce on Peak Oil & Energy Security, 2010). In his latest book, *Snake Oil*, Heinberg (2013) discusses the technique of hydraulic fracturing – or hydrofracturing – and critically assesses claims of an energy turnaround, America's energy independence and the end of Peak Oil.

Fracking is an old technique that goes back to the 1940s and involves injecting water at high pressure into wells to enhance the flow of oil or gas

(Deffeyes, 2005). In more recent decades, the exploration industry has further developed the technique that now involves injection of different types of fracturing fluids and fine sand into the rock. The injection is combined with horizontal drilling which now allows the effective reach of so-called tight oil (sometimes called shale oil, not to be confused with oil shale, see below) and shale gas from one single well (with up to 16 horizontal wells) (Heinberg, 2013).

Most fracking is currently for shale gas, although some shale rocks also contain tight oil. As discussed earlier, oil is normally kept in porous rock where it has migrated to from source rock. From there it is relatively easy to extract. Tight oil, however, is oil still in the source rock that could not migrate upwards into a more porous rock. Global resources could be vast. Currently the US is experiencing a massive increase in production of both gas and oil due to fracking. Most production comes from two 'plays': the Bakken in North Dakota and Eagle Ford in Texas.

While the media herald the success of fracking, Heinberg (2013) suggests that production prospects are totally inflated by the industry and readily picked up by both the EIA and the IEA. Claims such as the production of tight oil in the US exceeding that of Saudi Arabia (Maugeri, 2012) or 100 years of future production are unfounded and hugely exaggerated. While the oil resources might indeed be vast, unconventional resources are foremost restricted by the size of their 'taps' (Hughes, 2013). What counts more is how much of the oil can be physically, and even more importantly economically, recovered. As Cobb (2012: 2) notes, cynically: 'it is possible to recover rocks from the Moon. But we would never think of transporting rocks from the Moon to the Earth to make roadway aggregates'.

Heinberg makes a compelling case about the reasons for the hype (i.e. both political and financial with vested interests as far as Wall Street), the flaws in statements and the devastating environmental effects of fracking. Considering rapid decline curves and limited recovery (only 7% of the resource may be recoverable in the case of gas) he estimates that fracking will provide less than 10 years of current US consumption of gas. He further explores the situation for oil, which is even more problematic. According to production profiles of existing wells, the decline rate for wells is 81–90% in the first 24 months. This means that fracking results in a huge increase in production once wells are drilled – followed by an extremely rapid decrease. Rune Likvern (2012) of The Oil Drum reports that existing wells in the Bakken already produce diminishing returns. To make up for the decline, more and more wells have to be drilled (see Figure 4.12). Likvern uses the analogy of the Red Queen from Lewis Carrol's book *Through the Looking-Glass* which made the statement: 'It takes all the running you can do, to

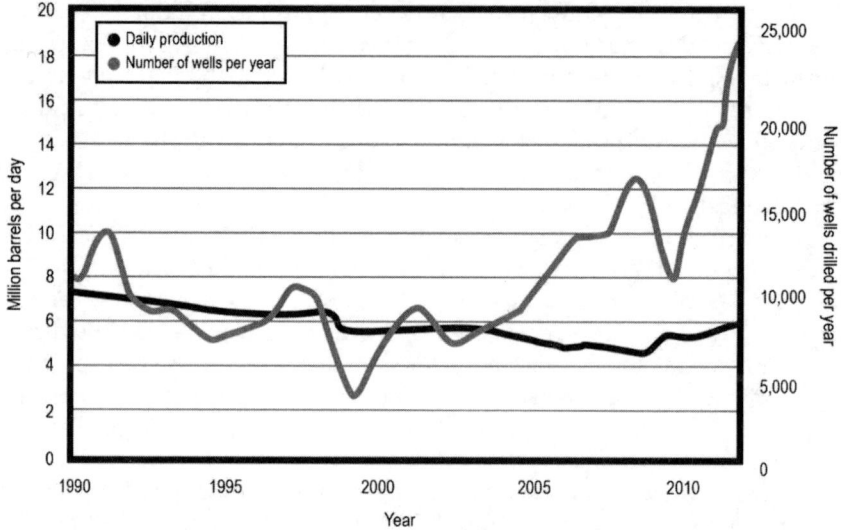

Figure 4.12 Oil well drilling rate in the US between 1990 and 2012 (12-month moving average)
Note: The number of wells drilled per year has increased by over 2.5 times since 2005.
Source: Hughes (2013).

keep in the same place.' Thus, the welcome relief from production through fracking may be short lived.

Hughes (2013) estimated that Bakken and Eagle Ford together may have 5 billion barrels of oil; which is less than 10 months of US oil consumption. Five billion barrels of oil would be classified as the top end of a giant oil field (see earlier); however, the net energy would be substantially less compared with oil from conventional giant oil fields. Estimates for the US are in the order of 24 billion barrels – or the same as 288 days of world energy demand (Cobb, 2012).

The outlook for fracking in other countries is not very promising, although many countries are seriously looking into the opportunities. Some countries have banned fracking (e.g. France), whereas others are cautiously assessing the potential, for example Poland, which is believed to have considerable resources of shale gas. Most countries still lack the technology and the equipment, which is mainly concentrated in the US. Other countries lack another key ingredient: water. Saudi Arabia, for example, lacks the water resources to exploit its shale gas resources. Fracking is extremely water intensive, and conflict with other users has already been observed in some parts of the US and Mexico (Heinberg, 2013).

Apart from the above production constraints, fracking has been associated with:

- chemical pollution of groundwater nearby fracking activity;
- contamination of wastewater in treatment plants when fracking water is disposed into plants;
- radioactivity of wastewater which is insufficiently dealt with;
- leakage of methane from wells and pipes (contributing significantly to greenhouse gas emissions and polluting drinking water);
- air pollution; and
- seismic activity and subsidence of land (destroying houses and infrastructure).

4.4.3 Other unconventional sources

Before briefly summarising the status of unconventional resources it is important to mention other *conventional* resources that might replace oil. Gas and coal are already being exploited conventionally, and some of the production is used to produce liquid fuel: gas-to-liquid and coal-to-liquid. Two more books could be written on these other resources, and they would explore similar questions: when will we run out of gas or coal? Information is no less hard to obtain as for oil, although estimates are available. Höök (2010) for example estimates the timing of a coal peak to be between 2020 and 2050. Understanding different types of fossil resources, and their possible substitution, is essential for the future planning of energy supply.

Historically, gas prices have been coupled closely with oil prices, but this relationship is now weakening, especially in North America, where domestic gas exploitation (see above, fracking) has driven prices to extremely low levels. For more information, readers are referred, for example, to the World Energy Outlook Special Report by IEA (2011) on 'The Golden Age of Gas' and coal statistics provided by the World Coal Association (2012). Peak Oil books, such as the one by Deffeyes (2005), also discuss gas and oil resources. Renewable energy sources will be discussed briefly in Chapter 7; and uranium as an energy source will not be explored in this book – although it is noted that physical constraints apply with that as well (Aleklett, 2012). The Wuppertal Institute for Climate, Environment and Energy (2009) state that, at present consumption, uranium resources will last for another 50 years. In the following, tar sands, deepwater resources and methane hydrates will be discussed briefly.

Tar (oil) sands: Tar sands have been found in over 30 countries (Deffeyes, 2005). The most significant discoveries are north of the Orinoco River in Venezuela and Alberta's tar sands in Canada. The Canadians refer to their resource as heavy-oil sand. Both resources are near-surface layers of rock that contain extremely viscose oil. Both are huge: the Alberta sands resource alone contains 1840 billion barrels – or about 60 years of global oil consumption (Heinberg, 2013). Only about 16% are currently under active development (IEA, 2011). Production rates are relatively small at this point at a level of 1.6 million barrels per day. This is projected to increase to 5 million barrels per day by 2013 (a fraction of world demand); an estimate that has to be taken with a grain of salt (Cobb, 2012). Moreover, the EROEI is very small at about 3:1 or 6:1, raising questions about net energy gains.

The product of tar sands is actually bitumen; it is 'thick, heavy and sticky, and turning it into anything useful takes an awful lot of work' (Strahan, 2007: 139). About 14,000 tonnes of rock per hour are dug up, crushed and then washed with hot water or steam (there are different types of processes, for more detail see Deffeyes, 2005) to separate the oil. Since bitumen is very thick it needs to be diluted with chemicals. Then it is transported via a pipeline to a facility for further upgrading and extraction of sulphur (Cobb, 2012). The final product is called Syncrude, because it is crude oil that is made synthetically with the input of hydrogen (derived from natural gas). Syncrude can then be refined to produce other fuels (Strahan, 2007).

In sum, the production of oil from tar sands is economical at high oil prices, but it is highly complex and requires the input of vast amounts of water and natural gas. Also, as Deffeyes (2005) notes, the investment required is considerable. He estimates that about US$2–5 billion is required before the first barrel can be produced. With profitability being highly bound by global oil prices, investors are understandably cautious. Finally, since tar sands are mined in an open-cast mine the exploitation brings with it considerable environmental destruction.

Tar or oil sands are not to be confused with oil shale, which is source rock for conventional oil that contains kerogen. Kerogen needs to be treated to form synthetic oil. Whilst there are large resources, especially in the Green River in the US, commercial exploitation is practically zero. Oil from oil shale is therefore insignificant for Peak Oil mitigation (Aleklett, 2012).

Deepwater resources: The IEA (2010) has reported that since 2000, over 50% of oil discoveries have been in deep water. So-called deepwater resources include those oil fields that are found under water columns of 500 metres of depth or deeper. Resources are mainly found in the Gulf of Mexico, Brazil, Nigeria, Angola and Congo, as well as in Alaska, America's Pacific and the Atlantic coast. The New Policies Scenario projects (or requires) annual discoveries of deepwater resources of about 9 billion barrels from 2015 onwards. Drilling technology in deep waters has progressed substantially, making more resources accessible and economically viable; the investments, however, are enormous. The drilling of one single well costs $100 million.

In their 2012 WEO, the IEA discusses Brazil as the most promising country for deepwater oil production. The Campos and Santos Basins off the country's south-east coast hold most proven reserves. In 2007, a consortium of Petrobras, BG Group and Petrogal discovered the Tupi field, which contains substantial reserves at a depth of 5000 metres below the seabed at a water column of 2000 metres. Petrobras estimates that Tupi (now renamed Lula) holds a recoverable resource of about 6.5 billion barrels of oil-equivalent. This might be an optimistic estimate, but highlights the enormous task of finding more than a Tupi every year in the future (see the estimate of nine billion barrels above).

The Gulf of Mexico is also believed to contain much oil at deepsea levels, for example in the geological formation called Jack. Jack caused considerable excitement and optimism in 2006 when it was discovered by Chevron. Jack is also an excellent example of how optimistic news reporting talked up the prospects of oil production from this formation, without robust evidence on actual size and economic recovery rates. It also sparked US President George W. Bush to express hope for future domestic exploitation when addressing a conference on renewable energy in October 2006 (in Aleklett, 2012: 164).

As you can tell, I'm excited about new technologies. But I think we've got to be realistic about the timing. And in order to become less dependent on foreign sources of oil, we've got to explore for oil and gas in our own hemisphere in environmentally friendly ways. And one of the interesting technological developments is the capacity to find oil in unique places.

Methane hydrates: Resources of methane hydrate around the world are huge, and Deffeyes (2005: 75) suggests that gas hydrates today are 'an opportunity for some young person to become richer than Bill Gates'. However, methodologies for extraction are highly uncertain. Methane hydrates are frozen hydrocarbons that exist in the Arctic tundra as well as in the outer parts of continental shelves, typically at a depth of between 600 and 2500 feet. When brought to the surface the gas might be useable as an energy source. Research on the economic recovery of methane hydrates is extremely limited. Heinberg (2013) reports that Japan is the country that has most invested to date. Japan's research programme has consumed about $700,000 over the last years – to produce the equivalent of $50,000 worth of usable gas.

In sum: conventional oil is a great resource that has facilitated the industrial revolution. It is a highly concentrated form of energy that can easily be extracted and made available for various end-uses. While oil consumption

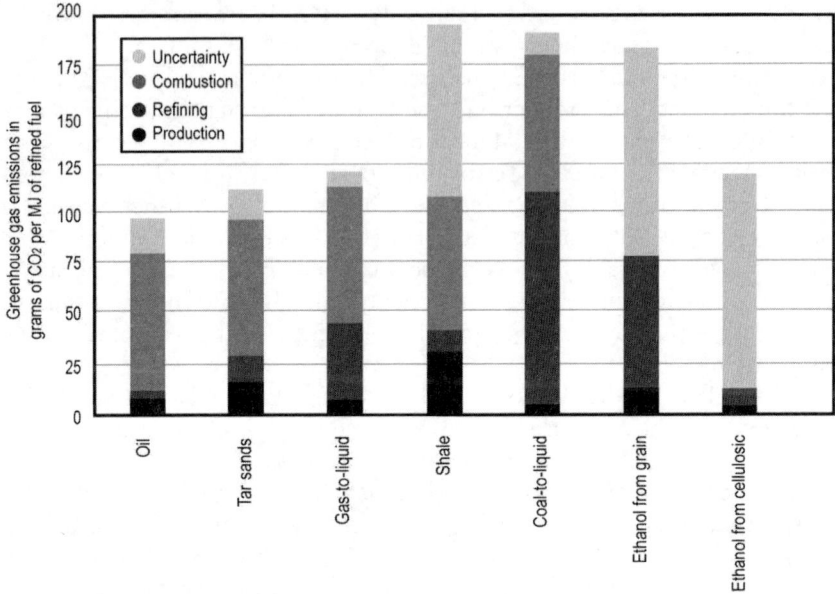

Figure 4.13 Greenhouse gas intensity
Source: After Brandt (2009).

has substantial negative effects, most notably the emission of greenhouse gas emissions that contribute to global climate change, Figure 4.13 shows that conventional oils are, indeed, the *least* carbon-intensive of liquid fuels. Increasing the production of alternative liquid fuels will inevitably lead to an increase in greenhouse gas emissions. McGlade and Ekins (2014) modelled that up to 600 billion barrels of oil (e.g. 40% of deepwater resources) need to be left in the ground if we want any chance of developing a low-carbon energy system that is compatible with global climate change goals. Other problems, such as excessive water use and pollution and environmental degradation, will also increase with the use of non-conventional fuels.

4.5 Conclusion

Discussions about Peak Oil are convoluted by different definitions and accounting frames of oil (Owen *et al.*, 2010). Traditional crude oil, or conventional oil, has peaked about five to seven years ago. The IEA (2010) announced this peak in conventional oil production, even though this fact was not promoted to being a dominant issue. Instead, the opportunities of unconventional resources have been discussed and future production targets have been set. Forecasts are typically following a predict-and-provide approach, where future energy demand is estimated based on econometric models, and oil production volumes are then estimated based on a favourable interpretation of known and unknown resources.

Resources of unconventional oil are huge. However, what counts more than the existence of oil resources is the amount that is recoverable. Unconventional oils have not been exploited up until now for a reason: they are hard to access and they are expensive. Thus, the low-hanging fruit have been picked, and production now moves to the higher hanging fruit. Cohen (2007) summarises that unconventional oil is plagued by three key constraints: (i) scalability in volume; (ii) scalability in time and (iii) low energy returns. Thus, whilst oil companies, governments and media are quick to jump at 'new discoveries' or 'technologies', they often fail to acknowledge that the production of most unconventional resources is tedious and will not produce the same volumes that conventional oil delivered. Technological progress is slow and investment is lagging behind – thus, mass exploitation of unconventional oil is many years away. Finally, and probably most importantly, the net energy gain of unconventional oil is very low.

In summary, the outlook is not rosy, when we accept that conventional oil has peaked, and unconventional oil will not be able to compensate for decline rates. As Benes *et al.* (2012) suggested, this could realistically result in a doubling of oil prices in the next 10 years. The implications of such a trend for tourism are discussed in Chapter 6 and possible responses are explored in Chapter 7.

Some analysts have put forward the concept of peak demand. The IEA 450 Scenario indicates such a peak, where demand for energy or more specifically fossil fuel is declining due to major improvements in energy efficiency, continuous growth in renewable energy sources and changing consumer behaviour. While energy demand in the OECD has, indeed, gone down, the UK Industry Taskforce on Peak Oil & Energy Security (2010) has argued that any reductions in wealthy countries are far from outweighed by growth in Asian economies and the Middle East. Different perspectives on the issue of Peak Oil, the use of data, and social representations shaped by lobby groups will be discussed in more detail in Chapter 5.

5 Socio-Political Challenges of Addressing Peak Oil

This chapter explores some of the challenges that obstruct addressing the risk of Peak Oil effectively. First, the lack of robust and freely available data will be discussed as a key barrier to understanding the magnitude and imminence of the risk. Some of the purposeful deception around oil statistics can be explained by geopolitics, whereby countries with higher oil reserves inevitably are perceived as having greater power. Geopolitics are changing, and there will be a range of new security risks – especially for oil importing countries – once global production of oil begins to decline. The public debate and social representation of Peak Oil are discussed in the last section of this chapter. As we will see in this chapter, representations do not reflect widespread concern, but a business-as-usual approach underpinned by neoliberal ideologies and a faith in humanity's ability to invent new technology to overcome possible supply constraints.

5.1 Uncertainty and Lack of Transparency

One of the biggest challenges for addressing short- or long-term oil crises is the limited knowledge of oil resources, and more importantly oil reserves. Partly, this is due to the fact that oil is buried deep in the ground and until it has been brought to the surface it remains anyone's guess how much there is. Geophysical methods of oil exploration are becoming increasingly sophisticated, but estimates of resources remain uncertain. Thus, supposedly simple questions, such as 'when is Peak Oil?', cannot be answered easily.

What is possibly an even greater problem is the lack of transparency of the *communication* of these estimates. The business of oil is dominated by vested interests and politics (see further below on geopolitics), and – different to the related issue of climate change – Peak Oil has not made it into a public arena of rigorous debate, measurement and data verification. Friedrichs (2011) argued that the Intergovernmental Panel on Climate Change (IPCC: 472) has acted as a 'strategic link between the science and the politics of climate change'. Peak Oil scientists have not managed to develop an equally strong global body to pursue regular updates on the state-of-the-art knowledge of oil supplies and demand.

More specifically, there is great uncertainty about three key elements of oil supply, namely: (i) production data and trends; (ii) discovery trends; and (iii) ultimate recoverable reserves (URR, see Chapter 4) (Bridge, 2010). There are many different reasons – both political and financial – why information on any of the above elements could be flawed or misrepresented (Chapman, 2013). In the following, some of the key problems associated with oil data are summarised.

5.1.1 'Creative accounting' by oil companies

> Overinflated industry claims could pull the rug out from optimistic [oil] growth forecasts within just five years. (Dr Nafeez Mosaddeq Ahmed, environment writer for *The Guardian* and bestselling author)

Public reporting of growth in oil reserves helps to spread optimism about the future security of oil supplies. Heinberg (2013) contends, however, that this 'reserve growth' is really often only a result of a reclassification of existing resources (e.g. from P2 to P1, see Chapter 4) or a purposeful inclusion of unconventional resources. For example, the recent accounting inclusion of Canadian tar sands as oil reserves paints an inflated picture, when compared with earlier reporting that was restricted to conventional (and therefore much cheaper to produce) resources. Agencies such as the International Energy Agency (IEA) have begun to talk about 'liquid fuels', which enables them to include alternative fuel sources (e.g. biofuel from sugarcane or corn) in their annual oil production statistics. These changes in reporting are not explicitly laid open and are likely to lead to misinterpretation by less critical or knowledgeable recipients of this information.

The pressure on oil companies to report annual replacement of depleted reserves is considerable. Replacement is normally achieved due to new oil discoveries. The case of Shell illustrates 'creative accounting' and lack of transparency in the oil industry. Back in 2005, Shell accounted for 550 million barrels of oil-equivalent as a proved reserve from a gas field in Australia, even though this would have required the development of a large liquefaction plant in a nature reserve, which had not yet been approved by the relevant authorities (Strahan, 2007). In addition, in 2004 Shell classified numerous reserves as proved, even though they did not meet the criteria of the United States (US) Securities and Exchange Commission. When this over-reporting was uncovered, it became clear that Shell had purposefully deceived the stock market and its shareholders by more than 4 billion barrels of oil (representing over one-fifth of its proven reserves) (Taylor, 2006; Treanor, 2009). Consequently, the share market value collapsed considerably and Shell was required to pay substantial fines.

Similarly, in 2005 Exxon Mobil announced oil discoveries that put them into a favourable position of 'more-than-replacement'. When examining the announcement more closely, however, it became clear that the company accounted for energy in the form of oil-equivalents. This allowed them to translate newly found gas reserves into oil, portraying that they had actually found oil and not gas. The reality was that Exxon had produced 1.6 million barrels of oil-equivalent (boe), and added new reserves of 1.8 billion boe (i.e. more than replacement). Much of the 1.8 billion boe stemmed from one gas field in Qatar, whereas the actual new additions of (pure) crude oil amounted to only 100 million barrels. This represented only 11% of production (Strahan, 2007) – a figure too low to report to shareholders.

The saga of BP's attempt to buy into Siberian oil fields in Russia with partner Sidanco is another example of the lack of credibility of available data sources. Describing the BP case, Strahan (2007: 149) concluded 'like most Russian oil companies at the time Sidanco had three sets of accounts: "one for a handful of insiders, another for its partners and a third even less flattering for the tax inspectors"'. Until recently oil data in Russia were officially treated as a 'state secret' (Chapman, 2013). BP lost several hundred millions of dollars because the resources were smaller than thought. Strahan interpreted BP's business strategies in Russia as a desperate attempt to gain control over new discoveries, because access to oil resources in the Middle East is becoming increasingly impossible for international oil companies (see below).

The examples above highlight the pressure that oil companies are under. At the same time they demonstrate the volatility of the share market, and explain why oil companies have no interest in acknowledging Peak Oil. Michael Rogers from PFC Energy – a major global energy consulting firm and now a subsidiary of IHS – noted that an admission of Peak Oil would send the message to the market that the oil industry is a 'sunset' industry (Strahan, 2007). Given already challenging conditions in terms of global investment in this industry, such a perception could be hugely detrimental to the future of oil production.

The recent growth in unconventional oil and gas production is also characterised by substantial inflation and lack of credible data (Heinberg, 2013). A report on the 'Shale Bubble' by the Energy Policy Forum estimates that shale resources are overestimated by up to 500% (Rogers, 2013). The study's author, Deborah Rogers, is a former Wall Street analyst and now acts as an advisor to the US Department of the Interior's Extractive Industries Transparency Initiative. Her report highlights the important role that Wall Street plays in the US shale business (see also Heinberg's assertions, 2013). Rogers summarises that Wall Street promoted the shale gas drilling fever and then profited from mergers, acquisitions and other transactional fees that occurred when prices plunged under production costs due to overproduction. In the light of this, she advised (Rogers, 2013: 4):

> It is imperative that shale be examined thoroughly and independently to assess the true value of shale assets, particularly since policy on both the state and national level is being implemented based on production projections that are overly optimistic (and thereby unrealistic) and wells that are significantly underperforming original projections.

5.1.2 OPEC production

According to its homepage, the Organisation of the Petroleum Exporting Countries (OPEC, 2013) is a permanent intergovernmental organisation of 12 oil exporting developing nations that coordinates its member countries' petroleum policies. According to OPEC's own statistics, member countries possess over 81% of global proven oil reserves amounting to 1200 billion barrels. Venezuela and Saudi Arabia hold the largest reserves (Figure 5.1).

OPEC oil data are majorly disputed (Owen et al., 2010). The key criticism is related to OPEC's system in which member countries are allocated export quotas depending on their reserves. Thus, each member country has great interest in inflating their reserves to ensure maximum quotas. None of the reserve figures provided by member countries' governments are audited independently. In fact, Strahan (2007) reports that OPEC countries provide their oil data often months after production and only through the great effort of external assessments afterwards can some judgement of accuracy be made. On this, Henry Groppe, an energy consultant in Houston, has stated: 'Everybody lies (...) the production information by the OPEC producers is absolutely unreliable' (Strahan, 2007: 159). Groppe's consulting company tried to reconstruct global exports of oil based on each individual country's import statistics (which is likely to be more accurate than OPEC's export claims). They found that there was up to 2 million barrels per day of exports that had never arrived anywhere. It is likely that they never existed and were invented by exporting countries for political reasons.

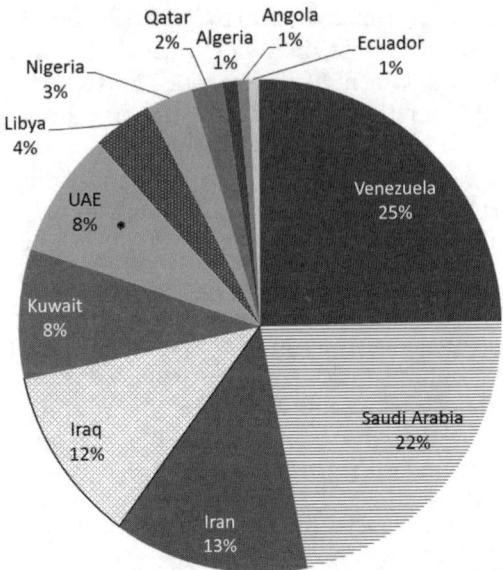

Figure 5.1 OPEC countries' share of OPEC oil reserves in 2012 according to its own statistics from the OPEC Annual Statistical Bulletin
Source: Based on OPEC (2013).

Global oil statistics show that in the 1980s the proved reserves in many OPEC countries suddenly increased dramatically. As an example, from one year to the other, Kuwait's reserves increased from 64 to 90 billion barrels, and three years later to 92 billion barrels. Similarly, Abu Dhabi's reserves tripled to 92 billion barrels; and Iran and Iraq increased their reserves from 49 and 47 to 93 and 100 billion barrels, respectively. Saudi Arabia increased its proved reserves from 170 to 258 billion barrels. No major discoveries had been made in these years, and observers have voiced great suspicion about these new figures, especially since most of the reserves are now almost the same size (between 90 and 100 billion barrels).

The globally very important question of 'how much oil does OPEC really have?' needs to be asked (Strahan, 2007). Table 5.1 provides official OPEC statistics and alternative estimates. It can be seen that OPEC's data are considerably higher than those from other sources. Strahan has reported that in the meantime, Kuwait has publicly admitted that its 1P reserves are not 102 but only 48 billion barrels. Interestingly, official statistics, including those of the BP Statistical Review in 2012 and 2013, are still using the 102 billion barrels figure.

Table 5.1 How much oil does OPEC really have?

	OPEC data (billion barrels)	IHS Energy (billion barrels)	Colin Campbell (key energy analyst) (billion barrels)
Kuwait	102	52	51
Abu Dhabi	98	54	39
Iran	138	135	69
Iraq	115	99	61
Saudi Arabia	264	289	159
Total	717	629	379

Source: Strahan (2007: 162).

As discussed in Chapter 4, Saudi Arabia's reserves are the largest and most important conventional oil fields in the world. For this reason, estimates about their size and depletion rates are critical for understanding global peaking. Several experts have questioned Saudi Arabia's publicly released statistics on their reserves, including former Saudi Aramco staff (e.g. Obaid Nawaf and Sadad Al-Husseini) who stated that Saudi Arabia has been producing at maximum capacity since 2006 and has no spare capacity left (Chapman, 2013). Aramco is Saudi Arabia's largest national oil and natural gas company. In 2008, *The Economist* news magazine wrote: 'Saudi Arabia and the United Arab Emirates are thought to be able to increase their output from today's levels, and even then, there are doubts, since Saudi Arabia, in particular, is secretive about the state of its oil industry.' Some fear that Saudi Arabia's reserves are overestimated by as much as 40%, if not more. If this is true, global reserves could be about 300 billion barrels less than currently believed and reported in key international statistics. There is evidence that the largest field in Saudi Arabia, Ghawar, is using enhanced recovery, in this case injection of water (Chapman, 2013). This is typically a sign of depletion.

5.1.3 Official energy statistics

Official forecasts are simply 'no worry' – business as usual will prevail, Peak Oil is a myth, while technical data shows the contrary. (Laherrère, 2012: 23)

The IEA has become the official global energy policy advisor and is the main provider of energy data through its annual World Energy Outlook (WEO) (Friedrichs, 2011). This was not the original mandate of the IEA when it was founded in response to the energy crisis in 1974. Since then, however, the IEA – and influenced by its mother organisation the Organisation for Economic Co-operation and Development (OECD) – has put considerable resources into monitoring global energy and oil markets. As Friedrichs noted, this has not been undertaken with a critical view of the actual availability of oil resources, but has been rested on a firm belief of (neoliberal) market dynamics.

As a result, the IEA has historically forecast oil data based on estimated demand, rather than physical or economical supply (see also Chapter 4). The 2008 WEO was the first report that indicated a shift from this position. Here, the IEA included a bottom-up analysis of producing oil fields and future discoveries and also reported a decline of 6% of currently producing fields. The report still refrained from explicitly 'decoding' this information into language that would have made it clear that there was a supply challenge (Aleklett, 2012). In their 2010 report, the IEA produced optimistic figures (once again), despite repeated exposure to problems identified in their earlier analyses (for more detail see Jakobsson *et al.*, 2009). Referring to the IEA's assertion by chief economist Fathi Birol that the world will be able to bring on line new production of oil four times the size of Saudi Arabia, Aleklett (2012: 145) responded:

> If the IEA made use of the information that we have published in peer-reviewed scientific articles then they would no longer be able to sweep Peak Oil under the mat.

Problems are not only restrained to the IEA. In a response to the BP Statistical Review 2012, Jean Laherrère (2012), a former petroleum engineer with the TOTAL Group and a key analyst of energy futures, criticised BP's latest increase in world proved oil reserves. BP reported a sudden growth from 1383 billion barrels in 2010 to 1653 billion barrels at the end of 2011. According to Laherrère, this was flawed for a number of reasons. In particular, the addition of non-conventional and conventional sources is inappropriate; they should be reported separately. Adding oil sands to the 'total world' resources is similarly misleading. Laherrère's critique goes into more detail, for example BP's 'ridiculous number of decimals down to the hundredth of a barrel' (2012: 4), which indicates that the original data were not thoroughly checked or cleaned. Finally, inconsistent definitions for oil supply (e.g. including biomass) and consumption (e.g. excluding biomass) decrease transparency and manipulate interpretation.

The BP data are based on the information countries provide in their official statistics. It is BP's policy not to question or change these data (see above on the credibility of 'official' data supplied by OPEC). The BP database, in turn, informs the IEA statistics. Chapman (2013) makes a very important point. He argues that if global reserves are systematically overestimated for reasons discussed above, oil prices are likely to be artificially lower than what they should be, assuming a functioning mechanism of scarce goods in global markets. In other words, if politicians, investors and markets acknowledged the true scarcity of oil, their behaviour and prices would change dramatically. Thus, by not providing vital data, decision-makers are denied important input into their future planning activities.

5.2 The Geopolitics of Oil

The lack of data is a real and pressing challenge, especially considering that data quality is lowest for those countries that possess most of the oil: the Middle Eastern countries. Moreover, many of these oil producing countries are subject to political instability or classified as potentially hostile regimes. Currently, OPEC countries produce about 40% of the world's oil, and their dominant position in terms of proven resources gives them political powers to pursue strategic goals (e.g. who to trade with). At the same time, their human rights record and compliance with international law is poor. In addition, 22% of global oil production is in states that support terrorism and are under US or United Nations sanctions. Countries such as Venezuela, Indonesia and Nigeria are characterised by high rates of corruption. Only a very small proportion (9% of the world's oil) is produced in countries that are considered free by Freedom House (The Institute for the Analysis of Global Security, 2003).

5.2.1 Dependence on rogue states and resource nationalism

Ever since the oil crises in the 1970s, Western countries have tried to reduce their dependence on imports from countries that jeopardise national energy security. The international energy situation in 1973 seemed bleak, and was further exacerbated by a report on the 'Prospects of Soviet Oil Production', which indicated a peak in the Soviet Union's oil production and its need to import oil in the future (Aleklett, 2012). Against the background of the Cold War, the resulting military involvement in oil-rich Afghanistan by the Soviet Union, was monitored with great concern by the newly elected US President, Jimmy Carter (Box 5.1).

It is very clear that there is a close relationship between oil resources, politics and military intervention. Strahan (2007) notes that it is not always

---

Box 5.1 Excerpt of the US President's State of the Union Address on 23 January 1980

Jimmy Carter's State of the Union Address on 23 January 1980:
The region which is now threatened by Soviet troops in Afghanistan is one of great strategic importance: It contains more than two-thirds of the world's exportable oil. The Soviet effort to dominate Afghanistan has brought Soviet military forces within 300 miles of the Indian Ocean and close to the Straits of Hormuz, a waterway through which most of the world's oil must flow. The Soviet Union is now attempting to consolidate a strategic position; therefore, that poses a grave threat to the free movement of Middle East oil.

This situation demands careful thought, steady nerves, and resolute action, not only for this year but for many years to come. It demands collective efforts to meet this new threat to security in the Persian Gulf and in southwest Asia. It demands the participation of all those who rely on oil from the Middle East and who are concerned with global peace and stability. And it demands consultation and close cooperation with countries in the area which might be threatened.

Meeting this challenge will take national will, diplomatic and political wisdom, economic sacrifice, and, of course, military capability. We must call on the best that is in us to preserve the security of this crucial region. Let our position be absolutely clear: An attempt by any outside force to gain control of the Persian Gulf region will be regarded as an assault on the vital interests of the United States of America, and such an assault will be repelled by any means necessary, including military forces.

Source: Aleklett (2012).

---

clear where one starts and the other one finishes. To illustrate this, he uses the case of the American Central Intelligence Agency (CIA) who contracted a former oilman, Louis Christian, to map Iraq's oil resources in the mid-1990s, and again in 2004 for Iran. There is a strong assumption that the existence and location of oil resources are linked to the military action in Iraq by US troops. More recently, events in the Middle East, with tensions in Egypt, Libya and Iran, and Syria, have shown, once again, how volatile oil prices are with respect to political conflicts in oil producing nations.

Concerns over energy security are evident in most countries, even in oil producing nations such as Norway (Kristoffersen & Young, 2010). The military organisations of Western nations are keenly interested in the Peak Oil question (for advances made by the CIA to gather information see Aleklett, 2012). In 2005, the US Army Corps of Engineers put together a report on energy trends, including a 'Conclusions about Petroleum' section, indicating clear concerns about peaking of oil production and impacts on national security (Fournier & Westervelt, 2005). One particular cause of concern is that the US military itself depends greatly on oil – the US military consumes about the same amount as some national economies, for example Greece (Bridge, 2010). An even more detailed report came from the German military, or more specifically a think tank of the Deutsche Bundeswehr (Zentrum für Transformation der Bundeswehr, 2010).

Assuming a peaking of global oil production in 2010, the German report discussed the implications of geopolitical shifts in power and new security risks. The functioning of the global oil markets, as we know them, presumes cooperation, trust, stable operating environments and secured infrastructure. Under scenarios of decreased oil availability and growing pressure on diminishing resources, these can no longer be taken for granted. The report argued that conflicts – military or otherwise – will become more likely and will not be geographically confined. Instead, they will likely have global reaches and involve different types of actors, including states and private corporations.

A scenario of an increasing importance of bilateral arrangements for oil export is conceivable. This would be at the expense of freely tradable oil on the commodity market. It is likely that oil exporting countries will be increasingly in a position to choose *who* they wish to trade with and *what* favours they demand in return for oil. Attractive goods and services may include technology, development assistance, weapons and scarce goods, such as nuclear material for alternative energy generation or potentially the development of weapons. Non-material favours could include political support (e.g. votes on the UN Security Council) or transit rights. This means that to be successful in securing access to oil, countries may have to apply greater pragmatism in their foreign energy policy at the expense of ethical aspects of international relations (e.g. respect of human rights as a condition for trade) (Zentrum für Transformation der Bundeswehr, 2010).

A major risk for the future of global oil exports and trade is resource nationalism. Here, oil producing countries may place national politics ahead of international market economics. Already, in many countries National Oil Companies (NOCs) dominate oil production within their national borders, making it almost impossible for International Oil Companies (IOCs) to gain access (Hirsch, 2008). Strahan (2007) provided a useful illustration of how IOCs (i.e. Exxon Mobil, Chevron, BP, Royal Dutch Shell) increasingly fight for a diminishing pie (see also above on creative accounting). The problem with NOCs is that they have to fulfil both political and business interests, whereby the efficient exploitation of oil often falls victim to political manoeuvres or inefficiencies.

Many countries in the Middle East rely on their NOCs to generate much-needed government revenues and development. In countries such as the United Arab Emirates, where oil income is used to subsidise social benefits for its population – with increasingly excessive lifestyles – limited funds are reinvested into oil field operations and maintenance, or new investments (Hirsch, 2008). If oil producing countries use a growing proportion of their own oil for domestic economic development, less oil is available on the world market. Such an 'oil exporter withholding scenario' is already being observed in Saudi Arabia, instigating the IEA to discuss the problem of 'runaway oil demand in Saudi Arabia' in their 2012 WEO (2012: 86). The resulting export problem, where global exports grow slower than global production, is a real concern (Heinberg, 2013). Resource nationalism of this kind also means that Saudi Arabia will be less likely to function as a so-called 'swing producer' (*The Economist*, 2004), where global shortfalls are quickly compensated for by increasing Arabian production.

5.2.2 The rise of China: New kid on the block

China now accounts for 28% of global industrial energy demand, up from only 16% in 2000 (IEA, 2010). Between 2004 and 2008 oil demand from China increased by 1.2 million barrels per day (mb/d), putting pressure on global oil markets (UK Industry Taskforce on Peak Oil & Energy Security, 2010). China's rapid development has come at a cost. In 1992, China was still a net exporter of oil; however, today its deficit has reached 60% (Figure 5.2). In 2011, China imported 7.2% of global oil production, or 6 mb/d – not at least to fuel its growing domestic tourism industry. In response to its increasing dependency on imports, China's 11th Five-Year Plan has set a target to reduce energy intensity (i.e. energy per unit of gross domestic product) by 20% between 2005 and 2010. As a result, the IEA in its New Policies Scenario assumes a growth rate of only 2% per year for the period 2008–2035, compared with 5–10% growth rates for energy demand in the last 10 years.

It is important to understand the role of domestic oil production in China in its development to a superpower. Facing a severe energy shortage in the 1950s, the news of the discovery of the Daqing oil field (translated: 'Great Celebration') was an important event for the government in Beijing. To develop the field as quickly as possible, a group of 40,000 workers (of which 30,000 were from the Red Army) were sent to the freezing conditions in the eastern province of Heilongjian. The first oil tank left Daqing only one year

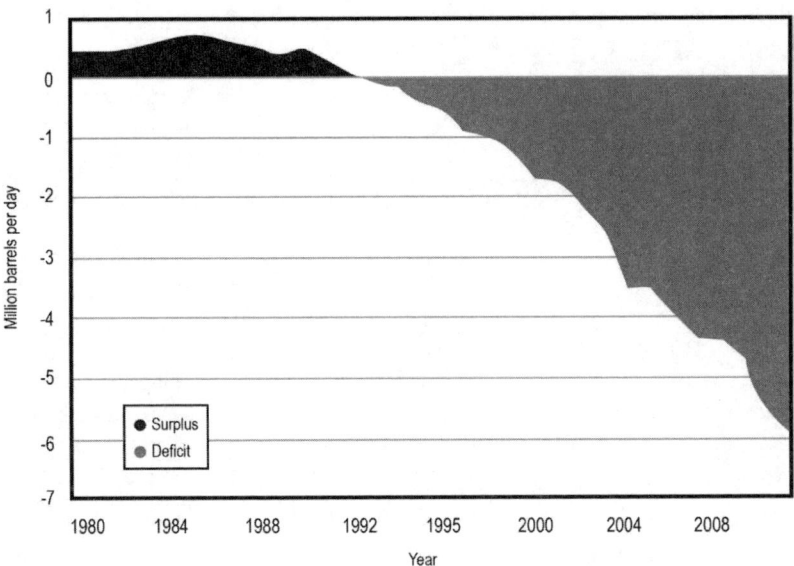

Figure 5.2 Oil production surplus and deficit in China from 1980 to 2011
Source: Hughes (2013).

later and energy self-sufficiency for China was achieved by 1963 (Aleklett, 2012). As is known today, Daqing is one of the top 10 largest oil fields in the world, with a URR of about 24.2 gigabarrels (Aleklett, 2012). Energy independence also meant political independence. Socio-politically, the hardworking women of the Daquing oil field, the so-called 'iron girls', became symbols of success in Mao's China.

Facing the reality of a growing deficit, China has begun to form partnerships with other oil producing nations. Since Western oil companies had already divided up many of the accessible oil fields in the world, China was forced to engage with new providers or those that had been avoided by Western countries on political grounds. Therefore, Chinese oil companies, for example Sinopec, China National Petroleum Corporation (CNPC) and China National Offshore Oil Corporation (CNOOC), have increasingly engaged with countries in Africa. China's foreign policy, based on non-interference with internal affairs (e.g. of troubled countries in Central Africa or Central Asia), was suited to and began to determine new 'rules of the game' (Zentrum für Transformation der Bundeswehr, 2010). For example, China's supply of weapons to some African nations may be seen as an attempt to cement its relationships in exchange for access to resources, rather than a purely economic transaction. China currently has military alliances with six African

Table 5.2 Ten largest recipients of official finance to Africa between 2000 and 2011 in billion US dollars

China	US	Development Assistance Committee of the OECD,
Ghana ($11.4 b)	Egypt ($7.6 b)	Nigeria (28.8 b)
Nigeria ($8.4 b)	Ethiopia ($6.9 b)	Democratic Republic of Congo ($21.9 b)
Sudan ($5.4 b)	Sudan ($6.8 b)	Tanzania (419.6 b)
Ethiopia ($5.4 b)	Democratic Republic of Congo ($5.8 b)	Mozambique ($17.9 b)
Mauritania ($4.6 b)	Kenya ($5.5 b)	Egypt ($16.5 b)
Angola ($4.2 b)	Nigeria ($4.2 b)	Ethiopia ($16.1 b)
Zimbabwe ($3.8 b)	South Africa ($3.6 b)	Kenya ($14.6 b)
Equatorial Guinea ($3.8 b)	Uganda ($ 3.5 b)	Sudan ($14.0 b)
Cameroon ($3.0 b)	Tanzania ($3.4 b)	Morocco ($12.6 b)
South Africa ($2.3 b)	Mozambique ($3.0 b)	Uganda ($12.0 b)

Source: Strange *et al.* (2013).

states, including the four oil producing nations of Sudan, Algeria, Nigeria and Egypt.

Many claims and much controversy surround Chinese investment in Africa, but the challenge is that there is very little publicly released information on where and how much China invests. To gain some appreciation of Chinese activities in Africa, Strange *et al.* (2014) compiled a database of thousands of media reports on Chinese-supported projects from 2000 to 2011. The database reveals a total investment of $75 billion across 50 African countries spread evenly across the continent, with the exception of those countries that are recognising Taiwan. Importantly, the report found that Chinese investment in development activities is quite comparable in size to that of the US, but differences exist in the top 10 receiving countries (Table 5.2).

5.2.3 Far-reaching changes in the security landscape

The peaking of conventional oil production has very broad and pervasive consequences beyond the most obvious shifts discussed above. These can be summarised as follows:

- 'run' on thus-far unexploited areas such as the Arctic;
- land use changes at the detriment of indigenous populations (e.g. in the Amazon);

- increased interest in the exploitation of gas resources as a substitute, involving new states and shifting power relationships, and creating numerous regional markets of gas supply (gas cannot be shipped as easily as oil);
- greater demand for nuclear material with a mounting risk of criminal intent and development of nuclear weapons;
- conflict over land resources due to increased production of biofuels, with likely increases in food prices, and potential hunger crises; and
- greater importance of private sector actors to help secure critical infrastructure, transport passages and land areas (e.g. for pipelines).

The pressure on natural resources, and specifically oil, is evident all around the globe with severe environmental and social implications in areas that have to date been spared of economic development and exploitation (Table 5.3). The Arctic, in particular, has been of growing interest to its bordering countries, despite great uncertainty over the actual size of oil resources and insufficiently defined territorial rights. Already, Russia and Canada have begun to invest in military infrastructure and 'flex' their muscles in relation to resource exploration in the Arctic. The reshaping of 'state space' and social negotiations over the conflicting goals of energy security and environmental protection, as well as the role of corporate versus public sector stakeholders, has also been illustrated for the case of Norway (Kristoffersen & Young, 2010).

The inevitable and lasting increase in food prices is a major security risk identified by the German military (Zentrum für Transformation der Bundeswehr, 2010). The German report reminds us of the so-called Tortilla crisis in 2006 in Mexico that resulted from the rapid increase in biofuel production from corn. It also warns that in addition to well-known regions of humanitarian crises (e.g. sub-Saharan Africa), nuclear powers, such as India and Pakistan, could be severely affected by food shortages or prohibitively high prices. The cascading price effects of global supply chains will also affect personal mobility. Tourism in particular could be impacted as transport costs rise, and people are faced with worsening economic conditions in their home countries (see Chapter 6). The German military suggested that a 'mobility crisis' could be symptomatic of an economic crisis resulting from Peak Oil.

5.3 Social Representation of Peak Oil

The public debate on Peak Oil is not well developed and restrained to a few 'whistleblowers and dissidents [who] fill a parallel world in the

Table 5.3 Examples of energy-conservation conflicts

Country	Issue	Source
Costa Rica	In 2008 Costa Rica's Congress rejected a proposed law intended to allow geothermal exploitation in national parks. The electricity industry is now working with environmental organisations to carry out experimental projects in low-level protected areas.	Guido-Sequeira (2010)
Ecuador	Yasuní National Park, in the core of the Ecuadorian Amazon, is one of the most biodiverse places on the planet. Proposed oil development projects represent a significant threat to the area's biodiversity.	Bass et al. (2010)
New Zealand	After massive protests from the population, the government abandoned controversial plans to mine sections of New Zealand's most pristine conservation land, and ruled out mining in the 7068 ha of conservation land it considered opening to mining interests.	Bennett (2010)
Peru	Oil exploration and extraction threaten both biodiversity and indigenous people and communities in isolated Amazon forests.	Finer and Orta-Martinez (2010)
South Africa	A new open-cast and underground coalmine is threatening Mapungubwe National Park near South Africa's border with Zimbabwe and Botswana. Having already obtained a mining and water-use licence, the company started infrastructure construction in 2010, and plans to use a coal-fired power plant.	Peace Parks Foundation (2010)
Tanzania	Sections of the Selous Game Reserve are threatened by the Mkuju River project, under which more than 22 million tons of uranium is expected to be mined over a period of 12 years. UNESCO's World Heritage Committee has asked the government of Tanzania to stop the intended mining activities immediately.	UNESCO (2011)
United States of America	Uranium and coal mining as well as gold exploration threaten the borders of wilderness areas, particularly in Glacier and Grand Canyon National Parks. In the latter, uranium claims have increased 2000% since 2004.	Carus (2011)

Source: Extending on Becken and Job (2014).

"blogosphere" where polemics and eschatological thinking loom large' (Friedrichs, 2011: 472). Bridge (2010) proposed that Peak Oil fits into a broader discourse of crisis relating to resource security, limits to growth and environmental carrying capacities. However, only a few studies have examined people's concern about different energy futures and relatively little is known about social representations of Peak Oil (Becken, 2014; Fischer *et al.*, 2012).

Heinberg, in his book *Snake Oil*, even questioned whether the general public can understand the complex messages around oil reserves, energy return on investment (EROI) and Peak Oil. He therefore suggests that a 'PR consultant might advise organisations discussing energy issues to stick with an easy message: "We are running out of oil", or "We are not running out of oil". Take your pick and make your case' (Heinberg, 2013: 124). This section explores how different public audiences perceive Peak Oil, and how alternative discourses shape social representations of energy security and oil depletion.

5.3.1 Peak Oil: A new idea?

While the theory of Peak Oil dates back to the 1950s, more popular discussions about oil depletion are relatively new. The current debate differs in nature from the oil discourse associated with the 1970s oil crises, which was mainly informed by discussions about political conflict, rather than geological constraints. Bardi (2009: 323) suggested that public perceptions of Peak Oil, just like other new ideas, follow a sequence of four phases:

(1) First phase: Never heard of it.
(2) Second phase: It is wrong.
(3) Third phase: It is right, but irrelevant.
(4) Fourth phase: It is what I had been saying all along.

The majority of views at present are probably between phases (2) and (3). One of the key arguments for rejecting the hypothesis of Peak Oil is that people believe in other factors that are perceived as responsible for the increase in the price of oil and temporary scarcities. Commonly cited reasons are the growing demand for oil from China and India, political unrest in the Middle East, a weakening US dollar, speculation on financial markets, and the lack of investment in much-needed oil infrastructure and refinery capacity. The latter point is avidly supported by agencies such as the IEA. Large oil companies also see the lack of reserve ownership, politics of access and the changing nature of the global oil industry as their key concerns, rather than physical limits (Bridge & Wood, 2010).

Some argue that it is simply false that a peak is being reached, as there are still plenty of discoveries and increases in production (Bardi, 2009). This apparent contradiction has been recognised by researchers who have pointed out that a peak in oil production is difficult to comprehend. Peaking will occur despite ongoing production or even discoveries of oil. There are just not enough discoveries to replace already consumed oil. Bridge (2010), as well as Bentley and Zittel (2013) therefore argued that the idea of Peak Oil is not intuitive.

There is a common misunderstanding that *peaking* implies that the world is 'running out of oil'. Instead, what it means is that the economically viable exploitation of known oil reserves is reaching its limits (Sorrell *et al.*, 2010). At the same time, some researchers have criticised that the problem is not so much about physical constraints, but the socio-economic systems of production and consumption (Bridge, 2010). Thus, the 'politics of Peak Oil' can not be understood by simply studying geological limits, but broader questions need to be conceptualised – the geological aspects are not even necessarily so relevant.

Those in the third phase believe that a peaking of conventional oil resources is not problematic as there are plenty of alternatives, for example unconventional oil resources or alternative energy sources. Such a view is often underpinned by belief in humanity's technological ability and the market forces that drive innovation and investment into new energy sources. Often, the problem of a very low EROI, as discussed in Chapter 4, is not considered in these arguments.

5.3.2 Business perceptions

As we have seen in Chapter 2, tourism is clearly dependent on oil. For some sectors, fuel is a core input factor and increases in price are of great business concern. A survey of chief executive officers (CEOs) in the aviation industry, for example, highlighted fuel prices as the dominant – and at the same time most probable – risk (Figure 5.3). Underlying questions of supply constraints, or even more explicitly Peak Oil, however, are rarely addressed.

Recent research on publicly traded oil companies has revealed that there is no consensus on Peak Oil (Bridge & Wood, 2010). While oil prices are an important aspect of the performance of both oil companies and other types of businesses, most companies are firmly anchored in a neoliberal growth paradigm that makes it imperative to believe in ongoing opportunities for growth and, almost by principle, deny ideas of finiteness. Such ideologies are fuelled by narratives by oil companies that legitimise the requirement for further production (e.g. of Canadian tar sands) and diminish the need to reduce consumption and adapt to a low-carbon future. Shell's scenarios are

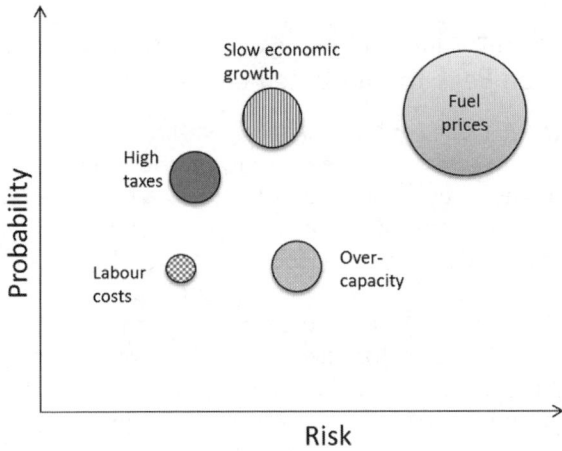

Figure 5.3 Threats to airline viability according to aviation-industry CEOs in 2012
Source: World Aviation Yearbook (2013).

an example of a strongly neoliberal discourse that 'serve as a tool for projecting a discursive future that through its very expression intervenes in the social perceptions that condition speculative markets' (Zalik, 2010: 552).

Ambiguous perceptions of the oil situation were observed at the 2004 'Oil and Money' conference, where the main discussions of the conference focused on how production was struggling, but key players appeared to be 'relentlessly optimistic' (Strahan, 2007: 59). When the IEA launched its 2006 WEO at this conference, stating that oil production would grow to 120 million barrels per day in 2030, Lord Browne of Madingley (CEO of BP at that time), UK stated that 'we have to demonstrate that there has been no shortage of oil, and there is no shortage age of oil, and that there never need be a shortage ... there is no reason why there should be any shortfall in the foreseeable future' (Strahan, 2007: 60). The IEA's persistent denial of Peak Oil has continued until today (Box 5.2). This is not surprising given the IEA's strong affiliation with the neoliberal agendas of its member states. The statement in Box 5.2 highlights that the IEA presents arguments typical of Bardi's (2009) phases (2) or (3) introduced above.

5.3.3 Future markets

To better understand how the future of oil supply is perceived amongst stakeholders, some have turned to examining future markets of oil. Labban (2010) notes that much greater quantities of oil are exchanged on a daily basis on future markets than those actually produced or consumed – a

---

Box 5.2 The International Energy Agency's declared stance on Peak Oil presented on its website

Where does the IEA stand in the Peak Oil argument?
Our analysis suggests there are ample physical oil and liquid fuel resources for the foreseeable future. However, the rate at which new supplies can be developed and the break-even prices for those new supplies are changing. Global oil production levels are also dependent on the production policy of OPEC, which holds between one and six million barrels per day of spare capacity in reserve. Declining oil production in any given year can occur for one of several reasons unrelated to peak production, including OPEC production decisions, unplanned field stoppages and the impact of earlier investment decisions by the oil industry. A combination of sustained high prices and energy policies aimed at greater end-use efficiency and diversification in energy supplies might actually mean that Peak Oil demand occurs in the future before the resource base is anything like exhausted.

Source: IEA (2013a).

---

disconnect that is rarely appreciated by those involved in the Peak Oil debate. Future pricing is an important component of oil trading and price shaping, and it is by nature speculative (Zalik, 2010). In the domain of tourism, airlines routinely engage in a strategy called hedging to protect them from future increases in the price of kerosene fuel. Some contend that oil futures are not an adequate indicator of real price development, especially considering that price is shaped my multiple and intertwined causes. On the other hand, de Almeida and Silva (2009) argue that the future price of oil is based on an informed decision by a large number of players and expert analysts. Indeed, Zalik (2010) confirms that future pricing is shaped by an elite group of traders whose daily business it is to assess supply and demand of oil.

The future price can therefore be used as a predictor of what people think the oil price will be. De Almeida and Silva (2009) revealed that future prices in 2005 did not show any recognition of a tightening oil market, but this changed in 2008. An analysis of the 2008 future price curve reveals very clear expectations of increasing oil prices, in the order of about $88 per barrel in 2009 to about $95 in 2016. The authors conclude that the observed change in price curves indicates that traders have become aware of a near-term peak in oil production. So, while oil market participants might publicly deny a nearing peak, their behaviour and market expectations show otherwise – a finding that was echoed by Matutinović (2009) in his analysis of the political economy of energy.

5.3.4 Media representation

Media reporting heavily influences public debate. Media inform societal discussions by facilitating people's familiarity with unknown issues, and their coverage of particular issues helps develop a shared meaning of particular phenomena (Gangl et al., 2012). The way media present a particular issue is called 'framing'. Media suggest 'what matters' and by defining salient issues and portraying them in a certain way they contribute to the development of social constructs. These are more than just descriptions of phenomena – they often become reality (Zamith et al., 2012). In other words, the physical phenomenon of resource depletion that exists in the material world only gains real meaning through the discourse surrounding it. The analysis of this discourse is therefore critical.

The cultural circuit has been discussed as a phenomenon where particular issues are received and re-communicated in a continuous flow between journalists, media outlets and information consumers (Carvalho & Burgess, 2005). Thus, an emerging discourse is negotiated between the media and the general public. Magazines have been relatively less researched in communication studies, but Becken (2014) undertook a framing analysis of Peak Oil in *The Economist* news magazine. *The Economist* is an elite newspaper that is popular with opinion leaders around the world, and its coverage is likely to influence elites in the policy and business domain. *The Economist* focuses on economic issues and current affairs, including those relevant to oil or more broadly energy.

Becken's research found that oil was an issue that received considerable attention in *The Economist*; however the particular risk of oil depletion was not prevalent. Instead, frames of oil dependence, investment, market dynamics and energy transformation were used to present news stories on oil. Researching representation of an issue in the media involves studying absences just as much as presences (Entman, 2001), and the particular phenomenon of Peak Oil was clearly not a dominant frame. Instead it emerged as a storyline within a broader frame of oil supply challenges. More intense – and more pessimistic – reporting was observed during periods of record-high oil prices in June, July and August 2008, and also in March to May of 2012 when prices surged once again.

In contrast, *The Economist*'s coverage from mid-2012 to the first quarter of 2013 was extremely optimistic and focused almost exclusively on the American 'energy transformation' and a resulting shift in global geopolitics in favour of the US. The discourse analysis also showed that *The Economist*'s language and coverage is very close to that of the IEA and its neoliberal ideology. The dominant discourse has prompted Aleklett (2012: 111) to comment 'There is nothing to indicate that the United States will become self-sufficient in oil production ... There is a real need for more critical analysis by the media in future when they report the exaggerated dreams of some members of the oil industry'. Overall, the analysis indicated denial of the Peak Oil challenge in *The Economist* and a tendency towards status quo framing (i.e. reinforcing existing knowledge and structures) (Becken, 2014).

5.3.5 The Peak Oil movement

Some have argued that a lack of concern about Peak Oil is reflective of a much broader denial of ecological crises, particularly evident in the US. Peak Oil could be conceptualised as an economic problem, but it is also discussed as an environmental risk because it is the depletion of a natural resource (e.g. like water) that is causing concern. With increasing exploration in ecologically sensitive areas, this constraint has truly become an environmental challenge. Denial of such crises is partly due to the prevailing neoliberal and capitalist ideology, the widespread scepticism of science, and the well-established psychology of denial (Schneider-Mayerson, 2013) (see also theoretical literature on climate change denial in particular). Nordhaus and Schellenberg (2004) even proposed 'The Death of Environmentalism', with climate change fatigue having been observed in risk perception surveys around the world (e.g. Leiserowitz *et al.*, 2010).

At the same time, there are a considerable number of individuals or groupings around the world that are concerned about Peak Oil. These include scientists, but also people of the general public that are sometimes labelled 'peakists' or, more derogatory, 'alarmists'. So, who are these people and what do they do? Dave Cohen (2007: 3) in his response to Cambridge Energy Research Associates (CERA) wrote:

> A final word about what Peak Oil is not: the hypothesis set forth here is not a catastrophist prophecy that the world is running out of oil. Once the world production does peak, views vary as to how severe the decline rate will be thereafter. Many reputable people from the oil and natural gas industry and elsewhere are concerned about Peak Oil. We are not a doomsday cult.

It is very important to study the people who believe in Peak Oil and are concerned about its impacts. Howitt (2001) emphasised that research on the political ecology of Peak Oil needs to go beyond the obsession of compiling inventories of oil resources and estimating supply gaps, but should provide a greater focus on people and the sociological systems they are part of (Schneider-Mayerson, 2013).

Aleklett (2012) refers to a 'Peak Oil moment', when people suddenly grasp the severity of the potential changes ahead. Schneider-Mayerson (2013) undertook some research to better understand the 'sub-culture' of the so-called Peak Oil movement. Peak 'Oilists' have made their belief in Peak Oil an integral part of their identity and lifestyle. For them, Peak Oil is more than a description of the geophysics of oil resources – it has become an ideology. The majority of peakists are very pessimistic about the impacts of Peak Oil, sometimes considering the future in an apocalyptic way. Transitions to alternative energy systems are deemed too little, too late. They envisage resource wars, social unrest and economic collapse, and in their views 'sustainable growth' is an oxymoron (Lloyd, 2007). In Schneider-Mayerson's research, negative views were more prevalent in America than in Canada or Europe. People who are concerned about Peak Oil were also found to be concerned about other environmental crises, including for example climate change, but also depletion of other resources, over-population and landscape degradation.

Peakists act at an individual scale; mainly to protect themselves and their immediate families. Despite recognising that collective action is essential to address the fundamental problem, they are not typically involved in collective networks. This is problematic and reflects a form of resignation and lack of belief in their ability to change the existing economic and political system. The distrust of government manifests in a lack of political involvement. According to Schneider-Mayerson, Peak Oil advocates in the US are even less likely to vote than other people (2013). This distinguishes the Peak Oil movement from earlier movements, such as the anti-nuclear one or the anti-Vietnam war factions. One respondent in Schneider-Mayerson (2013: 871) summarised this attitude by stating that 'all you can do is slow down [the] collapse to try and give all of us enough time to figure out how to best release ourselves from the age of oil to a simpler, more intimate way of life'. Transition towns are an exception (Chapter 7), as they are built on collective action and networks (Bailey et al., 2010). Lloyd (2007) questions whether such 'downshifting' will be effective, considering rapid economic development in parts of the world that far outweigh peakists in terms of population size.

5.4 Conclusion

In a nutshell, the diagnosis of the ultimate problem is simple; cheap oil and personal greed has enabled corporations to afflict people with affluenza,

> and affluenza together with population growth is causing resource deple-
> tion and anthropogenic warming. (Lloyd, 2007: 5812)

Not all people would agree with the above statement, and this chapter has provided some important background information on the socio-political challenges of addressing the Peak Oil problem. A problem that some would argue does not exist. One major challenge is the lack of reliable data and the basically non-existent international verification of the state-of-the-art knowledge in relation to oil resources and production. Too many vested interests and political power games dominate the global oil markets, and independent assessments are derived based on second- or third-hand information that is likely to be inaccurate and/or incomplete.

Due to the strategically critical role that oil is playing in nations' economic systems (and as a result, their social stability), the stakes are high and governments enage in difficult balances of national self-interest, foreign diplomacy and other political goals. Shifts in the geopolitical relationships between superpowers, oil exporting countries and other intersted parties (e.g. private corporations) are likely and carefully monitored. The role of China is particularly important in this context. Apart from a few exceptions it is not publicly known how governments really assess and address the security risks associated with global oil supplies.

Clearly there are different perspectives on Peak Oil, and they are quite polarised. On the one hand, there are those that believe that a peaking of global oil production is imminent (if not passed). These are often referred to as alarmists. On the other hand there are so-called 'cornucopians', namely those who believe in eternal (or long-lasting) economic growth. Cornucopians are often economists or business people – although Lloyd (2007) observes that most governments have subscribed to the axiom of economic growth. Cornucopians do not consider energy a critical input factor in production, and according to their neo-classical paradigm, energy is substitutable. Peak Oil believers criticise this growth paradigm and assert that it is in conflict with the physical finiteness of resources and the laws of thermodyanmics. Instead, they emphasise the unique role that oil as a concentrated form of energy has played in economic development.

Differences often reflect underlying beliefs and values rather than actual knowledge. While both groups claim they have a more accurate understanding of the future, none of them has exact knowledge about it. Balaban and Tsatskin (2010) provide an argument that the main reason for people or institutions to predict the future is to increase their own influence. Rather than what these people know *will* happen in the future (they cannot know), they portray what they *believe* it should be. Thus, future predictions reveal more about the predictor's beliefs, values and norms, than the actual future.

This chapter has shown that the common discourse is one of economic growth and scepticism towards Peak Oil. The social representations of oil are likely to relate to energy transformations (e.g. towards shale oil), technological advances and new discoveries of oil. They do not include the need for social change, reduction in wealth, 'downsizing' and a less globalised world.

Public discourse is often based on simple representations, for example catchy one-liners or iconic images. For the case of climate change, such a representation might be the polar bear floating on an iceshelf. To achieve a commonly accepted and recognised image or idea, it is necessary to reduce scientific complexity into something very simple and of general appeal. Scrase and Ockwell (2014) note that the outcome of such a simplification is a denominator that allows different groups to join in a common movement, even if these groups hold different interpretations and world views. This phenomenon is called a discourse coalition. The idea of sustainable development is a good example of such a discourse coalition.

Often the public debate is already occupied by dominating images or storylines (e.g. the economic growth paradigm) and it is difficult to promote new ideas. Such a shift is even more difficult when the new idea radically conflicts with existing and heavily institutionalised paradigms, as is the case for Peak Oil. Existing representations are often 'sponsored' by powerful groupings who have an interest in maintaining the status quo. Currently, the risk of Peak Oil is mainly advanced by scientists without major support by any particular government, industry corporation or other lobby groups. If the Peak Oil movement continues to be largely insular and individualist, it is unlikely to form a discourse coalition with these scientists or other interested or concerned groups.

To make progress on enhancing the discourse on global oil challenges, it is important to broaden the debate beyond geophysical assessments, and put greater emphasis on exploring political and societal choices (Bridge, 2010). This would also generate a better understanding of the validty of claims that a peak in demand is preceding a supply peak. A broader research agenda would also examine in more detail potentially hidden agendas of widely accepted and reiterated scenarios of future oil supply (Balaban & Tsatskin, 2010), which could ultimately lead to greater data transparency.

6 The Economic Impact of Oil Prices on Tourism

6.1 Introduction

As we have seen in earlier chapters of this book, the availability of cheap oil has been critical to the development of tourism. Cheap transportation has been at the core of the boom for many tourist destinations (see Figure 6.1) (Dobruszkes, 2006; Francis *et al.*, 2006). Affordable energy has also enabled economic growth around the world, leading to increasing incomes for many people. Accordingly, travel and tourism have grown rapidly. But what will happen if oil prices continue to rise? This chapter discusses the effects this will have on tourism, both at a macro level and for individual businesses. The content of this chapter presents insights into possible developments in principle, based on economic theory. However, a detailed destination-based or segment-based analysis goes beyond the scope of this chapter. Such analysis is encouraged for future studies.

6.2 Macroeconomic Effects

6.2.1 Oil vulnerability

Not surprisingly, the effects of changes in oil price on global economies are pervasive and multi-layered. There are two key effects: direct and indirect (Figure 6.2). Directly, consumers are affected by higher energy prices, for example when paying for their fuel at the petrol station. Indirectly, oil is a central input into the production of most goods and services, including those related to tourism. Higher oil prices will lead to higher production costs and changes of relative prices throughout the economy. The degree to which

Figure 6.1 Air Asia advertisement for flights from Singapore to Krabi, Thailand
Source: *Today Magazine*, 13 October 2013.

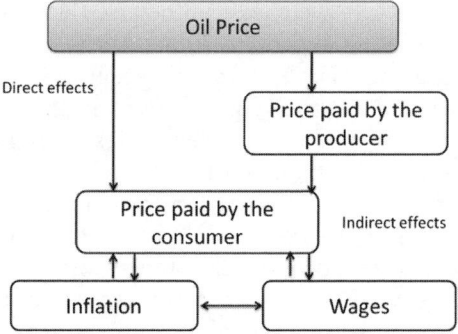

Figure 6.2 Direct and indirect effects of oil prices: Transmission mechanisms in the economy
Source: After Bijsterbosch (2008).

prices change, of course, will depend on the oil intensity of each of these goods and services. For example, for the case of food, the Organisation for Economic Co-operation and Development (OECD, 2011) estimated that energy accounts for more than one-third of the costs in the specific case of grain production. As a result, oil price increases of the last few years have contributed to major increases in food prices, resulting in a major food crisis following the 2008 oil spike.

As a result of changing production costs and changing purchase behaviour, an oil price increase will literally affect all key macroeconomic variables: real gross domestic product (GDP), employment, balance of trade and exchange rates, and inflation. The extent of inflation – as shown in Figure 6.2 – also depends on the ability of a country's monetary authorities to address inflation (OECD, 2011), highlighting the close link between oil prices and financial systems. A recent study from Spain has shown that about 50% of Spanish inflation in recent years has been driven by fluctuating oil prices (Álvarez et al., 2011). Further, a slowing economy due to higher oil prices will result in a decrease in tax revenue, which reduces government budgets and increases interest rates. Immediate price effects are more substantial than long-term ones, as both producers and consumers have time to adapt.

Not all countries will be affected equally, and it is useful to distinguish different types of oil risks. Gupta (2008) summarises three major risks: market or economic risk, supply risk, and environmental risk. Based on a number of indicators for the first two of these types of risk, Gupta developed an oil vulnerability index for 26 net-importing countries, with a higher index indicating higher vulnerability. Developing countries such as the Philippines, Korea and India emerged as most vulnerable in Gupta's analysis. Countries with a high ratio of domestic oil production to oil imports, such as Australia and the United States (US), were least vulnerable (Figure 6.3). Europe, as a major tourism region shows a medium vulnerability.

Most of European tourism is internal (i.e. intra-European), reducing dependency on long-haul tourism. This is shown in Figure 6.3 by a relatively short bar measuring outbound tourism departures leaving Europe (i.e. intercontinental). In contrast, outbound tourism from the US or China is substantial, meaning that tourism from these countries is likely to be more exposed to oil prices. It is useful to focus vulnerability analyses on international tourism as it typically involves longer travel distances and, as a result, oil inputs.

Net oil importers will experience negative economic effects from higher oil prices, depending on the share of oil costs in national income, the availability of alternative energy sources, oil efficiency of production and flexibility of the labour market to respond to changes in real wages (Gupta, 2008). Vulnerabilities are also closely tied to bilateral relationships and the

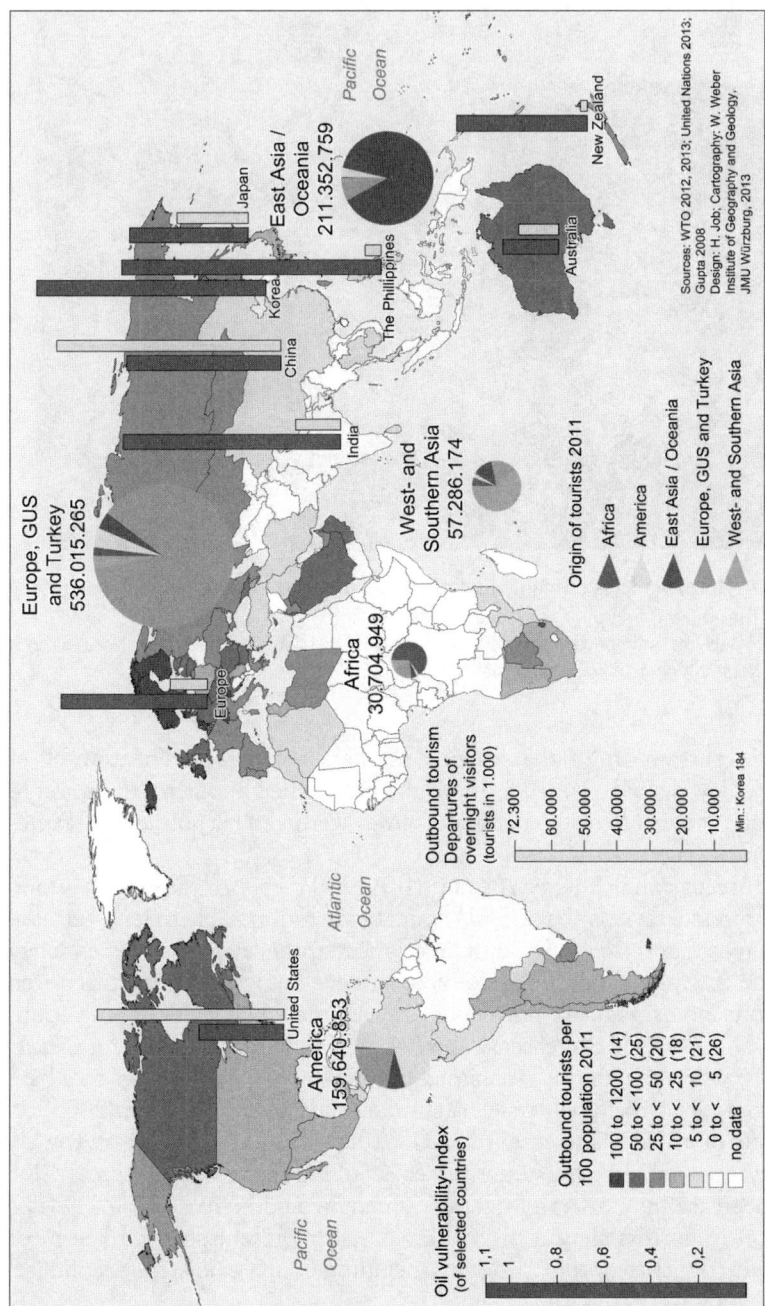

Figure 6.3 International outbound tourism and oil vulnerability index (higher index implies higher vulnerability)
Source: Based on Gupta (2008).

Figure 6.4 Motor vehicles lining up in Kathmandu, Nepal, to obtain limited amounts of rationed fuel during a supply shortage
Note: Nepal depends on imports from India, which may be restricted at times for various reasons, including Nepal's high debt for unpaid fuel imports.

geopolitics surrounding global resource markets (Chapter 5). The example of Nepal, which depends on fuel imports from its neighbouring India, highlights critical dependencies that are often exacerbated by political measures or sanctions (Figure 6.4).

An International Energy Agency (IEA, 2004) report based on a world economy model reveals that OECD countries are vulnerable to long-term oil price increases despite a substantial reduction in the level of oil dependency over time. The same report also found that developing countries suffer even more from increases in oil price. The IEA estimated that developing countries' real GDP would decrease by about 1.6% (compared with 1% for OECD countries) when the oil price increased by US$10 per barrel relative to a base case scenario of US$25 per barrel. A similar study by Huntington (2005) on the effects of a US$10 increase (from US$30 to US$40 per barrel) on the US economy showed that consumer prices would increase by 0.4%, real GDP would decrease by 0.5%, and unemployment would increase by 0.2%. The top 15 oil importers shown in Figure 6.5 also represent some of the most important countries of tourist origin, including China – now the second largest global oil importer.

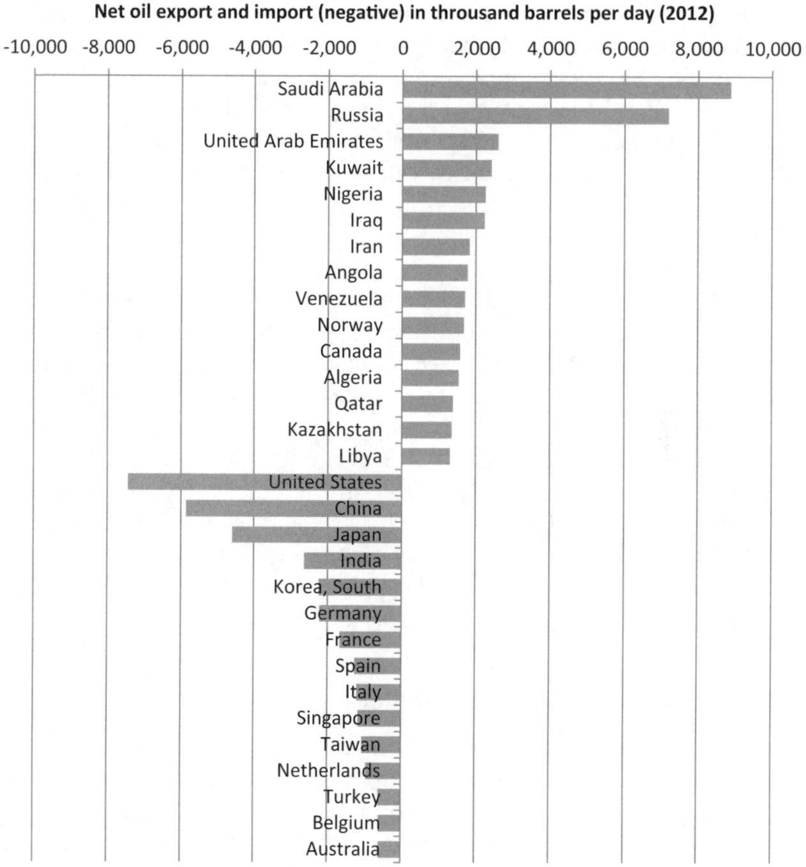

Net oil export and import (negative) in throusand barrels per day (2012)

Figure 6.5 showing a horizontal bar chart with x-axis ranging from -10,000 to 10,000 in increments of 2,000.

Countries (top to bottom): Saudi Arabia, Russia, United Arab Emirates, Kuwait, Nigeria, Iraq, Iran, Angola, Venezuela, Norway, Canada, Algeria, Qatar, Kazakhstan, Libya, United States, China, Japan, India, Korea, South, Germany, France, Spain, Italy, Singapore, Taiwan, Netherlands, Turkey, Belgium, Australia

Figure 6.5 Top 15 net oil exporters and importers in 2012
Source: US Energy Information Administration (EIA) (2013).

Oil exporting countries are generally less vulnerable than oil importing countries (see Figure 6.5). The reason for this is that, in the first instance, higher oil prices lead to greater income for all those countries that are able to export oil. However, the above IEA (2004) report showed that the positive effects on GDP in oil exporting countries are only observed in the short term. This is followed by a reduction in GDP growth after several years, because of decreasing exports of non-oil goods and services to the weakened oil importing countries. At the same time, countries that are likely to export goods and services to oil exporting countries are likely to benefit from higher global oil prices, at least in the short term. Lutz and Meyer (2009), for example, provide evidence that Germany would be less affected by high oil prices than other countries, because of its high share of exports to countries in the Middle East, for example automobiles and electronic equipment.

Several studies have examined the effects of oil price shocks on the economies of industrialised countries, rather than a sustained increase in the oil price over time. Such studies are only of limited value for understanding the impacts of Peak Oil. The main reason is that behaviours are likely to differ if people believe a shock is only short-term and does not require major adjustments. This will not be the case for a permanent decline in oil availability. Nevertheless, the findings of oil shock studies are of some interest. For example, Peersman and Robays (2009) investigated the economic effects of oil price shocks for a set of industrialised countries: the US, Euro Area, Japan, the United Kingdom (UK), Canada, Switzerland, Norway and Australia. The study found that the net oil and energy importing countries all face a permanent reduction in economic activity and a significant rise in costs of living, whereas the long-term output response in the energy exporting countries (Australia, Canada, the UK and Norway) is insignificant or even positive. As argued by Chatziantoniou *et al.* (2013), the nature of an oil shock, for example short-term versus long-term and supply versus demand driven, is highly relevant when assessing potential impacts.

6.2.2 Changes in tourism economies

As discussed above, some of the economic effects of higher oil prices are obvious and generally agreed upon, based on both economic theory and empirical evidence. However, assessing the overall impacts on tourism, as one sector in the wider economy, is more challenging, and has not been done systematically for the whole tourism system. Long-term changes in global oil price rises will be associated with changes in other commodity prices globally, as well as changes in exchange rates, and incomes. It is therefore useful to analyse the impacts of high oil prices on tourism from a general equilibrium perspective.

Computable general equilibrium (CGE) models are commonly used to study long-term economy-wide impacts of economic shocks. They have been applied widely in tourism to understand a broad range of changes (e.g. Dwyer *et al.*, 2010, 2013). A New Zealand tourism CGE model specifically focused on the impact of increasing oil prices (Becken & Lennox, 2012; Lennox, 2012). In this model, a global trade analysis project (GTAP) model was used to simulate a global negative productivity shock in the oil sector. The assumption was a 100% increase in world oil prices, which was imposed on the GTAP model and then a New Zealand tourism general equilibrium model

Table 6.1 Macroeconomic changes in New Zealand under the assumption of a 100% increase in oil price

	% change in volume	% change in real value
Real GDP	−0.9	n.a.
Imports	−3.8	−1.0
Exports	−2.6	−2.4
Tourism exports	−11.0	−9.0
Accommodation gross output	−4.6	−5.8

Source: Becken and Lennox (2012).

(NZTGEM) to simulate the detailed impacts on the New Zealand economy, including the tourism sector.

The New Zealand study showed that a doubling of oil prices (from a base of about US$60 per barrel) would lead to a 0.9% decrease in GDP and a reduction in the volume of imports of 3.8%, although the real value of imports decreases only 1.0%, due to the higher world prices of petroleum. Tourism would be affected much more severely than the economy on average, especially the transport components compared with, for example, accommodation (Table 6.1). The analysis also revealed that different markets would be affected differently. A price increase of the aggregated tourism 'basket' (in which oil prices are reflected) of 3.1% for South Korea, for example, would result in a quantity decrease of 17.2%. For the UK, a 7.9% price increase for holiday tourists is accompanied by an 18.6% decrease in quantity. Those visiting for other purposes, such as visiting friends and relatives, are less sensitive.

The New Zealand case provides an interesting perspective and might be useful for other countries that try to understand the possible impacts of Peak Oil. It is possible that New Zealand, due to its geographic remoteness, presents a worst-case scenario in terms of transport costs. However, further research needs to validate such assumptions, especially when the consumer behaviour of source countries is accounted for, which in the case of New Zealand may well reflect more affluent and less price sensitive customers.

Related research, using CGE models, focused on the impacts of a carbon tax on tourism. A carbon tax increases the price of fuel and is therefore broadly similar to oil price increases (Figure 6.6). Dwyer *et al.* (2013) analysed the potential economic effects of the Australian carbon tax introduced on 1 July 2012, but frozen in late 2013 by the new federal government. The

Figure 6.6 Last minute travel deals offered at Munich airport

tax was modelled to reduce growth in real GDP between 2012 and 2020. It showed a small contraction in output by the tourism industry and a slightly larger fall in employment in tourism relative to other sectors. The largest decrease in employment was observed in the accommodation sub-sector, followed by air and water transport, cafes, restaurants and food outlets. Note that Dwyer *et al.* (2013) only accounted for effects within Australia and not externally, as captured through the global trade model in the New Zealand study (Becken & Lennox, 2012).

6.2.3 Household income and travel propensity

The pivotal role of income and price in explaining the demand for international tourism has been thoroughly demonstrated empirically by the large number of studies that have been carried out over the past three decades. (Crouch, 1992: 660)

As we have seen above, increases in the price of oil will weaken economies all around the world. One consequence of this is that consumers' incomes will be reduced (Figure 6.7). In countries with relatively rigid wages, this can

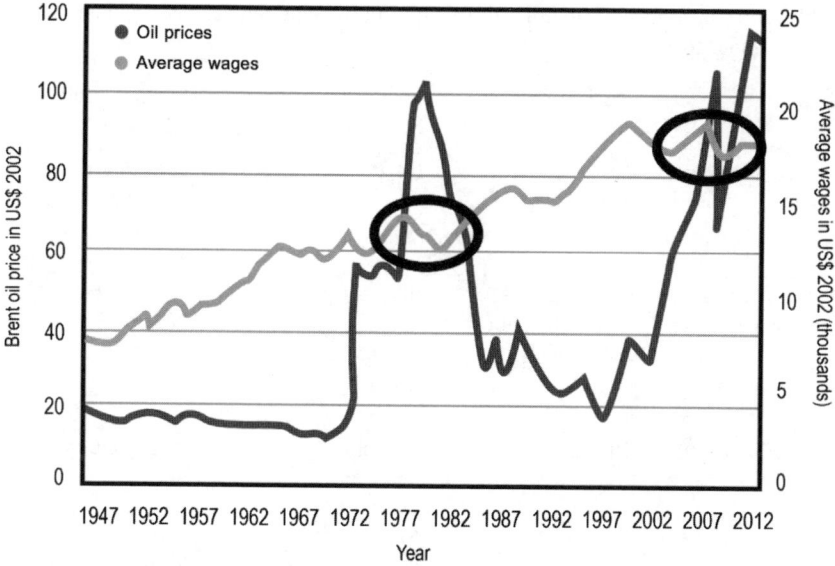

Figure 6.7 High oil prices are associated with depressed wages in the US
Source: Our Finite World (2013).

domino into high rates of unemployment. Such effects are highly relevant for global tourism, when less available income leads to reduced travel activity.

Income is a key variable in relation to travel demand. It is often argued that tourism is a luxury good and a discretionary spending activity, and as such it is relatively income-elastic (Davis & Mangan, 1992; Mervar & Payne, 2007). A large number of studies have investigated income elasticity of tourism. The income elasticity of demand is a measure of the responsiveness of the demand for a particular product or service relative to a change in the income of the people demanding this product, all else being equal. Income elasticity is calculated as the ratio of the percentage change in demand to the percentage change in income. An income elasticity of +2, for example, means that if incomes increase by 10%, the demand for a particular product increases by 20%.

Crouch (1995) reminds us that estimates of international tourism demand elasticities vary considerably, mainly due to different assumptions and methodological approaches. Thus, great care is required in the interpretation of reported elasticities. The examples shown in Table 6.2 generally show elasticities greater than one for a range of origin-destination pairs, which means that income increases have a positive effect on the demand for

Table 6.2 Examples of empirical results on income elasticity of demand for international tourism

Study	Destination	Origin(s)	Estimated income elasticity
Davis and Mangan (1992)	All	UK	2.10 (4.0 for low income households and 1.5 for wealthy ones)
Kulendran and Witt (2001)	Germany, Greece, Portugal, Spain, Netherlands	UK	Between 0.541 and 1.821
Munoz and Amaral (2000)	Spain	World	2.07
Song et al. (2003)	Thailand	Australia, Japan, South Korea, Singapore, Malaysia, UK, US	Between 2.046 and 4.922
Dritsakis (2004)	Greece	Germany, Great Britain	2.16 (Germany) and 6.02 (Great Britain)
Munoz (2007)	Spain	Germany	5.40
Bonham et al. (2009)	Hawaii	US, Japan	3.50 (US) and 2.23 (Japan)

international tourism. Crouch (1995) reported that about 70% of the income elasticity estimates in previous studies indicated income elasticity, typically between one and two. This finding was confirmed in more recent analysis by Song et al. (2009). It is important to note that research on price elasticities has mainly focused on international tourism, and there is a gap in understanding better the price sensitivities associated with domestic travel. For large countries, like the US or China, where domestic tourism is substantially larger than international tourism, and where travel distances are large, this is an important area for research.

In a recent study on understanding demand for tourism to Hong Kong, Song et al. (2009) employed a more sophisticated method to estimate income and price elasticities. Applying the bias-corrected bootstrap method, and generating confidence intervals rather than point estimates, they present strong evidence of a long-term relationship among demand, income and prices for all nine of the key markets investigated. Income levels were the key factor in driving tourism demand for Hong Kong, in particular for the long-haul markets from Australia, the UK and the US, and for the emerging economies of China and Korea.

Income not only influences travel propensity, but also the type of holiday tourists choose. A study by Fleischer and Rivlin (2008), for example, reported that higher incomes amongst Israeli households lead to increased demand for tourism, which is evenly split between more holidays and higher quality holidays. Travel distance between home and destination also seems to be influenced by income. Wealthy tourists with discretionary income are more likely to travel long-haul than tourists with lower incomes (Nicolau, 2008). In their case study of international travel to New Zealand, Lim *et al.* (2008) observe that as incomes increase in Japan, outbound tourism shifts from short-haul (e.g. into other Asian countries) to longer-haul travel.

The importance of available discretionary income for tourism consumption is obvious. However, very little research has been undertaken on the relative importance of tourism expenditure and possible substitution between tourism consumption and other discretionary consumption. A recent study by Crouch *et al.* (2007) reported that tourism in Australia attracts about 21% of discretionary income. Further, an increase in income results in a proportional increase of expenditure on tourism, with no evidence of significant cross-substitutions between tourism and other consumption categories. This study only looked at a one-off increase in available income. A longer-term decrease in income, as one might expect in the case of globally rising oil prices, was not examined in this study. Thus, further research on changing patterns in discretionary consumption in response to dropping incomes would be very useful.

6.3 Oil Prices and the Cost of Tourism

Higher oil prices will generally make tourism products and services more expensive. The extent of the price increase, and reduction of profitability, depends on several factors, for example whether oil can be substituted for other inputs in the production of the tourism service or product (Figure 6.8). Another factor is the potential for increasing energy efficiency of production. In addition to production costs, the impact on a business will also depend on changes in tourist behaviour. Different types of tourists will respond differently to increases in the prices for tourism products and services. Price elasticity of demand – as shown in Figure 6.8 – is an important factor when analysing the effects of higher prices of tourism products. As will be discussed below, other non-monetary factors also influence tourist decision-making.

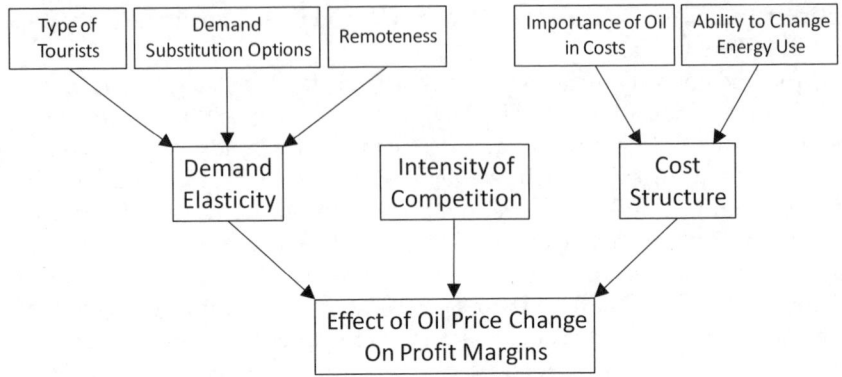

Figure 6.8 Overview of factors influencing the effect of a change in oil prices on profits for tourism businesses
Source: Becken *et al.* (2010).

6.3.1 Price and tourist decision-making

This chapter has provided evidence that higher oil prices tend to lead to lower incomes, especially for oil importing countries that are also often the major source countries of international tourism. In addition, higher oil prices are likely to increase the price of tourism, especially the transport component. Tourists' responses to lower incomes and higher prices can to some extent be explained with economic theories and measures such as elasticities (see earlier on income elasticity). There is a comprehensive body of literature on tourism demand, both in relation to explanatory modelling and forecasting (e.g. Crouch, 1992, 1995; Witt & Witt, 1995; Lim, 1997). Price elasticities of demand vary, but are typically negative in the order of −0.5 to −1.5. For the example of Spain, one of the most popular tourist destinations in the world, an average price elasticity of demand across markets has been estimated to be about −0.64 (Logar & van den Bergh, 2013). This means that a 10% increase in prices will reduce demand by 6.4%.

In summary, most empirical models assume that tourist arrivals and expenditure depend on the tourist's income, the price of the service, the prices of related goods (substitutes and complements), and other demand shapers (Mervar & Payne, 2007). The assumption that tourists respond to cheaper prices is somewhat verified in the fact that product discounts, last minute deals and other price-based campaigns are successful in engaging potential visitors to make travel-related purchase decisions (Figure 6.6).

The most direct effect on tourists from increased global oil prices is rising fuel prices. Figure 6.9 shows the increase in fuel prices for the UK (note that

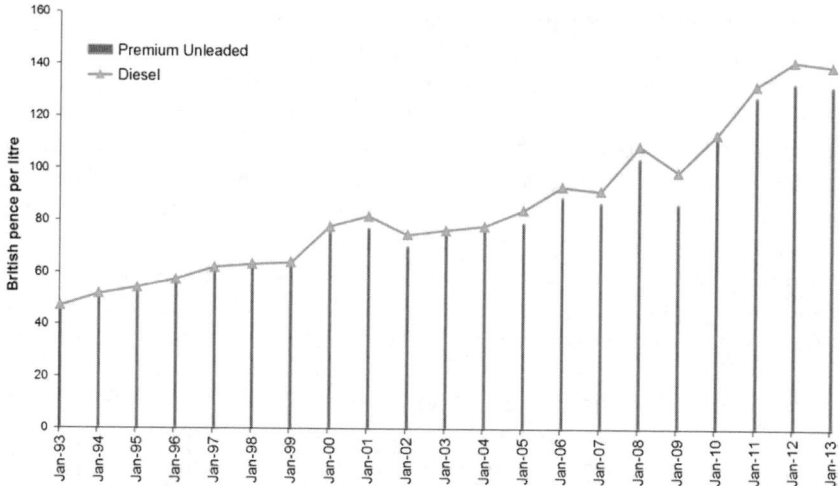

Figure 6.9 Petrol and diesel prices in the UK (1993–2013, not deflated)
Source: UK Department of Energy & Climate Change (2013).

end-user fuel prices also contain taxes, levies, etc.). Fuel prices for transport users almost tripled between 1993 and 2013; although based on general inflation rates of about 2% fuel prices should have only increased by 50%. While not the key driver of transport behaviour, Becken and Schiff (2011) provide evidence that transport costs have influenced local tourist travel in New Zealand for some segments. Using an input-output model for Spain, Logar and van den Bergh (2013) found that, under the assumption of an oil price of US$200 per barrel and an average price elasticity of −0.5, the demand for tourism-related air transport would reduce by 20.8%. Water transport would decrease by 13.2% and land transport would reduce by 5.3%.

Higher prices for transport influence travel behaviour, but there are also other possible behavioural adjustments and substitutions. Research on campervan tourists in New Zealand, for example, showed that tourists would be much more likely to change their recreational pursuits (e.g. participating in fewer activities or spending less at restaurants) than downgrading their campervan or reducing travel distance (Becken & Wilson, 2008). Similarly, Basham (2010) showed that spending on restaurants decreased markedly in 2009. Mainly this was explained by a general reduction in travel, with travellers making up between 15% and 40% of restaurant patronage. Research on the demand for different types of restaurants in the US following the recession highlighted no significant differences in people's choice of restaurants.

However, the research highlighted that, overall, fast food outlets were better able to cope with reduced demand (Koh *et al.*, 2013).

Different market segments display different sensitivities to price, as has been shown extensively for air travel. Typically, it is reported that business travellers are less price-sensitive than leisure travellers and short-haul travel is more elastic than long-haul travel (Gillen, 2004; Brons *et al.*, 2002). In terms of destination prices, both the differential relative to the tourists' origin as well as exchange rate effects are relevant (Dwyer *et al.*, 2001; Njegovan, 2005). To better capture tourism-specific changes in price that result from higher oil prices, some studies use tourism price indices that reflect typical tourist consumption bundles at the destination (e.g. Becken *et al.*, 2008).

In a detailed tourism consumption study of New Zealand, Schiff and Becken (2011) estimated demand price elasticities for 16 market segments. The price index and expenditure measures for each segment were expressed in foreign currency terms. The findings showed that New Zealand's traditional markets from the UK, the US and Australia are less price sensitive; however new markets from Asia appear relatively price sensitive. The research also indicated that effects of exchange rate fluctuations have been more substantial than changes in actual prices of tourism-related goods and services in New Zealand. It is important to note that exchange rates are strongly influenced by global oil prices.

Prices are important factors in tourist decision-making, but not the only ones (McKercher *et al.*, 2008). It is now widely acknowledged that earlier consumption models (Gross, 1987), including tourist destination choice models, were largely built on a positivist paradigm where the consumer would make their decision in such a way to maximise utility. This process involved rational consideration of the tourists' monetary resources, benefit derived from the consumption of goods and services, and available time.

The classic tourist destination choice models of the 'homo economicus' assume that the tourist maintains an 'evoked set' of potential destinations that he or she would like to travel to (Um & Crompton, 1990; Woodside & Lysonski, 1989). From these a final destination is selected, depending on a range of factors. Later models (e.g. Woodside & King, 2001) added details such as the influence of situational or psychographic variables, but decision-making was still essentially a rational process. Travel costs enter this process as the tourist learns more about the product and develops an attitude towards a specific destination (Decrop, 1999). Costs can then act as an inhibitor (e.g. 'too expensive') or be offset by other important destination attributes such as a positive image (e.g. 'worthwhile') or emotional attachment.

These models have been criticised as a simplification of what is rather emotional, opportunistic and hedonic behaviour (Hyde, 1999). It is now believed that tourists do not always have the cognitive competence to fully evaluate all possible tourist destinations in a cost–benefit sense (or an interest in doing so). They are also faced by 'bounded rationality' (Decrop, 1999), and are limited in their information search. Some tourists even enjoy a certain level of risk as they purposely delay decision-making and a hedonistic – sometimes serendipitous – unfolding of holiday decision-making (Hyde, 1999). The decision-making of independent travellers, for example, has been analysed in detail by Hyde (2008), who also proposed a model that includes both active and purposeful elements (e.g. information search) and more opportunistic or coincidental elements that affect trip decisions at the local level.

The above discussion indicates that economic variables such as tourists' income and the price of tourism are important but their manifestation is far from deterministic. Thus, while international tourist flows generally follow the theory of distance decay (i.e. further travel is more costly, and therefore less frequent; McKercher et al., 2008), this decay does not apply to all countries of origin and it may also take different shapes. Nicolau (2008) proposed the existence of a so-called Ulysses factor, where certain types of tourists feel a need to explore the unknown and purposefully travel larger distances than other tourists; thereby defying the 'tyranny of distance'. Similarly, emotional motives, such as visiting friends and relatives, result in longer distances travelled compared with other travel purposes.

6.3.2 Oil price and tourism businesses

In relation to airlines, the Centre for Aviation (2013) stated:

Frustratingly, the proportion of costs now dedicated to fuel barely makes 'non-fuel' cost reduction worth the effort. If so much pain is expended on reducing the residue of costs by 3% or 4% (which translates to perhaps 2% of total), the fact that a short burst in fuel prices of US$5 a barrel can neutralise that improvement is disheartening to management and staff alike.

Not all businesses are equally vulnerable to increased oil prices. In general, oil prices influence the variable costs of tourism businesses, that is, the costs that vary with the volume of output produced, such as the number of tourists served. Higher variable costs result in lower profitability. The question is whether the effect on profitability constitutes a significant business risk, in the sense that the tourism company can no longer generate an adequate return on the capital invested in it. It is possible that there will be potential winners that achieve an increase in their profitability despite higher oil prices, as these might be offset by reduced costs for other inputs such as labour. A business that is not overly energy-intensive, not located in a remote destination and is strongly focused on domestic tourism could possibly be such a relative winner.

Aviation is highly exposed to oil prices, despite substantial improvements in technological and operational procedures that have increased fuel efficiency (see also Chapter 2 and Box 6.1). Oil prices are likely to influence airfares for the foreseeable future. Fuel costs as a percentage of commercial airlines' operating costs and crude oil prices have increased substantially over time. Only 10 years ago, fuel costs made up 14% of operating costs, whereas now they constitute about 30%. The breakeven point for aviation fuel prices has risen from US$23.4 in 2003 to a substantial $116 in 2012. In a press release from March 2012, the International Air Transport Association (IATA) downgraded their profit forecast by US$500 million for the year 2012 because fuel prices were now estimated to average US$115 per barrel, instead of US$99 as previously forecast (IATA, 2012). The average price per barrel of crude oil in 2012 was US$111.2.

Since oil prices are so close to breakeven point, airline profit is very small and profitability is largely driven by oil prices. Brian Pearce, IATA's Chief Economist, points out that the average cost of transporting an air passenger globally is US$212.04. The average fare paid by a passenger, however, is only US$171.20. The shortfall is made up by additional revenue from cargo (US$31.30) and ancillary services (US$12.14), resulting in a net profit of US$2.56 (Pearce, 2013). The margin is therefore extremely tight. Reportedly, some airlines, for example in the US, have implemented strategies that only seats that cover the fuel cost will be sold. As a result, low fares of traditional low-cost carriers, such as Southwest Airlines, have risen by about 25% during recent years (Centre for Aviation, 2013).

Airlines have typically responded with fuel surcharges. However, the Centre for Aviation (2013) noted that fuel surcharges provide only temporary relief, especially since they are often charged on top of discounted tickets to remain competitive. Back in 2011, the Australian carrier Qantas, for example, increased fuel surcharges by about 40% across both international and domestic airfares. At the same time Qantas introduced fuel surcharges on frequent flyer award tickets. Flights between Australia and the UK, for example, were charged an additional US$290 for fuel costs. This was an increase of US$100 from US$190 of fuel surcharges on this route (Flynn, 2011).

Obviously, the greater the importance of oil in the costs of a tourism business (as we have seen for airlines), the more exposed it is to higher oil prices, everything else being equal. Chapter 2 provided some insight into the

Box 6.1 The impact of higher prices on the aviation sector: Example, Virgin Blue Australia

"In response to the escalating cost of fuel, over the past five years Virgin Blue has rigorously implemented measures throughout its business to reduce and minimise our fuel usage. Such measures include:

- investment in the latest and most technologically advanced passenger aircraft;
- the retro-fitting of winglets on aircraft to reduce fuel burn;
- the application of a polymer coating on our aircraft to further reduce drag;
- the use of the most up-to-date meteorological data in live flight planning resulting in a more efficient flight missions;
- an initiative, called *Weight Watcher*, which is minimising aircraft weight by reducing potable water loads, removal of ovens and utilising light-weight catering packaging to further reduce fuel burn; and
- more efficient design of flight plans and profiles, such as flex-tracks, which allow aircraft to take advantage of optimal winds.

Despite these ongoing initiatives, when fuel prices hit record levels earlier this year a programme of strategies to mitigate the impact on the business was required:

- an increase in ticket prices by an average of $5 across approximately 55% of Australian domestic routes;
- a 12% reduction in planned 2008/09 capacity growth via deferral of five committed aircraft deliveries into 2010/11;
- the redeployment of aircraft to trans-Tasman and Pacific routes, increasing frequencies and also launching new services on uncontested routes;
- an internal cost saving programme of an initial $50 million in 2008/09;
- ceasing to operate direct services on some under-performing routes (but not totally withdrawing from any markets);
- implementing a salary freeze for all management positions for the 2008/09 fiscal year;
- the introduction of new baggage fees; and
- an increase in the airline's flexible fares."

Source: Virgin Blue (2008: 1–2).

oil intensity of different types of tourism businesses. Broadly speaking, all profit-maximising firms will respond to an increase in marginal costs by raising their prices to some extent. The degree to which the cost increase is passed through to prices depends partly on the intensity of competition that a firm faces from its rivals. If competition is intense, pass-through will be higher. Firms that face intense competition will have relatively low profit margins already, and will find it difficult to absorb cost increases. For example, in the extreme of perfect competition, price equals marginal cost, so a cost increase will be fully passed through. In contrast, a monopoly firm will typically choose to pass through less than the full cost increase, and will accept lower profits.

In the long term, the impact of higher oil prices on the profits of tourism businesses depends on their ability to absorb the cost increase by passing higher fuel costs on to consumers, modifying their cost structure and accepting lower margins. The ability of a business to reduce vulnerability to high oil prices is influenced by:

- *The type of tourists served*: Budget-conscious tourists and/or those with lower incomes will likely be more sensitive to price increases. Thus, as a rule of thumb, businesses whose customers are young budget travellers with lower incomes are likely to face more elastic demand. Cultural aspects may play a role as well.
- *Cost structure*: Higher oil prices may be offset by modifying the businesses' cost structures. In the short-term such opportunities may be limited; however, over longer time periods, businesses can look to alternative sources of energy and new transport systems that are less dependent on fossil energy. Substitution potentials will differ greatly across different types of businesses. Airlines and other transport operators will have relatively limited immediate substitution possibilities, and will depend on efficiency gains due to technological improvements over time.
- *Substitution options available to tourists*: If tourists can identify adequate substitutes for the products or services provided by a business then they will be able to alter their choices relatively easily in response to a price change. This means that their demand will be more elastic compared to those businesses that have a unique product and service that is not substitutable.
- *Remoteness*: A business that is located in a remote destination will involve more time and expense for visitors to reach. Higher oil prices will increase the costs of travel to these places. Relatively remote businesses will therefore face relatively elastic demand, compared with those in more central tourist locations. The definition of remoteness

depends on the type of tourist destination, typical itineraries and tourist types travelling.

6.4 Conclusion

Oil prices have been characterised by extreme volatility with a general underlying trend of increasing prices. Given expected growth in demand for tourism – and consequently energy – and constraints in increasing supply, global oil prices are expected to continue to rise in the medium to long term. The recent global recession resulted in a temporary reduction of demand, resulting in a sharp fall in oil prices in 2009, but prices have continued to rise since then. This highlights the volatility of oil prices as they react quite dramatically to changes in market conditions.

Analysis of historic oil crises and increases in prices shows that negative economic impacts on oil importing countries are evident, at least in the short term but in some cases permanently. Several studies have demonstrated that the effects of oil price changes are reduced GDP, inflation and loss of employment. Effects are more severe in countries with high production oil intensities (e.g. China), high dependency on oil imports, and less flexible labour markets. Oil exporting countries, such as Canada and Norway, are likely winners from increased oil prices, although in the long term this also depends on how the economies of their trading partners fare. Many tourist generating countries (e.g. China, Germany, Japan) are net oil importers and therefore vulnerable to global oil price increases.

Reductions in GDP generally result in lower incomes and less discretionary income available for consumption, including tourism. The tourism literature clearly demonstrates that income is a key, if not the most important, variable in determining tourist travel. This is not only true in terms of trip generation, but also with respect to level of expenditure, length of stay and type of trip. Long-distance destinations are more dependent on high-income tourists than short-haul destinations. Factors such as tourists' specific desire to see distant and exotic destinations as well as emotional travel reasons (e.g. visiting friends and relatives) are positive factors that overcome financial inhibitors, at least for certain types of tourist. Relatively little is known about the price sensitivity and other relevant decision-making factors for domestic tourism.

Higher oil prices will also drive up transport costs, in particular for aviation where fuel constitutes a substantial proportion of operating costs, and where substitution options are very limited, particularly in the short term. Studies of price elasticity provide information about the extent to which tourist demand for travel will change given specific price changes. Again, it is important to distinguish between different market segments and types of tourists. For example, business travel has been found to be less price-sensitive to transportation costs than leisure travel. Similarly, long-distance travel is less price elastic than short-haul travel. While this is relatively positive for a long-distance destination, it does not negate the fact that there will be some price effect which will manifest in reduced tourist arrival numbers.

Just as tourists respond to higher transport prices to get to their destination, they are also likely to adjust travel behaviour and consumption at their destination if prices for tourism products and services increase. Energy, and in particular oil, is an important input into tourism production and increases in global oil prices will be reflected in higher in-country prices for tourism. Oil-intensive products (e.g. helicopter flights) will likely be more affected than those that rely only to a small extent on oil-related inputs. The accommodation sector, for example, is largely a user of electricity and as such not directly affected by oil price changes; however, it is important to note that increased global oil prices will also affect gas prices and as a result electricity prices.

The greater ability a business has to reduce its consumption of energy (and specifically oil) and improve its fuel efficiency (i.e. economic output per unit of energy input), the lower its vulnerability to increasing oil prices. The degree to which costs can then be passed on to customers depends on the level of competition, the type of tourists demanding a service and the characteristics of the service (e.g. remoteness). As indicated above, tourist decision-making is complex and price is only one factor among other determinants.

Hence, for a tourism business (or destination) the impacts of higher oil prices can be separated into those that affect the country as a whole (i.e. as a result of reduced consumption) or the business specifically. The latter impact depends on the specific business situation, its geographic location, customer base, production structure and ability to adjust. As such, there is some level of control on the part of the business to reduce its vulnerability to higher oil prices. In general, businesses, tourism products or local destinations within a country will be better placed to adjust to higher oil prices if the demand they face is less elastic, if there is less intense competition with other operators or substitute products or destinations, and if oil is less important in the cost structure or there are more opportunities to adjust the production technology to make more use of alternative energy sources or reduce energy use. Understanding the macroeconomic effects that might occur globally is an important piece of information that needs to be included in a business' decision-making and strategic planning.

7 Pathways to Post-Peak Tourism

Let's not let an oil crunch take us by surprise.
Sir Richard Branson at the launch of the 2010 report by the UK
Industry Taskforce on Peak Oil & Energy Security

The previous chapters have shown that tourism depends utterly on oil. Considering the growth that is expected from this sector, and in the absence of any major systemic changes to how tourism is conducted – this dependency is unlikely to change in the near future. Declining resources of conventional oil – cheap oil – and likely rises in the price of oil have the potential to throw a substantial obstacle in the way of not only tourism growth, but all the socio-economic development that surrounds it. So, it is not so much a question of the exact physical limits to oil production, but the socioeconomic and political implications of declining resources, and more specifically declining energy returns on energy invested (EROI) (Huber, 2008). No doubt, demand for tourism will continue to exist; but tourism systems and products are likely to change in a 'post-peak' (i.e. beyond the peak of oil production) world. This chapter explores some of these changes as well as opportunities to prepare for in a changing tourism world.

It has been recognised for about a decade that mitigation of or adaptation to a peak in oil production will require huge efforts, investment and change. Such a transformation will necessarily have to take place over several decades. Robert Hirsch (2008), co-author of the well-known 2005 Hirsch Report (one of the first explicit and authoritative reports on mitigating Peak Oil to avoid catastrophe, Hirsch et al., 2005) reminds us, once again, of the enormity of the task. Hirsch reasserts the undeniable fact that it is not possible to fully replace the current fuel-based vehicles and equipment with alternative forms of energy – let alone to do so quickly enough. Thus, transportation and food systems are at great risk. Because of the high stakes,

Hirsch stresses the need to begin mitigation early; well before the impacts of declining oil production are actually felt. Early action would most likely reduce long-term economic impacts and downturns, and also cushion social impacts. Thus, as argued for the case of climate change by Stern in 2006, early change will be less costly than reactive measures.

This chapter does not attempt to provide an analysis of different possible futures for tourism. As already discussed in Chapter 3, there is limited tourism-related information on future scenarios, let alone those relating to Peak Oil. The reason for this is that the tourism literature, with some exceptions (Dwyer *et al.*, 2008; Leigh, 2011; Peeters & Dubois, 2010; Yeoman, 2012) (Box 7.1), has not embarked on scenario exercises that consider major deviations from the status quo. In addition, it is not within the scope of this chapter to provide a complete systemic analysis of what might happen in the case of substantial increases in oil prices, for example by modelling behaviours (and geographic tourist flows) by segments and distance classes (for a similar approach, see for example Peeters & Eijgelaar, 2014). Instead, a qualitative discussion of potential dimensions of change is provided to deliver a platform for understanding future shifts in tourism geography, innovation, meaning, policy and management.

The broader literature provides some indication of where the world might be heading post-Peak Oil (and the interested reader is encouraged to consult further relevant literature on the theory of scenario development and applications relevant to the topic of this book). These scenarios are equally useful for the context of tourism. The City of Portland Peak Oil Task Force (2007), for example, identified three possible scenarios:

Scenario 1 – Long-term transition: Assuming a decline in oil supplies and increase in price at slow and incremental rates, this scenario assumes a longer-term and planned adaptation to reductions of fuel use in the order of 50% over the next 20 years.

Scenario 2 – Oil shocks: This scenario is similar to the first one, but characterised by additional periodic shocks where oil prices rise dramatically for short periods of time. Acute supply emergencies are also a real possibility. Additional preparations are required to cope with these sudden shocks.

Scenario 3 – Disintegration: This worst-case scenario sees the potential for severe social unrest, unemployment, hunger, crime and violence. Competition over resources (including food) will intensify. Failure of several global systems, including the financial one, is possible.

An interesting method for understanding post-Peak Oil trajectories has been presented by Friedrichs (2010). Friedrichs explored how different parts

---

Box 7.1 Tourism trends in an oil-constrained world proposed by Leigh (2011)

1. Any tourism types with large energy doses will be very expensive and scarce. While there may be esoteric luxurious facilities for the super-rich who will be able to afford air travel, for most people air travel and sumptuous holiday facilities will be out of reach.
2. Energy guzzling air travel will be greatly curtailed due to its high cost, and so only available for those with big budgets.
3. Most people will use efficient popular transport modes of train and bus, and ships for inter-continental travel, although sea travel may be quite expensive too.
4. There will be a high demand for local tourism. For the majority a holiday, for example, at a local beach or mountain resort (including forest or seaside camping) could be in reach.
5. Popular tourism will have to be simpler, less luxurious and more local-ised, to cut down on the total price and expensive consumption.
6. This means generally that there could be a great opportunity for sustainable tourism to become more serious and real, beyond lip service and window dressing.
7. Mass highly commercialised tourism will decline – smaller localised industry will (re)appear.
8. Generally people will travel less, and enjoy tourism with simpler cheaper requirements.

---

of the world might respond to oil shocks by taking an analogue approach based on three historic cases. The first case focuses on Japanese 'predatory militarism', which was evident during the Pacific War (1941–1945) at the end of World War II, when America imposed an oil embargo on Japan. Amongst others, Japan attacked the United States (US) Naval Base in Hawaii (Pearl Harbour) to gain access to the oil-rich East Indies. Friedrichs argues that some countries might follow this military-based model, especially countries that maintain considerable military power that could be imposed on resource-rich nations.

The second case, labelled 'totalitarian retrenchment', relates to North Korea's reaction to the end of subsidised oil deliveries from the Soviet Union at the end of the Cold War. The leadership elite in North Korea ensured a preservation of privileges, whilst the population experienced one of its worst famines in history. The third analogue was one of socio-economic adapta-tion in Cuba, following supply disruptions from the Soviet Union in the early 1990s. Different to the North Korean case, social networks in Cuban society held strong and communities displayed high adaptability by transforming urban spaces into agriculturally productive areas. Despite the economy as a whole having come to a stand-still, a widespread famine was not observed. The insights gained from Cuba's 'Special Period' have inspired a number of community groups to develop transition plans for a post-carbon society (e.g. Groundswell Group, 2007). Friedrichs suggests that, possibly, Western European countries might fall into this group – given their historically based dread of conflict since World War II.

Tourism developments in a post-peak world are also likely to be differentiated by region and destination. A number of aspects seem essential in determining vulnerability and change potential. Figure 7.1 highlights that post-peak tourism will most certainly have to tap into a much wider range of energy sources than just fossil fuels. Energy substitutes, energy conservation and energy efficiency will become more and more important. Similarly and intricately related to energy systems, transport systems will change. Broadly, transport will need to become more electrified (that is decarbonised) and integrated. These energy and transport supply-side measures may not be sufficient however, to make up for the declining availability of cheap oil. Changes to transport systems will result in a transition towards 'less expensive' and lower-carbon forms of tourist consumption – possibly

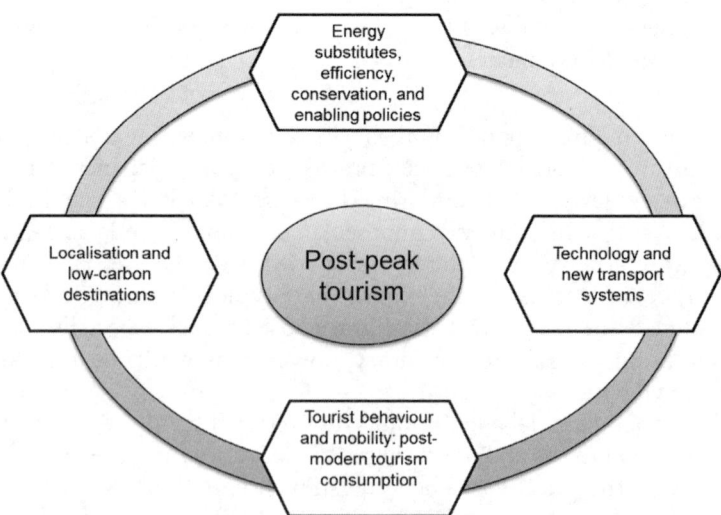

Figure 7.1 Achieving sustainable post-peak tourism: Key elements that will play a role in developing new tourism systems

reconceptualising tourism consumption more broadly. As a result, and also in direct response to oil prices, the way destinations operate and market themselves will evolve towards decarbonised forms of tourism.

In the following sections, each of these elements (Figure 7.1) will be discussed in more detail.

7.1 Renewable Energy and Enabling Policies

> The global renewable energy share can reach and exceed 30% by 2030. The technologies are already available today to achieve this objective.
> (International Renewable Energy Agency (IRENA), 2014)

How realistic is the optimism expressed in the quote above? Global primary energy consumption in 2008 amounted to 514 EJ (EJ = exa joules = 10^{18} joules). More than 80% of this energy use is met by fossil fuels (Moriarty & Honnery, 2012). Continuing on existing growth paths, energy demand will increase – including energy demand for tourism purposes (see Chapter 3). How much of this energy demand can be met by renewable energy sources? The IRENA (2012) has collected over 10,000 references globally on renewable energy to develop colour-coded maps for wind, solar, biomass, hydro, marine and geothermal energy potential, available on an interactive website. One difficulty of such assessments is that energy potential can be defined differently, ranging from a physical (theoretical) resource potential (e.g. wind speed), to the more limited technical, economic, and market potentials (see pyramid in Figure 7.2).

Estimates of renewable energy potentials differ vastly. Moriarty and Honnery (2012) compiled a range of estimates from the literature (Table 7.1), but warn that some of the upper-range values are not based on realistic assumptions. Economic potential, as indicated in Klimenko et al.'s (2009) estimates in Table 7.1, is often much lower than technical potential, for example by a factor of 10. The currently largest economic potential, for example, rests with hydro-power at 29 EJ. This, however, still only represents less than 1% of global energy demand. Thus, while it might be physically or technically possible to reach a 30% renewable energy share in the next 20 years (see quote above), it may be likely that political, economic and social barriers (witnessed and studied extensively in the context of climate change) prevent this from being achieved.

To truly understand the future energy supply situation it is critical to consider *net energy* (Heinberg, 2009; Moriarty & Honnery, 2012). All renewable technology requires the input of energy to be able to produce energy.

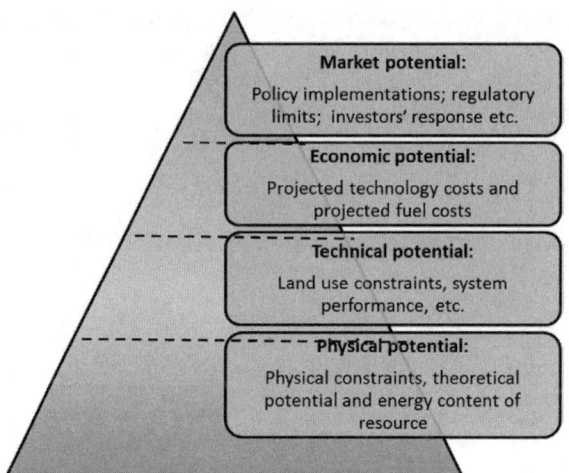

Figure 7.2 Different potentials for renewable energy sources: The market potential is the smallest and the physical (theoretical) potential is the largest
Source: After Department of Energy (DOE) Office of Energy Efficiency and Renewable Energy (2006).

For example, solar panels need to be manufactured. Wind turbines need to be put in place and connected to supporting infrastructure (access roads, transmission lines) and so forth. The net energy relates to the EROI (see also Chapter 4). If the EROI is under one (as is the case for some types of ethanol production, Heinberg, 2009), energy is 'lost' for human use.

For the case of photovoltaic systems (PV), Dale and Benson (2013) estimate that the total PV capacity installed to-date has not yet generated a net return on the energy invested. The costs of manufacturing PV are declining sharply, while installation is increasing – thus a point where a positive energy return can be achieved is likely to be in the foreseeable future. In addition, alternative energy is still relatively small compared with fossil fuels. Wind power, for example, constitutes only 2.5% of world electricity output despite substantial past investments in this energy market (Chapman, 2013). Recent investment has actually been shrinking for the last two years, with 14% less in 2013 compared with 2012, and 23% below the 2011 record (Frankfurt School-UNEP Centre/BNEF, 2014).

Notwithstanding recent trends of reduced investment, the International Energy Agency (IEA, 2012) predicts that development in emerging economies will lead to a 70% increased electricity demand between 2010 and 2035 – half of which will be met by energy from renewable sources. Already, in 2013 renewable energy, excluding large hydro projects, constituted 43.6%

Table 7.1 Estimates of renewable energy potential globally (technical potential unless indicated otherwise)

Study and year of estimate	Solar (EJ)	Wind (EJ)	Ocean (EJ)	Hydro (EJ)	Biomass (EJ)	Geothermal electricity (EJ)
Lightfoot and Green (2002) (range of values)	163 (118–206)	72 (48–72)	0 (1.8–3.6)	19 (16–19)	539 (373–772)	1.5
Gross et al. (2003)	43–144	72–144[a]	7–14[b]	NA	29–90	NA
Sims et al. (2007)	1650	600	7	62	250	NA
Field et al. (2008)	NA	NA	NA	NA	27	NA
Resch et al. (2008)	1600	600	NA	50	250	NA
Klimenko et al. (2009) ('economic' potential)	2592 (19)	191 (8.6)	22 (2.2)	54 (29)	NA	22 (3.6)
Cho (2010)	>1577	631	NA	50	284	NA
Tomabechi (2010)[c]	1600	700	11	59	200	NA
World Energy Council (2010)	NA	NA	7.6[b]	57.4	50–1500	1.1–4.4
All studies range	118–2592	48–600	1.8–33	50–95	27–1500	1.1–22

Notes: [a]Onshore only.
[b]Wave only.
[c]'Usable maximum'.
Source: Based on Moriarty and Honnery (2012).

of the new power capacity added in all technologies (Frankfurt School-UNEP Centre/BNEF, 2014). The largest investment in renewable energy sources has been observed in China ($56 billion investment in 2013) and Europe ($48 billion) (Frankfurt School-UNEP Centre/BNEF, 2014).

In a study funded by the Australian government, CSIRO (2008) proposed that governments have to play an important role in preparing for Peak Oil, because involvement by individuals and businesses is likely to be moderate – partly due to the above barriers associated with cost. Policies are required to increase the attractiveness of alternative energies, in particular to compensate for their higher production costs. In the US, for example, a kilowatt-hour of electricity from coal costs about two to seven cents, compared with 4.5 to 10 cents for wind, and 21 to 83 cents for solar photovoltaic

(Heinberg, 2009). Enabling policies include feed-in tariffs for renewable electricity, investment in research and development, tax breaks for renewable energy technology, subsidies, grants and education.

Germany is amongst the leading countries in the world where progressive energy policies are beginning to pay off. Germany's Energiewende ('Energy Transition') sets a long-term target to achieve a share of 60% renewable energy in final energy use by 2050. The government plans to achieve this with substantial renewable energy deployment in the electricity and district heat sectors, including innovative uses of solar thermal and heat pumps in district heat generation. An analysis by the German Advisory Council on the Environment (2011) highlights, however, how difficult it is to achieve a 100% renewable electricity system, even though it might be technically possible.

Research on renewable energy sources in tourism is comparatively sparse. An Australian study has established that the payback time of wind energy conversion systems is between three and four years, compared with six to seven years for PV systems (Dalton et al., 2008, 2009). Chan et al. (2013) undertook research into solar hot water options in Shenzen in China, mainly in response to rapidly growing tourism demand and mounting environmental problems. The research compared two different types of solar collectors and identified payback times for different scenarios between 0.8 and 3.8 years. Major barriers for installation were the limited roof space available (and its usage for other purposes, e.g. roof top restaurants) and noise associated with retrofitting and renovations. Another relevant study quantified the amount of renewable energy available from waste biomass created by 385 tourist attractions in the Yangtze River Delta (YRD) in China. The findings highlighted that about 6% (6740 TJ per annum; 1 TJ = 10^{12} joules) of the region's energy use in 2008 could be met with energy from waste biomass (Shi et al., 2013).

While there are attractive options for electricity generation and hot water supply in the tourism sector, IRENA's (2014) 2030 roadmap clearly identifies that the challenge will be the replacement of fossil *liquid* fuels. Transport energy use has always been tourism's Achilles heel in the context of climate change mitigation discussions (Becken & Simmons, 2005; Becken, 2005c), and it remains the key challenge in relation to Peak Oil. Technical options are available (for a tourism-related discussion, see Becken & Hay, 2007; Peeters et al., 2006; Peeters, 2010) including first (sugars and vegetable oils), second (various types of biomass) and third generation biofuels (waste products) (Figure 7.3).

However, it is the sheer scale of liquid fuel required that constitutes the problem. To put it into perspective: the current global production of conventional oil is in the order of 27,000 million barrels per year. Ethanol production

In the future, there will be no difference
between waste and energy.

HSBC ⟨X⟩

Figure 7.3 One example of the 'In the Future' campaign by London-based banking and finance group HSBC
Note: The advertisements convey future-oriented thinking, including reference to new fuels and resource alternatives.
Source: HSBC/JWT © Andy Rudak.

is about 260 million barrels per year (Heinberg, 2009), or about 1.86 million barrels per day in 2012 (Voegele, 2013). For the case of the US, Chapman (2013) reported that even if the whole crop of American maize production was used to produce biofuel, only 5% of domestic demand could be met. Peeters (2010) estimated that if biofuel for all global aviation came from Jatropha (a plant from the Euphorbiaceae family), an area the size of Germany, France, the Netherlands and Belgium combined would need to be cultivated with this crop. Notwithstanding, biofuel as an alternative to kerosene is heavily promoted by the airline industry (IATA, 2009).

Most alternative energy sources bring with them a range of environmental and social risks (Table 7.2), which means that technical or economic potentials are unlikely to be achieved fully. Major challenges associated with biofuel, for example, relate to the food-water-energy nexus, where problems arise when agricultural land area is used for energy rather than food production. Biofuel plantations can also directly conflict with tourism when ecologically attractive areas (e.g. rainforest) are made available for corn, sugarcane or palm oil, and are taken out of potential (eco)tourism use (Becken & Job, 2014). Similarly, windfarms have been controversial due to their visual impacts at

Table 7.2 Environmental and social impacts associated with different types of renewable energy sources

Renewable energy type	Environmental and social effects
Solar	Pollution from PV production; adverse effects on fragile semi-arid land ecosystems; competition for fresh water; depletion of scarce materials; albedo decreases.
Wind	Bird and bat deaths; possible habitat loss for other wildlife; noise and vibration pollution for nearby residents; visual impacts; possible adverse effects on marine mammals from offshore windfarms; possible climate changes for large-scale installations.
Ocean	Disruption to marine ecosystems; possible adverse effects on marine mammals from wave and current energy devices; shipping disruption.
Hydro	Loss of homes and livelihoods, and heritage sites; fresh-water biodiversity loss; inundation of land; possible increases in micro-seismicity and slope instability; increased downstream erosion; coastal land retreat and declining soil fertility from loss of sediment deposition; greenhouse gas emissions from submerged biomass.
Biomass	Competition with other biomass uses for fertile land and water; loss of existing uses for biomass wastes; biodiversity loss due to large monocultures.
Geothermal	Land subsidence; increase in micro-seismicity; air and water pollution.

Source: Based on Moriarty and Honnery (2012).

tourist destinations. Recent research on offshore windfarms in southern France, however, established that there is a distance decay effect, whereby turbines further away are perceived as lower impact. Moreover, the research found that some tourist segments actively appreciated the presence of windarms and wanted to learn more about them (Westerberg et al., 2013).

Thus, in summary, a wide range of renewable energy options exist, and these may go a long way in replacing fossil fuel-based electricity. For tourism, the greatest potential lies in the accommodation sector, mainly through solar hot water or PV installations. Some types of tourist transport may also benefit from PV (Figure 7.4). In summary, the criteria for the success of

Figure 7.4 Solar and wind-powered 'eco-vessel' for harbour cruises in Barcelona, Spain

alternative energy sources will depend on (a) scalability; (b) cost of production; (c) net energy yield (ideally more than 10:1); and (d) minimised environmental, social and political impacts.

Considering these constraints, and moving beyond electricity to specifically take into account the demand for liquid fuels, Heinberg (2009) concluded that *no combination* of alternative energy solutions will enable continuous economic growth at the scale we have experienced over the last century (see also Patzek (2007) for the same conclusion). This represents a major turning point for tourism. Clearly, other pathways need to be pursued in the face of peaking oil production to maintain tourism activity. Since it is critical to dramatically reduce the demand for transportation fuel, the next section summarises new transport technologies and systems.

7.2 Transport Technology and Systems

The literature on energy and transport and how to improve transport energy efficiency is vast (e.g. Bristow *et al.*, 2008; Moriarty & Honnery, 2008), and has also been integrated into tourism studies (Becken & Lane, 2006, Becken, 2009; Bows *et al.*, 2009; Dubois *et al.*, 2011; Lumsden *et al.*,

2006). Reducing the demand for transport fuel, however, is challenging, especially in tourism. One reason is that the energy intensity of transport, in particular air travel, is high and alternative sources are presently not viable at the quantities required. Another reason is the low elasticity (see Chapter 6) of tourist transport, meaning that even higher prices are unlikely to lead to substantial changes in transport behaviour. A third challenge is that fossil fuel-based transport is often highly subsidised, be it directly through fuel subsidies (e.g. Venezuela) or indirectly through tax benefits (e.g. for diesel use) and government investment into road and airport infrastructure (Newman, 2006).

The most promising pathways towards reduction of transport fuel use are:

(1) Improvements in vehicle efficiency and introduction of non-petroleum based energy sources;
(2) Operational practices; and
(3) System changes that provide alternative options to transport users.

7.2.1 Vehicle efficiency

The dominant technologies for propulsion are internal combustion and compressed ignition engines. Incremental improvements in fuel efficiency have been achieved, including gasoline direct injection, turbocharging, smart cooling systems, reduced engine friction, more efficient transmissions, lightweight materials and better aerodynamics (Sperling & Lutsey, 2009). While efficiency may be improved by up to 15% in the next decade (Sperling & Lutsey, 2009), gains are often outweighed by vehicle size and electronic functionalities. For tourism transport in particular, people often prefer larger vehicles with stronger engines to accommodate a larger number of passengers, luggage and maybe to tow a trailer or caravan.

Electric-drive technologies provide even greater saving potentials. It is not the purpose of the book to provide a detailed summary of the (fast-changing) technology in this area, including new applications like e-bikes, 'sky cars' (Wakefield, 2014), or other innovations. Broadly, technologies include hybrid gasoline-electric vehicles (HEVs), plug-in hybrids (PHEVs), battery electric vehicles (BEVs), and hydrogen-powered fuel-cell vehicles (HFCVs). The most realistic alternative in the short term is HEVs, because they rely on both internal combustion engines and electric propulsion. Vehicles, such as the Toyota Prius, are about 30% more fuel efficient than comparable conventional vehicles. PHEVs can be recharged externally, reducing fuel consumption by up to 75%; however, larger battery packs are required and the technology has not yet reached mass-market levels.

Figure 7.5 Green cabs: A taxi company in New Zealand that aims to appeal to customers through its plug-in hybrid fleet
Source: Green Cabs © Bradley Pratt, WhitePanda Media.

Similar issues apply to fully electrified vehicles, BEVs. While very efficient in terms of 'tank-to-wheel' energy efficiency, overall benefits depend on how the electricity was generated. Driving ranges of electric vehicles are still comparatively short (e.g. 150–200 km), reducing their appeal to a broader market, especially for tourism purposes. The main challenge for HFCVs is the lack of extensive refuelling systems, and questions surround how the hydrogen is produced. Again, those alternative technologies are better suited for daily inner-city travel and commuting, rather than for longer-distance holiday transport. Several taxi companies in different countries have capitalised on fuel-efficient and marketable green technologies, for example fleets made up of hybrid cars (Figure 7.5).

One of the key problems with alternative vehicle technologies is the initial cost, both for the development and infrastructure, and individual purchase prices. In the US, improved petrol or diesel vehicles with greater efficiencies cost about 10–30% more than conventional vehicles. Plug-in hybrid and fuel-cell vehicles cost 25–30% more than existing vehicles, and BEVs with comparable performance would be even more costly (Bandivadekar *et al.*, 2008). BEVs are most likely to be smaller in size and to be used for urban short-distance travel. In this scenario they are likely to payback during their lifetime due to fuel savings. Because of these constraints, Sperling and Lutsey (2009) conclude that evolutionary, rather than revolutionary, changes in road transport technology are more likely to make a real contribution to reducing transport fuel demand.

Just like technological improvements in efficiency are to be expected for road transport, advances are likely to be made in relation to rail efficiency, water transport and, importantly, aviation fuel consumption. It is beyond the scope of this book (and not the purpose of this chapter) to summarise these in detail but readers are referred to dedicated publications that specialise in the energy efficiency of the specific modes of transport, including those released by agencies such as the US Department of Energy, the International Energy Agency and the European Commission.

7.2.2 Operational practices

As has been discussed previously in the context of carbon dioxide emissions (e.g. Becken & Hay, 2007), fuel consumption depends substantially on driver behaviour and road conditions. 'Aggressive driving', as compared with 'restrained driving', for example, increases vehicle fuel consumption by as much as 30%. The use of air-conditioning increases fuel costs by 10–15%, and an additional 100 kg increases fuel use by up to 8% (Van den Brink & Van Wee, 2001). Direct feedback on driving style via fuel display instruments has the potential to educate drivers and reduce fuel consumption.

A recent study in Ontario, Canada, tested the deployment of vehicle monitoring technology (VMT) and eco-driver training as a means to improve fuel efficiency for a fleet of 14 vehicles operated by a large ski resort (Rutty et al., 2014). The research found that through eco-driver training the average daily speed of vehicles was reduced by 14%. Hard decelerations and hard accelerations also decreased significantly (−44% and −55%, respectively). Overall, the changed driver behaviour led to savings in fuel costs of about 8%. Rutty et al. (2014) conclude that the equipment and training are of very low cost and pay for themselves within less than one year.

In addition to driving style, improved vehicle maintenance has shown to lead to improved fuel efficiency per vehicle-kilometre. Inflating tyres, wheel alignment and regular replacements of oil and air filters, for example, produce measurable effects. In total, on-road improvements in efficiency from the above measures could increase fuel consumption by over 10% (Lutsey, 2008).

Similar to road transport, energy use in the aviation sector is strongly influenced by pilots' 'flying style' and operational practices. As discussed in more detail in Becken and Hay (2012), air traffic management is suboptimal in many regions of the world. In the fragmented European airspace, for example, an average of 50 km is flown unnecessarily per flight. Aviation policymakers around the world are working on agreements to reduce flight paths and decrease inefficiencies. The Single European Sky (SES), the Next Generation Air Traffic Management (ATM) system in the US, and the Pearl River Delta ATM system in Hong Kong are examples of such approaches.

7.2.3 Systemic changes

The most significant improvements in transport fuel use are likely to come from systemic changes. These are also the most difficult to achieve. Systemic changes include improvements to the current transport system, as well as the design of new systems, for example the development of coastal shipping routes to transport visitors efficiently across larger distances. One key component of reducing fuel use within the current system is better integration of subsystems, in particular individual and public transport (Lumsdon *et al.*, 2006). So, connectivity is the new buzzword. Improved transit arrangements between air, road and rail are central. Hong Kong is an excellent example of where air travel is seamlessly linked with a modern rail line into the city, and shuttle buses that take visitors from train stations to their hotels. It is important to note that improved connectivity with air travel may actually, paradoxically, increase air travel, and therefore oppose other trends of reduced air travel and slower forms of tourism (see below). Since oil price – different to the more moral approach to climate change mitigation – mainly manifests through increased transport costs, such effects are likely to be limited, with longer-haul travel being reserved for a small travelling elite.

Connectivity also improves access to walking and cycling and integration of these with other transport systems, for example bus and train transport (see Eaton & Holding, 1996, for an early example of public transport access to national parks). A wide range of policies can support modal shifts, including parking management and pricing, urban design and planning, the support of bicycle networks (see Lumsdon, 2000, on bicycle tourism), and information on transport options. Thus, connectivity and communication should lie at the core of the design and planning of any new transport systems.

The Trans-European Transport Network (TEN-T) is an example where a region-wide transport network is designed to maximise integration between roads, railways, airports and canals into one unified trans-European network. While not designed explicitly to address Peak Oil, the transport system will lead to greater efficiencies and enable freight and passenger movements within a defined geographic area (European Commission, 2013). The TEN-T will comprise nine major corridors to be completed by 2030: two north–south corridors, three east–west corridors; and four diagonal corridors. One core aim of the network is to improve east–west connectivity, but also to remove bottlenecks, upgrade infrastructure and streamline cross-border movements throughout the European Union. This will be achieved through:

- 94 main European ports with rail and road links;
- 38 key airports with rail connections into major cities;
- 15,000 km of railway line upgraded to high-speed;
- 35 cross-border projects to reduce bottlenecks.

The expansion of High Speed Rail (HSR, see also Chapter 2) is another example of a systemic change, where fuel-based transport (road and air) is transferred onto electrified alternatives that offer fast city-to-city linkages. The global network of HSR (speeds over 250 km/hour) comprises 21,365 km of lines in operation and a further 13,967 km of lines under construction (International Union of Railways (UIC), 2013). In 2012, the global traffic volume on HSR amounted to 1.15 billion passengers. Most of these passengers were counted in China (485 million), followed by Japan (300 million) and France (125 million). While HSR is expanding in several parts of the world, China has made the most progress: its network rose from zero to 10,000 km of HSR in just four years (UIC, 2013). The 2230 km line between Beijing and Guangzhou is currently the world's longest HSR line.

Of the roughly 1350 domestic city pairs served by airlines in China, about 200 are on the HSR network (Figure 7.6). Aircraft producer Boeing (2013) is keeping a careful watch on the HSR developments in China, noting that growth in rail traffic has been slower than domestic air travel. The average distance per rail trip in China has remained flat for the past few years, according to Boeing, whereas in other countries, average trip distance by rail has typically increased after the introduction of new HSR lines. Boeing sees these trends as evidence that the demand for air travel in China continues to be high and growing, despite rail options. There are some exceptions. For city-links with more than twice-daily air service, 17 have experienced more than a 25% reduction in capacity since 2009. Although airlines must adjust fares to compete with HSR, industry data show that average airline fares on the busiest Beijing-to-Shanghai route have remained high since the 2011 HSR inauguration (Boeing, 2013). For more scientific – and potentially less biased – research on HSR and tourism, please refer to (e.g. Amos et al., 2010; Becker & George, 2011; Yang & Zhang, 2012).

Figure 7.6 High Speed Rail in Hainan Island, China

To change a system, such as the present global transportation system, is a major challenge because of numerous lock-in effects and sunk investment, as well as established flows of trade, social practices and habits. Urry (2008) focuses on 'automobility' and asks whether it is possible to transform such an established system, or whether one has to wait for a 'tipping point', which by nature is not predictable. A tipping point would entail substantial changes in technology, policy, user behaviour, industry structures, and the symbolic meaning of mobility. Given the focus of the current system on the individualist, hedonic and consumerist culture, Urry argues that any new system is also likely to evolve around individual transport needs. He envisages a system made up of a wide range of dense forms of movement, including small and light 'vehicles' or 'pods' powered by battery or hydrogen. The pods are coordinated through a smart network where physical and 'virtual' (i.e. connecting via electronic channels) mobility are integrated. Individual systems would be complemented by larger mass transport. Urry does not elaborate on how these systems might be used by tourists, but a hub and spoke system of HSR, for example, combined with destination-based small vehicle/pod systems is conceivable. This could be completed by electric bicycles that are increasingly popular amongst locals, but maybe also tourists.

7.3 The Post-Peak Tourist?

The last 10 years have provided a substantial amount of research into tourists' environmental attitudes and behaviours. In particular, researchers have investigated in quite some detail how tourists perceive the particular issues of climate change, greenhouse gas emissions, and their own contributions to this global problem. The literature clearly indicates an increasing awareness of the greenhouse gas emissions associated with travel (Becken, 2007; Brouwer et al., 2008; Gössling et al., 2009; McKercher et al., 2010), but it also shows that actual travel behaviour is unlikely to be affected by perceptions or attitudes (Cohen et al., 2011; Cohen & Higham, 2010; Hares et al., 2010; Weaver, 2011). Thus, the more recent literature on climate change and tourism confirms earlier studies on transport behaviour that established that tourists are quite unwilling to use public transport and refrain from using personal vehicles, as long as there is an option to maintain car travel (Dickinson & Dickinson, 2006; Reilley et al., 2010). Partly, this can be explained by deeply entrenched associations of car travel and personal freedom (Hannam et al., 2014), especially in countries such as the US and Australia, and most recently China (Urry, 2008), where public transport systems are less developed and 'car cultures' form integral parts of social life.

Various researchers have explored causes for these apparent inconsistencies. Hares et al. (2010), for example, discuss an awareness-attitude gap (Antimova et al., 2012), building on more generic environmental behaviour literature and the well-established attitude-behaviour gap (Kollmuss & Agyeman, 2002). Hares et al. (2010) argue that tourists' awareness of climate change and transport's contribution to global emissions does not lead to changed attitudes, nor tangible behaviour. Another avenue of research relates to the so-called contextual gap (Ram et al., 2013), where social practices of environmental behaviour or actions (Verbeek & Mommaas, 2008) are not transferred from home to the holiday situation (Barr et al., 2010; Miller et al., 2010).

Very limited research has been undertaken to understand tourists' perceptions of Peak Oil or finite resources (Becken, 2011), and social marketing campaigns tend to focus on other aspects related to fuel consumption such as climate change or air pollution. The idea of placing warnings on pump nozzles, for example as shown in Figure 7.7, could be easily transferred from the initial climate change purpose to the Peak Oil issue. Overall, due to limited campaigning (Friedrichs, 2011) and discourse on Peak Oil (Becken, 2014; Wicker & Becken, 2013), and because of the well-established gaps on environmental behaviour, it is unlikely that tourists will choose to change their travel behaviour to save precious oil resources.

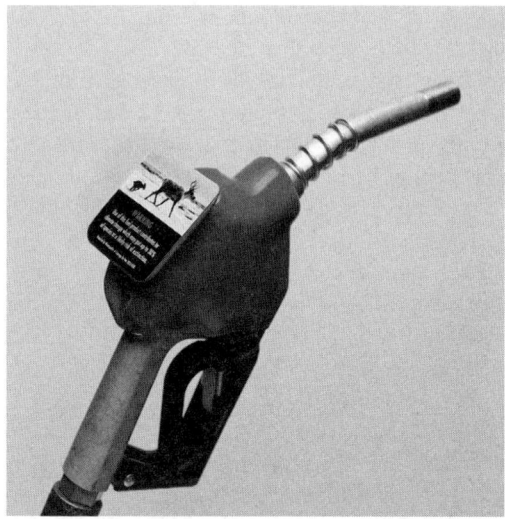

Figure 7.7 Social marketing campaigns and advocacy implement laws that provide information and feedback to consumers about the impacts of their fuel use
Source: With permission from Our Horizon (2014).

There is a fundamental difference between climate change mitigation behaviour and responding to Peak Oil. The former is typically based around environmental values and ethics, with tourists being asked to consider their carbon footprints on the grounds of sustainability or global equity (and even 'guilt', Cohen *et al.*, 2011). For Peak Oil, however, (and with exception of the 'peakists' discussed in Chapter 5) the matter of changing behaviour is less likely to be voluntary but may represent a forced adaptation to higher fuel prices. Thus, tourists, when faced with lower incomes and higher transport costs (see Chapter 6) will begin to reconsider their travel decisions. As already argued in the context of tourists' adaptations to climate change more broadly, tourists should be viewed as highly adaptive elements within the tourism system (Gössling *et al.*, 2012). They are free to make decisions in relation to destinations, travel modes and holiday types – and can adjust these rather rapidly when circumstances (e.g. costs) change.

Since long-distance air travel is the most expensive type of travel, it seems plausible that this will be reduced in the first instance (Ram *et al.*, 2013). Peeters and Dubois (2010) estimate that – to reduce emissions from tourism by 70% by 2050 – total air transportation volume would need to be reduced to 1970s levels, or 80% of all car use would need to be transferred to rail and coach travel with air transport stagnating at 2005 levels. Similar shifts could be witnessed in response to Peak Oil. Market-led changes may then be rationalised by individuals as well as policymakers by propagating other benefits associated with such changes, for example positive health outcomes and improved well-being. Ram *et al.*'s (2013) research on happiness illustrates that approaches of positive psychology might be more successful in changing deeply rooted transport behaviours than those appealing to the rationality of environmental decision-making.

New forms of tourism – post-peak tourism – may therefore materialise as 'slower travel, closer to home' (see also further below). For some this may seem like a step back into the past, but for others it has been interpreted as a new form of tourism with many benefits. Such post-modern tourism has the potential to reverse some of the meaninglessness of inauthentic and manufactured experiences available in the globalised tourism world (Altés Arlandis, 2012; Friedl, 2012). Arguably, modern tourism has made the 'Other' so accessible that experiences have become quite interchangeable and less special. Baumann (2000: 13) notes that tourists are often plagued by the thought that they could be here, there or anywhere, without any specific meaning attached to the place they are visiting at present. Boundaries between home and away, and between different places 'away' have become blurred or disappeared. As Altés Arlandis (2012: 4) notes:

> Such a blurring of distinctions does not amount to more than a metaphorical ending of tourism; the dissolving of tourism's specificity within liquid modernity is a change, a transformation of the ways in which we work, live and travel. Another trait of the post-modern condition.

It is possible that the consequences of Peak Oil will force tourism back into a more realistic conception of distance and experience. Distance decay, as previously researched in tourism (McKercher, 1998), will become, once again, meaningful. It has been argued that so-called 'fake fantasies', as epitomised in the tourist destination of Dubai (Altés Arlandis, 2012; Becken & Friedl, 2014), could make way for more 'meaningful' experiences closer to home. What will new experiences and destinations look like, and will there be a parallel evolution – or convergence – of post-peak tourism and post-oil destination development? The role of technology and the 'hybridization of virtual and physical spaces' (Hannam *et al.*, 2014: 178) is unclear, as it creates new networks, experiences and virtual travel companions on the one hand, but is also related to a new form of social exclusion, both from others and the place visited.

One major challenge in this 'contraction' of the world relates to the interconnectedness between tourism and migration, where families are spread over the globe and social networks have become dependent on (cheap) air travel to be maintained (Urry, 2011, 2012). Urry therefore asks, 'how can networking be achieved without the extensive travel and meetings culture that results in [. . .] global risks of consuming too much oil. . .' (2012: 29). He further concedes that there might be some bleak futures for the networks that we have become used to as it is increasingly difficult to sustain them or widen them to those parts of the world that have not yet participated in global networking and related mobility.

It is likely that a travelling elite will remain for whom Peak Oil is not relevant. This might include certain types of business travellers and those who are wealthy enough to afford high travel costs. Also, tourists who are dedicated to special-interest tourism (e.g. diving, hunting) are likely to continue their tourism activity as long as possible. For some destinations or businesses a focus on high-end or special interest tourism may well provide a lucrative niche. Virgin Airlines, for example, already appeals to its most valued (and well-off) customers in Australia through the possibility of a Velocity frequent flyer upgrade to 'space class' in partnership with Virgin Galactic.

By and large however, there is no doubt: a transition to post-peak tourism will be challenging and confronting. A glimpse can be gained from the stories presented in *Beyond Flying: Rethinking Air Travel in a Globally Connected World* edited by Chris Watson (2014). Bringing together a collection of personal stories of how people voluntarily gave up on flying, this book highlights how – despite major challenges and constraints – travellers are beginning to embrace the journey and engage with the people and places they visit. Again, the role of communication technology may be important, but is not explored further in this book.

7.4 Localisation of Tourism?

Some have suggested that one consequence of Peak Oil will be a contraction of our globalised world. Globalisation of trade is characterised by an international division of labour and production, with complex supply chains that involve the transport of goods from their country of production to the place of consumption. Over the last century, this has been facilitated by cheap oil. The movement of passengers, including tourists, is part of this process whereby the consumer travels to the location of production for enjoyment. For some origin-destination pairs, cheap air travel and cheap destination packages (typically in developing countries) have resulted in attractive offers to tourists that may even present savings compared with staying at home.

Curtis (2009) argues that both climate change and Peak Oil will lead to a shortening of supply chains and 'peak globalisation', whereby economic activity will increasingly be local or regional in nature. More localised tourism will be the result, and a shift from international tourism to domestic travel is possible. Whether local travel will supersede existing patterns of more frequent and further-away short breaks has been asked by a number of tourism academics, including Buckley (2011), Dickinson and Lumsdon (2010), and Fullagar *et al.* (2012). This new research on slower and shorter travel provides an antidote to previous research that focused on the particular role of transport and aviation (including low-cost airlines, e.g. Dobruszkes, 2006) in shaping destination development (Koo & Lohmann, 2013; Lohmann *et al.*, 2009).

The overarching term of more localised tourism is 'slow tourism', where tourists travel to destinations more slowly overland (i.e. not by air), stay longer and travel less whilst at the destination (Dickinson & Lumsdon, 2010). Bicycle tourism is an important component of slow travel. It is increasingly important and popular at many destinations, both as a means of transport and a leisure activity (Figure 7.8). While some proponents of slow travel

Figure 7.8 Bicycles available for short-term hire in Brisbane City, Australia

focus on the destination and what tourists experience on holiday, others include the travel between home and the destination. The latter approach is mainly related to developing low-carbon tourism with minimal total impacts on the global climate (Dickinson *et al.*, 2011), whereas the former focuses more on the tourist experience as such.

Dickinson *et al.* (2011) put forward that slow travel is not only a choice of transport, but it is a form of ethical purchasing behaviour and a conscious decision to negotiate space and immerse into the destinations that are traversed or stayed at. Thus, in line with the comments about post-modern tourism made earlier, slow travel presents an opportunity for superior tourism systems that provide satisfying tourist experiences. Developing destinations based on the ideal of creating high-quality experiences, instead of simply multiplying (mass) tourist arrivals, has also been advocated by Timms and Conway (2011) for the Caribbean islands. In some ways however, Timms and Conway's propositions regarding the development of slow tourism in marginal island destinations remind us of earlier discussions on ecotourism, alternative tourism, or community-based tourism, where small-scale operations with local participation and ownership are offered as a contrast to large-scale and foreign-owned mass tourism. One may ask whether slow tourism is nothing but 'old wine in new bottles'. In addition, the concept of slow tourism in island destinations is somewhat contradictory, unless travel to the island involves minimal transport energy.

To understand whether slow tourism could be a fundamentally new approach to tourism, let us look at movements outside of tourism where localisation processes can be observed. The concept of localisation is becoming popular more broadly, and insights can be gained from so-called 'eco-localisation' initiatives and transition towns (Bailey *et al.*, 2010; North, 2010). These build on the idea of developing new forms of smart low-carbon growth through local solutions. The focus of decision-making is shifting from profit maximisation to meeting the needs of local communities. North (2010) proposes that it is useful to distinguish *immanent* from *intentional* localisation. Immanent localisation is not underpinned by an ideology, but it rather represents a process that is occurring in response to changes in the economic environment. For example, due to higher transportation costs, new local opportunities might emerge that are more competitive than previous models. The increased popularity of locally grown food in tourism (e.g. the Eat Local campaign in South Australia) could be seen as an example of immanent localisation. This type of localisation is compatible with neoliberal ideologies: '...perhaps more like the middle of the last century. It is eco-business as usual, same exploitation, but carbon-free and with shorter supply and distribution networks' (North, 2010: 590).

In contrast, intentional localisation has normative connotations, which bode well with the Peak Oil movement discussed briefly in Chapter 5 (Note: this movement is inspired by the Australian permaculture movement in Australia in the 1970s in response to OPEC oil shocks). Advocates of intentional localisation do not believe that technological progress is sufficient to overcome oil constraints, and they also condemn contemporary capitalism with its diminishing returns on increasing complexities (Tainter, 1988) and 'catabolic societies' (Greer, 2008). Their interpretation of local solutions includes much wider reductions in resource use than just transportation fuel: reducing meat consumption, recycling material, smaller houses, reduced consumption of luxury goods, growing your own food (as increasingly incorporated into tourist resort operations, see Figure 7.9), and so forth. The essence of this type of localisation is to create low-energy livelihoods and forms of living. Some movements of localisation are inspired by Cuba's Special Period (see also earlier in this chapter and Friedrichs, 2010) and how communities adapted to fuel shortages, for example by reorganising land use and labour skills. Intentional localisation provides a 'radical alternative template of spatial relations to that of globalisation' (Bailey et al., 2010: 595).

The localisation movement has been criticised on a few grounds (North, 2010). Not everything can or should be produced locally, and there has obviously been a reason why a (geographic) division of labour has emerged. There

Figure 7.9 Shortening supply chains by growing food right at the tourist resort is a great opportunity for de-carbonising food and creating memorable tourist experiences

are some good reasons why certain goods and services can still be moved around in an overall attempt to increase efficiency; possibly distance and speed may need to be reconsidered for some products. Localisation also raises questions about justice. Some locations are better developed than others, and some enjoy a greater resource endowment than others – will this lead to protectionism? How would fair distribution of resources be ensured? Would cities become less attractive to live in or would there need to be some strategic alignment between cities that have to become more urban (i.e. more dense) and the countryside that needs to be more rural (more directly useful agricultural land use) (Newman, 2006)? For tourist destinations, the concept of tourism clusters might be useful in the development of viable and concentrated conglomerates of tourist attractions (Gardiner & Scott, 2014). A strategic decision to engage in intentional localisation processes could provide competitive advantages for some destinations.

Tourist destinations by definition involve some mobility, as the tourist would be coming from somewhere else. However, some destinations have begun to invest in low-carbon and slow local systems (Box 7.2), noting, however, that often these do not consider travel to the destination (often by aviation). With respect to tourist transport, for example, such destinations offer:

- Convenient low-carbon transport options that are well-integrated and affordable (see also earlier about transport systems);
- Detailed information on transport options and easy access to tourist attractions; and
- Tourist-friendly transportation, taking into account family needs, luggage provisions and experiential values of the travel component.

A very small number of destinations around the world have explicitly and strategically thought about Peak Oil. The Sunshine Coast, Australia, is one example. In its Sunshine Coast Climate Change and Peak Oil Strategy 2010–2020 (Sunshine Coast Council, 2010), the council identified the need to reduce oil dependency and enable a transition to alternative energy sources (detailed in an energy transition plan). Tourism was identified as one of the sectors vulnerable to high oil prices; which was seen as critical given that tourism contributes about 17% to the gross regional product. The fact that 91% of visitors to the destination are domestic at present was seen as a positive factor reducing vulnerability. The strategy also recommended careful analysis of the viability of further expansions at the Sunshine Coast Airport, due to the risk of rising oil prices in the future. Interestingly, risk assessments and strategic planning such as these have not influenced marketing strategies to date.

Box 7.2 Barcelona, Spain: Initiatives to improve the sustainability of the destination

Barcelona has a vision beyond a 'sustainable destination' approach, building on the idea that a city is a metabolism where locals and tourists live together in urban and natural environments. Key measures of success include:

- 85% of all trips within the city of Barcelona are made in sustainable modes, i.e. walking, cycling and public transport;
- Barcelona is counting more than 150,000 daily trips by bicycle;
- Thanks to more than 120,000 users of the public bicycle system, Bicing, Barcelona avoids emission of 9000 tonnes of CO_2 every year. Interestingly, the City had planned to offer Bicing to the city's visitors, but after strong protests from the city's bike rental firms, this idea had to be abolished;
- An excellent urban public transport network, including the Barcelona Bus Turistic;
- The Hotel Association of Barcelona and the City Council implemented the Mobec Hotels – a network of electric bikes located in different hotels in Barcelona; and
- Thematic walking tours around the urban landscape to discover the city's heritage.

Source: Pujol (2013).

Future planning of post-peak destinations could build on studies that have assessed the oil vulnerability of suburbs in a non-tourism context (e.g. Dodson & Sipe, 2008). Often, city centres are less vulnerable than outer areas, although these patterns may differ for smaller regional centres as shown in the case of Lake Macquarie in New South Wales, Australia where pockets of vulnerability have alternated with areas of relative resilience. Vulnerability was determined by, amongst others, indicators such as cars per capita, transport used for commuting to work and economic resources in the community (Institute for Sensible Transport, 2010). Systemic risk assessments, as evidenced in the University of Tasmania (UTAS) 'Peak Oil Risk Matrix' (Institute for Sensible Transport, 2012), would be highly beneficial for tourist destinations. The use of sustainability indicators that monitor destination transformations could be useful (McLennan *et al.*, 2012) in such assessments. Future research could also investigate whether there is an opportunity to include such resilience measures in destination marketing.

7.5 Conclusion

As has long been recognised for the risk of global climate change, early preparation for Peak Oil is likely to save costs and reduce adverse impacts. There are several dimensions to a post-peak world in which tourism will need to reconceptualise itself. As a very first critical step, it is essential to reduce dependence on fossil fuels and invest in alternative, that is renewable, sources of energy. This is particularly relevant for those tourism businesses that operate stationary businesses, for example accommodation providers and tourist attractions. Here the potential for producing renewable electricity is an important avenue to becoming more self-sufficient and, as a result, resilient to oil shocks.

Options for tourist transportation are more limited, but renewable energy opportunities do exist – and have been tested in tourism contexts. For transportation, the two key pathways are decarbonisation and integration. Electrified transport systems that provide high connectivity will be competitive in a post-peak environment. Thus, new technologies combined with new systems will provide future opportunities for global and local transportation. These are likely to differ from today's systems, but will nevertheless ensure some level of tourism mobility.

In a world where oil will be increasingly scarce and more expensive, tourists may have to rethink their travel behaviours and the types of experiences they seek to gain from their holidays and other trips. Different to the debates on ethical travel behaviour to minimise one's carbon footprint, the changes induced by higher oil prices will be less voluntary and more a response to economic signals. As such they are also likely to be more pervasive. People might start to choose 'cheaper' holidays and social norms will adapt to make such travel more socially acceptable and, in fact, desirable. Discussions on post-modern tourism with a greater emphasis of 'quality' rather than 'quantity' are relevant in this context.

A shift in travel behaviour and tourists' motivations will coincide with a 'contraction' of travel towards more localised – and maybe slower – forms of tourism. Travel to destinations that are closer will dominate. Those places that offer low-carbon transport systems and tourist attraction networks are likely to be more competitive than those destinations that remain highly vulnerable to high oil prices. Strategic assessments of destination oil vulnerability are rare in tourism but would assist in preparing for post-peak tourism.

8 Conclusion

This book has brought to the forefront a few key issues that are critical for the future of tourism. By analysing the energy and carbon intensity of tourism it became clear just how oil-dependent tourism is, in particular its transport component. Tourists use about 8% of global oil for transportation alone. In addition, the tourism industry consumes oil for tourist accommodation, attractions, activities and a wide range of other tourism services. This is estimated to add up to about another 2% of global consumption. Thus, tourism is a major contributor to oil demand, and at the same token oil is integral to tourism. Without oil, tourism would not operate the way it does today.

It is very obvious that most tourism organisations expect tourism to grow. Tourism is widely seen as a major force of economic development – especially in marginal areas – and governments, destinations and businesses invest accordingly. Tourism forecasts almost universally predict growth in the order of 4–5% per annum for the next few decades. Emerging economies predominately drive growth, and the case of China's tourism growth is particularly astonishing. It is difficult to imagine that tourism demand within and out of China will slow down in the short-term.

Tourism forecasts are typically built around more general projections of gross domestic product (GDP). Some also include oil prices as a moderating variable. However, rarely do forecasts include assumptions about 'limits to growth' or planetary boundaries. Thus, expectations for tourism demand assume no major changes to the availability or critical 'ingredients' (such as oil) of the tourism product. But what if oil suddenly or incrementally becomes more costly; much more costly? What if the predicted growth in tourism cannot materialise, and what if the natural resources available are not able to meet the undeniably increasing appetite for travel?

This book puts forward that the key question for the future of tourism should be around oil prices, and what will happen to them in the short, medium and long-term. But this question is not asked. Why? One reason is that oil is generally not discussed publicly – it does not appear to be viewed as a key issue or an important risk. It is not on the agenda of decision-makers or civic society, as for example is the case for climate change. Media coverage on oil is very limited, and if anything focuses on political tensions, energy policies and new opportunities such as 'fracking'.

The public debate is muted because of the lack of credible and reliable data on how much oil is being produced, how much is estimated to be left, and in what kinds of reservoirs. The absence of a widely accepted set of data on global oil production and supply can partly be explained by the fact that oil is an inherently political issue. Oil resources, and access to them, are highly correlated with geopolitical power, conflict, strategic investment, business interests and shareholder values. Importantly, no independent body or organisation has been powerful enough to demand transparency of 'official statistics', following the model of global greenhouse gas accounting. Therefore, it is not possible to be absolutely sure how imminent and how critical the onset of Peak Oil is. Questions around important aspects of Peak Oil, for example what would be the global decline rate after a peak, are modelled on second-best estimates of key parameters.

Scientists and energy experts, and with them members of the interested public, are left to put together various pieces of evidence to gain a coherent picture. Published academic research, for example in the journals *Energy*, *Energy Policy* and geological journals, clearly indicate increasing agreement on the precariousness of global oil production. The consistent message is that the peak might have passed, or is approaching soon. This point is even made by conservative agencies, such as the International Energy Agency, that has repeatedly published statements that a peak in conventional oil production was in the late 2000s. Often such messages are hidden in a wider narrative of increasing production – thanks to a growing exploitation of unconventional resources. Thus, the message of a global peak is 'smoke screens and mirrors' by official bodies.

In addition, there is evidence from people who have worked in the oil industry and who now provide informed insights into production data. A number of key experts have warned that oil statistics are inflated and that real oil supplies might fall short of those commonly stated in reports and forecasts. Indirectly, the future oil markets where investors reveal their expectations of trends in oil prices also confirm that oil prices are likely to increase. Finally, it is generally known that an increasing share of global production of liquid fuels comes from unconventional resources, which have much higher production costs (e.g. fracking or tar sands). Thus, if oil production is increasingly weighted towards costs of up to US$80 per barrel, instead of $10–20 per barrel, it is not difficult to predict that prices will only go one way, namely up.

Of particular concern is the declining energy return on energy invested (EROI), where more and more energy has to be spent to gain energy. For some sources of liquid fuel the EROI is close to one, for example for some types of biofuel, where basically no energy is gained from the production process. Such 'alternative resources' are obviously nonsensical. For some sources technological process will improve the EROI, but most are limited by physical factors that prevent them from ever reaching the EROI (up to 100) of conventional oil.

The question of Peak Oil is therefore 'not if but when'. The exact timing of a peak in global oil production is not necessarily obvious as production might fluctuate in the form of a plateau. Also, oil prices at any time depend on a complex mix of factors, including the present market forces, political factors and trading (including speculation). So, prices are not an accurate proxy for production potential. However, eventually there will be a point when oil production rates decline permanently and irreversibly. Unless demand drops suddenly at the same time, as has been witnessed in 2009 following the global financial crisis, then prices will inevitably increase.

What does this all mean for tourism? Higher oil prices (and associated with that higher costs of water and food) will clearly affect the economies more broadly, people will have less discretionary income and a lower propensity to travel, there might be more conflict globally, and transportation costs are almost certainly increasing. Thus, the signs are challenging for tourism as we know it. Building on a large body of tourism literature on income elasticities and price sensitivity, it seems likely that people will choose to travel less and shorter distances. This book did not provide a detailed model on global tourist flows and redistributions of long-haul and short-haul travel, or international and domestic, or high-end to lower-end, but these are all important tasks for future research.

It seems clear, though, that tourist behaviour and travel patterns will change, simply due to economic imperatives, and perhaps also because of a growing awareness of resource scarcity (although this would have to overcome the environmental gap already observed for climate change mitigation). Global tourist flows are likely to change as a result and destinations in close proximity to major source markets are likely to benefit. What will happen as a result to far-away and tourist-dependent nations is a question of great importance, and one that needs to be researched and addressed by policymakers with a matter of urgency.

Importantly, changes to global and local tourism systems can be reactive or planned. Proactive planning would enable destinations and businesses to reduce negative impacts, and even capitalise on new forms of tourism and products. This will include a niche opportunity for those who cater for a small travelling elite that is not majorly impacted by higher oil prices. Thus, luxury tourism might be an option for some players in tourism. For the majority, the pathway will be more likely one of decarbonisation and slower travel.

This book has provided a number of ideas for what post-peak tourism and destinations might look like. Very clearly, there is an urgent need for tourism businesses to invest in renewable energy sources where they can, and where the investment actually increases resilience. For example, investing in hydro-power in locations where increasing probabilities of drought are predicted may only increase risk. However, a number of technologies are well-established and proven to provide low-risk returns on investment, for example solar hot water for tourist accommodation. Overall, renewable energy is most beneficial for stationary tourism operations, such as hotels or tourist attractions.

The challenge is greater for transportation operators. Renewable liquid fuels will ever meet a small proportion of oil demand, especially when the growing demands of the global aviation industry are considered. The point could be made that aviation should be strategically prioritised for remaining fuel. Due to a likely 'run on the last (cheap) drop', new transportation technology and systems are needed. In a nutshell, changes relate to an electrification and integration of transport systems, and ongoing improvements in vehicle efficiency across all technologies. These new systems will cater for new forms of tourism, including those that are more focused on tourist experiences rather than maximising distance and quantity. Thus, debates around post-modern tourism and slow travel (including slow destinations) are very informative for the Peak Oil and tourism debate.

This book has not provided any suggestions for who is responsible for what, and what types of stakeholders should engage in what types of planning activities. The reason for this is that – different to other environmental issues – there is such a limited understanding of how tourism stakeholders view the challenge of Peak Oil that this author did not feel in a position to speculate on recommendations. It is important to undertake more research on how the different players in tourism view the oil challenge, and how much they are willing to engage in proactive planning to prepare for post-peak tourism.

This book has presented knowledge on what this author sees as the most critical challenge for tourism, but maybe also an opportunity to move onto more sustainable development pathways. It is highly unlikely that people will want to stop travelling. Thus, tourism will continue to exist – even in a 'post-peak' world. It seems, however, that the past decades in which we have seen a democratisation of air travel to an ever-increasing array of exotic destinations may come to an end. Instead there is likely to be a polarisation into a small travelling elite of luxury travellers, versus the majority of tourists who face contracting options of travel choices. Moving 'back in time' – or re-learning old practices – towards a more localised world represents more than a change of tourism practices, but reflects a much broader societal change of how we live and think. Tourism is then only symptomatic of a de-globalising world of shortened supply chains and increasing local identities with strengthened community networks and cooperation.

Areas for future research to support a transition to low-carbon, post-peak tourism will inevitably focus on a number of key areas. First, purposeful integration with the disciplines of engineering and transportation research will greatly benefit tourism research with a view of developing renewable energy technologies for tourism operations, as well as fossil-fuel free, efficient and smart transport systems. Second, sustainability science, with a focus on the sociology and psychology of consumption and 'happiness' (or subjective well-being), will help understand and shape new types of tourist behaviour. With that, values and norms will change as well. And third, more research into policy and governance for tourism in a resource constrained world is essential to enable necessary transitions and incentivise low-carbon models of tourist destinations and systems. Future tourism research can build on the growing body of research on sustainable tourism, climate change and tourism, and tourism resilience, but a clearer focus on resource constraints and oil efficiency will be necessary.

Peak Oil will force us to reconsider travel and tourism as a privilege and a 'special time'. It will also accelerate efforts to implement sustainable tourism and create new systems that are more viable and resilient. It is hoped that this book presents the beginning of a dialogue and cooperation for the future of tourism in an oil-constrained world, informed by critical thinking about the management of planetary boundaries.

References

Aall, C. (2010) Energy use and leisure consumption in Norway: An analysis and reduction strategy. *Journal of Sustainable Tourism* 19 (6), 729–745.

Airbus (2013) Future journeys 2013–2032. Global market forecast. See www.airbus.com/company/market/forecast/?eID=dam_frontend_push&docID=33752 (accessed 20 January 2014).

Aleklett, K. (2012) *Peeking at Peak Oil*. New York, Heidelberg, Dordrecht, London: Springer.

Aleklett, K., Höök, M., Jakobsson, K., Lardelli, K., Snowden, S. and Soderbergh, B. (2010) The peak of the oil age. *Energy Policy* 38 (3), 1398–1414.

Ali, Y., Mustafa, M., Al-Mashaqbah, S., Mashal, K. and Mohsen, M. (2008) Potential of energy savings in the hotel sector in Jordan. *Energy Conversion and Management* 49, 3391–3397.

Altés Arlandis, A. (2012) Towards the end of tourism: Global architecture, fantasy and void in the age of withdrawal. In International Forum on Urbanism (IFoU) (ed.) *6th Conference of the International Forum on Urbanism (IFoU): TOURBANISM* (pp. 1–9). Barcelona: International Forum on Urbanism-Escola Técnica Superior d'Arquitectura de Barcelona.

Álvarez, L.J., Hurtado, S., Sánchez, I. and Thomas, C. (2011) The impact of oil price change on Spanish and euro area consumer price inflation. *Economic Modelling* 28, 422–431.

Amadeus (2009) Future traveller tribes 2020. Report for the air travel industry. See www.amadeus.com/amadeus/documents/corporate/TravellerTribes.pdf (accessed 2 January 2013).

Amos, P., Bullock, D. and Sondhi, J. (2010) *High-Speed Rail: The Fast Track to Economic Development?* Beijing: World Bank.

Antimova, R., Nawijn, J. and Peeters, P. (2012) The awareness/attitude-gap in sustainable tourism: A theoretical perspective. *Tourism Review* 67 (3), 7–16.

Apelbaum Consulting Group (2007) *South Australian Transport Facts 2007*. Mulgrave, Victoria: Apelbaum Consulting Group.

Atmosfair (2010) CO_2 Emissionsrechner fuer Hochseekreuzfahrten. Dokumentation der Berechnungsmethode Version 1.1. See www.atmosfair.de/fileadmin/user_upload/Medienecke/Downloadmaterial/externeDoku_v1_1.pdf (accessed 20 November 2013).

Bailey, I., Hopkins, R. and Wilson, G. (2010) Some things old, some things new: The spatial representations and politics of change of the Peak Oil relocalisation movement. *Geoforum* 41 (4), 595–605.

Bakhtiari, A. (2004) World oil production capacity model suggests output peak by 2006–07. *Oil and Gas Journal* 102 (16), 18–19.

Balaban, O. and Tsatskin, A. (2010) The paradox of oil reserve forecasts: The political implications of predicting oil reserves and oil consumption. *Energy Policy* 38 (3), 1340–1344.

Bandivadekar, A., Bodek, K., Cheah, L., Evans, C., Groode, T., Heywood, J., Kasseris, E., Kromer, K. and Weiss, M. (2008) *On the Road in 2035: Reducing Transportation's Petroleum Consumption and GHG Emissions*. Cambridge, MA: Laboratory for Energy and the Environment, Massachusetts Institute of Technology.

Bardi, U. (2009) Peak Oil: The four stages of a new idea. *Energy* 34, 323–326.

Baron, T., Tuchschmid, M., Martinetti, G. and Pépion, D. (2011) *High Speed Rail and Sustainability. Background Report: Methodology and Results of Carbon Footprint analysis*. Paris: International Union of Railways (UIC).

Barr, S., Shaw, G., Coles, T. and Prillwitz, J. (2010) 'A holiday is a holiday': Practicing sustainability, home and away. *Journal of Transport Geography* 18 (3), 474–481.

Bartlett, A. (2000) An analysis of US and world oil production patterns using Hubbert-style curves. *Mathematical Geology* 32 (1), 1–17.

Basham, M. (2010) *Standard & Poor's Industry Surveys: Restaurant*. New York: McGraw-Hill.

Bass, M.S., Finer, M., Jenkins, C.N., Kreft, H., Cisneros-Heredia, D.F., McCracken, S., Pitman, N.C.A., English, P.H., Swing, K., Villa, G., Di Fiore, A., Voigt, C.C. and Kunz, T.H. (2010) Global conservation significance of Ecuador's Yasuni National Park. *PLoS ONE* 5 (1), e8767. doi:10.1371/journal.pone.0008767.

Baumann, Z. (2000) *Liquid Modernity*. Cambridge: Polity.

Becken, S. (2002a) Energy use in the New Zealand tourism sector. Doctor of Philosophy Thesis, Lincoln University. See http://researcharchive.lincoln.ac.nz/handle/10182/440 (accessed 1 October 2011).

Becken, S. (2002b) Tourism and transport in New Zealand – Implications for energy use. TRREC Report No. 54, July, Lincoln University.

Becken, S. (2005a) Harmonizing climate change adaptation and mitigation. The case of tourist resorts in Fiji. *Global Environmental Change – Part A* 15 (4), 381–393.

Becken, S. (2005b) The role of tourist icons for sustainable tourism. *Journal of Vacation Marketing* 11 (1), 17–26.

Becken, S. (2005c) Towards sustainable tourism transport – An analysis of coach tourism in New Zealand. *Tourism Geographies* 7 (1), 1–20.

Becken, S. (2007) Tourists' perception of international air travel's impact on the global climate and potential climate change policies. *Journal of Sustainable Tourism* 15 (4), 351–368.

Becken, S. (2009) Global challenges for tourism and transport: How will climate change and energy affect the future of tourist travel? In S. Page (ed.) *Transport and Tourism – Global Perspectives* (3rd edn; pp. 328–342). Harlow: Pearson Education Limited.

Becken, S. (2011) A critical review of tourism and oil. *Annals of Tourism Research* 38 (2), 359–379.

Becken, S. (2012) Shifters and shapers for the future of tourism. In C. Leigh, C. Webster and I. Stanislav (eds) *Future Tourism – Political, Social and Economic Challenges* (pp. 80–91). London, New York: Routledge.

Becken, S. (2013a) Developing a framework for assessing resilience of tourism sub-systems to climatic factors. *Annals of Tourism Research* 43, 506–528.

Becken, S. (2013b) Tourism and climate change – An evolving knowledge domain. *Tourism Management Perspectives* 6, 53–62.

Becken, S. (2014) Oil depletion or a market problem? A framing analysis of 'Peak Oil in *The Economist* News Magazine'. *Energy Research and Social Science* 2, 125–134.

Becken, S. and Carboni, A. (2008) Managing energy use in tourism businesses – Survey results. LEaP Report 4, Lincoln University. See www.leap.ac.nz (accessed 1 March 2013).

Becken, S. and Cavanagh, J. (2003) Energy efficiency trend analysis of the tourism sector. Research Contract Report: LC02/03/293. Prepared for the Energy Efficiency and Conservation Authority.

Becken, S. and Friedl, H. (2014) Dubai ... die letzte Erfolgsstory fossiler Wachstumsträume? Presented: 12. Salzburger Tourismusforum, Salzburg, Austria, 27–28 März.

Becken, S. and Hay, J. (2007) *Tourism and Climate Change – Risks and Opportunities.* Clevedon: Channel View Publications.

Becken, S. and Hay, J. (2012) *Climate Change and Tourism: From Policy to Practice.* London: Routledge.

Becken, S. and Job, H. (2014) Protected areas in an era of global-local change. *Journal of Sustainable Tourism* 22 (4), 507–527.

Becken, S. and Lane, B. (2006) Tourism and transport – The sustainability dilemma. *Special Issue: Journal of Sustainable Tourism* 14 (20).

Becken, S. and Lennox, J. (2012) Implications of a long term increase in oil prices for tourism. *Tourism Management* 33 (1), 133–142.

Becken, S. and Patterson, M. (2006) Measuring national greenhouse gas emissions from tourism as an important component towards sustainable tourism development. *Journal of Sustainable Tourism* 14 (4), 323–338.

Becken, S. and Schiff, A. (2011) Distance models for New Zealand international tourists and the role of transport prices. *Journal of Travel Research* 50 (3), 303–320.

Becken, S. and Simmons, D. (2002) Understanding energy consumption patterns of tourist attractions and activities in New Zealand. *Tourism Management* 23 (4), 343–354.

Becken, S. and Simmons, D. (2005) Tourism, fossil fuel consumption and the impact on the global climate. In M. Hall and J. Higham (eds) *Tourism, Recreation and Climate Change: International Perspectives* (pp. 192–206). Clevedon: Channel View Publications.

Becken, S. and Wilson, J. (2008) Environmental attitudes and fuel saving behaviour by KEA Campers customers. LEaP Report 6, Lincoln University. See www.leap.ac.nz (accessed 1 March 2013).

Becken, S., Frampton, C. and Simmons, D. (2001) Energy consumption patterns in the accommodation sector – The New Zealand case. *Ecological Economics* 39 (3), 371–386.

Becken, S., Simmons, D. and Frampton, C. (2003) Energy use associated with different travel choices. *Tourism Management* 24 (3), 267–278.

Becken, S., Carboni, A., Vuletich, S. and Schiff, A. (2008) Analysis of tourist consumption, expenditure and prices for key international visitor segments. LEaP Report 7, November. See www.leap.ac.nz (accessed 1 April 2013).

Becken, S., Ngyen, M. and Schiff, A. (2010) Developing an economic framework for tourism and oil. LEaP Report 12. See www.lincoln.ac.nz/leap (accessed 1 March 2014).

Becker, C. and George, B.P. (2011) Rapid rail transit and tourism development in the United States. *Tourism Geographies* 13 (3), 381–397.

Bell, A. (2009) *Peak Water: Civilization and the World's Water Crisis.* Cornwall: MPG Books.

Benes, J., Chauvet, M., Kamenik, O., Kumhof, M., Laxton, D., Mursula, S. and Selody, J. (2012) *The Future of Oil: Geology versus Technology*. IMF Working Paper. WP/12/09.

Bennett, A. (2010) People power forces government u-turn on mining. *New Zealand Herald*. See www.nzherald.co.nz/nz/news/article.cfm?c_id=1&objectid=10659967 (accessed 20 June 2010).

Bentley, R.W. and Zittel, W.G. (2013) Limits to global energy supply. Presented at the Global Energy Systems Conference, Edinburgh, 26–28 June.

Bijsterbosch, M. (2008) The macroeconomic impact of oil price shock and the policy response. EU Countries Division, Tallin, 21 August.

Boeing (2013) Current market outlook 2013–2032. See www.boeing.com/assets/pdf/commercial/cmo/pdf/Boeing_Current_Market_Outlook_2013.pdf (accessed 25 January 2014).

Bohdanowicz, P. and Martinac, I. (2007) Determinants and benchmarking of resource consumption in hotels – Case study of Hilton international and Scandic in Europe. *Energy Build* 39, 82–95.

Bonham, C., Gangnes, B. and Zhou, T. (2009) Modelling tourism: A fully identified VECM approach. *International Journal of Forecasting* 25, 531–549.

Bosshart, D. and Frick, K. (2006) The future of leisure travel – Trend study, Kuoni. See www.gdi.ch (accessed 5 January 2012).

Bows, A., Anderson, K. and Peeters, P. (2009) Air transport, climate change and tourism. *Tourism and Hospitality Planning and Development* 6 (1), 7–20.

BP (2012) *Statistical Review of World Energy*. London: BP.

BP (2013) *Statistical Review of World Energy*. London: BP.

BP (2014) *Statistical Review of World Energy*. London: BP.

Brandt, A.R. (2009) Greenhouse gas emissions from oil substitutes: Dynamics, resources, and systems behaviour. Stanford Energy Seminar, 3 September. See https://pangea.stanford.edu/researchgroups/eao/sites/default/files/Brandt_Stanford_Energy_Seminar_final_1.pdf (accessed 20 October 2013).

Brandt, A.R. and Farrell, A.E. (2006) Scraping the bottom of the barrel: CO2 emissions consequences of a transition to low-quality and synthetic petroleum resources. *Climatic Change* 84, 241–263.

Bridge, G. (2010) Geographies of peak oil: The other carbon problem. *Geoforum* 41 (4), 523–530.

Bridge, G. and A. Wood (2010) Less is more: Spectres of scarcity and the politics of resource access in the upstream oil sector. *Geoforum* 41 (4), 565–576.

Bristow, A.L., Tight, M., Pridmore, A. and May, A.D. (2008) Developing pathways to low carbon land-based passenger transport in Great Britain by 2050. *Energy Policy* 36, 3427–3435.

Brons, M., Pels, E., Nijkamp, P. and Rietveld, P. (2002) Price elasticities of demand for passenger air travel: A meta-analysis. *Journal of Air Transport Management* 8, 165–175.

Brouwer, R., Brander, L. and Van Beukering, P. (2008) 'A convenient truth': Air travel passengers' willingness to pay to offset their CO2 emissions. *Climatic Change* 90, 299–313.

Buckley, R. (2011) Tourism under climate change: Will slow travel supersede short breaks? *AMBIO* 40, 328–331.

Campbell, C. (2003) Industry urged to watch for regular oil production peaks, depletion signals. *Oil and Gas Journal* 102 (27), 38–45.

Campbell, C. and Heapes, S. (2008) *An Atlas of Oil and Gas Depletion*. Huddersfield: Jeremy Mills Publishing Limited.

Carus, F. (2011) Demand for uranium threatens Grand Canyon biodiversity. *Guardian*, 17 February. See www.guardian.co.uk/environment/2011/feb/17/uranium-demand-grand-canyon-biodiversity (accessed 20 October 2012).

Carvalho, A. and Burgess, J. (2005) Cultural circuits of climate change in UK broadsheet newspapers, 1985–2003. *Risk Analysis* 25 (6), 1457–1469.

Centre for Aviation (2013) *World Aviation Yearbook 2013: Global Overview*. See http://centreforaviation.com/reports/ (accessed 1 November 2013).

CERA (2008) No evidence of precipitous fall on horizon for world oil production: Global 4.5% decline rate means no near term peak. CERA/HIS Study. Cambridge, MA: Cambridge Energy Research Associations, Inc. See www.cera.com/aspx/cda/public1/news/pressReleases/pressReleaseList.aspxS (accessed 1 September 2010).

Chan, W.W., Li, D., Mak, B. and Liu, L. (2013) Evaluating the application of solar energy for hot water provision: An action research of independent hotel. *International Journal of Hospitality Management* 33, 76–84.

Chapman, I. (2013) The end of Peak Oil? Why this topic is still relevant despite recent denials. *Energy Policy* 64, 93–101.

Chatziantoniou, I., Filis, G., Eeckels, B. and Apostolakis, A. (2013) Oil prices, tourism income and economic growth: A structural VAR approach for European Mediterranean countries. *Tourism Management* 36, 331–341

Chèze, B., Gastineau, P. and Chevallier, J. (2011) Forecasting world and regional aviation jet fuel demands to the mid-term (2025). *Energy Policy* 39 (9), 5147–5158.

Cho, A. (2010) Energy's tricky trade-offs. *Science* 329, 786–787.

City of Portland Peak Oil Task Force (2007) Descending the oil peak: Navigating the transition from oil and natural gas. See www.portlandonline.com/shared/cfm/image.cfm?id=145732 (accessed 1 November 2013).

Cobb, K. (2012) Why unconventional oil will never provide the volumes we hope for. OilPrice.com. See http://oilprice.com/Energy/Crude-Oil/Why-Unconventional-Oil-Will-Never-Provide-the-Volumes-that-we-Hope-For.html (accessed 12 November 2013).

Cohen, D. (2007) Does the Peak Oil 'myth' just fall down? Our response to CERA. *The Oil Drum*. See www.theoildrum.com/story/2006/11/15/83857/186 (accessed 20 October 2013).

Cohen, S. (2001) *States of Denial. Knowing about Atrocities and Suffering.* Cambridge: Polity Press.

Cohen, S. and Higham, J. (2010) Eyes wide shut? UK consumer perceptions on aviation climate impacts and travel decisions to New Zealand. *Current Issues in Tourism* 14, 323–335.

Cohen, S., Higham, J. and Cavaliere, C. (2011) Binge flying: Behavioural addiction and climate change. *Annals of Tourism Research* 38, 1070–1089.

Cole, S. and Razak, V. (2009) Tourism as future. *Futures* 41 (6), 335–345.

Cox, W. (2012) The expanding economic pie & grinding poverty. See www.newgeography.com/content/003271-the-expanding-economic-pie-grinding-poverty (accessed 29 April 2014).

Crouch, G. (1992) Effect of income and price on international tourism. *Annals of Tourism Research* 19, 643–664.

Crouch, G. (1995) A meta-analysis of tourism demand. *Annals of Tourism Research* 22 (1), 103–118.

Crouch, G., Oppewal, H., Huybers, T., Dolnicar, S., Louviere, J. and Devinney, T. (2007) Discretionary expenditure and tourism consumption: Insights from a choice experiment. *Journal of Travel Research* 45, 247–258.

Cruise Lines International Association (CLIA) (2013) North America cruise industry update. See www.cruising.org/sites/default/files/pressroom/CruiseIndustryUpdate 2013FINAL.pdf (accessed 10 December 2013).

Cruise Market Watch (2013) 2013 cruise trends forecast. See www.cruisemarketwatch. com/articles/cruise-market-watch-announces-2013-cruise-trends-forecast/ (accessed 26 November 2012).

Commonwealth Scientific and Industrial Organisation (CSIRO) (2008) Fuel for thought – The future of transport fuels: Challenges and opportunities. See www.csiro.au/ Outcomes/Energy/Carbon-Footprint/Fuel-For-Thought-Report.aspx (accessed 20 February 2013).

Commonwealth Scientific and Industrial Organisation (CSIRO) (2013) The future of tourism in Queensland: Global megatrends creating opportunities and challenges over the coming twenty years. Report prepared for the Department of Tourism, Major Events, Small Business and the Commonwealth Games. See www.csiro.au/ en/Portals/Partner/Futures/Future-of-Tourism-in-QLD.aspx#move (accessed 20 September 2013).

Commonwealth Scientific and Industrial Organisation (CSIRO) (2014) *A World Without Wires*. EP 142132. Australia: CSIRO.

Curtis, F. (2009) Peak globalization: Climate change, oil depletion and global trade. *Ecological Economics* 69, 427–434.

Dale, M. and Benson, S.M. (2013) Energy balance of the global photovoltaic (PV) industry – Is the PV industry a net electricity producer? *Environmental Science & Technology* 47 (7), 3482–3489.

Dalton, G.J., Lockington, D.A. and Baldock, T.E. (2008) Feasibility analysis of stand-alone renewable energy supply options for a large hotel. *Renewable Energy* 33 (7), 1475–1490.

Dalton, G.J., Lockington, D.A. and Baldock, T.E. (2009) Case study feasibility analysis of renewable energy supply options for small to medium-sized tourist accommodations. *Renewable Energy* 34 (4), 1134–1144.

Daly, H.E. (1978) On thinking about energy in the future. *Natural Resources Forum* 3 (1), 19–26.

Daly, H.E. (2008) A steady-state economy. A thinkpiece. Presented at Sustainable Development Commission, UK, 24 April. See www.sd-commission.org.uk/data/files/ publications/Herman_Daly_thinkpiece.pdf (accessed 11 May 2014).

Davis, B. and Mangan, J. (1992) Family expenditure on hotels and holiday. *Annals of Tourism Research* 19, 691–669.

Davis, G. (2003) Meeting future energy needs. *The Bridge (National Academy of Engineering)* 33 (2), 16–21.

De Almeida, P. and Silva, P.D. (2009) The peak of oil production – Timings and market recognition. *Energy Policy* 37, 1267–1276.

Decrop, A. (1999) Tourists' decision-making and behavior process. In A. Pizam and Y. Mansfeld (eds) *Consumer Behavior in Travel and Tourism* (pp. 103–134). New York: The Haworth Hospitality Press.

Deffeyes, K.S. (2001) *Hubbert's Peak – The Impending World Oil Shortage*. Princeton, NJ: Princeton University Press.

Deffeyes, K.S. (2005) *Beyond Oil: The View from Hubbert's Peak*. New York: Hill and Wang.

Deloitte Access Economics (2012) Economic contribution of the cruise sector. See www. deloitte.com/assets/Dcom-Australia/Local%20Assets/Documents/news-research/Press

%20releases/Simon%20Rushton/The%20economic%20contribution%20of%20the%
20cruise%20sector%20to%20Australia.pdf (accessed 20 February 2014).

Dickinson, J. and Dickinson, J. (2006) Local transport and social representations: Challenging the assumptions for sustainable tourism. *Special Issue Tourism and Transport: The Sustainability Dilemma* 14 (2), 192–208.

Dickinson, J. and Lumsdon, L. (2010) *Slow Travel and Tourism*. London, Washington, DC: Earthscan.

Dickinson, J.E., Lumsdon, L. and Robbins, D. (2011) Slow travel: Issues for tourism and climate change. *Journal of Sustainable Tourism* 19 (3), 281–300.

Dobruszkes, F. (2006) An analysis of European low-cost airlines and their networks. *Journal of Transport Geography* 14 (4), 249–264.

Dodson, J. and Sipe, N. (2008) *Shocking the Suburbs. Oil Vulnerability in the Australian City*. Sydney: University of New South Wales Press Ltd.

Department of Energy (DOE) Office of Energy Efficiency and Renewable Energy (EERE) (2006) Report to Congress on Renewable Energy Resource Assessment Information for the United States, January 2011 (EPACT) Prepared by the National Renewable Energy Laboratory.

Draper, S., Goodman, J., Hardyment, R. and Murray, V. (2009) Tourism 2023. Four scenarios, a vision and a strategy for UK outbound travel and tourism. Forum for the Future. See www.forumforthefuture.org/projects/travel-and-tourism (accessed 15 January 2010).

Dritsakis, N. (2004) Cointegration analysis of German and British tourism demand for Greece. *Tourism Management* 25, 111–119.

Dubois, G., Peeters, P., Ceron, J.P. and Gössling, S. (2011) The future tourism mobility of the world population: Emission growth versus climate policy. *Transportation Research Part A* 45 (10), 1031–1042.

Dwyer, L., Edwards, D., Mistilis, N., Roman, C., Scott, N. and Cooper, C. (2008) *Megatrends Underpinning Tourism to 2020. Analysis of Key Drivers for Change*. Gold Coast, Australia: CRC for Sustainable Tourism.

Dwyer, L., Forsyth, P. and Rao, P. (2001) PPPs and the price competitiveness of international tourism destinations. Joint World Bank–OECD Seminar on Purchasing Power Parities. Recent Advances in Methods and Applications, Washington, DC, 30 January to 2 February.

Dwyer, L., Forsyth, P., Spurr, R. and Hoque, S. (2010) Estimating the carbon footprint of Australian tourism. *Journal of Sustainable Tourism* 18 (3), 355–366.

Dwyer, L., Forsyth, P., Spurr, R. and Hoque, S. (2013) Economic impacts of a carbon tax on the Australian tourism industry. *Journal of Travel Research* 52 (2), 143–155.

Eaton, B. and Holding, D. (1996) The evaluation of public transport alternatives to the car in British national parks. *Journal of Transport Geography* 4 (1), 55–65.

Energy Information Administration (EIA) (2006) *Definitions of Petroleum Products and Other Terms*. Washington, DC: US Energy Information Administration.

Energy Information Administration (EIA) (2010) *International Energy Outlook 2010*. Washington, DC: US Energy Information Administration.

Energy Information Administration (EIA) (2013) Countries. Top world oil net importers, 2012. See www.eia.gov/countries/index.cfm?topL=imp (accessed 20 September 2013).

Entman, R.M. (2001) Representations in mass media. In N.J. Smelser and P.B. Baltes (eds) *International Encyclopaedia of the Social & Behavioural Sciences*. Oxford: Pergamon.

European Commission (2013) New EU infrastructure policy website announcement, 17 October. See http://ec.europa.eu/transport/themes/infrastructure/news/ten-t-corridors_en.htm (accessed 20 February 2013).

European Travel Commission (2004) Tourism trends for Europe. See www.etc-corporate. org (accessed 20 October 2011).

Farrell, B.H. and Twining-Ward, L. (2004) Reconceptualising tourism. *Annals of Tourism Research* 31 (2), 274–295.

Field, C.B., Campbell, J.E. and Lobell, D.B. (2008) Biomass energy: The scale of the potential resource. *Trends in Ecology and Evolution* 23 (2), 65–72.

Finer, M. and Orta-Martinez, M. (2010) A second hydrocarbon boom threatens the Peruvian Amazon: Trends, projections and policy implications. *Environmental Research Letters* 2010, 5. doi: 10.1088/1748-9326/5/1/014012

Fischer, A., Peters, V., Neebe, M., Vavra, J., Kriel, A., Lapka, M. and Megyesi, B. (2012) Climate change? No, wise resource use is the issue: Social representations of energy, climate change and the future. *Environmental Policy and Governance* 22, 161–176.

Fleischer, A. and Rivlin, J. (2008) More or better?: Quantity and quality issues in tourism consumption. *Journal of Travel Research* 47 (3), 285–294.

Flynn, D. (2011) Qantas hikes fuel surcharges up to 40%, adds fuel charge to frequent flyer award tickets. Australian Business Traveller, 19 April. See www.ausbt.com.au/qantas-hikes-fuel-surcharges-up-to-40-adds-fuel-charge-to-frequent-flyer-award-tic kets (accessed 5 May 2013).

Fournier, D.F. and Westervelt, E.T. (2005) Energy trends and their implications for US Army installations. ERDC/CERL TR-05-21. See http://oai.dtic.mil/oai/oai?verb=getRecord&metadataPrefix=html&identifier=ADA440265 (accessed 3 January 2013).

Francis, G., Humphreys, I., Ison, S. and Aicken, M. (2006) Where next for low cost airlines? A spatial and temporal comparative study. *Journal of Transport Geography* 14 (2), 83–94.

Frankfurt School-UNEP Centre/BNEF (2014) Global trends in renewable energy investment 2014. Key findings. See www.unep.org/pdf/Green_energy_2013-Key_findings. pdf (accessed 19 April 2014).

Friedl, H. (2012) Globale Tourismusethik: Königsweg oder Utopie? Eine Abenteuerreise vom Wesen des Reisens zum nachhaltigen Tourismus. In U. Bechmann, and C. Friedl (eds) *Mobilitäten. Beiträge von Vortragenden der Montagsakademie 2011/12* (pp. 229–304). Graz: Grazer Universitätsverlag Leykam.

Friedrichs, J. (2010) Global energy crunch: How different parts of the world would react to a peak oil scenario. *Energy Policy* 38 (8), 4562–4569.

Friedrichs, J. (2011) Peak energy and climate change: The double bind of post-normal science. *Futures* 43, 469–477.

Fullagar, S., Markwell, K. and Wilson, E. (eds) (2012) *Slow Tourism: Experiences and Mobilities.* Bristol: Channel View Publications.

Gagnon, N., Hall, C.A.S. and Brinker, L. (2009) A preliminary investigation of energy return on energy investment for global oil and gas production. *Energies* 2, 490–503.

Gangl, K., Kastlunger, B., Kirchler, E. and Voracek, M. (2012) Confidence in the economy in times of crisis: Social representations of experts and laypeople. *The Journal of Socio-Economics* 41, 603–614.

Gardiner, S. and Scott, N. (2014) Successful tourism clusters: Passion in paradise. *Annals of Tourism Research* 46, 171–173.

German Advisory Council on the Environment (2011) Pathways towards a 100% renewable electricity system. Chapter 10: Executive summary and recommendations (provisional translation). See www.umweltrat.de/SharedDocs/Downloads/EN/02_Special_Reports/2011_01_Pathways_Chapter10_ProvisionalTranslation. pdf?_blob=publicationFile (accessed 1 November 2013).

Gillen, A. (2004) *Air Travel Demand Elasticities: Concepts, Issues and Measurements.* Department of Finance Canada.

Goodstein, D. (2004) *Out of Gas – The End of the Age of Oil.* New York: W.W. Norton.

Gössling, S. (2000) Sustainable tourism development in developing countries: Some aspects of energy-use. *Journal of Sustainable Tourism* 8 (5), 410–425.

Gössling, S. (2002) Global environmental consequences of tourism. *Global Environmental Change* 12, 283–302.

Gössling, S. (2010) *Carbon Management in Tourism: Mitigating the Impacts on Climate Change.* Oxford: Routledge.

Gössling, S., Haglund, L., Källgren, H., Revahl, M. and Hultman, J. (2009) Voluntary carbon offsetting by Swedish air travellers: Towards the co-creation of environmental value? *Current Issues in Tourism* 12, 1–19.

Gössling, S., Scott, D., Hall, C.M., Ceron, J.P. and Dubois, G. (2012) Consumer behaviour and demand response of tourists to climate change. *Annals of Tourism Research* 39 (1), 36–58.

Greer, J. (2008) *The Long Descent: A User's Guide to the End of the Industrial Age.* Gabriola Island, BC: New Society Publishers.

Gross, B.L. (1987) Time scarcity: Interdisciplinary perspectives and implications for consumer behaviour. *Research in Consumer Behavior* 2, 1–54.

Gross, R., Leach, M. and Bauen, A. (2003) Progress in renewable energy. *Environment International* 29, 105–122.

Groundswell Group (2007) The impact of peak oil on rural communities, Cornwall, July. See www.groundswellcornwall.org/files/u1/peak_oil_rural_communities.pdf (accessed 12 February 2014).

Guido-Sequeira, H. (2010) Geothermal energy exploration in environmental protected areas in Costa Rica. Proceedings of the World Geothermal Congress, Bali, Indonesia, 25–29 April. See http://b-dig.iie.org.mx/BibDig/P10-0464/pdf/0205.pdf (accessed 24 June 2011).

Gupta, E. (2008) Oil vulnerability index of oil-importing countries. *Energy Policy* 36, 1195–1211.

Hall, C.A.S. and Day, J.W. Jr. (2009) Revisiting the limits to growth after peak oil. *American Scientist* 97, 230–237.

Hall, M. (2010) Changing paradigms and global change: From sustainable to steady-state tourism. *Tourism Recreation Research* 35 (2), 131–143.

Hannam, K., Butler, G. and Paris, C.M. (2014) Developments and key issues in tourism mobilities. *Annals of Tourism Research* 44, 171–185.

Hares, A., Dickinson, J. and Wilkes, K. (2010) Climate change and the air travel decisions of UK tourists. *Journal of Transport Geography* 18, 466–473.

Hawaii Tourism Authority (2013) Historical visitor statistics. See www.hawaiitourismau thority.org/research/reports/historical-visitor-statistics/ (accessed 11 December 2013).

Henderson, J., Lim, C. and Wang, Y. (2011) Chinese outbound tourism and the market in Singapore. *Journal of Hospitality & Tourism* 9 (2), 56–75.

Heinberg, R. (2007) *Peak Everything. Waking Up to the Century of Declines.* Gabriola, BC: New Society Publishers.

Heinberg, R. (2009) Searching for a miracle: 'Net Energy' limits and the fate of industrial society. Post Carbon Institute & International Forum on Globalization, September. See www.postcarbon.org/report/44377-searching-for-a-miracle (accessed 20 February 2013).

Heinberg, R. (2011) *The End of Growth: Adapting to Our New Economic Reality*. Gabriola Island: New Society Publishers.

Heinberg, R. (2013) *Snake Oil. How Fracking's False Promise of Plenty Imperils Our Future*. Santa Rosa: Post Carbon Institute.

Hirsch, R.L. (2008) Mitigation of maximum world oil production: Shortage scenarios. *Energy Policy* 36, 881–889.

Hirsch, R.L., Bezdek, R. and Wendling, R. (2005) Peaking of world oil production: Impacts, mitigation and risk management. See www.netl.doe.gov/publications/others/pdf/Oil_Peaking_NETL.pdf (accessed 20 March 2014).

Höök, M. (2010) Coal and oil: The dark monarchs of global energy. Understanding supply and extraction patterns and their importance for future production. Digital comprehensive summaries of Uppsala dissertations from the Faculty of Science and Technology 760, Uppsala.

Howitt, O., Revol, V.G.N., Smith, I.J. and Rodger, C.J. (2010) Carbon emissions from international cruise ship passengers' travel to and from New Zealand. *Energy Policy* 38 (5), 2552–2560.

Howitt, R. (2001) *Rethinking Resource Management: Justice, Sustainability and Indigenous Peoples*. London: Routledge.

Hongkong and Shanghai Banking Corporation (HSBC) (no date) In the future. See www.hsbc.com/about-hsbc/advertising/in-the-future (accessed 12 April 2014).

Huber, M.T. (2008) Energising historical materialism: Fossil fuels, space and the capitalist mode of production. *Geoforum* 40, 105–115.

Hughes, J.D. (2013) Drill, baby drill: Can unconventional fuels usher in a new era of energy abundance? Post Carbon Institute. See www.postcarbon.org/reports/DBD-report-FINAL.pdf (accessed 12 November 2012).

Huntington, H. (2005) The economic consequences of higher crude oil prices. Energy Modelling Forum SR9. See www.emf.stanford.edu/files/pubs/22457/EMFSR9.pdf (accessed 12 November 2012).

Hyde, K. (1999) A hedonic perspective on independent vacation planning, decision-making and behavior. In A. Woodside, G. Crouch, J. Mazanec, M. Oppermann and M. Sakai (eds) *Consumer Psychology of Tourism, Hospitality and Leisure* (pp. 177–191). Wallingford: CABI Publishing.

Hyde, K.F. (2008) Independent traveler decision-making. In A. Woodside (ed.) *Advances in Culture, Tourism and Hospitality Research* (Vol. 2, pp. 43–151). Bingley, UK: Emerald Group Publishing Limited.

Institute for Sensible Transport (2010) Transport and oil vulnerability analysis for the Lake Macquarie Region. Prepared for Lake Macquarie City Council by the Institute for Sensible Transport, July. See www.sensibletransport.org.au/sites/sensibletransport.org.au/files/Lake%20Mac_01.12_0.pdf (accessed 19 May 2014).

Institute for Sensible Transport (2012) Peak Oil and the University of Tasmania. Risk assessment and response stage one. See www.sensibletransport.org.au/sites/sensible-transport.org.au/files/UTAS%20Peak%20Oil%20Risk%20Assessment%20%26%20Response_LOWRES.pdf (accessed 19 May 2014).

Intergovernmental Panel for Climate Change (IPCC) (2006) *IPCC Guidelines for National Greenhouse Gas Inventories*. See www.ipcc-nggip.iges.or.jp/public/2006gl/index.html (accessed 20 January 2013).

International Air Transport Association (IATA) (2009) The technology roadmap report. See www.iata.org/SiteCollectionDocuments/Documents/Technology_Roadmap_May2009.pdf (accessed 2 January 2011).

International Air Transport Association (IATA) (2012) Rising oil prices reducing profitability – Regional differences widen. Press release, March. See www.iata.org/ pressroom/pr/pages/2012-03-20-01.aspx (accessed 20 September 2013).

International Air Transport Association (IATA) (2013a) Fact sheet: Fuel. See www.iata. org/pressroom/facts_figures/fact_sheets/Documents/fuel-fact-sheet.pdf (accessed 20 December 2013).

International Air Transport Association (IATA) (2013b) Fact sheet: Industry statistics. www.iata.org/pressroom/facts_figures/fact_sheets/Documents/industry-facts.pdf (accessed 20 December 2013).

International Cruise Council Australia (2010) Cruise industry report Australia 2010. See www.cruising.org.au/filelibrary/files/australian%20cruise%20industry%20report% 202010%20final.pdf (accessed 20 February 2014).

International Energy Agency (IEA) (2000) *World Energy Outlook 2000*. Paris: International Energy Agency.

International Energy Agency (IEA) (2004) Analysis of the impact of high oil prices on the global economy. See www.iea.org/papers/2004/High_Oil_Prices.pdf

International Energy Agency (IEA) (2006) *World Energy Outlook 2006*. Paris: International Energy Agency.

International Energy Agency (IEA) (2010) *World Energy Outlook 2010*. Paris: IEA. See www.iea.org/publications/freepublications/publication/weo2010.pdf (accessed 1 March 2013).

International Energy Agency (IEA) (2011) Are we entering a golden age of gas? World Energy Outlook 2011 – Special report. See www.worldenergyoutlook.org/goldena geofgas/ (accessed 20 October 2013).

International Energy Agency (IEA) (2012) *World Energy Outlook 2012*. Paris: International Energy Agency. See www.iea.org (accessed 1 March 2013).

International Energy Agency (IEA) (2013a) About us – Frequently asked questions oil. See www.iea.org/aboutus/faqs/oil/ (accessed 25 December 2013).

International Energy Agency (IEA) (2013b) *Key World Energy Statistics 2013*. Paris: IEA. See www.iea.org

International Maritime Organisation (IMO) (2012) *International Shipping Facts and Figures*. Information Sources on Trade, Safety, Security, Environment. See www.imo.org/ KnowledgeCentre/ShipsAndShippingFactsAndFigures/TheRoleandImportanceof InternationalShipping/Documents/International%20Shipping%20-%20Facts%20and %20Figures.pdf (accessed 30 December 2013).

International Monetary Fund (IMF) (2011) Market-based instruments for international aviation and shipping as a source of climate finance. Background paper for the Report to the G20 on Mobilising Sources of Climate Finance. Report prepared with the World Bank, November. See www.imf.org/external/np/g20/pdf/110411a.pdf (20 November 2013).

International Union of Railways (UIC) (2013) High speed rail in Europe: Lessons learned and experiences. Presentation, 25 October. See www.unece.org/fileadmin/DAM/ trans/doc/2013/sc2/SC2-2013-Pres08e.pdf (accessed 12 December 2013).

International Renewable Energy Agency (IRENA) (2012) Studies on renewable energy potential. See www.irena.org/potential_studies/index.aspx (accessed 14 April 2014).

International Renewable Energy Agency (IRENA) (2014) REmap 2030. A renewable energy roadmap. See http://irena.org/remap/REmap%20Summary%20of%20findings_ final_links.pdf (accessed 12 April 2014).

Jackson, P. (2006) *Why the Peak Oil Theory Falls Down – Myths, Legends, and the Future of Oil.* Cambridge, MA: CERA Client Services.

Jackson, P. and Esser, R. (2004) *Triple Witching Hour for Oil Arrives Early in 2004 – But, As Yet, No Real Witches.* Cambridge, MA: CERA, Client Services, April 7.

Jakobsson, K., Söderbergh, Höök, M. and Aleklett, K. (2009) How reasonable are oil production scenarios from public agencies? *Energy Policy* 37, 4809–4818.

Joaquin Valley Geological Services (2013) Learn about oil. See www.sjvgeology.org/oil/index.html (accessed 4 November 2013).

Kelly, J. and Williams, P. (2007) Modelling tourism destination energy consumption and greenhouse gas emissions: Whistler, British Columbia, Canada. *Journal of Sustainable Tourism* 15 (1), 67–90.

Klimenko, V.V., Tereshin, A.G. and Mikushina, O.V. (2009) Global energy and climate of the planet in the XXI century in the context of historical trends. *Russian Journal of General Chemistry* 79 (11), 2469–2476.

Koh, Y., Lee, S. and Choi, C. (2013) The income elasticity of demand and firm performance of US restaurant companies by restaurant type during recession. *Tourism Economics* 19 (4), 855–881.

Kollmuss, A. and Agyeman, J. (2002) Mind the gap: Why do people act environmentally and what are the barriers to pro-environmental behavior? *Environmental Education Research* 8 (3), 239–260.

Koo, T.T.R. and Lohmann, G. (2013) The spatial effects of domestic aviation deregulation: A comparative study of Australian and Brazilian seat capacity. *Journal of Transport Geography* 29, 52–62.

Koppelaar, R. (2006) Oil supply analysis 2006–2007. Peak Oil Netherlands Foundation/ASPO Netherlands, Newsletter 5. See www.peakoil.nl/wp-content/uploads/2006/10/asponl_newsletter_5_2006.pdf (accessed 23 May 2014).

Koppelaar, R. (2007) Oilwatch monthly, November 2007. See http://www.peakoil.nl/wp-content/uploads/2007/09/oilwatch_monthly_september2007.pdf (accessed 03 September 14).

Kristoffersen, B. and Young, S. (2010) Geographies of security and statehood in Norway's 'battle for the north'. *Geoforum* 41 (4), 577–584.

Krumdieck, S., Page, S. and Dantas, A. (2010) Urban form and long-term fuel supply decline: A method to investigate the peak oil risks to essential activities. *Transportation Research Part A* 44, 306–322.

Kulendran, N. and Witt, S.F. (2001) Cointegration versus least squares regression. *Annals of Tourism Research* 28, 291–311.

Kuo, N.W., Lin, C.Y., Chen, P.H. and Chen, Y.W. (2012) An inventory of the energy use and carbon dioxide emissions from island tourism based on a life cycle assessment approach. *Environmental Progress & Sustainable Energy* 31 (3), 459–465.

Labban, M. (2010) Oil in parallax: Scarcity, markets and the financialisation of accumulation. *Geoforum* 41 (4), 541–552.

Laherrere, J. (2003) Will the natural gas supply meet the demand in North America? *International Journal of Global Energy Issues* 19 (1), 1–62.

Laherrere, J. (2007) *Limits to Growth Updated.* Ireland: Association for the Study of Peak Oil and Gas, July. See www.aspo-ireland.org/index.cfm?page=speakerArticles&rbId=9S (accessed 13 January 2014).

Laherrère, J. (2012) Comments on BP Statistical Review 2012. *The Oil Drum*, 13 August. See www.theoildrum.com/node/9389 (accessed 20 November 2013).

Leigh, J. (2011) New tourism in a new society arises from 'Peak Oil'. *Tourismos* 6, 1. See www.chios.aegean.gr/tourism/journal.htm

Leiserowitz, A., Maibach, E., Roser-Renouf, C., Smith, N. and Dawson, E. (2010) Climategate, public opinion and the loss of trust. Working Paper. New Haven, CT. See http://environment.yale.edu/climate/publications/climategate-public-opinion-and-the-loss-of-trust (accessed 24 September 2012).

Lempert, R.J., Popper, S.W. and Bankes, S.C. (2003) *Shaping the Next One Hundred Years. New Methods for Quantitative, Long-term Policy Analysis*. Santa Monica, CA: RAND.

Lennox, J. (2012) Impacts of high oil prices on tourism in New Zealand. *Tourism Economics* 18 (4), 781–800.

Lightfoot, H.D. and Green, C. (2002) An assessment of IPCC Working Group III findings in Climate change 2001: Mitigation of the potential contribution of renewable energies to atmospheric carbon dioxide stabilisation. Centre for Climate and Global Change Research (C2 GCR), C2 GCR Report No. 2002–5.

Likvern, R. (2012) Is shale oil production from Bakken headed for a run with 'the Red Queen'?, 25 September. See www.theoildrum.com/node/9506 (accessed 11 November 2013).

Lim, C. (1997) Review of international tourism demand models. *Annals of Tourism Research* 24 (4), 835–849.

Lim, C., Min, J.C.H. and McAleer, M. (2008) Modelling income effects on long and short haul international travel from Japan. *Tourism Management* 29 (6), 1099–1109.

Lipscy, P.Y. and Schipper, L. (2013) Energy efficiency in the Japanese transport sector. *Energy Policy* 56, 248–258.

Lloyd, B. (2007) The commons revisited: The tragedy continues. *Energy Policy* 35, 5806–5818.

Logar, I. and van den Bergh, J. (2013) The impact of peak oil on tourism in Spain: An input-output analysis of price, demand and economy-wide effects. *Energy* 54, 155–166.

Lohmann, G., Sascha, A., Koch, B. and Pavlovich, K. (2009) From hub to tourist destination – An explorative study of Singapore and Dubai's aviation-based transformation. *Journal of Air Transport Management* 15 (5), 205–211.

Lu, S., Wei, S., Zhang, K., Kong, X. and Wu, W. (2013) Investigation and analysis on the energy consumption of starred hotel buildings in Hainan Province, the tropical region of China. *Energy Conversion and Management* 75, 570–580.

Lumsdon, L. (2000) Transport and tourism: Cycle tourism – A model for sustainable development? *Journal of Sustainable Tourism* 8 (5), 361–376.

Lumsdon, L., Downward, P. and Rhoden, S. (2006) Transport for tourism: Can public transport encourage a modal shift in the day visitor market? *Special Issue Tourism and Transport: The Sustainability Dilemma. Journal of Sustainable Tourism* 14 (2), 139–156.

Lutsey, N. (2008) Prioritizing climate change mitigation alternatives: Comparing transportation technologies to options in other sectors. PhD Dissertation, UCD-ITS-RR-08-15, Institute of Transportation Studies, University of California, Davis.

Lutz, C. and Meyer, B. (2009) Economic impacts of higher oil and gas prices. The role of international trade for Germany. *Energy Economics* 31, 882–887.

Market Economics (2010) Auckland Airport future economic impact assessment: An assessment of the future contribution by Auckland Airport to the Auckland region and New Zealand economies. Report prepared for the Auckland Airport. See www.aucklandairport.co.nz/~/media/Files/Corporate/AIAL EIA Report 2021 and 2031 final 291010.pdf (accessed 15 November 2013).

Matutinović, I. (2009) Oil and the political economy of energy. *Energy Policy* 37, 4251–4258.

Maugeri, L. (2012) Oil: The next revolution. Discussion Paper 2012–10. Cambridge, MA: Belfer Center for Science and International Affairs, Harvard Kennedy School.

McGlade, C. and Ekins, P. (2014) Un-burnable oil: An examination of oil resource utilisation in a decarbonised energy system. *Energy Policy* 64, 102–112.

McKercher, B. (1998) The effect of market access on destination choice. *Journal of Travel Research* 37 (1), 39–47.

McKercher, B., Chan, A. and Lam, C. (2008) The impacts of distance on international tourist movements. *Journal of Travel Research* 47 (2), 208–224.

McKercher, B., Prideaux, B., Cheung, C. and Law, R. (2010) Achieving voluntary reductions in the carbon footprint of tourism and climate change. *Journal of Sustainable Tourism* 18, 297–318.

McLennan, C.J., Pham, T.D., Ruhanen, L.M., Ritchie, B.W. and Moyle, B.D. (2012) Counter-factual scenario planning for long-range sustainable local-level tourism transformation. *Journal of Sustainable Tourism* 20 (6), 801–822.

Meadows, D.H., Meadows, G., Randers, J. and Behrens, W.W. (1972) *The Limits to Growth*. New York: Universe Books.

Meadows, D., Randers, J., Meadows, D. and Behrens, W.H. (1974) *The Limits to Growth: A Report for the Club of Rome's Project on the Predicament of Mankind* (2nd edn). New York: Universe Books.

Mervar, A. and Payne, J. (2007) An analysis of foreign tourism demand for Croatian destinations: Long-run elasticity estimates. Working Papers 0701. The Institute of Economics, Zagreb. See www.eizg.hr/AdminLite/FCKeditor/UserFiles/File/EIZ-WP-0701.pdf (accessed 22 April 2014).

Miller, G., Rathouse, K., Scarles, C., Holmes, K. and Tribe, J. (2010) Public understanding of sustainable tourism. *Annals of Tourism Research* 37 (3), 627–645.

Moriarty, P. and Honnery, D. (2008) The prospects for global green car mobility. *Journal of Cleaner Production* 16, 1717–1726.

Moriarty, P. and Honnery, D. (2012) What is the global potential for renewable energy? *Renewable and Sustainable Energy Reviews* 16 (1), 244–252.

Müller, H.R. (1999) ETH-Pilotprojekt '2000 Watt Gesellschaft': Arbeitsgruppe 'Freizeit und Energie'. Bern.

Munoz, T. (2007) German demand for tourism in Spain. *Tourism Management* 28, 12–22.

Munoz, T. and Amaral, T. (2000) An econometric model for international tourism flows to Spain. *Applied Economics* 7, 525–529.

Nashawi, I.S., Malallah, A. and Al-Bisharah, M. (2010) Forecasting world crude oil production using multicyclic Hubbert model. *Energy Fuels* 3 (24), 1788–1800.

New Zealand Ministry of Business, Industry & Innovation (2013) *Tourism Research and Data*. See www.med.govt.nz/sectors-industries/tourism/tourism-research-data (accessed 31 December 2013).

Newman, P. (2006) Beyond peak oil: Will our cities and regions collapse? *Res Publica* 15 (1), 1–7.

Newton, J. (1987) *Uncommon Friends: Life with Thomas Edison, Henry Ford, Harvey Firestone, Alexis Carrel & Charles Lindbergh*. San Diego: Harcourt Inc.

Ng, D. (2009) What is the ecological footprint of Disneyland? *Science Blogs*, 5 May. See http://scienceblogs.com/worldsfair/2009/05/05/what-is-the-ecological-footpri-1/ (accessed 30 December 2013).

Nicolau, J.L. (2008) Characterizing tourist sensitivity to distance. *Journal of Travel Research* 47, 43–52.

Njegovan, N. (2005) A leading indicator approach to predicting short-term shifts in demand for business travel by air to and from the UK. *Journal of Forecasting* 24, 421–432.

Nordhaus, T. and Schellenberg, M. (2004) The death of environmentalism: Global warming politics in a post-environmental world. The Breakthrough Institute. See http://grist.org/article/doe-reprint/ (accessed 20 October 2013).

North, P. (2010) Eco-localisation as a progressive response to peak oil and climate change – A sympathetic critique. *Geoforum* 41 (4), 585–594.

Nygren, E., Aleklett, K. and Höök, M. (2009) Aviation fuel and future oil production scenarios. *Energy Policy* 37, 4003–4010.

O'Connell, J. (2011) The rise of the Arabian Gulf carriers: An insight into the business model of Emirates Airline. *Journal of Air Transport Management* 17 (6), 339–346.

Onut, S. and Soner, S. (2006) Energy efficiency assessment for the Antalya Region hotels in Turkey. *Energy and Buildings* 38, 964–971.

Organisation of Economic Development (OECD) (2011) The effects of oil price hikes on economic activity and inflation. OECD Economics Department Policy Notes, No. 4. Paris: OECD.

Organisation of the Petroleum Exporting Countries (OPEC) (2013) Homepage – About us. See www.opec.org/opec_web/en/17.htm (accessed 2 February 2013).

Our Finite World (2013) Peak oil demand is already a huge problem, 11 April. See http://ourfiniteworld.com/2013/04/11/peak-oil-demand-is-already-a-huge-problem/ (accessed 12 August 2013).

Our Horizon (2014) Homepage. See http://ourhorizon.org/our-name/ (accessed 28 April 2014).

Owen, N.A., Inderwildi, O.R. and King, D.A. (2010) The status of conventional world oil reserves – Hype or cause for concern? *Energy Policy* 38, 4743–4749.

Patterson, M.G. (1996) What is energy efficiency?: Concepts, indicators and methodological issues. *Energy Policy* 24 (5), 377–390.

Patzek, T. (2007) How can we outlive our way of life? Paper prepared for the 20th Round Table on Sustainable Development of Biofuels: Is the Cure Worse than the Disease? OECD Headquarters, Château de la Muette, Paris, 11–12 September. See www.oecd.org/sd-roundtable/papersandpublications/40225820.pdf (accessed 12 May 2014).

Peace Parks Foundation (2010) Peace Parks Foundation objects to the planned mine next to the Mapungubwe National Park and World Heritage Site in the Greater Mapungubwe Transfrontier Conservation Area. See www.peaceparks.org/news.php?pid=1097andmid=832ando=0andq=Greater%25Mapungubwe%25TFCA%25Objection%25to%25coal (accessed 20 December 2011).

Pearce, B. (2013) Cyclical gains but structural challenges. IATA presentation. See www.iata.org/whatwedo/Documents/economics/industry-outlook-presentation-march-2014.pdf (accessed 13 July 2014).

Peersman, G. and Robays, I. (2009) The economic consequences of oil shocks – A cross-country analysis. See www.wlu.ca/viessmann/rba09/Peersman.pdf (accessed 12 November 2012).

Peeters, P. (2010) Tourism transport, technology, and carbon dioxide emissions. In C. Schott (ed.) *Tourism and the Implications of Climate Change: Issues and Actions. Bridging Tourism Theory and Practice* (Vol. 3, pp. 67–90). Bingley, UK: Emerald Group Publishing Limited.

Peeters, P. and Dubois, G. (2010) Tourism travel under climate change mitigation constraints. *Journal of Transport Geography* 18 (3), 447–457.

Peeters, P. and Eijgelaar, E. (2014) Tourism's climate mitigation dilemma: Flying between rich and poor countries. *Tourism Management* 40, 15–26.

Peeters, P., van Egmond, T. and Visser, N. (2004) *European Tourism, Transport and Environment.* Final Version. Breda: NHTV CSTT.

Peeters, P.M., Middel, J. and Hoolhorst, A. (2005) Fuel efficiency of commercial aircraft: An overview of historical and future trends. NLR-CR-2005-669. National Aerospace Laboratory, November.

Peeters, P., Gössling, S. and Becken, S. (2006) Innovation towards tourism sustainability: Climate change and aviation. *International Journal of Innovation and Sustainable Development* 1 (3), 184–200.

Peeters, P., Szimba, E. and Duijnisveld, M. (2007) Major environmental impacts of European tourist transport. *Journal of Transport Geography* 15 (2007), 83–93.

Penner, J., Lister, D., Griggs, D., Dokken, D.J. and McFarland, M. (1999) *Aviation and the Global Atmosphere. Special Report of the Intergovernmental Panel on Climate Change.* Cambridge: Cambridge University Press.

Princess Cruises (2009) Sustainability report. See www.princess.com (accessed 3 March 2013).

Prior, T., Giurco, D., Mudd, G., Mason, L. and Behrisch J. (2012) Resource depletion, peak minerals and the implications for sustainable resource management. *Global Environmental Change* 22 (3), 577–587.

Pujol, T. (2013) The Barcelona citizen commitment to sustainability. A sustainable city vision beyond a 'sustainable destination' approach. Presented at the 7th International Conference on Responsible Tourism in Destinations, Barcelona, 3 October.

Rail Cooperative Research Centre (CRC) (2006) *Rail Research Industry Report: Project 24.* See www.railinnovation.com.au/research/downloads/1206-RailCRC-P24-IndReport.pdf (accessed 22 December 2013).

Rajagopalan, P., Wu, X. and Lee, S.E. (2009) A study on energy performance of hotel buildings in Singapore. *Energy and Buildings* 41, 1319–1324.

Ram, Y., Nawijn, J. and Peeters, P. (2013) Happiness and limits to sustainable tourism mobility: A new conceptual model. *Journal of Sustainable Tourism* 21 (7), 1017–1035.

Reilley, J., Williams, P. and Haider, W. (2010) Moving towards more eco-efficient tourist transportation to a resort destination: The case of Whistler, British Columbia. *Research in Transportation Economics* 26, 66–73.

Resch, G., Held, A., Faber, T., Panzer, C., Toro, F. and Haas, R. (2008) Potentials and prospects for renewable energies at global scale. *Energy Policy* 36, 4048–4056.

Robelius, F. (2007) Giant oil fields – The highway to oil: Giant oil fields and their importance for future oil production. Doctoral thesis, Uppsala University, Sweden.

Rogers, D. (2013) Shale and Wall Street: Was the decline in natural gas prices orchestrated? Energy Policy Forum. See http://shalebubble.org/wp-content/uploads/2013/02/SWS-report-FINAL.pdf (accessed 1 January 2013).

Rossello-Batle, B., Moia, A. Cladera, A. and Martinez, V. (2010) Energy use, CO_2 emissions and waste throughout the life cycle of a sample of hotels in the Balearic Islands. *Energy Build* 42, 547–558.

Rozenberg, J., Hallegatte, S., Vogt-Schilb, A., Sassi, O., Guivarch, C., Waisman, H. and Hourcarde, J.C. (2010) Climate policies as a hedge against the uncertainty on future oil supply. *Climatic Change* 101, 663–668.

Rutherford, D. and Zeinali, M. (2009) *Efficiency Trends for New Commercial Jet Aircraft 1960 to 2008*. International Council on Clean Transportation. See www.theicct.org/sites/default/files/publications/ICCT_Aircraft_Efficiency_final.pdf (accessed 20 December 2013).

Rutty, M., Matthews, L., Scott, D. and Del Matto, T. (2014) Using vehicle monitoring technology and eco-driver training to reduce fuel use and emissions in tourism: A ski resort case study. *Journal of Sustainable Tourism* 22 (5), 787–800.

Sanyé-Mengual, E., Romanos, H., Molina, C., Oliver, M., Ruiz, N., Pérez, M., Carreras, D., Boada, M., Garcia-Orellana, J., Duch, J. and Rieradevall, J. (2014) Environmental and self-sufficiency assessment of the energy metabolism of tourist hubs on Mediterranean Islands: The case of Menorca (Spain). *Energy Policy* 65, 377–387.

Schiff, A. and Becken, S. (2011) Demand elasticities for tourism in New Zealand. *Tourism Management* 32 (3), 564–575.

Schneider-Mayerson, M. (2013) From politics to prophecy: Environmental quiescence and the 'Peak Oil' movement. *Environmental Politics* 22 (5), 866–882.

Scott, D., Amelung, B., Becken, S., Ceron, J.P., Dubois, G., Gössling, S., Peeters, P. and Simpson, M. (2008) *Climate Change and Tourism: Responding to Global Challenges*. Madrid/Paris: United Nations World Tourism Organisation and United Nations Environment Programme.

Scott, D., Hall, C.M. and Gössling, S. (2012) *Tourism and Climate Change: Impacts, Adaptation and Mitigation*. Abingdon, Oxon: Routledge.

Scrase, J.I. and Ockwell, D.G. (2014) The role of discourse and linguistic framing effects in sustaining high carbon energy policy – An accessible introduction. *Energy Policy* 38 (5), 2225–2233.

Shell (2008) *Shell Energy Scenarios to 2050*. Netherlands: Royal Dutch Shell PLC.

Shi, Y., Du, Y., Yang, G., Tang, Y., Fan, L., Zhang, L., Lu, Y., Ge, Y. and Chang, J. (2013) The use of green waste from tourist attractions for renewable energy production: The potential and policy implications. *Energy Policy* 62, 410–418.

Simmons, C. and Lewis, K. (2001) Take only memories leave nothing but footprints. An ecological footprint analysis of two package holidays. Rough Draft Report. Oxford: Best Foot Forward Limited.

Simmons, M. (2003) Is the glass half full or half empty? In K. Aleklett, C. Campbell and J. Meyer (eds) *Proceedings of the Second International Workshop on Oil Depletion*, Paris, 26–27 May.

Sims, R.E.H., Schock, R.N., Adegbululgbe, A., Fenhann, J., Konstantinaviciute, I., Moomaw, W., Nimir, H.B, Schlamadinger, B., Torres-Martínez, J., Turner, C., Uchiyama, Y., Vuori, S.J.V, Wamukonya, N. and Zhang, X. (2007) Energy supply. In B. Metz, O.R. Davidson, P.R. Bosch, R. Dave and L.A. Meyer (eds) *Climate Change 2007: Mitigation* (pp. 251–322). Cambridge, UK: Cambridge University Press.

Skrebowski, C. (2004) Oil field mega projects 2004. *Petroleum Review*, January, 18–20.

Song, H., Witt, S.F. and Li, G. (2003) Modelling and forecasting demand for Thai tourism. *Tourism Economics* 9 (4), 363–387.

Song, H., Kim, J.H. and Yang, S. (2009) Confidence intervals for tourism demand elasticity. *Annals of Tourism Research* 37 (2), 377–396.

Sorrell, S., Speirs, J., Bentley, R., Brandt, A. and Miller, R. (2010) Global oil depletion: A review of the evidence. *Energy Policy* 38 (9), 5290–5295.

Sorrell, S., Speirs, J., Bentley, R., Miller, D. and Thompson, E. (2012) Shaping the global oil peak: A review of the evidence on field sizes, reserve growth, decline rates and depletion rates. *Energy* 37, 709–724.

Sperling, D. and Lutsey, N. (2009) Energy efficiency in passenger transportation. *Energy Efficiency* 39 (2), 22–30.

Stern, N. (2006) Stern review on the economics of climate change. HM Treasury. See www.hm-treasury.gov.uk/independent_reviews/stern_review_economics_climate_change/sternreview_index.cfm (accessed 14 November 2006).

Stoft, S. (2008) *Carbonomics. How to Fix the Climate and Charge it to OPEC*. Nantucket, MA: Diamond Press.

Strahan, D. (2007) *The Last Oil Shock: A Survival Guide to the Imminent Extinction of Petroleum Man*. London: John Murray.

Strange, A., Parks, B., Tierney, M.J., Fuchs, A., Dreher, A. and Ramachandran, V. (2013) China's development finance to Africa: A media-based approach to data collection. CGD Working Paper 323. Washington, DC: Center for Global Development. See www.cgdev.org/publication/chinas-development-finance (accessed 15 May 2014).

Strickland, J. (2009) Energy efficiency of different modes of transportation. Lecture notes. Stanford University. See www.builditsolar.com/References/EfficiencyTransport/strickland.htm (accessed 29 July 2014).

Sunshine Coast Council (2010) Climate change and peak oil strategy. See www.sunshine-coast.qld.gov.au/sitePage.cfm?code=cc-strategy (accessed 24 November 2010).

Sydney Water (2011) Best practice guidelines for water management in aquatic leisure centres, Sydney. See www.sydneywater.com.au/web/groups/publicwebcontent/documents/document/zgrf/mdq1/~edisp/dd_045262.pdf (accessed 2 August 2014).

Tabatchnaia-Tamirisa, N., Loke, M.K., Leung, P. and Tucker, K.A. (1997) Energy and tourism in Hawaii. *Annals of Tourism Research* 24, 390–401.

Tainter, J. (1988) *The Collapse of Complex Societies*. Cambridge: Cambridge University Press.

Taylor, B. (2006) Shell shock: Why do good companies do bad things? *Corporate Governance: An International Review* 14 (3), 181–193.

Tegg, D. (2011) Auckland Airport: Where pigs fly and bring untold prosperity. Oil Shock Horror Probe Blog. See http://oilshockhorrorprobe.blogspot.com.au/2011/01/auckland-airport-where-pigs-fly-and.html (accessed 17 November 2013).

The Carbon Trust (2005) Saving Energy at Leisure. Good Practice Guide. See www.worcester.gov.uk/fileadmin/assets/pdf/Environment/climate_change/Carbon_Trust_Good_Practice_Guide_Saving_Enegy_at_Leisure.pdf (accessed 3 December 2013).

The Economist (2004) Saudi Arabia and oil. What if? Special report, 27 May. See www.economist.com/node/2705562 (accessed 27 May 2014).

The Economist (2008) Energy: Double, double, oil and trouble, 31 May, p. 77.

The Institute for the Analysis of Global Security (2003) The geopolitics of oil. See www.iags.org/geopolitics.html (accessed 3 January 2013).

Tienhaara, K. (2010) A tale of two crises: What the global financial crisis means for the global environmental crisis. *Environmental Policy and Governance* 20, 197–208.

Timms, B.F. and Conway, D. (2011) Slow tourism at the Caribbeanis geographical margins. *Tourism Geographies* 14 (3), 396–418.

Tomabechi, K. (2010) Energy resources in the future. *Energies* 3, 686–695.

Tourism Research Australia (2013) *Tourism Forecasts – Spring 2013*. Canberra: Tourism Research Australia.

Tourism Victoria (no date) Trends affecting the world tourism industry. Strategic plan 2002–2006. See www.tourism.vic.gov.au/strategicplan/plan2002_2006/1_introduction/assets/intro_graph2.pdf (accessed 12 December 2012).

Treanor, J. (2009) Royal Dutch Shell to compensate shareholders for reserves scandal. *The Guardian*, 1 June. See www.theguardian.com/business/2009/may/31/royal-dutch-shell-compensation-shareholders (accessed 15 May 2014).

UK Department of Energy & Climate Change (2013) Statistical data set. Annual January prices of road fuels and petroleum products. See www.gov.uk/government/statistical-data-sets/oil-and-petroleum-products-annual-statistics (accessed 28 October 2013).

UK Energy Research Centre (2009) *Global Oil Depletion. An Assessment of the Evidence for a Near-term Peak in Global Oil Production*. London: UKERC.

UK Industry Taskforce on Peak Oil & Energy Security (ITPOES) (2010) The oil crunch. A wake-up call for the UK economy. Second report, February 2010. See http://peak oiltaskforce.net/download-the-report/ (accessed 3 June 2013).

Um, S. and Crompton, J.L. (1990) Attitude determinants in tourism destination choice. *Annals of Tourism Research* 17, 432–448.

United Nations Education, Scientific and Cultural Organisation (UNESCO) (2011) Decision 35 COM 7B.6 on Selous Game Reserve (United Republic of Tanzania) (N 199), adopted by the World Heritage Committee at its 35th session.

United Nations Environment Programme (UNEP) (2011) Decoupling natural resource use and environmental impacts from economic growth. A report of the Working Group on Decoupling to the International Resource Panel. M. Fischer-Kowalski, M. Swilling, E.U. von Weizsäcker, Y. Ren, Y. Moriguchi, W. Crane, F. Krausmann, N. Eisenmenger, S. Giljum, P. Hennicke, P. Romero Lankao, A. Siriban Manalang and S. Sewerin. See www.unep.org/resourcepanel/decoupling/files/pdf/decoupling_report_english.pdf (accessed 20 April 2014).

United Nations World Tourism Organisation (UNWTO) (2011) Tourism towards 2030: Global overview. See http://cestur.sectur.gob.mx/descargas/Publicaciones/Boletin/cedoc2012/cedoc2011/unwto2030.pdf (accessed 12 November 2013).

United Nations World Tourism Organisation (UNWTO) (2013) UNWTO Tourism Highlights (2013 edn). See http://mkt.unwto.org/publication/unwto-tourism-high-lights-2013-edition (accessed 20 January 2014).

United Nations World Tourism Organisation (UNWTO) (2014) World Tourism Barometer. Volume 12, January. See http://mkt.unwto.org/en/barometer (accessed 20 January 2014).

United States Congress House (1973) *Energy Reorganization Act of 1973: Hearings, Ninety-third Congress, First Session, on H.R. 11510.* p. 248.

Urry, J. (2008) Governance, flows, and the end of the car system? *Global Environmental Change* 18, 343–349.

Urry, J. (2010) Consuming the planet to excess. *Theory, Culture & Society* 27 (2–3), 1–22.

Urry, J. (2011) *Climate Change and Society.* Cambridge: Polity.

Urry, J. (2012) Social networks, mobile lives and social inequalities. *Journal of Transport Geography* 21, 24–30.

US Geological Service (USGS) (2000) *World Petroleum Assessment*. Washington, DC: USGS.

Van den Brink, R.M. and Van Wee, B. (2001) Why has car-fleet specific fuel consumption not shown any decrease since 1990? Quantitative analysis of Dutch passenger car-fleet specific fuel consumption. *Transportation Research Part D* 6, 75–93.

Verbeek, D. and Mommaas, H. (2008) Transitions to sustainable tourism mobility: The social practices approach. *Journal of Sustainable Tourism* 16 (6), 629–644.

Virgin Blue (2008) Submission for the information and consideration by members of the Senate Select Committee on Fuel and Energy. See www.aph.gov.au/~/media/wopapub/senate/committee/fuelenergy_ctte/submissions/sub0058_pdf.ashx (accessed 20 May 2014).

Voegele, E. (2013) IEA predicts global growth in ethanol production. *Ethanol Producer Magazine*. See http://ethanolproducer.com/articles/10005/iea-predicts-global-growth-in-ethanol-production (accessed 14 May 2014).

Wakefield, J. (2014) Sky cars to be built in Tel Aviv. BBC News Technology, 24 June. See www.bbc.com/news/technology (accessed 20 July 2014).

Walnum, H. (2011) Energy use and CO_2 emissions from cruise ships – A discussion of methodological issues. Western Norway Research Institute. See www.vestforsk.no/filearchive/vf-notat-2-2011-cruise.pdf (accessed 20 November 2013).

Walz, A., Calonderb, G.-P., Hagedornc, F., Lardellia, C., Lundströma, C. and Stöckli, V. (2008) Regional CO_2 budget, countermeasures and reduction aims for the Alpine tourist region of Davos, Switzerland. *Energy Policy* 36, 811–820.

Wan Lee, J. and Brahmasrene, T. (2013) Investigating the influence of tourism on economic growth and carbon emissions: Evidence from panel analysis of the European Union. *Tourism Management* 38, 69–76.

Wang, J.C. (2012) A study on the energy performance of hotel buildings in Taiwan. *Energy Build* 49, 268–275.

Watson, C. (2014) *Beyond Flying: Rethinking Air Travel in a Globally Connected World*. London: Green Books.

Weaver, D. (2009) Reflections on sustainable tourism and paradigm change. In S. Gössling, C.M. Hall and D. Weaver (ed.) *Sustainable Tourism Futures: Perspectives on Systems, Restructuring, and Innovations* (pp. 33–40). London, New York: Routledge.

Weaver, D. (2011) Can sustainable tourism survive climate change? *Journal of Sustainable Tourism* 19 (1), 5–15.

Westerberg, V., Jacobsen, J. and Lifran, R. (2013) The case for offshore wind farms, artificial reefs and sustainable tourism in the French Mediterranean. *Tourism Management* 34, 172–183.

Wicker, P. and Becken, S. (2013) Does concern about energy availability, climate change, and the economic situation influence consumer behaviour? *Ecological Economics* 88, 41–48.

Witt, S.F. and Witt, C.A. (1995) Forecasting tourism demand: A review of empirical research. *International Journal of Forecasting* 11, 447–475.

Wood, J. and Long, G. (2000) Long-term world oil supply (are source base/production path analysis). Report from the US Department of Energy, Energy Information Administration, presented in the Meeting of the American Association of Petroleum Geologists, New Orleans, Louisiana, 18 April.

Woodside, A.G. and King, R.I. (2001) An updated model of travel and tourism purchase-consumption systems. *Journal of Travel and Tourism Marketing* 10 (1), 3–26.

Woodside, A.G. and Lysonski, S. (1989) A general model of traveler destination choice. *Journal of Travel Research* 27, 8–14.

World Aviation Yearbook (2013) Global overview. See http://centreforaviation.com/reports/ (accessed 20 September 2013).

World Coal Association (2012) Coal statistics. See www.worldcoal.org/resources/coal-statistics/ (accessed 20 October 2013).

World Energy Council (WEC) (2003) *Drivers of the Energy Scene*. London: World Energy Council.

World Energy Council (WEC) (2010) *2010 Survey of Energy Resources*. London: WEC.

World Travel and Tourism Council (WTTC) (2013) *Travel & Tourism Economic Impact 2013: Country Profiles*. United Kingdom: World Travel & Tourism Council.

Wuppertal Institute for Climate, Environment and Energy (2009) *Energy Systems in OPEC Countries of the Middle East and North Africa. System Analytic Comparison of Nuclear Power, Renewable Energies and Energy Efficiency*. Berlin: Wuppertal.

Xydis, G., Koroneos, C. and Polyzakis, A. (2009) Energy and energy analysis of the Greek hotel sector: An application. *Energy and Buildings* 41, 402–406.

Yang, H. and Zhang, A. (2012) Effects of high-speed rail and air transport competition on prices, profits and welfare. *Transportation Research Part B: Methodological* 46 (10), 1322–1333.

Yeoman, I. (2012) 2050 – *Tomorrow's Tourism*. Bristol: Channel View Publications.

Yeoman, I., Greenwod, C. and McMahon-Beattie, U. (2009) The future of Scotland's international tourism markets. *Futures* 41 (6), 387–395.

Zalik, A. (2010) Oil 'futures': Shell's scenarios and the social construction of the global oil market. *Geoforum* 41 (4), 553–564.

Zamith, R., Pinto, J. and Villar, M.E. (2012) Constructing climate change in the Americas: An analysis of news coverage in US and South American newspapers. *Science Communication*. doi 10.1177/1075547012457470

Zentrum für Transformation der Bundeswehr (2010) *Peak Oil. Sicherheitspolitische Implikationen knapper Resourcen*. Strausberg, Germany: Dezernat Zukunftsanalyse.

Index